LOFTY ACHIEVEMENTS

SENIOR AUTHORS
Virginia A. Arnold
Carl B. Smith

LITERATURE CONSULTANTS
Joan I. Glazer
Margaret H. Lippert

READING
EXPRESS
MACMILLAN

Macmillan Publishing Company
New York

Collier Macmillan Publishers
London

ACKNOWLEDGMENTS

The publisher gratefully acknowledges permission to reprint the following copyrighted material:

"Atlantis" (originally titled "Priapus & the Pool, XII") is excerpted from the poem in COLLECTED POEMS by Conrad Aiken. Copyright © 1953, 1970 by Conrad Aiken; renewed 1981 by Mary Aiken. Reprinted by permission of Oxford University Press.

"Atlantis: The Lost Continent" is an excerpted/edited reprint of text from ATLANTIS: THE MISSING CONTINENT by David McMullen, Contemporary Perspectives, Inc., 1977. Reprinted from the Great Unsolved Mysteries series by permission of Contemporary Perspectives, Inc.

"Brady of Broadway: First Press Photographer" is from *Cobblestone's* April 1981 issue: Civil War Highlights. © 1981 Cobblestone Publishing, Inc., Peterborough, NH 03458. Reprinted by permission of the publisher.

"Courage" from ACROSS FIVE APRILS by Irene Hunt. Copyright © 1964 by Irene Hunt. Reprinted by permission of Modern Curriculum Press, Inc.

"Different Dreams" from DOGS & DRAGONS, TREES & DREAMS: A Collection of Poems by Karla Kuskin. Copyright © 1964 by Karla Kuskin. Reprinted by permission of Harper & Row, Publishers, Inc.

"Fifteen Reflections on Volcanoes" by Pamela Burnley from THE POETRY CONNECTION edited by Kinereth Gensler and Nina Nyhart. Copyright © Kinereth Gensler and Nina Nyhart 1978. Reprinted by permission of Teachers & Writers Collaborative.

"First Job" from IT WILL NEVER BE THE SAME AGAIN by Mike Neigoff. Copyright © 1979 by Mike Neigoff. Reprinted by permission of Henry Holt & Company, Inc.

"Frederick Douglass" is from INDEPENDENT VOICES by Eve Merriam. Copyright © 1968 by Eve Merriam. All rights reserved. Reprinted by permission of Marian Reiner for the author.

"Frozen Fire" adapted from FROZEN FIRE by James Houston. Copyright © 1977 James Houston. (A Margaret K. McElderry Book). Reprinted with permission of Atheneum Publishers, Inc. By permission also of the author.

"The Ghost on Saturday Night" from THE GHOST ON SATURDAY NIGHT by Sid Fleischman. Copyright © 1974 by Albert S. Fleischman. By permission of Little, Brown and Company in association with The Atlantic Monthly Press. By permission also of Bill Berger Associates, Inc.

"The Great Skinner Enterprise" from THE GREAT SKINNER ENTERPRISE by Stephanie S. Tolan. Copyright © 1986 by Stephanie S. Tolan. Edited with permission of Four Winds Press, an imprint of Macmillan Publishing Company. By permission also of Curtis Brown, Ltd.

"Help Wanted" from "The TeenAge Guide to Part-Time Jobs" edited by Nancy Rutter from the January/February 1986 issue of *TeenAge*. Reprinted by permission of TeenAge Magazine, New York, NY.

"Horse Power" is adapted from ANIMAL PARTNERS by Patricia Curtis. Copyright © 1982 by Patricia Curtis. Reprinted by permission of the publisher, E. P. Dutton/Lodestar Books, a division of New American Library. By permission also of McIntosh & Otis, Inc.

"A House Divided" from THE GOLDEN BOOK OF THE CIVIL WAR. Adapted by Charles Flato. © 1961, 1960 American Heritage. Reprinted by permission of Western Publishing Company, Inc.

Macmillan Publishing Company
866 Third Avenue
New York, N.Y. 10022
Collier Macmillan Canada, Inc.

Printed in the United States of America.

ISBN 0-02-172900-X

9 8 7 6 5 4 3 2 1

Cover Design: Bass and Goldman Associates

Illustration Credits: Charles Berger, 145, 148; Vince Caputo, 123, 139, 153, 165, 181, 193, 205, 339, 353, 369, 381, 391, 409, 419; Floyd Cooper, 178–179; Paul Cox, 96–106; Roland Descombes, 182–190; Donna Diamond, 194–200; William Pène du Bois, 392–402; Allen Eitzen, 276–287; Jim Findlayson, 351; Mark Fresh, 232–240; General Cartography, Inc., 410; Juan Gimenez, 430–443; Richard Hess, 340–349; Tim Hildebrandt, 166–176; Robert Jackson, 307, 391, 445–465; Doug Jamieson, 118–119; Chet Jezierski, 154–162; Hal Just, 471–495; Bernie Lowry, 319; Steve Madson, 52–63; Mike McKeever, 40–48; Verlin Miller, 271; Isidre Mones, 244–252; Alan Neider, 423, 426; Gabrielle Nenzione, 312–317; Hima Pamoedjo, 371; Steve Riedell, 404; Jonathan Rosenbaum, 15, 31, 39, 51, 67, 81, 95, 109, 231, 243, 257, 275, 291, 301, 311, 323; Roger Roth, 258–269; Ruda/Vannucci, 292–298; Joel Snyder, 354–365; Pat Soper, 124–136; Shannon Sternweis, 82–91; Jenny Tylden Wright, 32–36; Joe Veno, 16–26; Larry Winborg, 214–226; Frederic Winkowski, 324–334.

Cover Photo: The Image Bank: © Robert Kristofik

Photo Credits: AMERICAN GEOGRAPHICAL SOCIETY: 307. ANIMALS, ANIMALS: © Doug Allan, 374BR; © G. L. Kooyman, 372T; © Leonard Lee Rue, III, 375T. PETER ARNOLD: © W. H. Hodge, 305T. THE BETTMANN ARCHIVE: 120L, 120R, 140, 141, 206R. CULVER PICTURES: 144. © David Cupp, 69, 72, 74. DESIGN PHOTOGRAPHERS, INT.: © Ann Hagen, 305B. DORSET FINE ARTS—WEST BAFFIN ESKIMO COOPERATIVE: by Pootoogook, 367. DRK PHOTO: © M. P. Kahl, 376B. © Stephen J. Krasemen, 370–1T, 373T, 374TL; © Wayne Lankinen, 336. EARTH SCENES: © Doug Allen, 376TL: © James Brandt, 375B. JET PROPULSION LAB: 420–1, 424–5B. WOLFGANG KAEHLER: 372BL, 374TR, 374BL. KOBAL COLLECTION: 296BL, 296BR. LIBRARY OF CONGRESS: 146, 206, 208T, 210, 210BL, 210BR, 413. GIFT OF ANDREW MELLON: 143. MONKMEYER PRESS PHOTO: © Audrey Gottlieb, 113BL; © Freda Leinwand, 111. MOVIE STILL ARCHIVES: 296TL, 296TR. Loren McIntyre, 302–3, 303T, 303B. NASA: 422–3B, 423T, 424–5L, 424–5R. NATIONAL ARCHIVES: 147. COURTESY ELIZABETH BAKER SPOHR: 415, photo by Jim Goodnough. STOCK BOSTON: © J. Berndt, 113TR. THE IMAGE BANK: © Mel D'Giacomo, 12; © Cliff Feulner, 228, 254–5; © David Heiser, 376T; © Eric Schweikardt, 65; © Art Wolfe, 373. THE PHOTO SOURCE: 213. THE PICTURE CUBE: © Arnold J. Kaplan, 114T. THE STOCK MARKET: © Mark Ferri, 114B; © Alan Gurney, 370–1B. U.S. ARMY PHOTO: photo by M. Brady & A. Gardner, 208B. U.S. GEOLOGICAL SOCIETY: 410–11, 412–13, 414–15. U.S. NAVY: 372BR, 387; photos by P.M. Caulkus, 383, 384. WOODFIN CAMP & ASSOCIATES: © Dewitt Jones, 93.

Contents

UNIT ONE
LEVEL 14

WORKING
IT OUT

PREPARING FOR READING

Learning Vocabulary

1. Mr. Skinner left his company job to start an <u>enterprise</u> that would involve the whole family.
2. He was convinced that there would be many <u>potential</u> customers.
3. The flyers <u>generated</u> such a great response that the Skinners had to <u>temporarily</u> disconnect their phones.
4. Confusion on the first day of business made it difficult to put events in their proper <u>perspective</u>.

enterprise   potential   generated
temporarily   perspective

Developing Background and Skills
Literary Elements

Authors think about several important **literary elements,** or story parts, as they plan their writing. The story below and the discussion that follows will help you to understand these literary elements.

Amanda thought that having a business of her own would be an easy way to earn extra money. First she would have to think of something that the people of Profit, Iowa, would pay for. But it also ought to be something she *liked* to do. What could it be? She glanced at the clock. Had three hours really passed? Well, she would have to get serious. Finally, she came up with what she thought was a brilliant plan—she would listen to complaints. Everyone loved to complain, but no one liked to listen. Was it really eleven o'clock? Of course, all she had to do now was write an ad. That should be a snap. But somehow, she just couldn't get the first sentence right. Now it was midnight. A business of your own is certainly a lot of work, she thought.

Everything that happens in the story is part of the plot. **Plot** refers to the action of a story. Story events can be summarized to describe the plot. The plot of the story about Amanda can be summed up by *Amanda wants her own business but has a hard time getting started.*

The **setting** is the time and place of the story. The place may be real or imaginary. The author often tells you the place. In the story, it is the imaginary town of Profit. The time may be the past, the present, or the future. What clues help you know that the story takes place in the present?

The feeling that a story gives the reader is called the **mood.** Different stories may produce such moods as anger, horror, suspense, sorrow, and happiness. Would you agree that the mood of the story is somewhat humorous?

Theme is the general truth about life that a story conveys, that is, its overall message. The theme of the story about Amanda is *Things are not always as easy as they seem.*

Narrative point of view refers to the person through whose eyes the story is told. The point of view of the story above is third person from Amanda's point of view. This means that the author reports what Amanda sees, thinks, and feels. In the third person "all-knowing," the author knows everything and can reveal the thoughts and feelings of all characters. In a first-person narrative, a person called "I" describes all the events. The "I" can tell only what he or she knows or sees.

As you read the next selection, think about how you would summarize the main events in the plot. Decide how you would describe the story's setting, mood, theme, and narrative point of view.

THE GREAT SKINNER ENTERPRISE

STEPHANIE S. TOLAN

The changes in Jenny's conservative father are minor at first—a sporty moustache and colorful clothes. Then comes the day of the Ultimate Change, when Mr. Skinner abandons his middle-level executive job at McDougal and Son and arrives home in a brand-new van, with grand plans for the Skinner Family Enterprise. It isn't long before he has turned the dining room into Central Headquarters and incorporated the whole family into "At Your Service," a new-concept business designed for people who are too busy to do their own errands and odd jobs. When the flyers the family distributes around the neighborhood have the phones ringing nonstop, the Skinner Enterprise is put to the test.

When a person says "We're going to make it!" the way Dad said it, what's the picture that comes to mind? Success, right? Good things. Money and fame and sunshine and roses. By noon on Sunday, we had all realized that while Dad might have been

technically correct, making it was not going to mean 100-percent good things.

We'd gone around and unplugged all the phones after lunch on Saturday and had left them unplugged the rest of the day. Dad and Ben, making the massive sacrifice of *not* watching the Penn State football game on TV, closed themselves into the dining room with the computer. Ben came out from time to time to check on the game score and to moan about how hard it is for an adult to get truly comfortable with computers. Apparently, though, they were making progress at whatever it was they were doing.

Before we went to bed Saturday night, we plugged the phones back in in case of an emergency. Dad had decided we should begin At Your Service right away, instead of waiting a week. That way we wouldn't waste all the enthusiasm the flyer had generated or make people impatient. "We might as well jump right in and learn by experience," he said. "We'll do this first week on a free trial basis for the customers. It'll be good customer relations, and we can see how much time various jobs take and how much work is involved. I haven't worked out a fee schedule yet, and this will help us decide how much to charge."

The first call came on Sunday at 6:12 A.M. The Skinner family has hardly even been aware, through the years, that there *is* a 6:12 A.M. on Sunday. I pulled my blankets up over my head and went back to sleep. The business had been Dad's idea, so it seemed only fair that he should be the one to answer the phone before dawn on Sunday. I was vaguely aware that the phone rang several more times, but I did my best to ignore the sound.

Finally, the phone still ringing, I gave up and got out of bed. It was only eight then. When I got down to the kitchen, I discovered that Ben was the only one who'd been able to stay in bed. Everybody else was at the kitchen table in robes. Rick was drinking hot chocolate,

and Marcia was eating a bowl of puffed wheat. From the level of coffee left in the pot, I could tell Mom and Dad were not drinking their first cup of the day.

Dad was trying to keep a positive perspective, but he was having a little trouble. "It's really incredible," he was saying, "that three different people all thought of having someone pick up the Sunday *Times* for them and bring it to their door."

Mom shook her head. "What's incredible to me is that anyone would want the *New York Times* at six-thirty on a Sunday morning."

I looked out the window and saw that it was still raining—a steady, gray, cold-looking rain. No wonder people didn't want to get their papers themselves. It had to be much nicer to have someone else bring it—you wouldn't even have to get dressed.

"We'll have to do a new flyer," Dad said. "One that specifically says we do *not* do catering. That last guy wanted two orders of eggs Benedict and Swiss mocha almond coffee delivered with his paper!"

"Are you going to take their papers to them?" Marcia asked.

"Not until nine-thirty. I told

them we don't begin work on Sunday morning before nine."

"What about the eggs?"

"I agreed to pick up some Danish instead."

"What were the other calls?" I asked.

"A woman with a sprained ankle wants to be driven to church . . ." started Mom.

"And some man wants his Russian wolfhound walked—under an umbrella so the poor dog doesn't get wet and catch a cold," added Dad.

"Are you going to do all that?"

"What do you mean am *I* going to?" Dad poured himself another cup of coffee. "This is a family business, remember? *We* are going to do all that—after nine o'clock."

"For free?" Marcia asked.

"As an introductory offer. Next time we charge."

"Next time? Do you mean we're going to have to get up every Sunday morning at six-twelve?"

"I'm having a new flyer printed tomorrow. It will give our calling hours. We won't accept calls before seven on weekdays or nine on weekends."

"I think you should leave out that 'We do it all' slogan, too," Marcia said.

"Obviously."

"But what about days off?" I asked. "When do we get *our* weekend?"

"We'll work out a schedule," Dad said. "We'll alternate days off. But at least till we get the business on its feet, we need to be willing to do what people want done every day. And for this first week, we all just have to pitch in."

"This is a learning process," Mom said.

I thought of us spending Sunday mornings for the rest of our lives walking Russian wolfhounds and delivering Danish. It occurred to me that if I had to learn something, I'd rather learn Chinese. That would probably be easier.

When the phone rang again, I excused myself and went back up to my room. Whatever the day was going to be like, my part of it wasn't going to start until nine.

That day was certainly a day of learning. While Mom and Dad were getting dressed, they had Marcia answer the phone. That's when we learned we needed to have a form next to every phone that would tell us what information to get from each potential customer. When Dad got back downstairs, ready to head for the newsstand and the deli and take the lady to church, Marcia had two new jobs for him. One was another *Times* and Danish delivery. (Marcia had suggested the Danish, which the guy hadn't thought of himself.) The other was taking four kids to Sunday school and back so their father could sleep in. Neither would have been hard to do, but Marcia had forgotten to get an address for the Sunday-school kids. When Dad told her to call them back to get the address, it turned out she hadn't gotten a phone number either.

Dad lost his temper. "I can't wander up and down the streets looking for four kids who look as if they want to go to Sunday school!" he yelled.

"You didn't tell me what I had to find out," Marcia said.

"I'd have thought the address, at least, would have been obvious."

"I just forgot. It was my first time!"

"What's the name?" Mom asked. "We'll look them up in the book." Mom was keeping her head.

"Mr. Martin," Marcia said. "William Martin." At least she'd gotten the guy's name.

Unfortunately, there were enough William Martins in the phone book to fill half a column. Dad made Marcia call every single one of them until she found the right one. That's how we learned that most people named William Martin sleep late on Sundays. Marcia was crying by the time she finally found the right William Martin, so Mom had to talk to him. I thought Dad was being altogether too hard on Marcia, but I also knew she'd never again forget to get an address and phone number.

About the time Marcia broke down, Ben appeared, still in his robe. He immediately went into the dining room to word-process a phone form. Before Dad was ready to leave, Ben had had the printer print out ten copies. Rick had taken a couple of copies and a pencil to put next to each phone.

I had gotten dressed by this time—which turned out to be a mistake. "Eleanor," Dad said to Mom, "you can drop Jenny off to walk the Russian wolfhound. Be sure she takes an umbrella."

"Wait a minute," I protested. "I thought Marcia was supposed to do the dog walking."

"Don't argue with me, Jennifer Skinner."

Marcia, cleverly still in her robe, produced an umbrella from the front closet. Mom took the tissue on which the name and address had been written.

"How far do I have to walk him? How long is this going to take?"

"Ask Mr. Whatever-His-Name-Is how far he wants the dog walked. Our job is to please the customer."

Right, I thought. And the customer's job is to ruin my Sundays and probably my life.

So that's how I found myself walking for half an hour in the rain with a Russian wolfhound. They're very aristocratic, as the dog's owner informed me, and very delicate. Personally, I think they're sort of ugly.

I soon found out that you can't stay under an umbrella yourself and still keep it over a dog. In fact, it's hard to keep it over a dog at all, when all the dog keeps doing is rushing one way and then another to sniff at every tree and bush and telephone pole it can find. I probably looked like a maniac, rushing around after a dog, trying to keep an umbrella over it, while the rain ran off my raincoat hood and into my face.

When Mom came back to pick me up after I'd finished, I could tell that walking a dog in the rain wasn't the only rotten part of that day. "We've got to go to the bank," she said.

"Bank? On Sunday? Why?"

"Because if you're going to deliver newspapers and Danish to people who won't be paying for them until they get them, you have to have cash. Your father tried to write a check at the newsstand, and the guy just laughed in his face. Besides, they only had three copies of the *Times* left, and he had to go to two other places before he found enough. No wonder that man wanted to get his so early. By the time your father had gathered enough papers, he was out of cash,

and he hadn't bought the Danish yet. Irving, at the deli, wouldn't take a check either. Dad's delivering the papers for the people who didn't order breakfast, while we get the cash for the Danish. Thank heaven for computer banking!"

Mom wasn't thanking heaven five minutes later when we got to our bank and found the sign that said the automatic teller was temporarily out of service. The nearest branch with an automatic teller was in the next town—the opposite direction from the deli.

When we got home, Ben was printing out more phone forms. Rick had ruined several while trying to take calls, and the rest had been used up.

Rick greeted Mom at the front door, all dressed in his raincoat and boots, with a plastic bag full of flyers. "I'm going out to deliver more flyers," he announced.

Mom didn't even say anything. She just took the flyers out of his hand and put them in the front closet. Then she looked at the handful of phone forms Marcia held out, shook her head, and went into the bathroom, closing the door firmly behind her. The lock clicked. We didn't see Mom for quite a while after that.

She was still in the bathroom when Dad arrived to pick up the cash. He gave me a handful of change, told me to put it in the shoe box next to the computer in the dining room, and took the bills. Marcia tried to give the new calls to him, but he waved them away. "I'll be back as soon as I've made the Sunday school return run," he said. "Have your mom decide what to do about those."

So it was an hour or so before we could decide what to do about the man who needed shirts washed before Monday and the woman who wanted to know if we could keep her son's guinea pigs until he got over the flu and the guy who needed someone to find half a dozen fresh artichokes before guests arrived for the dinner party he was giving.

When Mom finally came out of the bathroom, she assigned the jobs—mine was to wash the shirts. I decided to take them to the Laundromat where I'd be safe from the phone. My friend Sarah went with me. Between incoming calls I did manage to reach her, though we got interrupted once by Call Waiting. I decided that doing laundry was definitely better than

dog walking. For one thing, it was inside work. For another, there was all that free time while the stuff was in the washer and then in the dryer. So while the shirts were getting done, I told Sarah about the early-morning calls and the likelihood that At Your Service was going to kill us all.

"Oh, Jenny, don't exaggerate," she said. "Things'll calm down when you get used to it. I told you it would work. You'll all be rich."

By dinnertime (we hadn't had an official "lunchtime" because everybody was too busy), I had decided I didn't even want to be rich. Marcia and Ben weren't speaking to each other because of some argument they'd had about the phone forms. Dad had reduced Rick to tears because Rick had promised somebody we'd meet him at the train station and take him to his house. Rick didn't realize that the house we were to take him to was thirty miles away. (That's how we learned that we'd need a zip-code map to see how far away people were.) Mom got mad at Dad for yelling at Rick, then Dad got mad at Mom because she hadn't been there to oversee the calls. Then Mom got madder at

Dad because she'd been off picking up an enormous cage full of guinea pigs, who were now taking up the whole downstairs bathroom. The cage had been too big for Mom to get up the stairs, and the bathroom was the only place on the first floor where they could be kept safe from Czar Nicholas, our cat. All evening Czar Nicholas sat outside the bathroom door, his tail twitching as he listened to the guinea pigs rustling around and whistling inside.

We'd unplugged the phones again at five o'clock, and Mom was mad about that, too. She was afraid some emergency would happen and nobody would be able to reach us to tell us about it. "Emergency?" Dad yelled. "Like what? Like the van getting a flat tire in the rain, halfway from the train station to East Nowhere while I've got an eighty-year-old passenger in the back?" (That had actually happened, and it was hard to blame Dad for being in such a lousy mood.) "Well, Eleanor, I don't see how there can be an emergency worth hearing about since we're all in this room together and not one of us is out in the world creating further disaster!"

Mom headed for the bathroom at that, remembered the guinea pigs, and went upstairs. Dad stormed off and closed himself into the dining room again. We cleared the table in silence and went our separate ways. I, at least, had homework to do. Buffy, our dog, who'd clearly been feeling ignored all day, especially when I came home smelling like male Russian wolfhound, went with me. Sitting on my bed with Buffy curled up against my legs and my history book in my lap, I wondered if all successful businesses began this way.

Questions

1. By the end of Saturday, what decision had Mr. Skinner made about beginning and running the family business?

2. How would you describe the first Sunday's business of At Your Service? Support your answer with examples.

3. Do you think the Skinners' Sunday problems could have been avoided by more careful planning? Give an example of a problem that might have been avoided by careful planning.

4. If you were part of At Your Service, what services would you want to provide?

Applying Reading Skills

Write the best answer to each question below about "The Great Skinner Enterprise."

1. Which sentence best states the plot of the story?
   a. Mr. Skinner leaves his executive job and makes plans for a new family business.
   b. Unexpected complications arise when the Skinners start their family enterprise.

2. What is the setting of the story.
   a. a city area in the future
   b. an American town in the present

3. Which word best describes the mood of the story?
   a. pride   b. suspense   c. amusement

4. What is the theme of the story?
   a. Success never comes without hard work.
   b. Working together brings families closer.

5. From which narrative point of view is the story told?
   a. first person, Jennifer's point of view
   b. third person, "all-knowing" point of view

WRITING ACTIVITY

WRITE A HUMOROUS STORY

Prewrite

"The Great Skinner Enterprise" is a humorous story about one family's attempt to start a business. What makes the account funny to many readers may be the unexpected things that happen, the frantic or fast pace of events, and the reactions of the different characters. Another reason the story may be funny is that it reminds readers of their own family experiences.

Everyone has had a funny experience in his or her life. Trying out a new recipe and discovering the results, a day when just about everything seemed to go wrong, or a first day on a new job are some possibilities.

You are going to write an account of a funny experience. It can be based on a real-life experience, or it can be entirely imaginary. Look back at pages 14 and 15 to review the literary elements of a story. Then complete this story plan.

MY STORY PLAN

Characters:
Setting: (Time and place)
Problem: (For example, I tried to bake a pie and . . .)
First Event: (An opening paragraph that introduces your reader to the problem of your story.)
Other Events in Story: (List possible events in the order in which they happened.)
Solving the Problem: (For example, I fed the pie to the dog and left for the bakery.)

You need to consider your point of view, that is, who will tell the story, and the funny mood you are trying to create. The conversations of your characters, your choice of words, and the use of the unexpected are important parts of a funny story.

Write

1. Review the ideas in your story plan.
2. Introduce the problem with a paragraph about your first event.
3. Introduce the characters and setting.
4. Continue to write about the remaining events in the sequence you planned.
5. Conclude with a paragraph about how you solved (or maybe didn't solve) your problem.
6. Use your Glossary or dictionary for spelling help.

Revise

Read your story. Have someone read it and point out what was really funny and what seemed unnecessary. Remember, whether you are writing about a real or an imaginary experience, the funniest things are often the ones that really could or do happen in real life. Sometimes a writer tells too much and the action of the story seems to drag. What can you add or take out to make your story more interesting to readers?

1. Proofread for end punctuation in your sentences.
2. If you use conversation, check your use of commas and quotation marks.
3. Rewrite your story to share.

PREPARING FOR READING

Learning Vocabulary

1. Sergio Abramof's job <u>criteria</u> were enjoyable work and use of his abilities.
2. He began as an <u>apprentice</u> to a cook but soon moved to a position in which he was <u>supervising</u> others.
3. Margaret Dosland consulted a counselor who helped her select <u>relevant</u> courses to take at college.
4. Eventually Margaret enrolled in an <u>internship</u> program to acquire practical experience.

criteria   apprentice   supervising
relevant   internship

Developing Background and Skills
Make Judgments

A **judgment** is a decision. Even simple decisions involve some steps.
1. Think about what you already know.
2. Gather information.
3. Evaluate, or figure out the value or importance of, what you know and what you found out.

Read the following paragraph.

Ted wanted a job. The newspaper said it would hire Ted to deliver papers for $35 a week. However, Ted did not have a bicycle, which would make the work easier, and the hours would cut out baseball practice. The grocery store offered Ted an eight-to-four job bagging groceries at $75 a week. This would leave him free for baseball practice, but Ted thought the work would be boring. K & K Lawn and Garden Service also offered Ted an eight-to-four job at $75 a week. The work would be mowing lawns and trimming hedges, things that Ted liked to do.

To decide what job to take, Ted might set up a chart like the one below.

JOB	BENEFITS	DRAWBACKS
delivering papers	$35 a week	no bicycle, hours would cut out base-ball practice, lowest earnings
bagging groceries	$75 a week, free for base-ball practice	boring job
mowing lawns and trimming hedges	$75 a week, free for base-ball practice, enjoyable job	

The chart shows the benefits and drawbacks of each job possibility. Which job has the most drawbacks? Which has the most benefits? Based on his evaluation, Ted chose the job at K & K Lawn and Garden Service. Ted might have provided himself with more information if he had applied for and been offered another job. How might this have influenced his decision?

The selection that follows includes two autobiographical sketches. As you read, think about how the authors evaluated their situations to make important career decisions.

GOING ON INSTINCT

Sergio J. Abramof

It's the end of a busy Saturday night. Tonight, my crew of five and I have prepared more than 200 dinners, each one cooked to order.

I am happy with the results. As the head chef of a 120-seat, formal Northern Italian restaurant, I have cooked many beautiful and delicious meals. The most important critics, our customers, have for four years in a row named us their favorite restaurant in this city. All of the hard work has paid off.

This career of mine was not planned with any foresight at all. Rather, it kind of snuck up on me and then blossomed unexpectedly.

The beginnings of my career were typical: I was out of college, broke, and in debt. When I set out to look for a job, my criteria were simply to find something that I enjoyed, and to use my natural ability. I decided to try cooking.

At first, I wondered whether or not I had made a wise choice. My first cooking position exposed me to all of the evils of the restaurant business. There were the owners who cared only about the bottom line, and the managers who knew nothing about food and who cared even less.

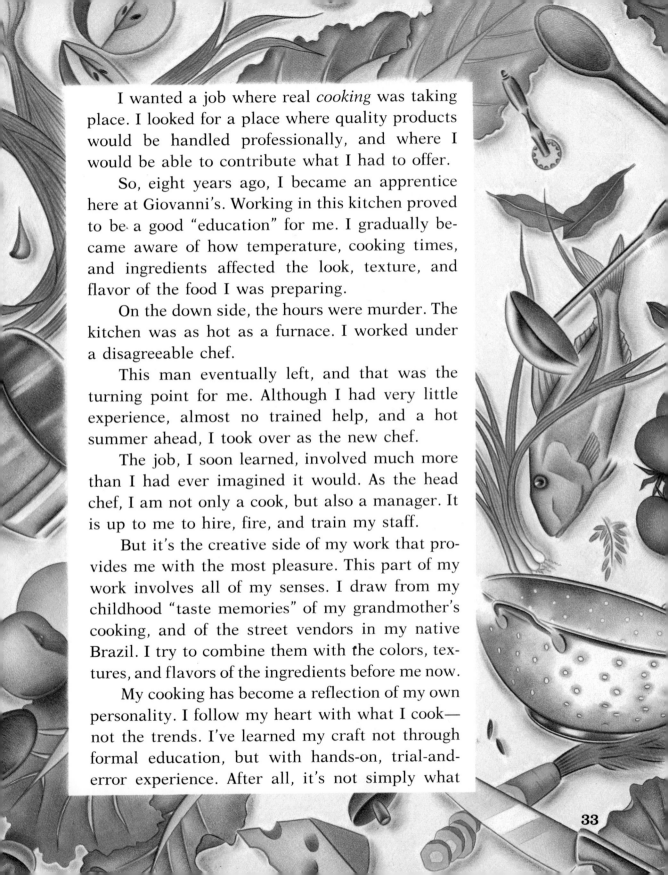

I wanted a job where real *cooking* was taking place. I looked for a place where quality products would be handled professionally, and where I would be able to contribute what I had to offer.

So, eight years ago, I became an apprentice here at Giovanni's. Working in this kitchen proved to be a good "education" for me. I gradually became aware of how temperature, cooking times, and ingredients affected the look, texture, and flavor of the food I was preparing.

On the down side, the hours were murder. The kitchen was as hot as a furnace. I worked under a disagreeable chef.

This man eventually left, and that was the turning point for me. Although I had very little experience, almost no trained help, and a hot summer ahead, I took over as the new chef.

The job, I soon learned, involved much more than I had ever imagined it would. As the head chef, I am not only a cook, but also a manager. It is up to me to hire, fire, and train my staff.

But it's the creative side of my work that provides me with the most pleasure. This part of my work involves all of my senses. I draw from my childhood "taste memories" of my grandmother's cooking, and of the street vendors in my native Brazil. I try to combine them with the colors, textures, and flavors of the ingredients before me now.

My cooking has become a reflection of my own personality. I follow my heart with what I cook— not the trends. I've learned my craft not through formal education, but with hands-on, trial-and-error experience. After all, it's not simply what

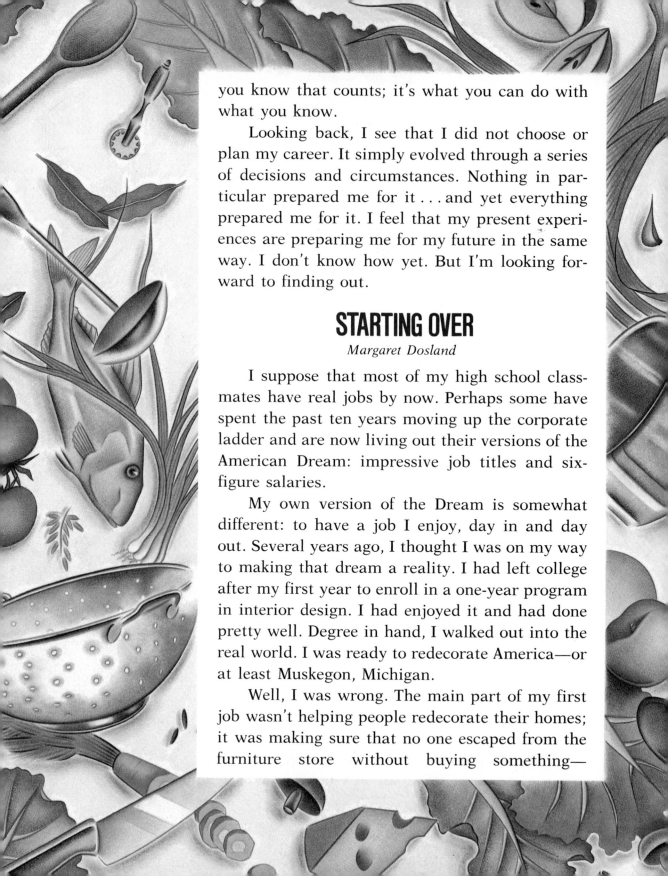

you know that counts; it's what you can do with what you know.

Looking back, I see that I did not choose or plan my career. It simply evolved through a series of decisions and circumstances. Nothing in particular prepared me for it . . . and yet everything prepared me for it. I feel that my present experiences are preparing me for my future in the same way. I don't know how yet. But I'm looking forward to finding out.

STARTING OVER

Margaret Dosland

I suppose that most of my high school classmates have real jobs by now. Perhaps some have spent the past ten years moving up the corporate ladder and are now living out their versions of the American Dream: impressive job titles and six-figure salaries.

My own version of the Dream is somewhat different: to have a job I enjoy, day in and day out. Several years ago, I thought I was on my way to making that dream a reality. I had left college after my first year to enroll in a one-year program in interior design. I had enjoyed it and had done pretty well. Degree in hand, I walked out into the real world. I was ready to redecorate America—or at least Muskegon, Michigan.

Well, I was wrong. The main part of my first job wasn't helping people redecorate their homes; it was making sure that no one escaped from the furniture store without buying something—

anything! I began to wonder about my career choice. Hadn't I entered the interior design field because I thought I would be using my artistic ability? Was selling an art? Maybe, but not the type that I appreciated.

So I quit. I spent the next two years jumping from job to job, trying to figure out where I fit in. Finally, I realized what my real problem was. I had never put much careful thought into my career decisions.

I decided to take matters into my own hands. I would return to college—and take an organized approach to pursuing a career.

Now, I wasn't all that sure how to do that. Fortunately, while looking over the course booklet, I found a listing for a class that promised to help. It was a career planning course. Taking it turned out to be one of the smartest moves I ever made.

We spent many of the class periods taking tests designed to help us pinpoint our areas of interest. The questions on these tests were often hard to answer. "Do you enjoy cooking?" Well, yes, I remember thinking, but so what? Does that mean I should be a chef? Or does it simply mean I'm hungry? I answered all of the questions honestly.

The tests revealed that my "interest areas" included graphic arts and dietetics. When I got

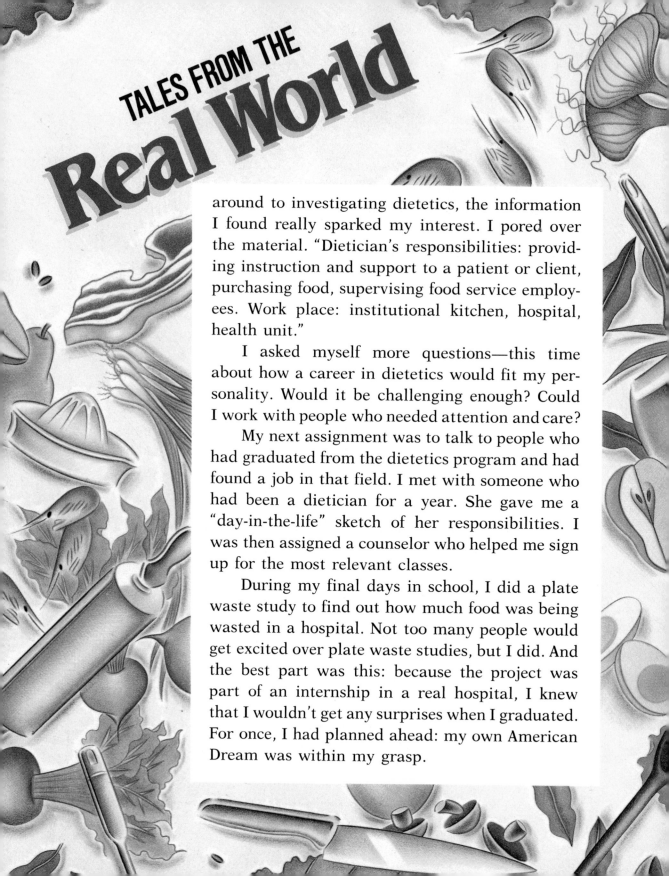

around to investigating dietetics, the information I found really sparked my interest. I pored over the material. "Dietician's responsibilities: providing instruction and support to a patient or client, purchasing food, supervising food service employees. Work place: institutional kitchen, hospital, health unit."

I asked myself more questions—this time about how a career in dietetics would fit my personality. Would it be challenging enough? Could I work with people who needed attention and care?

My next assignment was to talk to people who had graduated from the dietetics program and had found a job in that field. I met with someone who had been a dietician for a year. She gave me a "day-in-the-life" sketch of her responsibilities. I was then assigned a counselor who helped me sign up for the most relevant classes.

During my final days in school, I did a plate waste study to find out how much food was being wasted in a hospital. Not too many people would get excited over plate waste studies, but I did. And the best part was this: because the project was part of an internship in a real hospital, I knew that I wouldn't get any surprises when I graduated. For once, I had planned ahead: my own American Dream was within my grasp.

Questions

1. What is Sergio Abramof's job? Does Margaret Dosland have a "real job"? Explain.
2. In what way did the careers of Sergio Abramof and Margaret Dosland follow different paths?
3. Do you think that career planning is important? Give reasons for your answer.
4. Name a career that interests you. Explain what you might do to decide whether the career is a good choice for you.

Applying Reading Skills

Read each passage below, which is based on "Tales From the Real World." Then write the answers to the questions.

Sergio Abramof decided to try cooking as a career because he had a flair for it and enjoyed it. His first job was a disaster. Then he became an apprentice at Giovanni's. He eventually became the chef, but discovered the job involved a great deal of work, including hiring, firing, and training the staff. However, the creative side of his work provides Abramof with great pleasure.

1. In your judgment, should Abramof continue in his present job? Give the best reason for your answer.

After completing an interior design course, Margaret Dosland took a job with a furniture store. She disliked selling, so she quit and went back to college to take a career planning course. When tests revealed that dietetics was one of her interests, she decided to investigate that field. Through "hands-on" involvement, Dosland has retained her interest, although she has not, as yet, found a job.

2. In your judgment, did Dosland make the right decision in going back to school? Give the best reason for your answer.

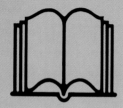

PREPARING FOR READING

Learning Vocabulary

1. Ever since he could remember, Jōi (jō′ ē) knew that being an artist would be his <u>occupation</u>.
2. No one could <u>dissuade</u> him from his goal.
3. When Jōi went to see a master cartoonist, he felt that the apprentice <u>resented</u> him.
4. The master was convinced of Jōi's dedication when Jōi <u>defiantly</u> refused to consider changing his mind.

occupation   dissuade
resented   defiantly

Developing Background and Skills
Character's Motives or Feelings

Characters in stories like people in real life have **feelings**. In real life, people's feelings are revealed by what they say and the way they say it, by what they do, and by the way they look. Writers reveal the feelings of characters in the same ways. Read the paragraph below.

As the door opened, Kim stood trembling outside. The man who answered the door asked, "How can I help you?" Kim replied hesitantly, "I'm not sure . . . not sure that I should have come." She looked very pale. Then she turned to leave.

Several clues let you know how Kim felt.

- what she did   stood trembling, later turned to leave
- what she said   "I'm not sure . . . not sure I should have come."
- how she said it   hesitantly
- how she looked   very pale

These clues let you know that Kim was feeling afraid and unsure of herself.

Writers also reveal a character's **motives**, or reasons for acting. Sometimes the connection between a motive and an action is directly stated. For example:

Kim spent long hours sketching
because she wanted to improve her drawing skills.   MOTIVE

Sometimes you will have to decide for yourself what motive a character had for an action. You should ask, "Why did the character do that? What were his or her reasons?" By reading carefully, you will find the answer or clues that will lead you to the answer. Read the passage below. See if you can figure out Kim's motive for going to see Dr. Huang.

Kim's art teachers had always praised her drawings. But Kim still wasn't sure about her ability. Surely there was *someone* who could tell her whether or not she had talent. Dr. Huang was a famous art expert. Kim made an appointment with Dr. Huang, and on Thursday she went to see him.

Would you agree that Kim's motive for visiting Dr. Huang was to get his opinion of her talent?

As you read the next selection, try to figure out the feelings of the different characters. Notice how the feelings of the main character, Jōi, change throughout the story. Try also to determine the motives the different characters have for their actions.

THE
INK-KEEPER'S APPRENTICE

ALLEN SAY

Drawing on his own boyhood experiences, the author tells the story of Jōi (jō' ē), who is thirteen and living in Tokyo soon after World War II. Although he attends a good school, drawing is his main interest. So when he reads in the paper about Japan's leading cartoonist, he goes to the building where Noro Shinpei (nô' rô shin pā') has his studio.

40

ENGLISH CONVERSATION SCHOOL, said a small hand-painted sign on the door. I looked at the crumpled newspaper article in my hand to check the address, and my heart sank. No mistake, I'd come to the right place.

I had never been in this part of Tokyo, and the shabbiness of the neighborhood depressed me. The dead-end street was full of cracks and puddles, and the two-storied office building in front of me looked more like a run-down barracks than a place of business. The place just didn't seem like the home of the great man I'd come to meet.

I stood there a good five minutes, hoping for someone to come out of the building—for anything to happen. But nobody came out, and nothing happened. Finally, I rushed through the front door.

The long hallway was dark and empty, smelling of mildew. I went from door to door, reading the nameplates, but the man I was looking for was not on the first floor. It was almost a relief.

The second floor wasn't much better, except a dirty skylight in the ceiling cast a shaft of light along the corridor

41

and made the place seem a little more cheerful. Another **ENGLISH CONVERSATION SCHOOL** sign was posted on the wall at the top of the staircase, with an arrow pointing to the far end of the hallway. I followed the arrow, and went past the school until there was only one door left. Something small and white glowed on the door, right below the frosted glass. It was an ordinary calling card, pinned there with a thumbtack.

Noro Shinpei, read the four characters. I touched the crisp card to see if it was real. My heart began to beat fast, then I laughed silently. I'd finally found the man I'd come to meet. Feeling weak in my knees, I tapped twice on the glass.

"Enter," said a man's voice. It was more like an order than an invitation. I cracked open the door and peeked inside. Two figures were seated at a long desk, peering up at me with curiosity.

"A-are you Master Noro?"

"You've found him. Come in and close the door."

Quickly I closed the door and looked around the room. Books and magazines and pieces of paper were scattered everywhere. The desk was cluttered with pens and nibs[1] and

---

1. **nibs:** penpoints.

pencils, brushes of all sizes, and more ink-pots than anybody could use in a lifetime.

"Well, pull up a chair and sit," he said. "Put the books on the floor, anywhere."

Noro Shinpei was in his late thirties. His long hair looked as if it was always combed with fingers, and he wore a long kimono. Not many men wore kimonos anymore, and he looked old-fashioned, sitting there with his hands inside the long sleeves.

Tokida (tô′ kē dä), the youth sitting next to him, kept staring at me suspiciously.

"And your name?" asked Noro Shinpei.

"Jōi, sir."

"That's an unusual name. How do you write that?"

I wrote the two characters on a piece of paper.

"Kiyoi (kē oi′)." He misread my name.

"It's Jōi, sir." I corrected him.

"And what can I do for you?"

"I want to be a cartoonist, sir."

"I see . . ."

A long pause.

"And you want to be my pupil, is that it?"

"Yes, sir."

My ears felt hot, and my shirt collar felt tight.

"How old are you, Kiyoi?"

"Thirteen, sir. I'll be fourteen in August."

"Where do you go to school?"

"Aoyama Middle School, sir."

"A very good school. Is this spring vacation?"

"Yes, sir, two weeks."

"Do your parents know you came to see me?"

"Yes, sir."

"Did you tell them why?"

"Yes, they don't mind, sir."

"You're quite sure about that? Even if you are a genius, you're a minor and I have to respect your parents' wishes. What is your father's occupation?"

"He's a merchant, sir."

"Now that's a sly answer. He could be anything from a street peddler to a department store tycoon. I get the feeling you're the oldest son."

"Yes, sir."

"Where is your sense of filial duty?"[2]

---

2. **filial** (fil′ ē əl) **duty:** respect and obedience owed to parents by their children.

"What do you mean, sir?"

"What does your father feel about his heir wanting to become a cartoonist?"

"He doesn't mind, sir, he really doesn't. He only wants me to stay in school. He says I'm going to change my mind when I grow older," I said desperately.

"And do you think you'll change your mind?"

"No, sir," I admitted.

"Of course not. At least that's what you think now. What about your mother?"

"She doesn't mind either, sir, as long as I do well in school."

"You're blessed with a wise mother. So tell me, why do you want to be a cartoonist?"

The question surprised me. Somehow I didn't expect such a question from a famous cartoonist.

"I'm not sure, sir, but I've always drawn. I'm not good at anything else. I'd rather draw cartoons than anything, sir."

"Drawings before dumplings." He rephrased an old saying. "Tell me, if I don't take you on, what will you do?"

"I don't know. . . . I'll draw on my own, sir," I said defiantly, though I suddenly felt tired and hopeless.

"I like your spirit," he said and began to laugh. His laughter took me aback.

"So what have you been drawing?"

"I've been copying mostly, sir. I've copied a lot from your strips."

"Draw something for me then," he said, handing me a drawing pad. "Let's say a horse. Yes, draw a horse, and don't try to imitate my style—or anybody else's for that matter. I want you to draw it in your own way. Tokida and I will go about our business, so relax and take your time."

I didn't move. I couldn't. My knees would have buckled under me if I tried to stand up. I picked up a pencil and licked the lead. I wished Tokida would leave the room, but he showed no sign of getting up. He's probably enjoying the scene, I thought, waiting for me to make a fool of myself. What if my hand shakes, I thought suddenly.

The first thing I drew was an ear, the side view of it. Then I drew another ear, slightly overlapping the first. Then the slanting line of the forehead, a little bump over the eye, and the dipping "dish nose" of an Arabian horse. I heard the soft lead of the pencil sliding over the paper. My hand didn't shake, and I wasn't afraid anymore.

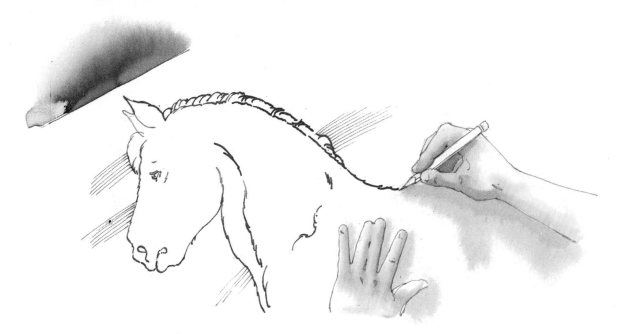

Soon a side view of a horse appeared on the page. I could have drawn the horse from some other angle but didn't think of it. I was happy with the way the horse was coming out. The snout was about the right length, the legs had all the joints, the tail turned out a little too bushy, and the eye was a bit like a human eye, but it was a horse, all right, and not a bad one. I shaded the animal here and there and handed the drawing to the great cartoonist.

He looked at it, squinting his eyes. Tokida craned his neck to peer at my drawing, but the cartoonist closed the sketchbook.

"The horse was an excuse," he said. "I wanted to see how you draw. Most boys your age draw like this," he said, drawing a straight line with many jerky strokes. "You seem to have survived your art teachers."

I thought he was paying me a compliment, but wasn't sure, so I said nothing.

"So you want to devote your life to the serious business of cartooning?" he asked.

"Yes, sir."

"What can I do to dissuade you?"

"Nothing, sir."

"Then I have no choice but to take you on."

"You mean I can be your pupil, sir?"

"If that is what you want."

Speechless, I nodded my head.

"Then I accept you as my pupil. But there's one thing, Kiyoi. Any talk about money and out you go; is that clear?"

"Yes, sir."

"Don't worry, Kiyoi, I'll make you earn your keep." He laughed. "Tokida here is three years older than you. Think of him as your partner, an older brother."

Tokida gave me a thin smile. I knew very well he resented me for barging in to share his master. I had read about him in the paper, the youngest budding cartoonist.

"If you have nothing else to do, stay for supper," said my new master.

"Thank you, sir, but my family is expecting me," I lied, and bowed several times to the two of them. I walked out as calmly as I could. I floated down the dusty staircase, swam through the hallway, and burst out the front door. Puddles were still there on the pavement, but now the rainbow of the oil slick caught my eye. I looked up at the ugly building, and somehow the shabbiness of it all seemed wonderful.

Questions

1. Why was Jōi depressed by the neighborhood in which Noro Shinpei had his studio?
2. Why do you think Noro Shinpei asked how Jōi's mother and father felt about his wanting to become a cartoonist?
3. How do you think Noro Shinpei will train Jōi to become a cartoonist?
4. Describe your favorite cartoon or comic strips. What features do you enjoy the most?

Applying Reading Skills

A. The sentences below are from "The Ink-Keeper's Apprentice." Write a word or phrase to describe the feelings of the character whose name is underlined. Then write one or more of the following phrases to show what helped you decide: character's words; way character spoke; character's actions; character's appearance.

1. "A-are you Master Noro?" (Jōi)
2. My ears felt hot and the shirt collar tightened around my neck. (Jōi)
3. "I like your spirit," he said and began to laugh. (Noro Shinpei)
4. "I don't know. . . . I'll draw on my own, sir," I said defiantly, though I suddenly felt tired and hopeless. (Jōi)
5. Tokida gave me a thin smile.

B. Each sentence below describes an action by a character in "The Ink-Keeper's Apprentice." Write a sentence describing the motive the character had for the action.

1. Jōi touched the card with the name Noro Shinpei on it.
2. Noro Shinpei told Jōi to draw a horse.
3. Tokida stayed in the room while Jōi did his drawing.

PREPARING FOR READING

Learning Vocabulary

1. The sheepherder showed his concern for the mules by being <u>painstaking</u> in arranging the heavy loads they had to carry.
2. He warned his young helper that a dog should never get the <u>notion</u> that it was the boss.
3. After the <u>din</u> and bustle of departure, the first day on the trail seemed an <u>eternity</u> of <u>oppressive</u> silence and dust.
4. The young herder's memories caused him to <u>grieve</u> for his home and friends.

painstaking	notion	din
eternity	oppressive	grieve

Developing Background and Skills
Literary Elements

Thinking about the **literary elements** in a story and how the author has used them can help you to appreciate what you read. The main literary elements include the following:

PLOT: the events or actions in the story, including everything that happens to the characters

SETTING: the time and place in which the story takes place

MOOD: the general feeling the story creates in the reader

THEME: the idea or message of the story, often not stated but revealed through what characters learn

NARRATIVE POINT OF VIEW: the person through whose eyes the story is narrated, or told.

A story map is a visual way to show an author's plan for a story. Some stories involve a journey in which a character follows a path and returns to the place he or she started from. The story map for that kind of story could be drawn as shown below.

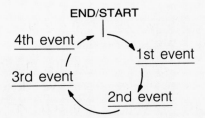

END/START

4th event

3rd event

1st event

2nd event

Other stories are more complex. Events take place in the present, but the plot also includes a flashback. In a flashback, a character recalls events from the past. The story map for such a story might be drawn as shown below.

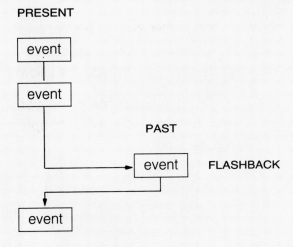

PRESENT

event

event

PAST

event **FLASHBACK**

event

The author of the next selection included a flashback. Through this plot device, you will learn more about the main character. See if you can tell when the flashback begins and when it ends.

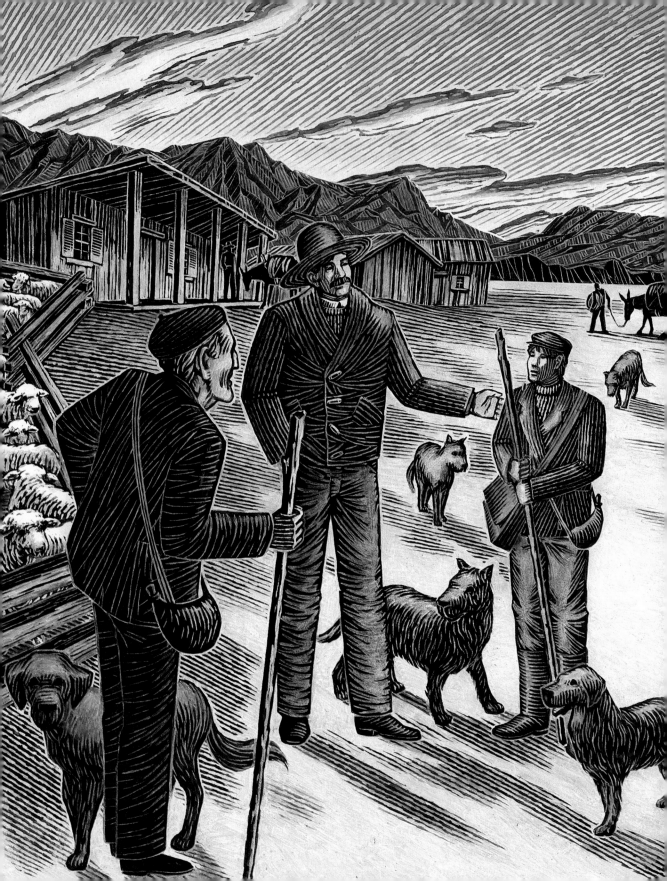

THE OLD HERDER AND THE NEW

Ann Nolan Clark

In 1910, when he was sixteen, Kepa (kā pə) went from his small village in the Spanish Basque (bäsk) country to start a new life in Idaho. He was summoned by his godfather, Pedro, to help herd sheep across the great Northwest frontier. His godfather apprenticed him to Tío (tē' ō) Marco, his most experienced sheepherder.

The day of departure began early. In the shadowy dawn the ranch house, the bunkhouse, and the commissary[1] were filled with milling men; the horse and sheep corrals with neighing, kicking mules, bleating sheep, and baaing lambs. Barking dogs were everywhere.

On his way to the bunkhouse, Tío Marco was stopped by Pedro, who beckoned Kepa to join them. The older herder had not spoken to the boy, although Kepa had noticed that often he had been watching him keenly. "This is Kepa, the boy I spoke to you about," Pedro said. "As I told you, I am placing him in your good hands for training."

"Well, I can train a sheep dog, I guess I can train a boy." Tío Marco spoke unhurriedly, giving no indication of pleasure or displeasure. "Although," he continued, "in my day a young herder trained himself." Looking directly at Kepa, he said, "On my first day I was given a dog, a mule, and three thousand sheep and told to take them to summer range and bring them back."

---

1. **commissary:** a store where food and general supplies are sold.

"I know," Pedro spoke quietly. "The same thing happened to me. That's why I want it to be different for young Kepa."

Suddenly Tío Marco clapped Kepa on the shoulder. "The boy and I will get along," he told Pedro. "No?" he asked, looking at Kepa, who nodded. At least Kepa hoped they would. Pedro laughed, leaving them together.

"Come on. I begin the training," the herder said.

The old herder and the new, young one went to the corral to get their mules. Tío Marco was given the same one he had last year. "You two seem to understand each other," the ranch foreman told him, "but the one the boy is getting is young and frisky. Stubborn, too, and mean." The man looked at Kepa as if wondering if the boy could handle a stubborn mule. Apparently he decided that the boy could, saying, "Better show him quick which one is master before the brute gets the notion he is boss."

"I will," Kepa answered, again hoping that was the way it would be.

Tío Marco supervised Kepa's packing; the wooden packsaddle first, and on it the folded tent, the bedroll, his roll of clothing. Then the food—"grub," they called it —— from the commissary.

Again Tío Marco supervised Kepa's packing half the grub supply, and added a plate, bowl, spoon, coffee pot, and fry pan. "My mule will carry the Dutch oven,[2] the kettle, lantern, canteens, and ammunition, along with the rest of my load. We understand each other, my mule and I." Tío Marco put Kepa's carbine[3] in its scabbard[4] and tied it onto the boy's packsaddle, not trusting it to his

2. **Dutch oven:** a large, heavy pot or kettle, usually of cast iron and with a tight lid, used for slow cooking.
3. **carbine:** a light shoulder rifle with a short barrel.
4. **scabbard:** a sheath or container for a sword or rifle.

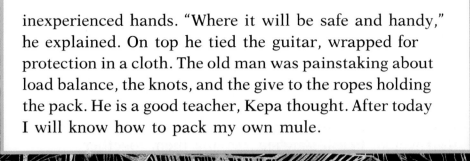

inexperienced hands. "Where it will be safe and handy," he explained. On top he tied the guitar, wrapped for protection in a cloth. The old man was painstaking about load balance, the knots, and the give to the ropes holding the pack. He is a good teacher, Kepa thought. After today I will know how to pack my own mule.

While Tío Marco packed his own mule, Kepa had a word with his. "I'm calling you Patto-Kak," he told the skittish animal. "Not because you remind me of the Patto-Kak, ponies of the Pyrenees,[5] but to remind myself that I, being Basque, am more stubborn than you are." The mule rolled his eyes wickedly, trying to rid himself of the wooden packsaddle and the heavy pack.

Tío Marco, leading his mule, and Kepa, with the newly christened Patto-Kak on a tight lead, went into the yard where the sheep dogs were waiting, tense and eager, for the first sight of their masters and the signal to go. Tío Marco's signal was so quick Kepa did not see it. The dogs did and rushed to his side.

---

5. **Pyrenees** (pir′ ə nēz′): the mountain range between France and Spain, where the Basque people originated.

The two dogs looked very much alike. They were small, black and white, with tan trim, their outer coats stiff and coarse. But Kepa, remembering Tinka, his dog back home, knew their inner coats were soft and thick to insulate them from heat or cold. The younger dog had one dark eye and one light one. Although as alert as the older dog, he seemed quieter and not as confident.

The sheep had wakened at the first ray of sunrise and now were moving under the flockmaster's tally out of their corrals. For each twenty-five ewes, a bellwether, a leader sheep, was put in the moving line and a black sheep for every hundred. There were twenty-five hundred sheep in Tío Marco's band.

Tío Marco's band was the first one to leave on the trail. As usual, at the beginning, there was noise and confusion, the tinkle of the bellwethers' bells adding to the din. But once set on the trail there was silence. The dogs, ever watchful of a straying sheep or a lagging lamb, ran before, beside, behind the browsing band, nipping a leg where necessary. The sheep feared and respected them.

The pack mules, resigned to their loads, followed the sheep, now that they were on the trail not needing to be

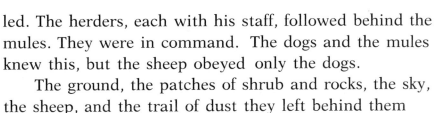

led. The herders, each with his staff, followed behind the mules. They were in command. The dogs and the mules knew this, but the sheep obeyed only the dogs.

The ground, the patches of shrub and rocks, the sky, the sheep, and the trail of dust they left behind them were one color—earth color—with no contrasting hue to sharpen or relieve the drabness. Slowly the sun moved across the sky; slowly the day moved across the eternity of time. Slowly the sheep moved across the desert, and the dust trail flattened itself over the land. The silence was oppressive, as heavy and as suffocating as the dust. Occasionally, it was broken by the tinkle of the bellwether's bell or the shouted command of the old herder to his dogs,

but instantly it closed again, choking sound into still-ness. Kepa wished that Tío Marco would talk or sing—anything to break the unreality of the silent world. He looked at the old herder and wondered how many years and miles he had walked this trail in silence, having no one to talk to. But he has me now, the boy thought and wondered if the old herder were lost in his own thoughts, if the habit of silence had imprisoned him or if there was nothing he wanted to say.

Midday came. The sheep stopped grazing to rest in the small shade of shrub and sagebrush, each ewe sheltering with her body her own small lamb from the sun's hot rays. The pack mules drowsed. The old dog curled up by his master. The young one lay alone. "Don't hurry him," the old herder said. Kepa was surprised. He had thought the old man had been napping.

They ate lunch, and Tío Marco began to talk. "The sheep will rest until late afternoon. Then they will graze until sunset, and at sunset we will make overnight camp."

A question had been bothering Kepa. "How do you count them?"

The old herder explained patiently what he thought the boy should know. "You mark the count by the bell-wethers and the black sheep. They keep their places in the moving band. In a few days all the ewes also will have decided their own places in the band. There will be the leaders, the followers, and the tailers. Even though they scatter for a time they will find their own places again. You soon will learn where each belongs and will be able to tell if some are not in their usual places."

Kepa looked at the resting sheep. They looked alike to him. How could he ever learn to know which ones were not in their right places? Then he remembered his small flock at home in the Pyrenees. He had known each one of them very well. "Twenty-five hundred is a lot of sheep," he said. The old herder did not answer. His gaze was on the distant hills. The boy sensed that conversation for now was ended.

In late afternoon the sheep roused and began to graze again, the dogs urging them on, slowly. By sunset they had reached night camp. Kepa could see that the place had been used as a campsite before, perhaps many times before. There was a bed of dry brush on the ground, stakes for a tent, rocks making a campfire place for cooking. How did the herder know, he wondered, that the sheep would reach this camp by sunset? He looked around for a spring or stream or water hole. "No water here," Tío Marco said, sensing the boy's unspoken question. "The sheep will get the water they need from the dew on the plants they eat in the early morning. If there is dew they do not need water every day."

The sheep had bedded down for the night. The man and the boy took off the packs from the mules and tethered the animals out to graze. Tío Marco showed Kepa how to cut sagebrush for under his bedroll.

The old herder put up his tent and helped Kepa
with his. "You store the food and your clothing and whatever you have inside the tent to keep them dry and safe.
If it is not storming you sleep on the ground outside,
with your carbine always handy."

The old man cleared most of the ashes from the
rock-rimmed fireplace, made a fire, and cooked their
dinner. He was as deliberate and thorough with these tasks
as he had been in loading the pack mules. When dinner
was cooked the old man fed his dog first, giving him bits
of food by hand, but when Kepa tried to do the same, the
young dog would not accept the food handed to him.
The herder spoke harshly. "Put the food on the ground near
him. He will eat only out of his master's hands. Don't push
him, boy." Then he said more kindly, "A herder learns
to take his steps one at a time so he may never need re-
trace them."

They ate their meal in silence. Dusk had come to the night camp; the shadows had lengthened; the sheep were still. The old man lighted the lantern and stirred the fire coals. "Get your guitar, boy, and sing to the stars. It helps." Then as if he spoke only to himself, he added, "I had a harmonica once, but I lost it somewhere along the trail and. . . ." He sat looking at the smoldering campfire. "And with it, I guess, I lost my songs."

Singing, Kepa found out, did not help. It made loneliness a sharper pain, bringing home closer and yet keeping it farther away. In memory the boy saw his father's *caserío* (kä sä rē′ ō), the big ancient house cupped in a valley of the Pyrenees, surrounded by its fields, its pasture, its vineyard, and the encircling forest.

In memory he climbed the wide stone steps leading to his mother's bright, friendly kitchen, but even in thought he dared not stop there for he knew that he would see his father and mother, his sisters, and probably José, his godfather's brother. He dared not stop to picture them, nor to pat Tinka, asleep on the mat by the door.

The remembered sights and sounds and smells of home smothered him, choked him with unshed tears. No, he thought sadly, singing brings memories, and memories bring no comfort. Aloud he said, "I do not know how to sing to the stars. I can sing only to what's in my heart."

Kepa put the guitar in his tent. The old herder was asleep, wrapped in his bedroll, his old dog asleep beside him. The boy looked over at the young dog asleep by the fire. "Tinka," he whispered, but the name did not fit. The boy unrolled his blankets and crawled in between them, but he could not sleep. He could not push from his mind the thoughts of home. He thought of the last time he had seen Tinka, and the last talk he had had with his father.

Now he was not in his bedroll under the stars in a strange world called America. He was home again in a Pyrenees valley, ready to set forth to an unknown land across the ocean, but still at home among the things he knew and loved.

The boy and his family, a line of ten, went single file down the wide stone steps, through the wide doors, past the dooryard, where Tinka was asleep on the door mat and the little donkey was patiently waiting for the portmanteau[6] and the sack full of food to be tied on his rounded, fat sides, one weight balancing the other.

"But where is Tinka's sled?" Kepa asked in surprise.

Father motioned for the others to start down the mountain trail. He put his hand on his youngest son's shoulder, but he did not look at him. There was a moment of silence. At last Father spoke, "Tinka cannot make the journey down the mountain and back up again, my son. He is too tired from a lifetime of service and too old from a lifetime of years. He has earned his rest. Do not grieve that today he sleeps and cannot go with you."

Again Father was silent, thinking of the words he must choose for this last talk with his young son, this boy beginning his manhood journey into the years. Abruptly, he said, "Today you come to the first fork in your trail. Remember, my son, although *you* travel a new trail, the old one is still there for the people who walk it."

The man again stopped talking and began anew. "What I am trying to say, Kepa, is that once you leave home you have, in a way, left it forever. Two things will hurt you when you come back. One is that living has not stopped just because you have gone. It has taken place as

6. **portmanteau** (pôrt man′ tō): a large leather suitcase.

it always has, only you have not been a part of it. The other thing is that what was real yesterday may not exist tomorrow. Let that knowledge, my son, steel your heart against hurt when you return to us." Kepa hoped he understood. He was not certain.

Father stopped to unbuckle the wide leather spike-studded collar from around Tinka's great neck, wakening the dog from his sleep. "Take this, young Kepa, to remember your love for your first dog and to help you share that love with your new one in America." Kepa took the collar and, blinded by tears, stooped to pat his dog good-bye.

"Do it quickly," Father urged. "Pat him once and go on. It would only disturb him if you communicate your grief. Learn now and never forget it—if you must grieve, keep it locked within you. Do not show it. This is the Basque way."

Kepa moved, turned, sat up, still wrapped in his blankets. Stars shone down on a sleeping world. The campfire glowed. This was not the Pyrenees. This was America. He had wanted to come and now he was here. The boy lay again on the hard ground beneath his blanket. Finally sleep came to bring him comfort.

Questions

1. Why did Kepa's godfather want Kepa to accompany Tío Marco on his first trail drive?
2. How did Tío Marco feel about being with Kepa? How did Kepa feel about being with Tío Marco?
3. Why do you think Kepa began to think of his old home the first night on the trail?
4. Describe an experience you have had that involved learning how to do something.

Applying Reading Skills

A. Use complete sentences to answer the questions below about "The Old Herder and the New."

1. What is the setting of the main part of the story?
2. What are the important plot events in the main part of the story?
3. What is the setting of the flashback?
4. What are the important events in the plot of the flashback?

B. Write the answer to each of the following questions about "The Old Herder and the New."

1. What is the narrative point of view?
   a. third person, from Tío Marco's point of view
   b. first person, from Kepa's point of view
   c. third person, from Kepa's point of view
2. Which statement best expresses the theme?
   a. Even animals have feelings.
   b. Each person has a path to follow.
   c. Change is not always easy to accept.
3. Which word best describes the mood?
   a. uncertainty   b. hope   c. fear

Different Dreams

When dusk is done
And the gray has gone
And the stars blow out
That once were on,
Then the pale moon casts
Its frozen gleams
And the hollow of night
Fills up the dreams:
Cats of mice
Elves of trolls
Cooks of silver spoons and bowls.
Poets dream of winds of Rome.
Sailors dream of ships and home.
Princes dream of foreign lands
To conquer
And of ladies' hands.
Dogs dream dreams
Of hounds to hares,
The red fox dreams
Of grass-green lairs.
While deep in your sleep,
With your dark eyes shut tight,
You dream of the day
That will follow the night.

Karla Kuskin

PREPARING FOR READING

Learning Vocabulary

1. Participation in sports and other physical activities can be <u>therapeutic</u> for many people with physical and mental <u>disabilities</u>.
2. Physical therapy often helps handicapped people gain confidence and <u>self-esteem</u>.
3. Alexandra felt <u>exhilarated</u> when she realized that Joey had made a real <u>breakthrough</u> in relating to others.

therapeutic	disabilities	self-esteem
exhilarated	breakthrough	

Developing Background and Skills
Summarize

A **summary** gives the most important information about something. Many newspapers have a feature called "News Summary." The business covered during a meeting is summarized in the minutes.

To write a summary, you must read all the information and decide what the main ideas are. You already know how to find the main idea of a paragraph. The main idea of a paragraph is really a summary of the paragraph. You can go about summarizing several paragraphs, an article, or even a book in the same way. Read the paragraphs below and think about how you might summarize them.

Just then a woman in a wheelchair came rolling into the barn. She was severely disabled, but there was nothing weak or timid about the way she pushed herself in the chair.

"Hi, Maria," said Cathy. "We'll bring Silver out for you in a minute. Boy, does he need brushing. We'd like you to do a really good job on him today."

"Brush him!" Alexandra thought with dismay. "Do they seriously expect that woman to groom a horse? I doubt if she can even stand up."

To summarize the paragraphs, first find the main idea of each. Then combine the information into a summary statement. The following is a list of the main ideas and a summary statement.

1. A handicapped woman appeared in a wheelchair.

+

2. Cathy told Maria that she wanted her to give the horse a good brushing.

+

3. Alexandra doubted that Maria could even stand.

↓

Alexandra doubted that the handicapped woman could groom the horse.

Summaries can be complete or incomplete, but no summary is ever "right" or "wrong." And no two people will summarize in exactly the same way. Can you think of another way to summarize the paragraphs above?

A great deal of information is presented in the selection that follows, "Horse Power." As you read, think about the main idea of each paragraph or each group of closely related paragraphs.

HORSE POWER

PATRICIA CURTIS

I saw the sign that read "Oaklands Riding Center" and turned in the driveway. On their business stationery it had said "Therapeutic Equitation" (thãr′ ə pū′ tik ek′ wə tā′ shən) in smaller letters under the title.

I had just graduated from college. I had majored in physical education and taken equestrian science because of my love of horses and riding. I'd heard about therapeutic equitation, the fancy name for horseback riding for the handicapped. In therapeutic equitation programs, blind people, amputees,[1] cerebral palsy[2] victims, paraplegics,[3] mentally retarded people, and many others with disabilities can have the exercise and pleasure of riding, with the help of professional instructors and specially trained horses.

---

1. **amputees** (am′ pū tēz′): people who have had a limb amputated, or cut off, especially by means of surgical removal.
2. **cerebral palsy** (sãr′ ə brəl pôl′ zē): a condition characterized by lack of muscle control, resulting from damage to the brain before or during birth.
3. **paraplegics** (pãr′ ə plē′ jiks): people whose legs and all or part of their trunk are paralyzed.

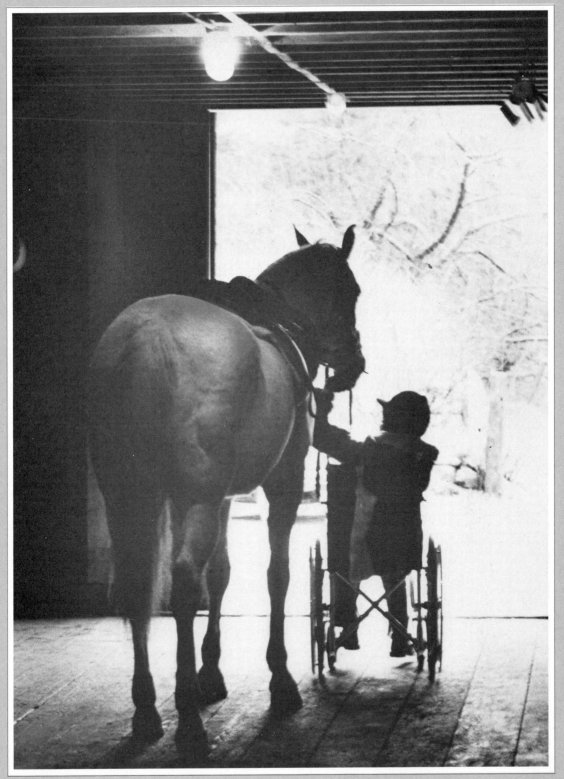

I wanted to see this firsthand. So, I'd written ahead and gotten permission from the director to visit and learn something about therapeutic equitation. I parked my car and walked around to the stable. A young woman about my age, dressed in riding clothes and carrying a bridle, came over to me.

"Hi—I'm Alexandra Snow," I said. "I've come to observe for the day."

"Hello—we're expecting you." The girl smiled in a friendly way. "I'm Cathy, one of the instructors."

Just then a woman in a wheelchair came rolling into the barn. She was severely disabled, but there was nothing weak or timid about the way she pushed herself in that chair.

"Hi, Maria," said Cathy. "We'll bring Silver out for you in a minute. Boy, does he need brushing. We'd like you to do a really good job on him today."

Brush him! I thought with dismay. Do they seriously expect that woman to groom a horse? I doubt if she can even stand up.

I was in for a surprise. Cathy led Silver out of his stall and casually handed the reins of his bridle over to Maria. Leading the horse with one hand, Maria wheeled herself out of the barn. I tagged along and leaned against the fence to watch.

In front of the stable, Cathy took Silver's bridle while Maria wheeled her chair right up beside him. Most horses would have flinched at that, but Silver didn't bat an eye. Then, Cathy handed Maria a brush. Maria struggled to her feet and brushed the horse thoroughly on one side. It took a lot of effort on her part. Then Cathy had the disabled woman go around to brush the other side. I thought Cathy was sort of hard on Maria, but Maria just laughed and did as she was told. Cathy did help her put the saddle on at least.

Another instructor, whose name was Bill, soon joined

them, and he and Cathy teased Maria a lot. Maria kidded them right back. I got the impression that beneath all the kidding around, Cathy and Bill respected Maria greatly.

Then, the two boosted the handicapped woman into the saddle. Silver just braced his feet and stood perfectly still as Maria's weight landed awkwardly on his back. Maria gathered up the reins and, with Cathy walking beside her, rode down the hill to the riding ring.

I could hardly believe my eyes when I saw Maria ride at a trot. Her head bobbed a good deal, but she managed to post,[4] pushing herself up and down in the stirrups. Cathy ran, leading Silver, and someone else ran alongside just in case Maria started to fall, which she didn't. Silver acted as if he knew he should pick up his feet carefully and not stumble, swerve, or break his stride.

Flashback to five or six years earlier, when I was in high school. I had my own horse; his name was Blaze. I took complete care of him myself, including buying his feed and paying for his care with the money I earned babysitting and working part-time at the supermarket. I rode him every day.

One fine autumn day we were walking past a house on our way home, and I happened to glance at some people beside a car in the driveway. They were unfolding a wheelchair, while a man lifted a girl about my own age out of the car. She was a really pretty blonde girl, but pale and fragile looking. I saw her legs were withered and in braces. The man set her in the wheelchair, and just then she looked across the lawn at me. Blaze was prancing a little, exhilarated by the good gallop we'd just had. The girl watched us, and our eyes met. I'll never forget the way she looked at me. Something very strong stirred inside me. A lot of mixed feelings

---

4. **post:** to rise and fall in the saddle in rhythm with the horse's gait while trotting.

pushed their way into my mind—pity for her, pride in myself and my horse, and at the same time a lot of guilt. Why should I be able to do this marvelous thing, while she could not?

Then Blaze and I passed on down the road, but I thought long and hard on my way home. An idea began to form in the back of my mind. Okay, the girl couldn't walk, but did that necessarily mean she couldn't ride? Would it hurt her if she did? Would she be scared? Couldn't somebody walk or run beside her and hold her on the horse's back? Had anybody ever tried it?

Although I rode past the house many times after that, I never saw that girl in the wheelchair again. I didn't forget her though.

I thought of becoming a veterinarian when I grew up, so I could be around horses. I figured that if I really knocked myself out in college I might possibly get into veterinary school. But later on, I discovered a field of college study that I liked even better. I had always loved sports—baseball, basketball, soccer, swimming, skiing, and best of all, riding. I decided to major in physical education in college, and take equestrian science.

College was a pleasure; the four years flew by. I wasn't sure exactly what sort of job I'd look for when I graduated, but I felt I was learning skills that would be useful to me in some way.

The idea of teaching riding to the handicapped interested me. You can imagine how I felt when I saw Maria at Oaklands that day. Here was someone like the girl I'd seen that afternoon, years before, with Blaze. But this girl was riding, just as I had wished that other girl could.

I was greatly impressed by the day I spent at Oaklands. I liked the fact that horses were used this way as full partners in therapy for people who needed them. I did some homework to find out more about therapeutic equitation. I learned

it's not a brand-new idea. There are references in the earliest of medical writings, from ancient times, to the use of horses in the treatment of certain disabilities. As medicine became more of a science, therapeutic riding fell into disuse—I suppose because it didn't seem scientific.

In 1970, the Cheff Center for the Handicapped, the first institution in North America specifically built and staffed for teaching riding to disabled people, opened in Augusta, Michigan.[5] Its director, Lida McCowan, a lifelong horsewoman, had trained for this work in England. Some two hundred-thirty disabled adults and children ride at Cheff every week.

Cheff offers a three-month intensive program to train instructors. After visiting Oaklands, I applied to that. I thought the course would be easy for me, but it was tough.

We were taught routine horse care and stable management. We also learned about physical therapy, and much about the various disabilities we would be likely to encounter in our work. Physically handicapped people are the ones who seem to benefit most from riding therapy. But emotionally disturbed children and retarded people gain confidence, self-control, and self-esteem that cannot be underestimated.

I'll never forget all I learned at Cheff—about horses and teaching, and about the disabled.

So—here I am now, working as a therapeutic riding instructor at Green Haven, a school for retarded children. It doesn't look as if I'll be rich and famous any time soon, but I couldn't be happier. Every day, unless the weather is too wet or too cold, kids come down to the barn for their riding lessons. Some have physical as well as mental disabilities. And all of them benefit from what the other instructors and I teach them.

---

5. Today there are about three hundred fifty centers in the United States and Canada that are accredited by the organization, North American Riding for the Handicapped.

Our star rider is a great kid named Joey. He is about twelve physically and maybe six mentally, active and cheerful and eager to try everything. But it wasn't always so. When he first came to Green Haven, Joey was a very withdrawn child. When the counselors brought him for horseback riding, he would meekly let himself be put on a horse and led around, but he didn't show any emotion one way or the other. He never responded to affection either. The staff here is very caring. The kids get a lot of physical contact—hugging, patting, that sort of thing—and in turn most of them are extremely affectionate. But not Joey, not in those days.

Then one day when he was hanging around the horses and ponies waiting his turn to ride, he went up to Willing. He's a wonderful, big, gentle horse who's just like his name. Joey began to put his fingers in Willing's nostrils and mouth. One of the instructors started to interfere—afraid not that Willing would bite, but that Joey would annoy him. Just then Joey laid his cheek tenderly against the horse's warm velvet nose and stood there like that for a few minutes.

"Nice Willing, nice Willing," the boy said softly.

The instructor stood back—she knew she was witnessing a real breakthrough. In fact, no one had been aware that Joey even knew the horse's name.

Joey began to improve in every way after that. Now he is so sunny and outgoing, it's hard for me to picture him as the sad and passive child he once was.

In this business, we get rewards like that every so often. I consider myself extremely lucky to be involved in work that keeps me happy and interested. Not only am I around horses all the time, but my work is useful and needed. To see a handicapped child struggle and then finally accomplish a goal, and see so plainly what this means to that child—this makes me feel good. To me, there couldn't be any work that's more rewarding.

Questions

1. Describe what Alexandra observed on her visit to the Oaklands Riding Center.
2. How did Alexandra's early interests, her college career, and her visit to Oaklands influence her decision to apply to the Cheff Center and prepare her for the training there?
3. Do you think Alexandra made a wise decision for herself in becoming a therapeutic riding instructor? Explain your answer.
4. Many athletes have overcome disabilities to excell at their sports. Give an example of such a person and describe his or her achievement.

Applying Reading Skills

Reread "Horse Power" and then study carefully each paragraph below. Decide which paragraph is the better summary of the selection. Explain why you decided as you did.

a. Alexandra Snow's job as a therapeutic riding instructor reflects her love of horses as well as her interest in rehabilitation of the handicapped through sports participation. A teenage experience led her to think about how people with disabilities could participate in sports activities. Alexandra's college major—physical education—and an equestrian science course helped further pave the way toward her career. A visit to Oaklands convinced her to enroll at the Cheff Center, where she received the final training necessary for her job.

b. At Oaklands, Alexandra Snow watched a handicapped woman skillfully handle a horse. The woman was named Maria. Alexandra was reminded of a teenage experience. At the Cheff Center she later learned about horse care and stable management, and how the disabled can benefit from riding therapy. Today she is a therapeutic riding instructor.

WRITING ACTIVITY

WRITE A JOB SUMMARY

Prewrite

"Horse Power" describes an interesting and unusual career—
therapeutic equitation. Suppose your class decides to plan a booklet that features information about different jobs or careers. Each
person will investigate a job or career and write a summary about
it for the booklet.

Here are some ideas to help you organize your investigation.
First, choose a career of interest to you. Second, find out about it.
Go to the media center in your school or public library for information. Ask your school's guidance counselor or a teacher how to
contact state and local employment agencies. Work with your class
to make a list of jobs or careers of parents, other family members,
and adult friends. Add employees in the school such as teachers,
principals, nurses, librarians, cafeteria and maintenance workers.

If possible, plan to interview a person in your chosen career or
job. Call for an appointment, confirm the time and date by a short
note, and plan your questions. Ask permission to tape record the
interview to help you recall information completely and correctly.

These questions can be used for your interview and also as a
way to organize your summary. Add or take away from the list as
you wish.

1. What are the qualifications for the job or career?
2. What education or special training is required?
3. What other work experiences could be helpful?
4. What is the approximate starting salary?
5. What hobbies or special interests would be helpful in preparing
   for this kind of work?
6. How many openings are there for this kind of work where I live
   now? In other places?
7. What other information can you share?

Write

1. Read the notes from your interview and research.
2. Begin your first paragraph with a sentence that names the job or career and gives an interesting fact to attract the interest of the reader. Continue the paragraph by explaining the answers to questions 1 through 6 on your list.
3. Add another paragraph for any special information.
4. Use your Glossary or dictionary for spelling help.

Revise

Read your summary. Check to make sure you included the important facts about the questions on the list. To make your summary more interesting to your readers, add a personal example or quotes from the interview.

1. Proofread your summary for correct spelling.
2. Check the end punctuation and capitalization in each sentence.
3. Be sure to use quotation marks and commas correctly in the quotes from your interview.
4. Rewrite your summary, and work with your teacher and class to publish a booklet about jobs and careers.

PREPARING FOR READING

Learning Vocabulary

1. Emilia found it difficult to <u>conform</u> to her cousins' lifestyle on a dairy farm.
2. In a voice clearly <u>audible</u> to everyone, Mrs. Ramsden told Emiglia she would have to learn to <u>cope</u> with the situation.
3. For Emiglia's cousin Carrots, field work was enjoyable, not <u>drudgery</u>.
4. Her body and <u>reflexes</u> took over the job while her mind dwelt on other things.

conform   audible   cope
drudgery   reflexes

Developing Background and Skills
Summarize

You know that a **summary** gives the most important information about a topic. No summary is right or wrong, but a summary can be complete or incomplete. Here are some guidelines for writing a summary.

1. It should be short.
2. It should include only the most important points.
3. It should *not* include unimportant details.

The paragraphs below are taken from the story you will read next. Read both paragraphs. Write the main idea of each. Then combine the main ideas into a summary.

A good half of the field was done by noon. The family didn't take the time to go back to the house for lunch but ate sandwiches out of the box Mama had packed earlier. Sitting on the edge of the creek on a big rock that was streaked with red from its iron content and yellow from something else unknown, Carrots dabbled her feet in the water and enjoyed the almost-chill of the shadowy air.

Too soon it was time to brave the blazing sun again. This time there was no escaping into daydreams. Dust and prickles from the grass stung eyes and throat, stuck into the sweat that trickled down sides and back and front. Faces flushed scarlet. Even hats stuffed full of green leaves didn't keep their hair from becoming soggy masses beneath the straw crowns.

The main idea of the first paragraph could be stated as: *When half of the field was done at noon, the family stopped for lunch.* The main idea of the second paragraph could be stated as: *It was soon time to return to the hot, dusty work.* The summary might be stated as: *The family stopped for lunch at noon when half the field was done, but they soon returned to the hot, dusty work.*

Reread your main idea and summary statements. Were they like the ones given above?

As you read the selection "Trial by Sweat," think about how you would summarize its most important sections.

TRIAL
—BY—
SWEAT
A R D A T H   M A Y H A R

When Charlotte Ramsden, nicknamed Carrots, learned that her cousin Emiglia was coming to live with them, she knew life was going to be different. Emiglia had been born in Hungary and raised in London. Now she was an orphan with no place to go except the Ramsden East Texas dairy farm. Emiglia, dubbed Miggle by Carrots' little sister Cherry, had no idea that people worked so hard. The idea that even children worked like paid hands on a farm was horrifying to her, and she did not hesitate to say so.

The east field was baled and all the hay stored in one of the huge barns before the showers began, but those only lasted a day and a half. Then it was time to cut the huge hayfield that fronted on the major creek flowing through Bobcat Ridge.

As soon as milking was done, the equipment cleaned, the floors washed, and the breakfast consumed hurriedly, the real work of the day began. Carrot's brother Glen drove the pickup, loaded with extra gasoline and water jugs, while Mama took the larger tractor and Carrots the smaller.

Cherry and Miggle were left on their own to freeze the peas that all had worked at shelling each evening.

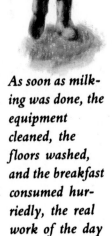

As soon as milking was done, the equipment cleaned, the floors washed, and the breakfast consumed hurriedly, the real work of the day began.

The shadows from the surrounding wood still stretched long fingers across the big field.

The next day, when the hay had cured enough for baling, all hands would be needed in the field.

The shadows from the surrounding wood stretched long fingers across the big field. Along its western edge the thick woods that lined the creek huddled secretly, bound together with wild vines. Glen headed the pickup in that direction, backed to a low point along the creek-bank, and off-loaded the water jugs into the shade.

While that was being done, Mama hooked up the drive on her big rig and came over to help Carrots hitch the old sickle mower to her smaller tractor. Then both took off, Mama hitting the heavy Johnson grass along the creek terraces, and Carrots cutting the lighter Bermuda grass growing on the higher edge of the field. The machinery clack-clack-clacked, the tractors muttered and groaned, and rabbits and snakes and insects fled frantically at this invasion of their home territory.

But for Carrots the job of mowing wasn't drudgery. It was something her hands and reflexes could do almost unattended, while her mind soared away into other dimensions entirely. She flew with the buzzard patrolling the field, looking down, in her imagination, through his high-borne eyes at the snorting tractors and the tiny figures guiding them. She made up silly rhymes about the grasshoppers and the cottontail rabbits.

A good half of the field was done by noon. They didn't take the time to go back to the house for lunch but ate sandwiches out of the box Mama had packed earlier. Sitting on the edge of the creek on a big rock that was streaked with red from its iron content and yellow from something else unknown, Carrots dabbled her feet in the water and enjoyed the almost-chill of the shadowy air.

Too soon it was time to brave the blazing sun again. This time there was no escaping into daydreams. Dust and prickles from the grass stung eyes and throat, stuck into the sweat that trickled down sides and back and front. Faces flushed scarlet. Even hats stuffed full of green leaves didn't keep their hair from becoming soggy masses beneath the straw crowns.

But by four o'clock the job was done. The worst of the day's work was over. After this, the evening milking looked positively leisurely. They raised the mower blades, loaded the equipment back onto the pickup, and got everything ready to go.

The house was ominously silent when Carrots and Mama entered the back door. Cherry's tear-stained face popped over the stair-rail as they came into the hall.

"Mama, make Miggle be good!" she sniffed.

On the heels of that, Emiglia came from the kitchen, her face pinkish with emotion. "Cousin Ginevra, I must protest. It is shocking to make children do such hard and continuous work. Cherry is only five, after all. She has been convinced that this is the way it is proper to live. She will never make a lady. I don't even mention Charlotte, who is lost to anything decent already. But there would still be hope for Cherry, if she were sent away to school and taught how civilized people behave."

Mama was tired and hot, and her blood pressure was elevated by her hard day's work. This was too much. "Civilized people earn their keep. Civilized people do not expect all lifestyles to conform to those they are used to."

She looked at the girl sharply. "Do you have supper on the table, as I asked you to?"

Miggle looked sheepish.

Cherry piped from above, "I made sandwiches and iced tea. Miggle said she wasn't anybody's servant."

Mama turned even pinker than the heat and her blood pressure could account for. She looked sternly at Miggle.

Mama was tired and hot and her blood pressure was elevated by her hard day's work. This was too much.

"Emiglia, there are certain things you need to know about living as part of this family. The first is that you are expected to see what needs to be done and to do it without being either asked or told. None of us really enjoys some of the dirty, difficult jobs we have to do. But they are necessary, and we all do them, right down to Cherry, who understands that what she does helps us all to survive. We have no time and no energy to devote to childishness, and a lack of willingness to do what you can to help earn your way is just that."

Miggle turned even redder than Mama. Her mouth opened to protest, but Mama spoke first.

"Tomorrow you will find out what haying is all about. You will not be expected to cook, for you will be too exhausted to hold your head up. As we are now. Until then I think you should take a sandwich to your room and think long and hard about what it means to pull your own weight in the world. There is a world out here that demands all that you have, and more. If you are to survive, you'd better learn about how to live in it and cope with it."

"One who does her level best, no matter what the circumstances," Mama said.

Miggle's mouth closed with an almost audible snap. Her cheeks were flaming. She turned and went into the kitchen. In a few minutes she returned and made her way up the stairs.

Cherry came down as her cousin went up, and went to Mama to put her arms about her waist. "What's a lady, Mama?"

"One who does her level best, no matter what the circumstances," Mama said.

Cherry relaxed. "Oh. Then we don't have to worry about *that*, do we?"

Mama laughed and hugged her. Then she went, steps dragging, toward the bathroom to change into her milking clothes.

The next morning, when Carrots reached the house for breakfast after finishing the milking, Mama had the sandwiches packed, small water jugs iced and ready, and Miggle's haying gear laid out in the back bedroom. Breakfast didn't take long, for everyone was keyed up and ready to go. Only Miggle hung back.

Thinking about it, Carrots realized that this was going to be something as strange and frightening for her cousin as a trip to London would be to any of the Ramsdens. She felt a qualm as she watched Emiglia stalk into the kitchen, clad in one of her khaki shirts, a pair of washed-out jeans (new ones were entirely too hot), and the wide straw hat with the pink scarf tied under her chin. She looked as if she were going into battle.

Carrots grinned at her. "It's not that bad. Kind of fun, really. You're not going into something terrible."

But as they jounced along on the back of the pickup, she began thinking about the heat. That was going to be the worst thing for Miggle, and there was nothing that could be done about it. However, they were in the field before she could warn her cousin about moving slowly and keeping in the shade as much as possible.

This time the pickup was stopped in the woods on the east edge of the field, opposite the side where the creek meandered. Tools and gasoline cans and water jugs were unloaded, and each of the Ramsdens set about getting ready for the day's work.

Carrots checked the oil in the little tractor, filled both tanks, and pulled loose straw out of the radiator grill. Miggle watched her as she worked, her eyes big.

"You . . . know how to do all those things, like a man?" she asked.

"No. Not like a man. Like a farmer, which I am," she answered. "Didn't your mother know how to do anything?"

She looked as if she were going into battle.

Miggle looked down at the toes of her borrowed boots. "Mama embroidered beautifully. She was a gourmet cook. She kept a shining apartment. But never in her life did she touch anything mechanical. I did not know that women and children could do such things."

Cherry had finished settling the water jugs in their places on both tractors. Now she climbed onto the seat that had been built for her on the front of the big tractor and waited for Glen to begin raking. Carrots climbed onto her steed, also, and set her toe on the starter bar. The machine ground, then caught, and the small tractor grunted into life.

Glen waved her toward the south end. "Hay's lighter there. Won't work the tractor so hard. I'll take a few turns until there's enough to start on, then Mama can rake, and I'll get the baler ready to go. Mr. Newman's bringing his big Ford over in a while to pull the baler, so we can all move at the same time."

Carrots growled away in a whirl of dust and crickets and began making regular sweeps around the lower end of the field. After a time she looked up and saw that Mama had relieved Glen. Twisting in her seat, Carrots saw the Newmans' low-bodied Ford pulling the baler. Glen was driving that. The pickup was moving behind it, and one of the Newmans' hay hands was pitching bales into the bed.

Miggle must be doing her part. Carrots relaxed and settled into the rhythm of the day.

By noon the upper end of the field was dotted with bales. Looking, you could barely realize how many the pickup hands had already hauled to the barns and stacked. They sat in the shade with Mr. Newman and Saul, his helper, and ate sandwiches and drank cool water. The scent of the hay was sweet, the shade cool as leaves stirred in the light breeze.

She growled away in a whirl of dust and crickets and began making regular sweeps around the lower end of the field.

Mama turned to look at Miggle. "So how was your first morning as a hay hand?" she asked.

Emiglia was sweaty and dusty, as they all were. The pickup moved so slowly that it didn't make much breeze. She was flushed with heat, and her hair, freed from the hat, was wet.

She gulped a swallow of water before answering. Then she said, "I didn't think I could drive! And it is easy!"

Glen nodded. "But don't mistake pulling up a pickup in the hayfield for real driving. You stay in low gear, and there's no other traffic. Cherry could do it nicely, as she does the tractor, if she wasn't too short to see out. But I have to say that you did well."

Emiglia blushed redder. "But I still think that you should hire men to do this work."

"There's no money," Glen said. He nodded toward Mr. Newman. "If we didn't swap out work with our neighbors, we'd have to do every bit ourselves. Carrots and I will be going to Al's next week to help him, just the way he's helping us today. That's the only way we can make it."

"But I thought that all Americans were rich!"

"That's the same kind of thinking that thinks all Texans are cowboys," put in Carrots. "Didn't your Dad ever warn you not to buy a horse without looking at its teeth?"

Emiglia looked bewildered; but before anything more could be said, Mama stood and gestured toward the sun-drenched expanse. "Back to the salt mines!"

Cherry was left to nap in the shade while the rest went to work. As Carrots moved toward the spot where her tractor had been left, she saw Miggle climb into the pickup.

"If we can keep her going for a while, we may be able to make something out of her!" she said to a passing monarch butterfly. She cranked her machine and turned once more into the scorching heat of the field.

Questions

1. What jobs had to be done every day on the Ramsdens' dairy farm?
2. Why did Emiglia find it difficult to adapt to life with the Ramsdens?
3. Do you think it was reasonable of Mrs. Ramsden to expect Emiglia to see what needed to be done and to do it without being either asked or told, or do you think Mrs. Ramsden was too hard on her? Explain your answer.
4. Have you ever had to do a job or task that you did not like or did not want to do? Describe what you did and explain how you felt before and afterward.

Applying Reading Skills

Reread the passages from "Trial by Sweat" listed below. Then use your summarizing skills to follow the directions. Remember to list the main ideas before you try to write a summary.

1. Write a summary of the first three paragraphs on page 86.
2. Write a summary of the paragraphs on page 88.
3. Read the summary below. Then find the two paragraphs in the story that it summarizes. Write the numbers of the paragraphs and the numbers of the pages on which they are found.

   Cherry and Carrots climbed onto their tractors and listened as Glen explained what everyone was to do.
4. Write a summary of the first four paragraphs on page 90.

WORK

Let me but do my work from day to day,
   In field or forest, at the desk or loom,
   In roaring market-place or tranquil room;
Let me but find it in my heart to say,
When vagrant wishes beckon me astray,
   "This is my work; my blessing, not my doom;
   Of all who live, I am the one by whom
This work can best be done in the right way."

Then shall I see it not too great, nor small,
   To suit my spirit and to prove my powers;
   Then shall I cheerful greet the labouring hours,
And cheerful turn, when the long shadows fall
At eventide, to play and love and rest,
Because I know for me my work is best.

Henry van Dyke

PREPARING FOR READING

Learning Vocabulary

1. Mr. Larsen's manner was <u>brisk</u> as he explained that the job was not a <u>glamorous</u> one.
2. Sid knew that if he didn't arrive at work on time he would be <u>violating</u> his agreement.
3. Mr. Larsen advised Sid to concentrate on the important work and not waste time on the <u>nonessential</u> details.
4. As Sid cut the film strip into <u>segments</u>, he discarded the frames that were too <u>dense</u> to make good prints.

brisk	glamorous	violating
nonessential	segments	dense

Developing Background and Skills
Character's Motives or Feelings

Characters' **feelings** usually change throughout a story. We can figure out a character's feelings at different times in several different ways. Read the chart below.

CLUES TO CHARACTER'S FEELINGS	EXAMPLE	FEELING
what author directly tells us	Sid was unsure about what to say.	uncertainty
what character says or thinks	"I've had it!" Sid shouted.	anger
how character speaks	"I did exactly as you asked," Sid said triumphantly.	pride

what character does	Sid drummed his fingers on the table as he waited.	nervousness
how character looks	Sid had a big smile on his face.	happiness

Characters usually have **motives**, or reasons, for acting as they do or for saying what they say. How do we know what their motives are?

Often you can make the connection between motive and action by reading with some questions in mind. For example, "Why did the character do or say that? What reason did he or she have?"

A help in finding the answers can be thinking about your own past experience. Read the sentences below.

Sid dialed Mr. Larsen's number and let the phone ring seven times. No answer. Well, he would just have to try again later.

Your own experience tells you that Sid's probable motive in calling Mr. Larsen was that he wanted to talk with him. You can also tell that it was important for Sid to reach him. He let the phone ring seven times, and he planned to call back.

As you read the next selection, try to figure out the feelings and motives of the characters. Ask yourself which character's feelings and motives you learn most about. Try to relate your answer to the story's narrative point of view.

FIRST JOB

Mike Neigoff

I don't know how long I waited, but it seemed hours. All there was to look at was that small office with desks cluttered with papers. There were some typewriters and an adding machine that looked old enough to belong in a museum. The desks could have been there forever. The pastel-colored office telephones with rows of buttons were the only modern touch.

Then the door at the rear opened and a short, stubby woman, all shoulders and square jaw, came shuffling in.

"Yes?" she asked in a hard, brittle voice.

I cleared my throat.

"Well?" she asked impatiently.

"It's about the job," I stammered. "For the student with photographic skills."

"Wait here," she ordered, and shuffled back through the rear door and shut it behind her. She was wearing bedroom slippers.

I didn't wait as long this time. The door opened again, and a gray-haired man came into the room and glanced at me.

"You came about the job to help around here?" he asked.

I nodded.

"Lift up that leaf at your left and come in," he said.

I saw what he meant. I pushed up on the leaf and came into the room. The man pointed to a chair by one of the desks and I sat down. He dropped into the chair behind the desk.

He pulled out a sheet of paper from the mess on the desk and then unclipped a ballpoint pen from the pocket of his sport shirt.

"Name?"

I gave him my name, address, and age, the school I attended, and previous work experience: none.

"Are you a hotshot photographer?" he asked in a brisk tone.

What was I supposed to say to that one? If I said yes, he'd ask me to prove it, and I had no idea what he considered a hotshot photographer. And if I said no, then he'd ask me why I was wasting his time.

"I don't think so," I finally said. When in doubt, tell the truth.

"That's a relief," the man said in the same brisk tone. I couldn't tell if he was joking or not.

The door opened and the same woman stuck her head in. "Phone for you, Joe. On six."

He grunted and pushed one of the illuminated buttons on the phone.

"Joe Larsen," he said, and listened.

"I think we can do that, Mr. Salmon. I'll send Jerry around to see you Monday."

Now I knew his name. Joe Larsen. He was listed in the paper as editor and publisher. Under his iron gray hair there was a hard face with all the features making angles and not curves. No fat on his body that I could see, and I could imagine him jogging every morning while everyone else was still asleep. That kind of hard-nosed guy.

He put the phone back, and he had no trouble picking up where he had left off in talking to me.

"I've had a dozen kids come in here, lugging their photographs. All self-proclaimed artists. I'm not looking for an artist. I'm looking for a kid to do some darkroom work. Do you know anything about photographic processing?"

"A little," I said. "I have a small darkroom at home and develop my black and white films and do some enlarging."

"I pay four dollars fifty cents an hour," he said. "I expect to get four dollars-and-fifty-cents' work out of the kid I hire. You understand?"

"Yes," I said.

But Mr. Larsen glared at me behind his wire-rimmed glasses and asked, "What do you want this job for?"

"I need the money," I said. "There are some things I want to do and I can't ask my folks. My dad just lost his job."

"What line of work is he in?" Mr. Larsen shot back at me.

"Newspaper reporter," I said. "He was on a city paper."

"You should know something about newspapers, then," he said.

"Not much," I admitted.

"At least you're not a know-it-all," Mr. Larsen said. There wasn't a touch of softness in his voice.

"Do you know the kind of job we're talking about here?" he asked.

I shook my head.

"I need someone to help. It's not a glamorous job. You'll push a broom around the floor and you'll soup the rolls of film the reporters bring to you. You'll print up proof sheets and then you'll enlarge the ones they mark and you'll crop them the way they direct you to and not to suit your own ideas of art. Understood?"

I understood. All "souping" films meant was developing the exposed film into a negative, and while I didn't know all there was to know about cropping, I knew that the term meant cutting out the nonessential parts of the photo.

"I'll give you a chance at the job," Mr. Larsen said. "But remember this. I'm hiring you to work, not to goof off. I expect you to do the things I tell you to do and do them quickly and as best you can. You understand all that?"

I nodded again.

"All right. Come in Monday at eight-thirty and I'll break you in. But remember, you're on trial here. You goof off, and you're out the door."

"Thanks," I said. "I'll do my best."

"You had better," Mr. Larsen said sharply. "Eight-thirty Monday. Don't be late."

"I won't," I said and made it out the door before anything wrecked the deal.

Monday morning came about much too fast. There I was in bed with Dad pulling at a leg and shouting, "Come on, Sid, get up, you're a working man now!"

I squinted at my alarm clock, and it was only seven o'clock! Getting up at seven on the first day of summer vacation was violating the contract of students.

"I don't have to be there until eight-thirty," I told Dad and grabbed the pillow and pulled it over my head.

He pulled the pillow away from my head.

"Take a shower. Get dressed. Your mother is making you a big breakfast."

I didn't want a big breakfast. I wanted to go back to sleep. But Dad was still standing guard in my room, a sentry in a blue bathrobe.

The shower woke me up, and after throwing on some jeans and a clean tee-shirt, I went down to the kitchen.

"You're going to work looking like that?" Mom asked.

"What's wrong with it?" I asked. "My white tie and tails are at the cleaners."

"This time, he's right, Ann," my

father said. "He's not going to be sitting at a desk but getting his hands dirty."

"I've fixed you a good, hearty breakfast," Mom said and plopped down a plate with two fried eggs staring up at me.

"Mom, I'm not going out to plow the back forty," I said. "What am I supposed to do with all this food? I want my usual juice and a roll."

"You're going to be working," she said, "and you need to have a good breakfast."

"O.K.," I agreed. I had one of the eggs and felt that my belt buckle would burst open. So Mom had the other egg. She can't stand to see food wasted.

They pushed me out of the house early enough so I could spend hours waiting for the *Arbor News* office to open.

Mom offered to drop me off at the paper on her way to the village, but I decided to take my bike.

I took the long way there but still was early. There's a private parking lot next to the paper office and I chained the bike to a fence and stalled as much as I could, but finally there was nothing left to do but walk through the door into the office.

There were people in it this time. They were reading the morning papers and didn't even look up as I came in. I waited at the counter, but I was being ignored. Finally, I said aloud, "I'm supposed to see Mr. Larsen. He hired me."

One of the young men looked at me and pointed with his thumb to the rear door. So I lifted the leaf and walked through the office to the rear door.

It was another office with some desks cluttered about and with long tables piled high with newspapers and paste pots and other junk. A woman was standing at the table marking up copy for an advertisement.

"I'm looking for Mr. Larsen," I said.

"He's in the composing room," she said, not looking up.

How was I supposed to know where the composing room was? At this rate, it would take all day for me just to find Mr. Larsen.

"Through that door," she said, pointing with her head. I got the idea. There was another door. I sucked in my breath and opened the next door. Now I was in a large room with a lot of long tables and low-hanging light fixtures, and there were people everywhere.

I looked around and finally saw a gray head of hair bending over one of the long tables. There were pages of the newspapers spread out along the ledge. He had tweezers in his hand and was moving pieces of typed matter around one of the pages. A woman wearing glasses was at his side.

I went up to his elbow and waited.

"Just move that story around under the picture," he said. "That should do it for this page."

He slipped his tweezers into his shirt pocket and said to me, as if he had expected me to be in that spot, "Come with me."

So I followed him. He stopped off to scan another page and told someone, "Reset that three-column head a size larger." He stopped again, with me tailing him as though I were on a leash, and scrawled an O.K. on some copy.

We went through another door, and I recognized the room we were in now as the photographic darkroom. I saw a sink and counters and an enlarger.

Mr. Larsen marched to one of the counters and picked up a film spool in its cassette. "This is Tri-X film," he said. "Process it."

It was all too quick. I hadn't processed Tri-X film before. I knew the developing time for Plus-X which is what I used in my camera. And where was the tank and the hypo* and developer?

"You've got some questions?" Mr. Larsen asked in a voice that was punishing.

---

* **hypo** (hī′ pō, short for *hyposulfite*): a salt, used especially as a fixing agent in photography.

Yes, I had questions and I wasn't about to flunk my first test because I didn't ask them.

"I've never worked with Tri-X before," I said. "What's the developing time? What developer are we using? Where's the daylight tank?"

He reached up and snapped up a printed sheet from some place. "Here are the developing times for the various films. You'll make up a fresh batch every Monday. I've done it already this morning. At 68 degrees, developing time is five-and-a-quarter minutes. The tanks are on the shelf in front of you. All the chemicals are on the shelf, too, all clearly marked. Look around. If you have any more questions, ask them now because I'm going to leave you to develop this roll. I'll be back in about twenty minutes, and by

that time you should have the film out of the tank and ready to be washed. We'll see how well you've done. One more thing, lock the door as I leave so no one lets light in accidentally by opening the door. Any questions?"

I shook my head. I'd work it out on my own. Besides, he made me nervous and tongue-tied. He left and I locked the door.

I looked around and set up the equipment on the counter. I checked to make sure everything was there. I set the timer for five-and-a-quarter minutes, so all I had to do when I had the film in the solution was push the button. There was even a darkroom rubber apron. I put it on.

I filled the tank with developer, made sure the reel and cover were where I could find them in the dark, picked up the cassette, and killed the lights.

In the dark, I pretended I was at home in my own darkroom and loading my own daylight tank. Nothing special about it.

That calmed me down, and I didn't have the trouble I sometimes do getting the film to roll easily upon the reel.

It was routine after that, and I

even had time to look around and check the enlarger while I waited for the developer and hypo to do their magic.

There was a loud banging on the door. I unlocked it, and Mr. Larsen came bursting in.

"Aren't you washing the negatives yet?" he asked.

"Another minute," I said, glancing at the timer. "I leave them in the hypo for fifteen minutes."

"Ten is enough," he said. "It's fresh hypo. Remember we have to save minutes where we can."

The timer buzzed. I poured the hypo out of the tank and back into the beaker. This was the moment of truth. I opened the tank, and with a pair of tongs, unreeled the film.

Mr. Larsen took the film from me and held it up to the light. I winced. Some of the frames were too dense and some too thin. There were a couple of normal frames though.

"The kid who shot these doesn't know his elbow from a camera," Mr. Larsen grunted, "but the processing is all right. Throw these into the wash and note the time. Might as well wash it for a full hour. I'll be back with more film for you to process in a few minutes. You do know how to make proof sheets?" he asked.

I said I did.

I processed three more rolls of film, and by that time, the first roll was dry. So I clipped it into segments and made a contact print and processed that through the trays set up next to the enlarger.

Mr. Larsen came in from time to time to bark out more orders and to ask, "Aren't those proofs ready yet? We've got to keep things moving."

I was moving as fast as I could, but there wasn't time to tell him that. He was already out the door.

The last proof sheet was dry, and I sat on the stool and took a break. And Mr. Larsen came rushing in.

"They're dry?" he asked.

I nodded.

"Well, don't goof off, wasting time. I'll show you where you deliver them, and make sure the film goes with the sheets. The reporters have to mark up the ones they want printed, and I'm not going to be your messenger."

So I grabbed the film and the proof sheets and ran after him to the front office where he showed me a wire basket where I was to dump the film and proofs. There was another basket next to it with a sign marked "Darkroom."

"This is where you pick up your work," he said. "Now, follow me."

I followed. We went back into the next room which was the advertising and art department, and in a corner was his office.

It was the size of a closet, with just enough room for two file cases, a desk, and two chairs. And like everything in the place, the desk was piled high with papers and file folders.

He reached under the mess and came up with a slip of paper. "What's your Social Security number?"

"I don't have one," I said, and saw my job vanishing.

"Get one," he said. "Have to let the government know that you're earning money so it can get its cut. For the time being, you'll work mornings from eight-thirty to twelve-thirty, unless I need you longer. Understood?"

I nodded.

"O.K., get back to the darkroom and clean it up so you'll be ready to go again in the morning. We like things neat here."

I held back a grin. Neat? The place was a mess. There wasn't a neat desk in the shop.

So through the doors again, somehow I found the darkroom though I made a few false turns. I wiped up some messes and poured chemicals back into their bottles and stacked the trays. Everything was neat enough to please my mother. I hung up the rubber apron and then looked at my watch. It was twelve-thirty.

It couldn't be, I thought. It felt like I'd been here for days. It was the first time all morning that I'd looked at my watch. I'd been too busy with all the hurry-up by Mr. Larsen.

Now what did I do? Did I just walk out because he said I'd work until twelve-thirty, or did I wait to be dismissed?

I clicked off the light and walked out, expecting I'd see the boss and nod at him pleasantly, so he'd know I was leaving. But I hadn't come across him by the time I was at the front door, so I just kept going.

It hadn't been bad, I decided as I pedaled back to the house. It might get to be a drag after a while, but it hadn't been too dismal. And I hadn't loused up one roll of film. Now that was something!

Questions

1. What job did Sid apply for and get?
2. Why did Mr. Larsen, rather than someone else, interview Sid?
3. Do you think Mr. Larsen was as helpful as he might have been in getting Sid started in his new job? Why might Mr. Larsen have acted as he did?
4. Describe a job that you are interested in and explain your qualifications.

Applying Reading Skills

A. The sentences below are from "First Job." Write a word that describes the feelings of the character whose name is under-lined. Then write the clue from the chart on pages 94 and 95 that helped you decide.

1. "Well?" she asked impatiently. (woman in office)
2. "It's about the job," I stammered. (Sid)
3. "You've got some questions?" Mr. Larsen asked in a voice that was punishing.

B. Write the phrase that best completes each sentence below, based on "First Job."

1. Sid gave Mr. Larsen his name, address, age, school, and previous experience because he ___ .
   a. wanted to comply with Mr. Larsen's request
   b. thought Mr. Larsen would need them

2. When Mr. Larsen asked Sid if he were a hotshot photographer, Sid said "I don't think so," because he ___ .
   a. wanted Mr. Larsen to think he was modest
   b. thought it best to tell the truth

PREPARING FOR READING

Learning Vocabulary

1. Teenagers are not always aware of all the job <u>options</u> they have.
2. It is important to try to match your skills, personality, and <u>aptitudes</u> to job requirements.
3. Most companies and businesses hiring workers require them to fill out <u>applications</u>.
4. First impressions are often important, so how you present yourself in an interview can be <u>crucial</u> in landing a job.
5. An <u>employer</u> may ask applicants how they think they can benefit the business or company.

options   aptitudes   applications
crucial   employer

Developing Background and Skills
Make Judgments

You know that a **judgment** is a decision. Many of the decisions we make are important to us: *What kind of career do I want for myself? How can I find out if it is a good choice for me? Should I change jobs?*

In making judgments of these kinds, we must evaluate information, or determine its importance. Read the following paragraph and the questions and choices that follow.

    Ben wanted a summer job. The list of "positions available" he got from the school counselor was long—more than 100 jobs were listed. Looking through the list, Ben noticed that some descriptions said "minimum age: 16." Ben was only 14. Others stated "some Saturdays and Sundays." Ben didn't want to work on the weekends because that was when his swim team practiced. Ben wanted a full-time Monday-through-Friday job to earn as much money as possible. Some of the jobs listed were half-day only.

What is the most reasonable decision for Ben to make?
  a. to apply for all the jobs.
  b. to apply for none of the jobs
  c. to apply only for the jobs that meet his requirements
     and for which he is qualified

Do you agree that **c** is the most reasonable decision? By limiting his applications to jobs that meet his requirements and for which he is qualified, Ben can save a great deal of time. He is more likely to receive offers of jobs for which he is qualified. He is also more likely to accept offers that meet his requirements. Why wouldn't **a** and **b** be better choices?

The following selection, "Help Wanted," is an informative article with a great deal of practical advice. As you read, think about how you can evaluate the information and advice to reach important decisions about jobs and careers for yourself.

HELP WANTED

THE TEENAGE GUIDE TO PART-TIME JOBS

This article was researched and written by TEENAGE magazine Editorial Interns Sara-Ellen Amster, 17, of Farmingdale, New York; Anne Cloutier, 20, of Claremont, New Hampshire; Joan Goldfarb, 21, of Cincinnati, Ohio; and Mark Woodlief, 18, of Newton, Massachusetts.

Good Jobs Are Hard To Find

But Six Million Teenagers Found One Last Year

By the time most teenagers turn 16, an allowance doesn't go very far. There are records to buy, concerts and movies to attend, and there's college to save for. And there's only one way to earn the money: you've got to work for it.

If you head for the job market this year, you won't be alone. In 1983, some 5,833,000 American teenagers held down part-time jobs in a variety of industries. They flipped hamburgers, took care of kids, counted out cash at banks, and bagged countless orders of groceries. And while many of the jobs teenagers tackle aren't exactly glamorous, they can provide you with a good introduction to the working world.

Sticking With It Gets Results

Give Yourself a Goal, and Reach for the Phone

The biggest mistake young job-hunters make, says Jo Cavender of Jobs for Tennessee Graduates, is "giving up—not continuing to persevere. Sometimes it takes ten contacts to get one interview. It can be devastating." Even more devastating is the number of books, articles, and resources that instruct high school students on the fine art of landing a job. It's a job just to tackle these references so you can determine how to go about looking for work.

The experts recommend many things: planning, building self-confidence, writing a good resumé, using personal contacts, setting goals, being enthusiastic. But really, there's just one sure-fire way to get a job: go out there and look, look, look. Here are some pointers that should make that looking easier and your job hunt more successful.

TAKE STEPPING STONES

You may want to get a snazzy, high-paying job (who doesn't?), but for many teenagers, those jobs are next to impossible to find. Yet any job is a good start. Says Leonard Corwen, author of *How to Find and Land Your First Full-Time Job,* "Don't be too choosy in looking for your first job. Get some general experience first. You can get more selective when you've got some experience under your belt." Adds Cavender, "Jobs should be stepping stones."

You can't begin to step, though, until you start to look. Cavender says

111

the best way to handle the hunt is to set clear-cut, short-range goals. "Get a reasonable goal, like 'I will fill out five applications today,'" she recommends. "Or 'I will set up three interviews tomorrow.'" Dr. Thomas D. Bachhuber, director of the Career Development Center at the University of Maryland, agrees. "Don't hunt too haphazardly," he says, "or in a hit-or-miss fashion. Be organized and think through the steps you'll take in getting a job."

KNOW THYSELF

You may think landing a job at a fast-food restaurant is a cinch, but not every teenager is handed a uniform simply because he or she has walked in the door. You have to sell yourself to any prospective employer. That, says Corwen, is easier if you know yourself.

"Try to match your skills, personality, and natural aptitudes," Corwen says, "with the requirements and demands of jobs in specific fields and industries." Failing to sum yourself up could cost you a job. Most job-hunters aren't effective at communicating to an employer how they can benefit the organization. Anyone who can offer an employer reasons his or her personality can benefit the company, then, is one step ahead of the rest of the crowd.

SHOW OFF YOUR BEST

To land *any* job, you'll have to meet an employer face-to-face. How you present yourself in an interview is crucial. Cavender says that first impressions are the most important.

"An employer's first glance is at a person's grooming," she says. "Then an employer will notice a person's first words, look for eye contact, and expect a firm handshake." Good, solid answers to questions are important, too. But if you look messy or stare at the floor when you first arrive, you may have already lost the job before you begin to speak.

Corwen also recommends arriving early for an interview (about ten minutes or so), sitting up straight, smiling, calling the interviewer by name, being courteous, showing enthusiasm for the job and the company, and thanking the interviewer before leaving. On the "don'ts" side, he says an applicant should never chew gum, fidget, ask questions about benefits or vacations at the outset, or interrupt the employer while he or she is speaking.

Jobs Most Often Come With Pickles, Relish

Even the Most Unskilled Can Cook a French Fry

If you're looking for a part-time job, get ready to hold the pickles, the lettuce, and maybe the onions.

Fast-food chains offer vast employment opportunities for American teenagers. According to Philip Rones, an economist for the Bureau of Labor Statistics (BLS), about 85 percent of all working 16- to 19-year olds in 1983 found their jobs in the service-producing businesses. These include fast-food restaurants and department stores.

Teenagers are more easily employed in the service sector of the economy because those jobs don't require specialized working skills. "Teenagers tend to have the fewest skills in the work force," says Rones. "They have an incomplete education and are inexperienced. They're suited for unskilled work. It's not that difficult to cook french fries."

113

BEYOND THE BURGER

There *are* jobs in the service industry that don't require flipping burgers. Jobs in mall stores, supermarkets, and even day-care centers all fall into that growing category of "service" in the economy. Teenagers may have an even better chance than adults at getting jobs in companies that cater to the youth market, like record stores, sneaker shops, and blue jeans outlets.

Still other part-time jobs exist for students in banks, offices, insurance agencies, and hotels. The BLS lists the clerical field as the second largest employer of teenagers. The health field is opening up more jobs for young people as well. There are unskilled jobs in places like hospitals and nursing homes.

Matching Jobs And Careers Makes Sense

But They Sure Take a Lot of Hard Work to Find

At first glance, it may not seem as if a part-time job would help to advance your future goals. But many part-time and after-school jobs can introduce you to a profession, and (just as important) that profession to you.

Teenagers who know what career they're likely to pursue have a head start when it comes to matching a job with a future goal. For example, if you're interested in medicine, it makes sense to take a job that has something to do with the medical profession, even if that job is an unskilled position.

NARROWING THE FIELD

Not everyone knows what career he or she will choose, though. "Kids don't always know the kind of options they have," says Allan B. Goldenthal, author of *The Teenage Employment Guide*. "There are easily 20,000 careers to choose from."

To narrow the field, he says, take inventory of your abilities and your preferences. It's also important to look into what challenges a particular career involves. "Most public libraries have career guidance sections," says Goldenthal, "with books that list and describe possible careers." In addition, your state division of labor and the U.S. Department of Labor offer a number of publications that describe careers in detail. The phone directory can lead you to the right state or federal agency for more information.

Poring over career reference guides doesn't necessarily mean you'll decide upon a career at 16. And even if you uncover career options you want to investigate, you may not be able to find a job in that field. That's not cause for despair, though. You can turn even the most ordinary job into a career opportunity, if you look at it in the right way. If you start a lawn-mowing service, you are forming a business, doing the marketing, getting the clients, and keeping the books. Any job is a way to learn about a particular business.

Talking Back To Boss Not A Great Idea

Once You Find a Job, You've Got To Work at Keeping It

There are a number of ways first-time employees can help ensure job security, says Kathleen Nicholson, a youth program director. The key to keeping a job, she notes, is good work habits. That, according to Nicholson, means that first-time employees should:

• Be dependable. Show up on time each day. If an emergency comes up, notify the employer as soon as you can.

• Be neat. Good grooming and good dress are important. You don't need to wear a tux, but scruffy, torn jeans and sneakers with holes generally aren't good business dress, unless the job is a dirty one. Being neat also applies to keeping a clean work area.

• Be efficient. Get your assignments and do them promptly.

• Be honest. Don't steal company time by taking long breaks. Don't waste company money by making personal, long-distance calls from the office or snitching office supplies to take home.

• Be "part of the team." Proceed on your own only after you've learned your job and your role in the company. Try to integrate yourself into the company's mode of operation.

• Be friendly and courteous. Be the person everyone says is easy to get along with.

• Be willing to learn. Follow the directions you are given, but don't hesitate to ask for help if you don't understand an order or procedure. Try to accept constructive criticism from colleagues and supervisors. It'll all pay off in the long run.

Questions

1. According to the selection, what are some of the things teenage job-hunters can do to make a job hunt successful?
2. Why can a job applicant with experience be more selective about work than one without experience?
3. Do you agree or disagree with the list of rules on page 116? Which rule do you think is the most important? Why? Can you think of any other rule to add to the list?
4. Describe a job you have had. Explain how you got the job and what you learned, not only about the job but about yourself.

Applying Reading Skills

Based on information in "Help Wanted," decide which lettered statement is the best reason for each numbered judgment. Write the statement you choose for each judgment.

1. It is a good idea for teenagers to have a job.
   a. By working, teenagers can earn needed money and gain valuable experience.
   b. Working teenagers can help prove or disprove textbook theories about jobs.
   c. Companies benefit by hiring teenage workers.
2. If you fail to find a job at first, you should keep trying.
   a. You were probably not enthusiastic enough in your interviews
   b. The biggest mistake young job-hunters make is giving up.
   c. You were probably too selective.
3. You should be well-groomed and present yourself at your best in a job interview.
   a. You will feel better about yourself if you do.
   b. A good appearance will make up for lack of experience or skill.
   c. First impressions are often the most important.

THE JOB INTERVIEW

OUT TO GET A JOB TODAY,
WENT ABOUT IT IN THE FUNNIEST WAY.
GOT UP TOO LATE,
MISSED THE BUS.
IT RAINED ON MY HAIR,
ALL THAT TIME AND FUSS!
FINALLY GOT THERE,
TOOK THE ELEVATOR,
GOT THE SPACE BEFORE SOME MAN,
ACCIDENTALLY KNOCKING HIS HAT FROM HIS HAND.
THE DOOR SLID CLOSED,
AND CRUSHED HIS HAT,
BOY, MISTER, AM I SORRY FOR THAT!
NOW IT SEEMS I REMEMBER SEEING BEFORE,
THAT MAN — YES, DOWN ON THE VERY FIRST FLOOR,
I BUMPED INTO HIM AND HIS BRIEFCASE AND BOOKS,
GEE, DID HE EVER GIVE ME SOME LOOKS!
SO NOW AS I SIT DOWN FOR MY INTERVIEW,
OH, NO, A CRUSHED HAT!
IT'S WITH — GUESS WHO!?!!!
CONSIDERING ALL OF MY MANY MISTAKES,
I WASN'T SURPRISED BY HIS DOUBLE TAKE,
BETTER LUCK NEXT TIME,
YOU'RE QUICK TO SAY,
BUT NO, I FIND
SINCERITY PAYS
(NOT TO MENTION MY NEW JOB)!

REAGAN LEE BRENNEMAN, 14
LANCASTER, PENNSYLVANIA

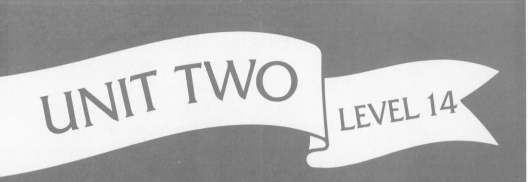

HOME
OF
THE BRAVE

PREPARING FOR READING

Learning Vocabulary

1. Rose's mind was in a <u>turmoil</u> as she put out her hand toward the woman and found nothing there.
2. Susan blinked at Rose in <u>consternation</u> and asked, "Where did you come from?"
3. "Susan is the girl I saw in Aunt Nan's house," thought Rose. "Well, really in *this* house," she <u>amended</u>.
4. The children told stories of violent storms on the lake, <u>boisterous</u> jokes, and long-lasting fights.
5. A sad-looking woman appeared in the doorway and asked <u>plaintively</u>, "Is that you, Will? Are you coming in now?"

turmoil   consternation   amended
boisterous   plaintively

Developing Background and Skills
Sequence of Events

Events take place in a sequence, or order. In real life, the **sequence of events** is chronological. That is, events follow one another in time.

In articles or stories, writers may rearrange the sequence of events. For example, they may describe the most exciting or dramatic event first. Then they may tell about the events that led up to it. Read the following newspaper story.

Atlanta, Georgia, December 14, 1939—The Civil War film *Gone With the Wind* opened here last night. For author Margaret Mitchell, it was another important event in her novel's history. Published in 1936, the novel took more than ten years to write. At the end of only one year, more than one million copies had been sold. In 1937, Mitchell was awarded the Pulitzer Prize. Then the book was turned into a motion picture.

Compare the sequence of events listed below. Notice how the writer rearranged the sequence to attract the interest of the reader.

SEQUENCE OF EVENTS IN THE STORY	ACTUAL SEQUENCE OF EVENTS
1. The film version of *Gone With the Wind* opened in Atlanta.	1. Margaret Mitchell spent more than ten years writing the novel *Gone With the Wind*.
2. Margaret Mitchell spent more than ten years writing the novel *Gone With the Wind*.	2. More than one million copies were sold.
3. More than one million copies were sold.	3. Mitchell won the Pulitzer Prize.
4. Mitchell won the Pulitzer Prize.	4. The book was turned into a motion picture.
5. The book was turned into a motion picture.	5. The film version of *Gone With the Wind* opened in Atlanta.

Watching a film set in the past—Civil War times, for example—is almost like traveling back in time. While we watch the movie, we can almost imagine being in a time and place that no longer exists. The next selection is a time-travel fantasy. In the story, the sequence of events depends on the character's point of reference. The main character, a girl living in the present, travels to the past. Characters from the past travel to the present.

THE ROOT CELLAR

Janet Lunn

When orphaned Rose Larkin's grandmother dies, she has to leave New York City to live with her Uncle Bob and Aunt Nan Henry and her twin boy cousins. Rose finds it difficult to adjust to living in the Henrys' farmhouse in Ontario, Canada. She sometimes sees an old woman named Mrs. Morrissay and a young girl in the farmhouse, yet the Henrys never refer to them. Rose begins to wonder if she has just imagined the two figures. Then as she sits in her bedroom one afternoon, Mrs. Morrissay appears once again.

"Mrs. Morrissay!" A shudder like an electric shock ran through Rose. "What are you doing?" Rose whispered.

Mrs. Morrissay said nothing. She didn't move. She stood half in the twins' room, half in Rose's, a blue and orange kerchief tied around her head, a dust mop in her hand, looking very ill at ease.

Rose was trembling. Her hands were wet with cold sweat and she could hardly focus her eyes. Mrs. Morrissay came the rest of the way through the wall and into the room. She was no longer half visible. She was solid, three-dimensional.

"You're a ghost." Rose heard her own voice, strange and shrill and accusing.

"I'm no ghost." Mrs. Morrissay was indignant. "I'm just plain myself, minding my own business and it happens."

"Happens?"

"I shift! I'm going along minding my own business like I said, hoeing or scrubbing or mopping, and right in the middle—I shift. I'm in my kitchen, then quick's a cow's tail after a fly, I'm in yours—or your bedroom."

"Mrs. Morrissay, you have no right to be here!" Rose could barely control her shaking voice. Her sense of how things ought to be had never been so disturbed, not even by her grandmother's death. "You don't belong here, Mrs. Morrissay—" Rose stopped abruptly, her fear, and her shock, subsiding before Mrs. Morrissay's smile.

"It's my house. I grew up in it. I was married in it. I'm like to die in it and"—Mrs. Morrissay finished with a sigh—"it seems I shift in it."

She reached over and took Rose's hand. Rose snatched it away. "It's all right," said Mrs. Morrissay soothingly. "Rose, I told you, I'm no ghost. I'm just shifted, and I don't know how no more than you do. It just happens, like I said. Rose, I want you to make things right in my house for me."

"Mrs. Morrissay, I can't fix your

house. It isn't my house and anyway I don't even like this house. I'm not going to stay here. I'm going back to New York."

Rose realized that she was actually talking to the old woman as easily as she had used her name, Mrs. Morrissay. "How do you know so much about me? Who are you?"

But Mrs. Morrissay was staring at Rose in alarm. As if she hadn't heard her question, she said,

the window, she caught sight of something blue and orange moving across the glade.

"There she is!" Rose said excitedly. "There's her kerchief!"

She flew down the stairs and out of the house. But there was no sign of Mrs. Morrissay in the clearing. Rose slumped down against the little hawthorn tree.

She sat there, dejectedly scuffing the leaves with her feet, her mind going over and over what had happened. Her toe struck something metal. Surprised, she sat up straight and pushed at it with her foot. It clinked. She went over on her hands and knees to look. She brushed away the leaves and discovered that there were boards underneath with a metal latch of some sort.

"It's a door, a door in the ground. How odd." Excitedly she began to pull at the vines and thick grass that had grown over the boards. When she had pulled most of them away she saw that, indeed, it was a door, two doors in fact, with rusty hook-and-eye latches that secured them together. With much pulling and wrenching she managed to loosen them and slowly, slowly,

"Don't talk about going off like that, Rose." Mrs. Morrissay looked at Rose in alarm, opened her mouth to say something and disappeared, not slowly the way she had come but instantly, like a light being turned off.

Rose started back. Fearfully she put her hand toward the spot where Mrs. Morrissay had been standing. There was no one, nothing. Her mind was in a turmoil. At that moment, through with a great deal of straining and heaving she pried them open.

There were steps inside that had been made by cutting away the earth and laying boards across. The boards had all but rotted away, but the earth steps were still there. At the bottom, facing her about three feet away, was another door, upright, also fastened with a hook-and-eye latch. The doorway was so low she had to stoop to get through.

Inside she found herself in a kind of closet with shelves along the sides on which stood crockery jars and glass sealers.

"I don't understand. If Aunt Nan keeps her pickles and things here, why is it so hard to get into?" she thought. She lifted the lid off one of the crocks and found it full of beets. She looked up. Someone behind her was blocking the light. Quickly she turned around.

A girl, smaller but probably about the same age as she, stood at the top of the steps with a jar in her hands. It was the girl she had seen in the bedroom with the four-poster bed. She wore quite a long dress made of some dark brown material, with a white apron over it. On her feet she had awkward looking ankle-high boots. She had dark brown hair in one long braid down her back, a plain round freckled face, a small nose, a wide mouth, and bright black eyes. They were blinking at Rose in consternation.

"Where'd you come from?" she demanded. "You'd best get out of our root cellar." The girl came down the steps. "Missus will be terrible cross." She reached up to the top shelf and brought down one of the crocks. All the while she kept turning around to stare nervously at Rose.

Rose stared back.

"You'd best come along now."

The girl frowned. "Honest, Missus doesn't like having strangers around." She started back up the steps.

"Look"—Rose followed the girl—"look, isn't this—" She'd been going to ask, "Isn't this Aunt Nan's root cellar?" but the words never got spoken. At the top of the steps she found herself standing beside a little garden with rows of young plants set out in it. Behind it, the creek bubbled merrily. Down past the creek a cow and a small flock of sheep were browsing. Beyond, where there should have been a field of crab grass and burdock, was an apple orchard in full bloom.

"This time it's me," whispered Rose. "I've shifted."

"Susan!" A fretful voice called from the house.

"Oh, there she is again," sighed the girl. "I don't know where you come from, but you best go back there right soon." She paused. "You aren't lost or nothing?"

"Susan!" cried the voice.

"Stay here. I'll be back."

Rose sat down at the edge of the garden. She couldn't believe what had happened.

"It's true," she whispered. "I have shifted. And that girl— Susan—*is* the girl I saw making the bed in Aunt Nan's house— in this house," she amended. Although it looked new and bright, this was the same house she hated so much for being old and ugly. Dazed, she got up and started walking around to the front.

The tangle of bushes that grew so close to the eastern side of the Henrys' house was gone. Instead there were three large lilac bushes in full bloom.

Nearby someone played a few notes on a flute. Rose looked around. There was no one in sight. The notes sounded again, above her. She looked up and saw a boy with blond hair sitting on the roof of the drive-shed. He was intent on his music and had not seen her. Susan came around the corner of the house.

"There you are," she said, coming toward Rose.

"Who's that?" called the boy.

"I dunno. I think he's lost," said Susan.

"What are you playing?" asked Rose.

"I'm trying to talk to the birds. It's an experiment," answered the boy crossly.

"Mebbe the birds don't want to talk to you," said Susan good-naturedly. "Come along down off of there and help this boy find out where he belongs." She turned to Rose. "You can't have come far," she said reassuringly. "Strangers don't much find their way down the road—unless mebbe you came off a schooner docked over the other side of the bay. Did you?"

"I don't . . . ." Rose hesitated, not sure what to say. "I come from New York City. Yes, from New York, and I'm not a boy, I'm Rose."

"I thought you were pretty for

a boy," said Susan, "only your hair is awful short and girls don't wear britches around here." She looked at Rose's jeans. Although she said nothing more, surprise showed clearly in the way her eyes widened. "Well, I'm Susan, and this here's Will."

"How do you do?" Rose put out her hand, and Susan took it shyly.

"New York City's quite a piece away. It must be awful hard with the war on and all that."

"Oh," said Rose vaguely, wondering what Susan could mean. "It's big and noisy in New York. I think this place is better."

"Is it?" Will peered down at her from the roof as though she were some exotic bird that had just dropped into the yard. "City folks don't generally care much for the country."

"See here," Susan asked anxiously, "is your schooner like to go off without you?"

"Schooner?"

"Your schooner, the ship you come over on."

"Oh, my schooner, uh—no, it's all right. It's going to be here for ages."

"That's grand," said Susan. "I got my half-day tomorrow, and Will can show you around if you like. I'm hired girl here and I got to get back to work now but Will, he belongs here, so he can help you find where your ship's docked. Does your pa own it? Has all the boys gone to war? Is that why you're dressed like a boy?"

"Yes, my father owns the ship, so it's all right for me to stay here tonight." The words tumbled out of her in her anxiety not to appear too outlandish.

"You can't stay here," said Susan. "I don't think so," said Will, both at the same time.

"You see," Susan apologized, "Will's ma doesn't open her house much to strangers. I guess I'm the most stranger that's been near the place since her son Adam died, except for the hired man who used to come and do the heavy chores."

"Susan! Susan!"

"There's the missus. Will you come back later?" she asked eagerly. Rose promised and Susan smiled. Susan ran off as Will slid down from the roof and dropped to the ground.

Rose could see now that Will was a year or so older than she was and almost a foot taller, a serious-looking boy with a thin face and blue eyes. He was wearing a heavy gray shirt and brown woolen britches. His boots were laced to the knees. He stuffed his flute into a pocket and started toward the road.

"Come along," he said curtly. He strode toward the bay, and, not sure what else to do, Rose followed him down to the water where a small rowboat was tied to a dock.

"You get in first," he said.

Will rowed steadily across the bay. He anchored close to the shore by a little wood. He sat back, listening. Rose listened, too. The redwing blackbirds mixed their metallic complaints with the pretty songs of the orioles and the bluebirds.

Will picked up his flute and played a few notes. Rose listened. She forgot where she was. She forgot who she was. She knew only the sounds of the birds and the flute.

Rose felt a smile grow inside her, almost in spite of herself. She felt very happy. "What date is this, Will?"

"Why, it's the tenth of June."

"But what year is it?"

"Year? 1862, same as it was yesterday."

1862. Then it was the Civil War they were talking about. Rose remembered lessons with her grandmother. The American Civil War, the war between the North and the South, Abraham Lincoln's war. "Is the war on here?" she asked.

"No. The war's got nothing to do with us, though there's strong feelings about it. We don't mostly hold with the South. We don't believe in slavery. There's a few fellers gone over to join the Union army for the North. Mostly we're not much for war around here, but some of us have come over from the States. My ma comes from Oswego in the States so all her relatives are there. Now I'll bring us in. I got to get back."

Will rowed them swiftly to the shore, leaped out, and tied up the boat. Rose jumped out after him.

"I'll see you after dinner," he promised, and off he went whistling up the slope.

Rose stayed a long while by the water thinking about Will now she was alone. "How odd," she thought. "Here I am with Will, and down in the United States the Civil War is happening."

"The American Civil War was one of the worst wars in the history of the world." She could still hear her grandmother's rich voice in her head. "Your great-great-grandfather and his brothers fought on opposing sides in that war. He was a Union man—they were for the Confederacy, for the South. When it was over, his brothers were dead, and he came to live in the North. He was never happy, but he believed in the Union, in one country, and he hated slavery so he had to fight. I remember him talking about it when he was an old man

and I was a small child." Rose had never forgotten those words, partly because it was such a sad story and partly because of the passion in her grandmother's voice as she had told it.

It seemed only a few minutes later when she glanced up to see Will going into the house.

"It can't be dinnertime already. It's not dark." She hurried up the slope and stationed herself beside a big maple tree not far from the root cellar. In a few moments Will came out, and Susan was with him. Will was carrying a large basket. Susan smiled and waved. "Here you are," she called, "and we've brought our dinner to have with you. Come along and let's take it out to the orchard."

When they had eaten everything, Rose and Susan sat with their backs against the trees and Will stretched out on the ground.

Rose looked from Will to Susan. "I don't know if you'll believe me, but I'm going to tell you anyway. I came to live with my aunt and uncle in this house one week ago—only, of course, it isn't this house. I mean it *is* this house, only it's more than a

hundred years from now. I don't know how it happens. It started with Mrs. Morrissay, so I think she has something to do with it." Rose told them the story of her meeting with Mrs. Morrissay, of Aunt Nan, Uncle Bob, and the twins. She told them how she had found the root cellar.

"That's a fine tale!" Will sat up. "You've even put us Morrissays in it. It's like some of the stories Susan's gran used to tell about ghosts and strange critters back where she came from in Scotland. It's the kind of story you could almost make a song out of." He pulled his flute out of his pocket and played a few notes. "It's kind of sad too, but I guess it's like Susan says, it doesn't matter where you come from. I guess what matters is where you belong. Me, I'm not always sure. I was born here, but Ma comes from across the lake in the States. Now they got this war, I feel like it's got something to do with me."

They told other stories about the neighborhood, tales of storms on the lake that sank whole ships in five minutes, of boisterous practical jokes, and fights that went on for days. Rose could hardly imagine some of the scenes they described. She realized that Will's name was Morrissay. She learned that Susan's parents had been killed when their sleigh upturned through the ice on the bay and that Will did not want to farm even though he loved the land.

Both Will and Susan listened, fascinated. When Rose had finished, Susan shook her head slowly. "It doesn't matter where you come from, Rose." Rose could see that Susan did not believe a word she had said, but she did not mind. No one had listened to her with such interest.

Susan talked about being an orphan, too, and coming to work for Will's mother. "I'm twelve now. Been here three years." Rose could hardly believe Susan was the same age that she was.

It didn't seem like more than a few moments before the sun was low over the bay, and the trees were making long shadows against the ground. Reluctantly Susan got up.

"What are we going to do about you, Rose?" asked Will. "I guess mebbe you could stay in the barn for one night."

Susan agreed. "We'll just have to figure out something else after tomorrow. But first thing in the morning you'll have to be getting back to where you come from—or finding a place that'll take you on as a hired girl. I'm coming, Pearly!"—as the cow bellowed to be milked, and off went Susan, skirts flying, to bring her in.

Will did not get up at once. Now and then he glanced over at Rose. "The things you said were awful funny," he said finally. "No mind. I guess I might as well show you the barn."

They gathered up the cloth and the empty plates and bowls and carried them to the house. At the kitchen door Will took what Rose had carried. "I best go in alone," he said.

From inside, his mother called plaintively, "Is that you, Will?"

Through the screen door Rose could see a woman approaching. She was tall with a long, gaunt face, large sunken eyes and gray-blond hair in a tight bun at the back of her head. Suddenly Rose was frightened. It was the look of the woman, so drab, so obviously wretched in a world that was so beautiful. She leaped back. Without thinking where she was going, she ran to the root cellar, pulled open the doors, and scurried down the steps.

Seconds later, feeling foolish, she went back up the steps—and out into the cold autumn evening of the Henrys' backyard.

If you continue reading The Root Cellar, *you will discover that Rose returns to 1862. She gains first-hand knowledge about the Civil War. You will have an opportunity to learn more about this time of crisis in our nation's history as you read the selections in this unit.*

Questions

1. What was so unusual about Mrs. Morrissay's entrance into Rose's bedroom?
2. What clues led Rose to believe that she had shifted?
3. What could Rose do to prove to someone that she had traveled back in time to the year 1862?
4. Rose's "doorway to the past" was the root cellar. What other time-travel device could the author have used?

Applying Reading Skills

Use complete sentences to answer the following questions about "The Root Cellar."

1. What important events are described in the introduction? List them in chronological sequence.
2. What season of the year is it when Rose discovers the root cellar? How do you know?
3. What season of the year is it when Rose shifts to 1862? How do you know?
4. What season of the year is it when Rose returns to the present? How do you know?
5. Which time line shows events from Rose's point of view? Which time line shows events from Mrs. Morrissay's point of view?

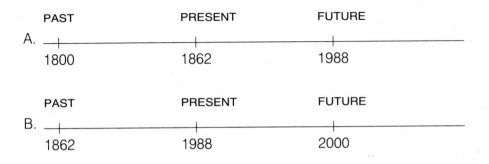

PAST   PRESENT   FUTURE

A.   1800   1862   1988

PAST   PRESENT   FUTURE

B.   1862   1988   2000

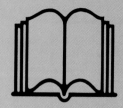

PREPARING FOR READING

Learning Vocabulary

1. During the 1858 campaign, Abraham Lincoln and Stephen Douglas held a stirring series of <u>debates</u> on the slavery question.
2. Lincoln was known as a <u>moderate</u> who did not have extreme views.
3. Congress had tried to prevent war by working out a <u>compromise</u>.
4. The <u>Fugitive</u> Slave Act provided for the capture and return of runaway slaves.
5. By 1860, the nation stood on the brink of war over the very important, indeed the <u>momentous</u>, issue of slavery.
6. In December of that year, South Carolina voted for <u>secession</u> and became the first state to withdraw from the Union.

debates	moderate	compromise
fugitive	momentous	secession

Developing Background and Skills
Cause and Effect

As you read, you discover how events and actions are connected or related to one another. One way in which events are related is called **cause and effect**. In a cause-and-effect relationship, one event or action—the cause— leads to another event or action—the effect. The sentence below is an example.

Because the troops did not want the supplies to reach the fort, they destroyed the bridge.

In this sentence, the effect—the destruction of the bridge— was caused by the desire of the troops to prevent supplies from reaching the fort. The word *because* signals a cause-

and-effect relationship. Some other cause-and-effect signal words are: *so that, since, in order to.*

Writers do not always use signal words. Often they only imply, or suggest, a relationship or connection. The same cause-and-effect relationship stated in the sentence above is implied in the sentences below.

The troops destroyed the bridge. They did not want the supplies to reach the fort.

Two questions can help you determine cause-and-effect relationships: *What happened? Why did it happen?* The answer to the first question tells you the effect. The answer to the second tells you the cause. Try the questions on the paragraph below.

Harriet Beecher Stowe's novel *Uncle Tom's Cabin* was published in 1852. It was a book about slaves and slave-owners. Thousands of people who had never thought much about slavery were touched and troubled by the book's message.

How would you state the cause and effect presented in the paragraph? One way would be:

CAUSE	EFFECT
Harriet Beecher Stowe wrote a novel about slaves and slaveowners.	Many people who read the book were touched and troubled about slavery.

In the selection that follows, you will learn about the period in our nation's history between 1820 and 1861. As you read, look for cause-and-effect relationships.

A HOUSE DIVIDED

CHARLES FLATO

On April 12, 1861, at 4:30 A.M., the Civil War began with the Confederate attack on Fort Sumter in Charleston Harbor.

Fort Sumter was a U.S. Army fort in the harbor of Charleston, South Carolina. Although Confederate authorities claimed the fort, Union troops still occupied it. In April 1861, the Union commander reported that his troops' supplies were almost used up. President Lincoln ordered that supply ships be sent. As soon as the ships neared the mouth of the harbor, however, Confederate gunners opened fire on the fort. The shelling lasted 34 hours. Union troops, low on food and ammunition, surrendered on April 13. The Civil War had begun.

The firing on Fort Sumter was a mighty explosion at the end of a long quarrel between the North and the South. Many things were involved in the quarrel, but the most important was slavery. Without slavery, the problems between the two sections could probably have been worked out in one way or another. With slavery, they could not be solved.

Processing cotton in factories involved feeding cotton into a carding machine which formed the cotton fibers into ropes called slivers. The slivers were then drawn into a strand known as a roving, which was spun into yarn.

Slavery

Early in the nation's history, slavery itself was not perceived as a problem. There were slaves in all parts of Colonial America. Nor did there seem to be much difference between the North and the South. Most people in both sections made their living by farming.

After the Revolution, the big change began. In the North, commerce and industry grew rapidly. Hundreds of immigrants arrived. Great cities came into being almost overnight. The South remained agricultural, with few immigrants and few large cities. It manufactured little.

Trade between the North and the South was brisk, but it was the cause of much bad feeling. A good part of the South's crops went north to be processed. Cotton, for example, was made into cloth in Northern mills. As the largest buyer, the North set the price, which the Southern planters always thought too low. At the same time, the South bought most of the manufactured goods it needed from the North. Again the North set the

price, and to the planters it seemed too high.

Other things divided the two sections. Their ways of living and thinking were different, and each side often misunderstood the other. But the big thing that set them apart was slavery.

Slavery gradually died out in the North, simply because it did not pay. At the beginning of the nineteenth century, most Americans, Southerners and Northerners alike, thought that in time slavery would go out of existence everywhere. And then a Connecticut Yankee, Eli Whitney, invented the cotton gin.

Whitney's invention was a simple device that made it possible for textile mills to use the short-staple cotton the Southern states could grow so easily. Within a few years, cotton was being planted on every acre where it could grow. The world had a great appetite for cotton, and the textile mills gobbled up every bale that was produced. More and more slaves were needed to work in the fields, and on the plantations there was no more talk of slavery going out of existence.

In the South, cotton was King, and the kingdom was growing. Planters looked westward for new land, to the black soil of Alabama and the yellow-gray loam of Mississippi. After that, King Cotton's rule extended into Mexican Texas and Missouri. And in Missouri came the first head-on clash between the North and the South. It happened in 1818, when Southern settlers in the territory applied for admission to the Union as a slave state. This would end the even numbers of free and slave states.

To Thomas Jefferson, this was a dangerous signal. The "momentous question," he wrote, "like a firebell in the night, awakened and filled me with terror." He feared that the republic he had helped to establish would split apart over the slavery issue.

Compromises

The split was prevented, at least for a time, by the Missouri Compromise of 1820. Missouri was admitted as a slave state, Maine as a free state. Congress also said that it would admit no more slave states north of the parallel that marked Missouri's southern boundary. Americans everywhere hoped that the argument over slavery was ended once and for all. But John Quincy Adams knew better. He called the compromise merely "a title-page to a great, tragic volume," and what happened after the Mexican War proved him right.

Henry Clay became known as the Great Compromiser because of his efforts to settle disputes between the North and South.

As a result of the war, the United States gained an immense new territory. It included areas that would later be the states of Texas, California, Arizona, and New Mexico. A Congressman from Pennyslvania, David Wilmot, was determined to keep slavery out of the new lands. He introduced a bill, known as the Wilmot Proviso, forbidding slavery in any part of the territory.

A Congressman from Georgia answered him angrily: "In the presence of the living God, if by your legislature you seek to drive us from the territories...I am for disunion."

Disunion...the ugly word had been used at last. But, after much wrangling and argument, another compromise was reached. Called the Compromise of 1850, it was the work of three giants in the Senate—Daniel Webster from the North, John C. Calhoun from the South, and Henry Clay from the border state of Kentucky.

California was to be admitted as a free state. New Mexico and Utah would come into the Union as either free or slave states, depending on the wishes of the settlers there. The slave trade in the District of Columbia was abolished. The Fugitive Slave Act, providing for the capture and return of runaway slaves to their masters, was made much stronger.

Once again, people hoped that the slavery issue had been settled for good. This hope soon exploded, mostly because of the Fugitive Slave Act. As manhunts for runaway slaves became common in the streets of cities and towns, Northerners grew more and more opposed to slavery. Some broke open jails to release captured slaves. Others worked for the Underground Railroad, a system by which slaves were helped to escape to Canada. In 1852, with the excitement at a high pitch, Harriet Beecher Stowe brought out her novel, *Uncle Tom's Cabin*. She had tried to write "something which would make the whole nation feel what an accursed thing slavery is," and she succeeded—at least in the North. The book sold 300,000 copies in its first year and won over many of its readers to the cause of anti-slavery.

An advertisement for a play based on *Uncle Tom's Cabin*.

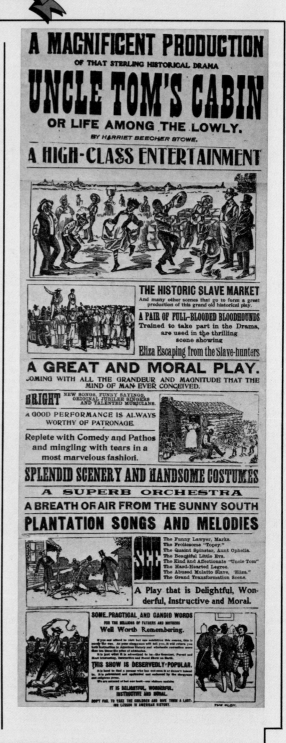

The Kansas-Nebraska Act

Two years later, Senator Stephen A. Douglas of Illinois introduced the Kansas-Nebraska Act. The bill created the territories of Kansas and Nebraska, but it did much more than that. It did away with the Missouri Compromise, and stated that the people of each territory would decide for themselves, when time for statehood came, whether or not to allow slavery.

The Kansas-Nebraska Act was passed, and the feeling between the North and the South became even more bitter. Many Northerners who had been friendly to the South now felt that the "slave power" was trying to extend slavery across the nation. Abolitionists[1] angrily called for an end to slavery. In the South, the "fire-eaters"[2] spoke just as angrily. There were moderates in both the North and the South, but their voices could not be heard in the uproar. Worse yet, Kansas was thrown open for settlement under conditions that made bloodshed practically certain.

Into Kansas, from the North, came settlers determined to make Kansas free soil; from the South came settlers just as determined to win Kansas for slavery.

---

1. **Abolitionists:** people who wanted to end slavery.
2. **fire-eaters:** pro-slavery people who quoted the Bible to try to prove that slavery was good.

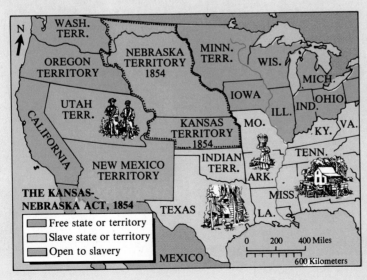

THE KANSAS-NEBRASKA ACT, 1854

Free state or territory
Slave state or territory
Open to slavery

The Kansas-Nebraska Act started a race to win Kansas as a slave or free state. Fierce fighting broke out between proslavery and antislavery groups as each side tried to form a majority. There was so much violence over the issue of slavery that this troubled territory was called "bleeding Kansas."

145

The Dred Scott Decision

With the country torn by mistrust and hatred, the Supreme Court added to the bitterness. It announced its decision in the case of Dred Scott, a Negro slave. Scott's master had taken him to Illinois, and later to Wisconsin, both states where there was no slavery. Scott sued for freedom, stating that he lived in free territory and could not be held in bondage. The court ruled against him, which was no surprise. But the reasons given by the court stunned the North. A Negro born of a slave could not be a citizen of any state, had no rights, and could not sue anyone. Even more alarming, the Constitution gave slavery ironclad protection. Congress had no right to forbid slavery in the Northern territories. In fact, there was no legal way to keep slavery out of any territory.

Truly, the United States seemed a house divided against itself. And, as a lawyer in Illinois said, "A house divided against itself cannot stand. I believe this government cannot endure half slave and half free."

That lawyer from Illinois was Abraham Lincoln, and in 1858 he ran for the Senate against Stephen A. Douglas. The two toured the

The Lincoln-Douglas debates made Abraham Lincoln well known as a person who did not want slavery to spread to the territories.

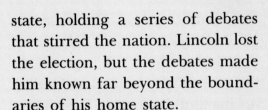

state, holding a series of debates that stirred the nation. Lincoln lost the election, but the debates made him known far beyond the boundaries of his home state.

Although Lincoln was clearly opposed to slavery, he was no abolitionist. He was against bringing more slave states into the Union. At the same time, he was against interfering with slavery where it existed.

Like the nation itself, the political parties were hopelessly split in the 1860 election. The Democrats ran two tickets, one Northern, one Southern. The border states ran their own candidates. The Republican candidate was Abraham Lincoln. He won the largest number of electoral votes, although he did not receive a majority of the popular vote.

Lincoln was a moderate on the slavery issue. He believed that the Federal government did not have the power to interfere with slavery in the states where it already existed. But the Republican party represented the industrial North and was a threat to the still agricultural South.

Secession

When the election returns came in, the South Carolina legislature was in session. The palmetto-tree flag of the state was unfurled; the flag of the United States was rolled up and put away. South Carolina was preparing to leave the Union. On December 20, 1860, a state convention voted for secession. The people celebrated this great and fearful event with the ringing of bells and a display of fireworks.

Other states soon followed South Carolina's example. On February 8, delegates from South Carolina, Mississippi, Alabama, Georgia,

Jefferson Davis of Mississippi, a former soldier, congressman, and Secretary of War, became President of the Confederacy on February 18, 1861.

Florida, Louisiana, and Texas met at Montgomery, Alabama. There they set up a new nation, the Confederate States of America. Jefferson Davis of Mississippi, a former Senator and Secretary of War, was elected President.

Meanwhile, Lincoln was preparing to move from Springfield, Illinois, to Washington. With his own hands he tied up the family trunks and labeled them "Executive Mansion, Washington." On February 11, he began the twelve-day journey, and on March 4 he stood on the steps of the Capitol, delivering his inaugural address. The Union, he said, would remain "unbroken." But he warned the South: "In your hands, my dissatisfied fellow-countrymen, and not in mine, is the momentous issue of civil war."

In April, the guns roared at Fort Sumter.

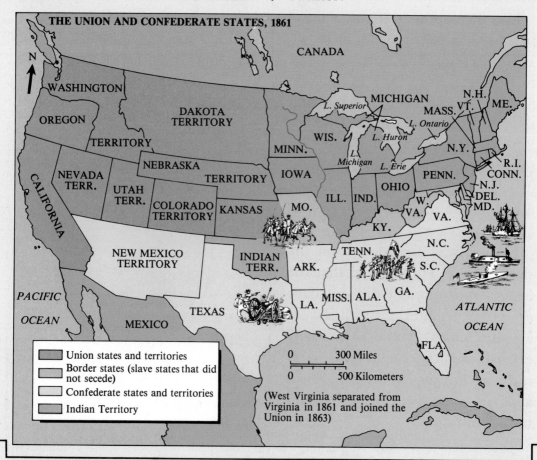

THE UNION AND CONFEDERATE STATES, 1861

N

CANADA

WASHINGTON

OREGON

DAKOTA TERRITORY

TERRITORY

NEVADA TERR.

UTAH TERR.

NEBRASKA TERRITORY

COLORADO TERRITORY

KANSAS

CALIFORNIA

NEW MEXICO TERRITORY

INDIAN TERR.

TEXAS

PACIFIC OCEAN

MEXICO

L. Superior

MICHIGAN

WIS.

MINN.

IOWA

MO.

ILL. IND.

OHIO

KY.

TENN.

ARK.

LA. MISS. ALA.

N.H.
VT. ME.
MASS.
L. Ontario
L. Huron
L. Michigan
L. Erie
N.Y.
R.I.
CONN.
PENN.
N.J.
DEL.
MD.
W. VA.
VA.
N.C.
S.C.
GA.
ATLANTIC OCEAN
FLA.

- Union states and territories
- Border states (slave states that did not secede)
- Confederate states and territories
- Indian Territory

0   300 Miles
0   500 Kilometers

(West Virginia separated from Virginia in 1861 and joined the Union in 1863)

Questions

1. What four things did the Compromise of 1850 provide for?
2. What did the Supreme Court decision in the Dred Scott case say about the rights of people whose parents were slaves?
3. Why didn't Abraham Lincoln receive a majority of the votes cast by citizens in the election of 1860?
4. How did the Civil War affect the history of your state?

Applying Reading Skills

Copy and complete the charts below about cause-and-effect relationships described in "A House Divided."

A.

CAUSE	EFFECT
1. The troops in Fort Sumter ran low on food and ammunition while under fire.	
2. The United States won the Mexican War.	

B.

CAUSE	EFFECT
	1. Slavery gradually died out in the North.
	2. Missouri was admitted a slave state, Maine as a free state.

WRITING ACTIVITY

WRITE TEST ITEMS

Prewrite

The selection "A House Divided" presents many facts about the events leading up to the Civil War. The article is divided into sections, and each section has a heading naming its topic. This kind of selection is very similar to the kind of writing you find in your social studies textbook.

For most textbooks there are tests provided for the teacher to give to students. True/false questions and multiple-choice items are the most common forms of test questions. You have probably taken many tests; now you are going to write one. Your test will consist of true/false and multiple-choice questions about the selection "A House Divided."

Make a chart like the one below to help you plan the number of test items and their content. For each section of the article, identify three main ideas you think students should remember. You will write three test items for each section. Decide which items will be multiple choice and which will be true/false.

Section	Main Ideas	True/False	Multiple Choice
Introduction	Surrender of Ft. Sumter Slavery, most important issue	2 items	1 item

To write a true/false test item, select a main idea and write a sentence about that main idea which is true or false.

Example: T F The book *Uncle Tom's Cabin* won many supporters for the anti-slavery cause.

150

To write a multiple-choice item, select a main idea, and write the first part of a sentence about that main idea. Then write three possible endings that could complete the sentence. One ending should be completely correct. The others should be partly or totally incorrect.

Example: The invention of the cotton gin ___.

    ___ a. made slavery die out in the North

    ___ b. kept slavery in the South because of the need for cheap labor

    ___ c. made more states choose to keep slavery

Write

1. Write the test items for each section of the article.
2. When you have completed the test items, combine all the true/false items into Part One of the test. All multiple-choice items will make up Part Two of the test.
3. Write directions for completing each part of the test.
4. Refer to "A House Divided" for spelling help.

Revise

Read your test items. Exchange tests with another student and take each other's test. Then revise the unclear items. Make sure you use complete sentences in both kinds of test items.

1. Proofread for correct spelling and punctuation.
2. Make sure the subject and verb agree in each item.
3. Rewrite your test and prepare to give it to other students.

PREPARING FOR READING

Learning Vocabulary

1. Robert E. Lee gained a <u>reputation</u> as a talented young officer in the Mexican War.
2. In 1860, Lee felt the nation was approaching either <u>anarchy</u> or civil war.
3. Lee hoped the country could bypass, or <u>avert</u>, war, which he knew would be a great <u>calamity</u> for both North and South.
4. Lee did not <u>waver</u> from his decision to do his duty as he saw it.
5. When Virginia's secession was approved by the convention, Lee was certain the people would <u>ratify</u> it.

reputation	anarchy	avert
calamity	waver	ratify

Developing Background Skills
Make Generalizations
Read the paragraph below.

The Union commander surrendered Fort Sumter to the Confederates on April 13, 1861. At the Battle of Bull Run, three months later, the attacking Union army was forced to retreat. Confederate troops stopped several other Union invasions in the East during the first year of the war. The Southern victories were largely the result of General Robert E. Lee's leadership. Lee defeated Union armies outside Richmond, at the Second Battle of Bull Run, at Chancellorsville, and at several other places in Virginia. The Northerners outnumbered the Southerners, but the Southerners managed to drive them back. Lee's reputation for intelligence and daring grew. Meanwhile, the Union grew discouraged at not finding a commander to match him.

If you were asked to make a general statement based on the information in the paragraph, what would you say? You might say *The South was successful in the East during the early part of the Civil War largely because of Lee's leadership*. A statement of this kind is called a **generalization**. A generalization should be supported by facts or other evidence. Nearly every sentence in the paragraph above provides a fact or a piece of evidence to support the generalization. The evidence and facts are listed below.

1. Fort Sumter surrendered to the Confederates.
2. Confederates won the Battle of Bull Run.
3. Confederate troops stopped several other Union invasions.
4. Lee defeated Union armies outside Richmond, at the Second Battle of Bull Run, at Chancellorsville, and at several other places in Virginia.
5. Northerners outnumbered Southerners, but the Northerners were driven back.
6. Lee's reputation for intelligence and daring grew.

A generalization such as the one above that is supported by many specific facts or details is said to be valid.

A generalization not supported by facts or details, or supported by too few facts or details, is said to be invalid. For example, *The Union army never found a general to match Lee*.

Most of the time you do not know all the details about a particular subject. For this reason, it is a good idea to avoid words such as *never*, *all*, *every*, and *always* when making generalizations.

In the selection that follows, you will be presented with a great many facts and details. Think about what generalizations you can make based on the information.

Robert E. Lee's Decision

Burke Davis

Robert E. Lee was born in the mansion Stratford Hall in Virginia. Not far away was the room where, by family tradition, two signers of the Declaration of Independence had been born before him. He was an honor cadet at West Point, and had fought in the war with Mexico under General Winfield Scott. The general's admiration for Lee amounted almost to awe. Lee emerged from the Mexican War with a reputation as the army's most talented young officer. He had since filled a number of choice posts. He had headed projects of the Engineer Corps in New York, Florida, Baltimore, Savannah, and St. Louis. He had been West Point's superintendent and, until lately, he had been second in command in frontier Texas.

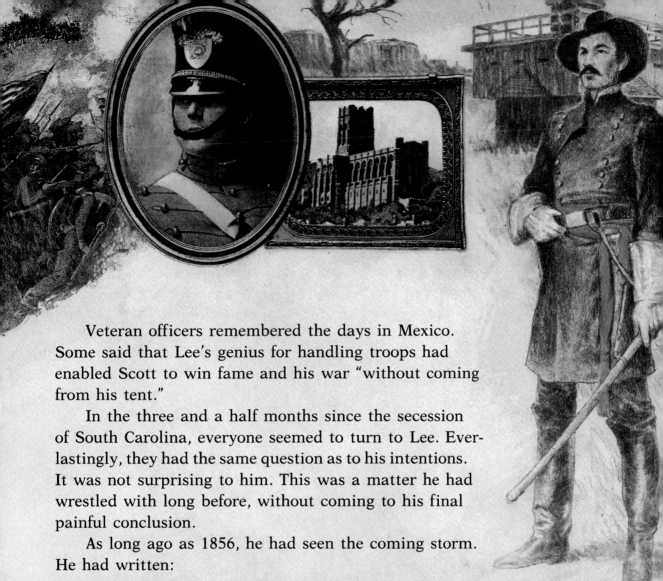

Veteran officers remembered the days in Mexico. Some said that Lee's genius for handling troops had enabled Scott to win fame and his war "without coming from his tent."

In the three and a half months since the secession of South Carolina, everyone seemed to turn to Lee. Everlastingly, they had the same question as to his intentions. It was not surprising to him. This was a matter he had wrestled with long before, without coming to his final painful conclusion.

As long ago as 1856, he had seen the coming storm. He had written:

Mr. Buchanan, it appears, is to be our next President. I hope he will be able to extinguish fanaticism both North and South, cultivate love for the country and Union, and restore harmony between the different sections.

He had also expressed himself on slavery at about that time:

There are few, I believe, in this enlightened age, who will not acknowledge that slavery as an institution is a moral and political evil....

155

In Texas, where Lee was stationed in the winter of 1860, he had clung to hope for the Union. He wrote his family that he would not permit himself to believe that the Union would be wrecked "until all ground for hope is gone." He added a note of hopelessness, however.

. . . As far as I can judge by the papers, we are between a state of anarchy and civil war. May God avert both of the evils from us!

. . . I see that four states have declared themselves out of the Union; four more will apparently follow. . . . Then, if the border states are brought into the gulf of revolution, one half of the country will be arrayed against the other.

I must try and be patient and await the end, for I can do nothing to hasten or retard it.

Lee was often called upon to declare himself in pre-war Texas, and his statements were unvarying. He stood for the Union, but could not think of making war on Virginia. R. W. Johnson, who served with Lee on the Indian frontier, saw Lee as he was leaving Texas, called to Washington headquarters.

"Colonel, do you intend to go South or remain North?" Johnson asked.

Lee replied, "I shall never bear arms against the United States. But it may be necessary for me to carry a musket in defense of my native state. In that case, I shall try to do my duty."

The Federal commander in Texas, General Twiggs, surrendered his command to state troops. In effect, he was delivering all to the Confederacy. Mrs. Caroline Darrow told Lee the news in San Antonio. She later wrote: "His lips trembling and his eyes full of tears, he exclaimed, 'Has it come so soon as this?'" At night, she overheard Lee praying in his hotel room.

Lee did not waver from his course, but he seemed unable to speak or write of it without emotion. In a letter to a son, he revealed the depths of his feelings.

. . . I can anticipate no greater calamity for the country than a dissolution of the Union. It would be an accumulation of all the evils we complain of, and I am willing to sacrifice everything but honor for its preservation.

I hope . . . that all constitutional means will be exhausted before there is a recourse to force. Secession is nothing but revolution. . . .

It is idle to talk of secession. . . . Still, a Union that can only be maintained by swords and bayonets, and in which strife and civil war are to take the place of brotherly love and kindness, has no charm for me.

I shall mourn for my country and for the welfare and progress of mankind. If the Union is to be dissolved and the Government disrupted, I shall return to my native state and share the miseries of my people, and save in defense will draw my sword on none.

And he had come home in that mood, just a few troubled days ago. The days had been full, and the country's tension had mounted rapidly. Twiggs had been dismissed from the army and replaced. Lincoln had been inaugurated. South Carolina had cut supplies from Fort Sumter in Charleston harbor. Near the end of March, Lee had flattering offers. One was a commission as a full colonel, signed by Lincoln. The other was a letter from L. P. Walker, now styled Secretary of War, Confederate States of America. Walker offered the rank of brigadier general in the new army.

Many of his brother officers were acting, but Lee could not. He was not convinced that Virginia would come to secession. There was wild talk of it everywhere, but he hoped there would be calm heads in Richmond.

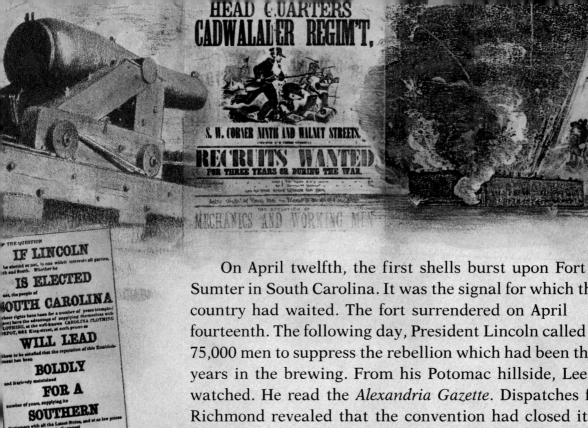

On April twelfth, the first shells burst upon Fort
Sumter in South Carolina. It was the signal for which the
country had waited. The fort surrendered on April
fourteenth. The following day, President Lincoln called for
75,000 men to suppress the rebellion which had been thirty
years in the brewing. From his Potomac hillside, Lee
watched. He read the *Alexandria Gazette*. Dispatches from
Richmond revealed that the convention had closed its
doors for secret session. The natural assumption was that
secession would follow. Lee learned of the closed meeting
on April seventeenth.

On the same day he was called into Washington by
two messages. One was a note from his cousin John Lee,
asking him to come to meet Francis P. Blair, an old
newspaper editor and a power in the Lincoln administra-
tion. The other message came from General Scott. It was
a request to report to his office.

On the morning of April eighteenth Lee dismounted
at Montgomery Blair's house, just opposite the War
Department, and went in to meet Francis Blair. They
talked alone. Blair did not mince matters. Lee could have
command of the enormous Federal Army if he wished it.
Secretary of War Cameron had ordered this offer of
command through Blair. There was the strong impression
that the proposal came from Lincoln himself. Lee dismissed the affair in sparse words.

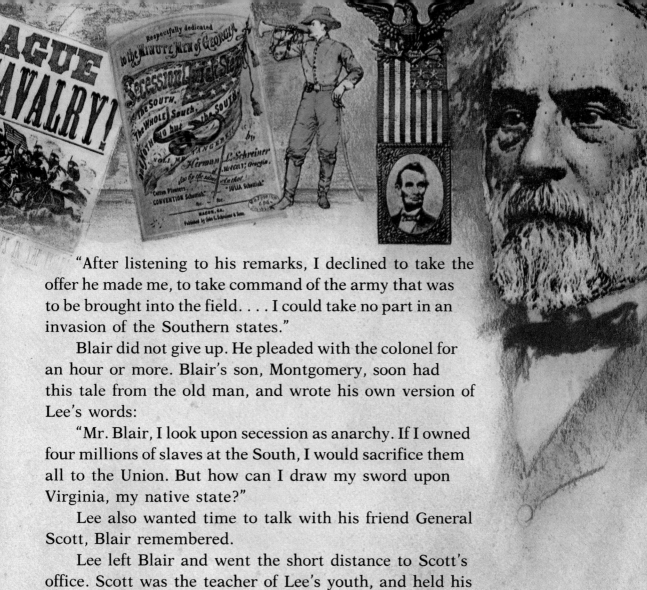

"After listening to his remarks, I declined to take the offer he made me, to take command of the army that was to be brought into the field. . . . I could take no part in an invasion of the Southern states."

Blair did not give up. He pleaded with the colonel for an hour or more. Blair's son, Montgomery, soon had this tale from the old man, and wrote his own version of Lee's words:

"Mr. Blair, I look upon secession as anarchy. If I owned four millions of slaves at the South, I would sacrifice them all to the Union. But how can I draw my sword upon Virginia, my native state?"

Lee also wanted time to talk with his friend General Scott, Blair remembered.

Lee left Blair and went the short distance to Scott's office. Scott was the teacher of Lee's youth, and held his respect. Lee told the general of his refusal of Blair's offer.

"Lee, you have made the greatest mistake of your life," Scott said, "but I feared it would be so."

"The property belonging to my children, all they possess, lies in Virginia," Lee said. "They will be ruined, if they do not go with their state. I cannot raise my hand against my children."

As Lee left the capital he saw signs of excitement. The Washington papers were screaming the news of Virginia's secession, but it was not yet official.

Lee rode into Alexandria the next day. He saw volunteers at drill on vacant lots. The rooms of the Young Men's Christian Association were filled with women sewing at uniforms.

Lee saw the dread news in print in the *Alexandria Gazette*: Virginia's secession was approved by the convention. Within a month the people of the state would vote on the act. They were certain to ratify it. He went into a pharmacy shop to pay a household account and sighed as he stood at the counter.

"I must say that I am one of those dull creatures that cannot see the good of secession."

The merchant was so struck by these words that he scribbled them on his ledger, adding, "Spoken by Colonel R. E. Lee, when he paid this bill, April 19, 1861."

The colonel went home. After supper, he went upstairs to his own room. His wife, Mary, listened as he paced the floor above; she waited through long periods of silence. It was after midnight—long after—when he came down with a letter in his hand.

"Well, Mary," he said, "the question is settled. Here is my resignation and a letter I have written General Scott."

There was a brief note to Secretary of War Cameron, and the longer one to Scott.

"I must say that I am one of those dull creatures that cannot see the good of secession."

Spoken by R.E. Lee who paid his bill April 19, 1861

Arlington, Va., April 20, 1861

General:
Since my interview with you on the 18th . . . I have felt that I ought no longer to retain my commission in the Army. I therefore tender my resignation, which I request you will recommend for acceptance. I would have presented it at once, but for the struggle it has cost me to separate myself from a service to which I have devoted all the best years of my life and all the ability I possessed.

During the whole of that time—more than a quarter of a century—I have experienced nothing but kindness from my superiors and a most cordial friendship from my comrades. To no one, General, have I been as much indebted as to yourself for uniform kindness and consideration. I shall carry to the grave the most grateful recollections of your kind consideration, and your name and fame will always be dear to me.

Save in defence of my native State, I never desire again to draw my sword. . . .

R. E. Lee

On Saturday, April twentieth, there was a note from Judge John Robertson, who had come up from Richmond. Lee was asked to meet the judge in Alexandria the next day. Lee replied that he would meet him after church.

After the service at Christ Church, he was approached by three men. They talked for a long time. When Lee left the mysterious men, family and neighbors were still in suspense. This was soon to be ended. That night there was another message from Judge Robertson, saying he had been detained in Washington. He asked Lee to accompany him to Richmond the next day.

Lee accepted without hesitation.

On Monday morning, April twenty-second, people at the Alexandria station watched Lee climb aboard to ride to Richmond with Judge Robertson.

The train shuddered and clanked into motion, and fled southward, trailing a pall of wood smoke. By late afternoon they were in Richmond. Colonel Lee was installed in the heart of the city's bustle, at the Spotswood Hotel. Soon he was closeted with Honest John Letcher, the political lawyer from the Shenandoah Valley who was Governor. Letcher offered command of all Virginia forces, with the rank of major general. Lee accepted.

Questions

1. What decision did Robert E. Lee have to make? What did he finally decide to do?
2. Why was it difficult for Lee to make his decision?
3. How would you describe Robert E. Lee? What qualities did he have?
4. If you could interview Robert E. Lee, what questions would you ask him?

Applying Reading Skills

A. Read the paragraphs in "Robert E. Lee's Decision" listed below. Then choose the generalization that can be made based on the facts found in each paragraph. Write the generalization on your paper.

1. First paragraph on page 154
   a. All the Lees were prominent people.
   b. Winfield Scott was responsible for winning the Mexican War.
   c. Lee had a great deal of military experience.

2. First paragraph following Lee's letter on page 157
   a. Events were happening fast and furiously.
   b. Lincoln's inauguration was a great event.
   c. The times were troubled.

3. Lee's letter on page 161
   a. Lee was grateful for his years in the army.
   b. General Scott was a kind man.
   c. Lee owed a great debt to General Scott.

B. Find five facts in "Robert E. Lee's Decision" to support the following generalization. Write the facts on your paper.

   Few men were as reluctant as Lee to go to war.

PREPARING FOR READING

Learning Vocabulary

1. The two runaway slave girls found protection from the storm in a makeshift shelter.
2. The next day dawned bright and clear. It was hot but still humid, even though the rain had stopped.
3. The man the girls met was startled and looked cautiously down the road before he spoke.
4. Liza chided Julilly for believing everything anyone said.
5. Julilly was awestruck to learn that their friends had been in the same cabin just a week before.

makeshift   humid   cautiously
chided   awestruck

Developing Background and Skills
Sequence of Events

The **sequence of events,** or order in which things happen, can help you follow the plot of a story. Keeping track of what characters have done in the past can help you predict what they might do in the future. Remembering what characters did in the past can help you understand their motives and feelings in the present.

Read the paragraph below.

The two girls felt secure as they sat in the warm, snug cave. As soon as they finished eating, they began to talk. It seemed incredible to them that only twelve hours had passed since they had left the plantation. But long before that, they had begun planning their escape. They had saved scraps of food from each meal and carefully bundled them up with the clothing they would need. Then had come the frightening moment when the overseer had inspected the slave quarters. Now, as they drifted off to sleep, the girls thought about the new life of freedom they would have in Canada.

If you read the paragraph carefully, you will probably agree that the events took place in the following order.

1. The girls planned their escape.
2. They saved food and bundled it up with needed clothing.
3. The overseer inspected the slave quarters.
4. The girls left the plantation.
5. The girls sat in the warm, snug cave, feeling secure.
6. They ate.
7. They began to talk.
8. They drifted off to sleep and thought about their new life of freedom in Canada.

Which of the events helps you to understand why the girls felt secure in the cave? What preparations had they made?

What events are the girls looking forward to? What events do you predict will take place before the girls reach their goal?

As you read the next selection, use what you know about the sequence of events to help you understand the events in the plot. How is one event connected to another? How do past events influence later events?

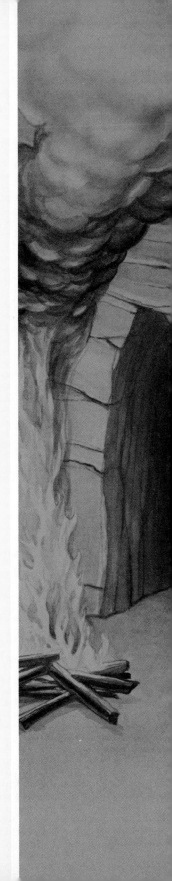

Runaway To Freedom

Barbara Smucker

Julilly and her friend Liza, who is crippled, are slaves who have escaped from a Mississippi plantation run by a cruel overseer. Disguised as boys, they head north toward Canada, where they hope to find freedom. They travel a hazardous route, journeying mainly at night and hiding by day, sometimes eating nothing but nuts and berries. When the girls see two other slaves, Lester and Adam, captured by slave catchers, they become more worried about their situation. But help comes unexpectedly from those who work on the Underground Railway.

There wasn't much danger from slave catchers on the high mountain paths at night. But even without them, this wild place was terrifying and strange for Julilly and Liza. High-pitched animal cries that they had never heard before echoed in and out of the tall black mountain peaks. Their path sometimes became "slim as the string bindin' a cotton bale," as Liza exclaimed.

The girls held on to one another, and once Julilly had to grab a swaying tree limb to keep from slipping down the mountain's side. Liza fell against her, hanging to her waist. They climbed up again on their hands and knees.

"If that North Star wasn't up there steady, beckonin' to us," Julilly shuddered, "I couldn't go on."

Before long, a strange, nervous wind began to blow. It skittered about—twirling up the stones along the path—then jumping into the trees and making ugly, swaying brushes of the giant pines.

A cloud smashed across the moon and erased their path. It was dark now, as dark as the deep end of a cave. The air began to chill. Julilly and Liza stopped climbing and held on to the trunk of the nearest tree. The wind lashed around them like a slave owner's whip.

Someplace nearby there was a long, cracking noise and then a thud. When the flashes of lightning came, Julilly and Liza could see a giant tree, torn from the earth with its raw, useless roots exposed to the storm. Thunder pounded in the sky, and then rain swept down like moving walls of water. Another flash of lightning. This time the girls saw a flat place close at hand, shielded by an overhanging rock.

"Get all the tree limbs you can find, Liza, and pile them under that rock," Julilly screamed above the wind.

The pile grew high. They dragged heavy limbs that could not blow away.

"Now we'll dig a place under this rock," Julilly screamed.

They scraped and grovelled. Their hands bled; but a small shelter did take shape, big enough for the two of them to squeeze inside. They shoved their bundles ahead of them.

"It's dry in here." Liza rubbed her hands over the ground.

But their newly patched clothes dripped with water, and they shivered each time the wind blew through their makeshift hovel. There was nothing to do but take their clothes off, wring the water from them as best they could, and hang them over branches that were still dry. They covered themselves with pine needles and bunches of dried leaves and dug deeper with sticks into the dry earth.

Somehow they slept, and when they woke the wind had stopped blowing. Mountain birds chirped their early morning songs, and a faintly pink sun spread shyly across the sky. The girls peered through their shelter of branches. Fallen limbs and scattered leaves crisscrossed over the ground.

"Looks like somebody stirred the whole place up with a big wooden spoon." Julilly pushed her head clear of the branch above her.

"Nobody is gonna come look' for runaway slaves in this mess." Liza shook the still damp clothes and hung them carefully over a limb in the warming air.

The sun rose. It was humid and hot. The damp clothes steamed, and then blew stiff and dry. Gratefully the girls dressed and ate a small amount of food.

"We'd best walk in the daylight," Julilly said. "There's no paths left and no signs of people."

"Tryin' to step over these sticks and stones when night comes is more than my two legs can manage," Liza agreed.

They decided to stay near the covering trees at all times and take cover at once if any stir of life was heard around them. They trudged along whatever trails they could find. Sometimes furry little animals jumped across

their paths, but the wild beasts that howled in the night seemed to take cover for the day. The girls climbed on and on, only stopping for drinks from the flooded mountain streams. Their guide was the needle of the compass which never left Julilly's hand.

The land was getting flatter and flatter, and the protecting mountain peaks were behind them. That night they rested uneasily in a cornfield near a road.

In the very early morning, Julilly saw an old man hobbling along the road, pulling a cart behind him. She crawled quickly from their hideout and walked up to him. She had no fear of this ancient white-haired, black-faced man.

"Can you tell me what town I'm comin' to next?" she asked.

The old man jumped a little. Julilly startled him. It seemed as if he had trudged this road a thousand times and never had a black girl bound out right in front of him before. He stopped his cart and looked at her carefully.

"Lexington, Kentucky," he answered kindly. Then he whispered, "You a slave? You runnin' away?"

Julilly didn't have to answer. The old man knew. He looked cautiously down the road behind him as though expecting someone. Then he pulled his cart to the side of the road and lowered the handles to the ground. He reached inside his loose jacket and drew out a half loaf of bread.

"This is for you, child," he said softly. His wise old eyes lighted on her briefly, then focused far away with tired patience.

"If I was a young man, I'd go 'long," he said. He peered again down the road. "Hide in those bushes, child. When night comes, follow the railroad tracks to Covington. There's a free colored man named Jeb Brown lives there. He'll get you 'cross the Ohio River in his little boat. You've got to cross the Ohio to get to Canada."

Julilly held his hand and thanked him from her heart.

The old man's back was more bent than Liza's, she noticed. His shabby clothes barely covered it. But he had strong arms and steady feet, and he had a pleased look on his face since giving Julilly the bread. He started toward his cart, when a man on horseback swerved around the corner of the road and stopped beside him.

Julilly ran quickly to the shelter of the cornfield.

The man on horseback pulled in the reins of his horse and glared down at the old man.

"What you mean, Joe," he cried out, "restin' by the road so early in the morning? Get along there." He twirled a whip in the air.

The old man leaned down and picked up the handles of his cart and plodded on down the road.

Julilly and Liza held each other and sobbed.

"He's a slave, too," Julilly cried. "He'll be hungry today. He gave us all his food."

She held the bread gently in both her hands.

*T*he tracks were their guide. The North Star shone steadily above them, but Julilly and Liza were frightened and ill at ease. It was light as day. Anyone could see them striding along the uncovered tracks. They crept down into a grove of trees, feeling hungry and tired: there had been nothing to eat since they finished the old man's bread. A field of corn waved in the night wind, its ears hung heavy with grain.

"We'll start us a fire and roast some of those ears," Julilly decided.

They were starting to gather dry sticks, when a dog came bounding and barking out of the field toward them. They ran for the nearest tree. Julilly lifted Liza up into the lowest branch and then swung herself up beside her. The dog circled and barked around the trunk. The girls were tense, and their hearts pounded so fast it was hard to breathe. Could this be a sniffing old slave catcher's dog, they wondered.

Then they heard a sharp whistle. The dog stopped barking and began to whine. Footsteps crunched nearby.

"What you chased into that tree, Pal?" a low-pitched voice asked eagerly. "Somethin' for us to eat?"

Liza and Julilly looked down. It was a black man!

"Joy and praise the Lord!" Julilly cried, loud enough for the man to hear.

"You hush, Julilly"—Liza grabbed her arm—"you trust people too soon."

But it was too late to be quiet now.

"You Jeb Brown?" Julilly called down to him.

The girls were silent. The man hadn't answered. Finally he said, "No, and I don't aim to get mixed up with him. It's a dangerous business he's in."

The girls climbed higher into the tree.

"Don't you be afraid of me," he called to them.

There was a long silence. Julilly and Liza were still tense and afraid.

"Now listen to me," the man said in a low voice. "You come down out of that tree when my dog and me leave. You walk straight ahead through those trees to the north until you hear the running water of the Ohio River. Then you look along the riverbank till you see a little house with one candle lighted in the window. That's all I got to say."

The man whistled for his dog and together they crunched into the bush and off into the crackling leaves of a cornfield until there was no sound from them.

They slid down the tree with Julilly keeping a firm grasp on Liza's arm.

*I*t was easy to walk north through the grove of trees and then down a row through a cornfield where the leaves twisted with the wind like hundreds of waving arms.

At the end of the field they heard the steady splash of moving water.

"The Ohio River, Liza," Julilly whispered. "We've reached the Ohio River!"

They walked toward the sound, but stopped abruptly when they saw the flickering light of a single candle from the window of a small log cabin.

"That's the cabin of Jeb Brown," Julilly said and started toward it. Liza pulled her back.

"You believe everybody," she chided. "That man could be tellin' lies."

Julilly didn't listen, but dragged Liza with her toward the cabin. When they reached the door, Julilly rapped softly.

A dog growled inside. Then came a man's voice.

"Who's there?"

"A friend with friends." Julilly used the faithful password.

A door creaked open exposing a big, straight man with crinkly gray hair and coal-black skin. Beside him growled a large brown dog.

"You Jeb Brown?" Julilly asked.

"I'm the man," he said, urging them inside.

"Quiet, Pal." He patted the dog's head and then called, "Ella, we got freight—two packages of dry goods."

A sprightly little brown-skinned woman stood there. Her eyes twinkled above the candle which she carried in her hand. Her white hair was piled about like fresh-picked cotton.

Jeb hurried about pulling down shades over all the windows. Ella walked behind a cupboard of dishes, motioning for the girls to follow. She pushed against the wall, and it opened like a door! Ella and the girls slipped through, followed by Jeb, and the wall closed behind them.

"You stay out there, Pal," Jeb said to his dog, "and this time you bark as much as you want if you hear any noises."

The room behind the wall was small but cosy. There were mats on the floor and a long spread-out table with benches around it. The only window was above them, cut into the roof.

"Looks like you were expectin' us." Julilly now felt that she could speak out loud.

Liza slumped to the floor—too tired and hungry to walk another step.

"Poor child." Ella leaned over her. She looked closely at her face, then laughed. "I thought you two were girls. We've been lookin' for you since your friends Lester and Adam were here."

"Lester and Adam!"

"Now you two just rest on those mats," big, kindly Jeb said, settling himself on one of the benches. "I'll explain about everything, while Ella fixes us some supper."

Ella went out through the secret door.

There was no way the girls could rest now. They stood in front of Jeb demanding to know about Lester and Adam at once.

"Well, they came one night more than a week ago," Jeb said quietly. "Chains were hangin' from their wrists. They'd rubbed through the skin and both were bleeding."

Julilly closed her eyes wondering if she really wanted to know the rest of the story.

"Lester had a sprained arm. The big man, Adam, had a swollen foot—so sore he could hardly lift it."

"How'd they know to come here?" Julilly was awestruck that all of them should come to this lone cabin on the Ohio River.

"They came 'cause we're a station of the Underground Railway," Jeb answered simply. "Isn't that why you two came?"

Ella interrupted by swinging through the secret door. Her arms held a tray with steaming food. She placed the lighted candle in the center of the long table and around it spread a feast of fresh venison, warm corn bread, wild honey, milk, and butter.

They bowed their heads, and Jeb prayed. It was a good prayer, full of hope and promise for the end of slavery.

"Amen," Liza added at the end of it with deep emotion.

Julilly and Liza filled their plates and Jeb told his story—how Lester and Adam had jumped from the slave catcher's wagon during the night they were captured, into a swamp, even though they were handcuffed together. For a whole night they stayed in the water to throw off their scent from the hunting dogs. They rubbed their chains against a jagged rock until it broke and they were free from each other. They drank swamp water and ate watercress. "Lester knew names of folks along the Underground Railway which he'd pledged to Massa Ross to keep secret—even from the two of you."

"Those boys were poorly and mighty sick," Ella interrupted. "I nursed them for a week in this very room. When they could walk, they left. They told us to watch for the two of you."

Julilly sat on her mat and cried. She had thought and dreamed of Lester and Adam dragging their heavy chains back to Mississippi. Now Jeb said they might be free right now in Canada. Inside her there was a welled-up fountain of joy. The tears came from its overflowing.

"But what's this Underground Railway?" Liza asked.

"You don't know 'bout the railway?" Jeb laughed. "The slave catchers gave us the name. They said runaway slaves just seem to disappear underground and that there must be a railway down there."

"We Abolitionists use the railway all the time," Ella laughed softly. "Colored and white folks work together on it. Our homes, where we hide you slaves, are the 'railway stations.' The roads you all follow are the 'tracks.' You runaway slaves are the 'freight.' The women are 'dry goods' and the men are 'hardware.'"

So that's why Jeb had announced them as packages of dry goods when they came to his cabin door. Julilly chuckled to herself.

"We aim to send you from here to the 'president' of the Underground Railway, Levi Coffin," said Ella. "He's a Quaker, and he lives across the river in Cincinnati."

Questions

1. Why did Julilly and Liza decide to travel by day instead of by night?
2. Who was the man who told the girls how to get to Jeb Brown's house? What makes you think so?
3. Which parts of "Runaway to Freedom" are based on fact? Which parts are completely fictional?
4. If you have been Julilly or Liza, when would you have been most afraid? When would you have felt most hopeful?

Applying Reading Skills

Follow the directions below using information about the sequence of events in "Runaway to Freedom."

1. The introduction explains that Julilly and Liza had seen Lester and Adam captured by slave catchers. Reread the section in which Jeb and Ella explain what happened to the two men. Then copy the events listed below in sequence.

   Lester and Adam were able to walk and left for Canada.
   The two men spent the night in a swamp.
   Lester and Adam were handcuffed together.
   Ella nursed the men for a week.
   Lester and Adam came to the Browns' house.
   The two men escaped from the slave catcher.

2. List in order the places Julilly and Liza visited on their journey. Begin your list with the plantation they escaped from. End your list with the names of places they will visit after they leave the home of Jeb and Ella Brown.

3. What event had prepared Jeb and Ella Brown for the arrival of Julilly and Liza?

Motherless Child

Sometimes I feel like a motherless child,
Sometimes I feel like a motherless child,
Sometimes I feel like a motherless child,
A long ways from home,
A long ways from home.

Sometimes I feel like I'm almost gone,
Sometimes I feel like I'm almost gone,
Sometimes I feel like I'm almost gone,
A long ways from home,
A long ways from home.

Sometimes I feel like a feather in the air,
Sometimes I feel like a feather in the air,
Sometimes I feel like a feather in the air,
And I spread my wings and fly,

I spread my wings and I fly.

—Black Spiritual

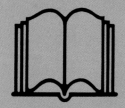

PREPARING FOR READING

Learning Vocabulary

1. Frederick Douglass, the man with the golden voice, was well known as an <u>orator</u>.
2. As a slave, Douglass had performed many <u>menial</u> tasks—hoeing, shoveling, digging, and shining shoes.
3. From his youth on, Douglass viewed freedom as an <u>entity</u> that could be attained.
4. Now Douglass stood before a large audience, <u>exhorting</u> an end to slavery.
5. The audience rose in <u>unison</u> and loudly applauded his speech.

orator   menial   entity
exhorting   unison

Developing Background and Skills
Facts and Opinions: Persuasive Devices

A **fact** is a true statement that can be tested by experience or by observation. An **opinion** is a statement that expresses a personal belief or judgment. Most stories and articles you read include both facts and opinions. Sometimes authors want to persuade, or convince, the reader to share their views (opinions), or to act in a certain way. To do this, they may use specific propaganda techniques. Propaganda is an effort to spread opinions or beliefs for the purpose of persuading others. A technique is a method or way of doing something. Some common propaganda techniques are described below.

- In **name-calling**, the writer says something bad about someone or something in hopes of turning the reader against that person or thing.

Abolitionists are troublemakers who will destroy our nation.

- A **testimonial** is a statement that someone, usually a famous person, makes in support of another person, thing, or action.

  The President stated, "The Union must be preserved."

- A **glittering generality** is a broad statement not supported by facts. In this technique, the writer promises "something for everybody."

  This candidate will help us put the nation back on its feet. He will work in the best interests of all groups—for Southern landowners and Northern businessmen, for factory workers, clerks, and farmers.

- A writer using the **bandwagon technique** tries to convince the reader to go along with something that he or she says "everybody else is doing."

  Shall we sit idly by while our sister-states are joining the Confederacy? It is time for us to act!

- In the **plain folks** approach, the writer attempts to connect a person, thing, or idea with basic honesty, good value, simplicity, or thrift.

  A vote for Lincoln is a vote for the people. Lincoln is an "ordinary" man, one of us. He knows what it means to work hard for a living.

Sometimes authors use a combination of these techniques. Or they may use one of the following persuasive devices:

- repetition
- a long list of examples or details

As you read the next selection, notice the techniques and devices the author uses to express her view of Frederick Douglass.

FREDERICK DOUGLASS

EVE MERRIAM

Frederick Douglass was born in 1817 and grew up on a plantation in Maryland. In 1838, he escaped to the North and became active in the anti-slavery movement. As founder and editor of the abolitionist newspaper the *North Star*, Douglass worked for the rights of blacks. The daring and courage of this "Prince of Abolitionists" compelled poet Eve Merriam to describe him in a poetic biography.

Women's Council   Washington, D.C.
February twentieth, eighteen hundred and ninety-five

Susan B. Anthony led him onto the platform:
a legend while he was still alive.

Prince of abolitionists,
man with the golden voice and the silver pen.
Orator, editor of the *North Star*.
Adviser to President Lincoln.
Minister to Haiti and Santo Domingo.
United States Marshal.
Titles, honors, badges too many to tabulate.
Douglass Hall named for him in Baltimore.
His statue in the University of Rochester:
a marble monument
and the man not even dead!
But he never would be,
for he was immortal Douglass,
everlasting champion
of the rights of all.

Look at him standing there,
taller than ordinary men,
still upright,
still going strong. . . .
The crowd of delegates cheered loud and long
for the giant with the flaming white hair and beard.
He looked a little like God,
had God a thundercloud dark face
and God been born a slave.
He had raised himself as high as heaven,
as high as human dignity:
behold,
Frederick Douglass, *free!*

On the twisting road from slavery,
was there a manual menial job
that he had missed?
His hands had planted, hoed,
sawed wood,
shoveled coal,
carried dung,
dug cellars,
shined shoes,
swung a crane,
wielded bellows,
rolled barrels of oil,
hauled cargo,
hoisted his weight and more in sweat, in pain, in pride.

What he held inside his hands no master could take away.

What you got there boy?
Open your fist and show.

Nothing, sir.

Don't try no trick now boy.
Give it to me quick.

The hands forced open wide
showed nothing inside.
Merely blisters, scars, cuts,
a bloodhound's bite
from an early runaway day,
welts from master's whip,
slip of the knife,
gash, lash, scab,
an oozing sore,
but dark blood can't hurt
the same as white,
so there was nothing there,
no special sight . . .

All right boy,
I see there's nothing.
Get on with your chores.

Alone, he would cup his hands
and stare at his secret.
Without shape or form
and colorless as water,
invisible as air,
he could feel it all the same—
alive, pulsing, warm.
It was all he had,
but it was all his own:
what could one call it?
It was himself, his entity:
a wish, a will, a dare:
its name was *free*
and it was always there.

The sky above the head of a slave
is the sky above a deep deep grave.
Nothing but dirt and stone and endless night.
No horizon for you to sight.
The way you're born,
that's the way you stay,
and the only release
is Judgment Day.
Tears dry up and leave no stain.
And what's one more cry in a world of pain?

Cornmeal,
ashcake,
cold clay floor.
Work
till you drop
and then
work some more.

And every sensible master knows
how to keep Uncle Tom and good old Mose.[1]
Let them sing and let them pray
and track down every runaway.
You'll hardly need to tighten the chains
if you just make sure they don't use their brains.

    A pail of water
    and a nosebag of feed,
    and don't let them learn
    to write or read.
    Just that sloppit of water
    and a big enough crumb
    to keep them alive
    and keep them *dumb*.

A slave's to fetch,
a slave's to bring,
a slave's not a person:
a slave's a thing.

A piece of kindling,
like wood to burn,
and a piece of wood's
got no need to *learn*.

A slave's a field
to plow and sow;
step on a field
and it won't even know.

---

1. **Uncle Tom and Mose:** characters in Stowe's *Uncle Tom's Cabin* who
   represent any blacks who are extremely humble or overly respectful
   to whites.

A field's just dirt
where seeds can grow
and the place of a field
is down below.

The sky above the head of a slave
is the sky above a deep deep grave.
How to make a breakaway?
How to tunnel through night to the light of day?

Dig a hole deeper into the ground?
No matter how deep, soon be found.
Have to aim higher for freedom's flight:
aim to learn how to read and write.

Master, master,
beware young Fred:
revolution
in his head!

Master's wife starting
the boy on his way;
shows him the Bible
and what the words say.

Master comes by
and takes it away.

Then whip him until
the boy is half-dead;
but all that he's read
stays safe in his head.

Take away one book,
he finds another;
learns dangerous words
like *helper* and *brother*.

And his favorite word
like a high-flying bird
over the sea
is *free.*
F as in *Frederick.*
F as in *Free.*

Now horrors, now Hades,[2]
new frightening sight:
grabbed onto a pencil—
he's starting to write!

He'd get by on water
and a crust of bread,
but his mind was starving
to be fed.

Where there was a book,
there was Fred:
books at his workbench,
books in his bed.

Letters of the alphabet
each like a root
reaching to a tree
bearing freedom fruit.

Learning the marks,
funny squiggly lines
untangling to grow
into freedom signs.

---

2. **Hades** (hā′ dēz): in Greek mythology, a place to which the dead go.

How beautiful those dark lines of writing came to be:
and most beautiful of all—
spelling *Frederick Douglass, free.*

How long ago,
how very long ago.

Slavery and the Civil War
were ancient history—
or partly so.

Now here he was, with hair as white as snow.
On this platform today
to support the rights of women,
the rights of labor,
free education for all;
exhorting the end
of every kind of slavery
that remained
to hold the human mind enchained.

The hall rocked with applause
as the women delegates in unison
waved their handkerchiefs,
little white sailboats
timidly bravely setting out upon
the thundercloud dark sea.
He was that great dark sea,
eternal Frederick Douglass,
freedom's forward tide,
never to be contained.

That evening he died.

Farewell, farewell,
toll the cold iron bell.
Black mourning crepe draping Douglass Hall.
The marble statue remote and classic-browed.
The flag lowered to half-mast.
Judges and senators filing past
to see the great man lying in state.[3]
Grieving, the crowd of mourners came
and came and came
in stumbling waves of disbelief.

 That majestic white-maned head
 no longer to be lifted high?
 His passionate words no more
 to blaze against the sky?
 How could the great dark father ever say goodbye?

 Then bitterly rejoice
 that only death
 could still his freeman's voice.

 And with it gone,
 that others echo on:

 that myriad
 dear dark
 sons and daughters
 embark
 upon the future's
 unknown boundless waters.

---

3. **lie in state:** to lie with certain honor and ceremony in some public place
   prior to burial.

Questions

1. What were some of the titles and honors Douglass achieved?
2. Why would Douglass have been invited to speak to a group of women who were working for women's nights?
3. In what way is Frederick Douglass immortal?
4. How does the poetic biography of Douglass differ from other biographies you have read?

Applying Reading Skills

Answer the following questions based on information in "Frederick Douglass."

1. Reread page 183. What terms does the poet use to refer to Douglass? List them in the order they appear. Why do you think the poet chose these terms? What impression do they create in your mind? What kind of a person do you "see"?
2. Find two passages in the poem that make use of repetition. List the word or phrase that is repeated.
3. Imagine what statement Douglass might have made in support of women's rights. Use this statement to write a testimonial urging people to support women's suffrage, or right to vote.
4. Reread the passage on page 184 beginning "On the twisting road. . . ." What is the author trying to persuade you to believe? Is her means of persuasion direct or indirect? What persuasive device does she use?

PREPARING FOR READING

Learning Vocabulary

1. Mary Chesnut allowed herself no sad foreboding about where secession might lead.
2. If the fort commander was obstinate and did not surrender, the Confederate troops would open fire on the fort.
3. The fear that the attack on the fort would end in great bloodshed turned out to be a delusion.
4. As the war dragged on with its many separations and uncertainties, Mary was filled with melancholy.
5. Mary began to keep a journal, in hopes that her memoirs might someday prove useful.
6. When Richmond, the Confederate capital, fell to the Union, the government archives, or records, were lost.

foreboding	obstinate	delusion
melancholy	memoirs	archives

Developing Background and Skills
Facts and Opinions: Persuasive Devices

Writers often try to persuade or convince readers to support their opinions by using a number of techniques and devices.

Glittering generalities are often used by writers when they try to describe an entire group. For example: Northerners have no respect for history. For Southerners, the past is important.

You know that a valid generalization is based on facts. If a generalization is too broad it is difficult to support. How could you prove that *all* Northerners have no respect for history, or that *all* Southerners value the past?

Writers often use **name-calling** to turn their readers against someone or something. For example: Their soldiers are untrained and disorganized.

Writers use the **bandwagon technique** when they appeal to a reader's feelings about their state or country. For example: We Southerners are all in this together.

Writers and speakers who want to gain support for their opinions also use a variety of **persuasive devices**. Read the paragraph below.

Last night Major Anderson lowered the Union flag that once flew so proudly over Fort Sumter. Now *our* flag flies in its place for all to see! This is just the beginning of the Confederate march to glory.

The writer uses the Union and Confederate flags as **symbols**. The lowering of the Union flag and the raising of the Confederate flag symbolizes Union defeat and Confederate victory.

Read the following paragraph. How does the writer try to convince you as a reader that the Confederates will triumph?

We have all heard the depressing accounts of recent Union victories. These reports should not discourage us. When this conflict began, we knew the road to victory would be difficult. Remember our victories at Bull Run and Chancellorsville! Our loyal commanders and troops will not be overcome. We have only begun to fight!

Notice how the writer avoids discussing the Union victories. Instead, Confederate victories are recalled. This **focuses attention on the positive** and **downplays the negative**.

The next selection includes excerpts from a Southern woman's journal. As you read, notice how she reports events. What propaganda techniques and persuasive devices does she use or describe?

MARY CHESNUT'S
CIVIL WAR

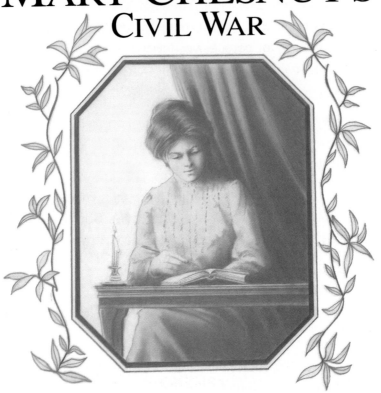

Mary Boykin Chesnut had kin and friends who lived
throughout the Confederate states. Her husband James
Chesnut, Jr., was a senator from South Carolina. He did not
favor secession, but he sided with the Southern delegation
when war approached. Later he served as military aide
to General P.G.T. Beauregard (bō′ rə gärd′) and Confederate
President Jefferson Davis.

In 1860, Mary Chesnut began keeping a journal.
Reading this journal today gives readers a chance to learn
about history from a person who was living through what
she described.

Montgomery, Alabama

February 18, 1861. *I do not allow myself vain regrets or sad foreboding. This Southern Confederacy must be supported now by calm determination and cool brains. We have risked all, and we must play our best, for the stake is life or death. I shall always regret that I had not kept a journal during the two past delightful and eventful years. . . .*

Charleston, South Carolina

March [no day] 1861. *"Now this is positive," they say. "Fort Sumter is to be relieved and we are to have no war." Poor Sumter—not half as much as we would be.*

After all, far too good to be true.

If there be no war, how triumphant Mr. Chesnut will be. He is the only man who has persisted from the first, that his would be a peaceful revolution. Heaven grant it may prove so.

April 7, 1861. *The air is too full of war news. And we are all so restless. News so warlike I quake. My husband speaks of joining the artillery.*

Things are happening so fast.

My husband has been made an aide-de-camp of General Beauregard.

Three hours ago we were quietly packing to go home. The convention has adjourned.

Now he tells me the attack upon Fort Sumter may begin tonight. Depends upon Anderson[1] and the fleet outside.

---

1. **Major Robert Anderson:** Union commander at Fort Sumter.

April 12, 1861. *Anderson will not capitulate.*

I do not pretend to go to sleep. If Anderson does not accept terms—at four—the orders are—he shall be fired upon.

I count four—St. Michael chimes. I begin to hope. At half past four, the heavy booming of a cannon. I sprang out of bed . . .

There was a sound of stir all over the house—pattering of feet in the corridor—all seemed hurrying one way. I put on my double gown and a shawl and went, too. It was to the housetop.

The shells were bursting. In the dark I heard a man say "waste of ammunition."

I knew my husband was rowing about in a boat somewhere in that dark bay. And that the shells were roofing it over—bursting toward the fort. If Anderson was obstinate—he was to order the forts on our side to open fire. Certainly fire had begun. The regular roar of the cannon—there it was. And who could tell what each volley accomplished of death and destruction . . .

Do you know, after all that noise and our tears and prayers, nobody has been hurt. Sound and fury, signifying nothing. A delusion and a snare.

April 15, 1861. *I did not know that one could live such days of excitement. . . . The crowd was shouting . . . good news. . . . Fort Sumter had surrendered.*

Montgomery, Alabama

April 27, 1861. *At Mrs. Davis's[2] reception, dismal news, for civil war seems certain.*

A General Anderson from Alexandria [or?] D.C., I think, was in doleful dumps. He says they are so much better prepared than we are. They are organized, or will be, by General Scott. We are in wild confusion.

---

2. **Mrs. Varina Davis:** wife of the Confederate President, Jefferson Davis.

Camden, South Carolina

June 10, 1861. I have been busy too. My husband has gone to join Beauregard. Somewhere beyond Richmond.

I feel blue-black with melancholy. But I hope to be in Richmond before long myself. That is some comfort. . . .

I am always ill. The name of my disease is a longing to get away from here and to go to Richmond.

Camp Pickens, Virginia

July 9, 1861. Our battle summer. May it be our first and our last. So-called. After all, we have not had any of the horrors of war. Could there have been a gayer or pleasanter life than we led in Charleston? And Montgomery, how exciting it all was there. So many clever men and women congregated from every part of the South.

Flies and mosquitoes and a want of neatness and want of good things to eat did drive us away.

Richmond, Virginia

July 13, 1861. Now we feel safe and comfortable. We cannot be flanked.

Yesterday as we left the cars,[3] we had a glimpse of war. It was the saddest sight. The memory of it is hard to shake off.

Sick soldiers—not wounded. There were quite two hundred (they said) lying about as best they might on the platform. Robert Barnwell[4] was there, doing all he could. These pale, ghastly faces. So here is one of the horrors of war we had not reckoned on. There were many good men and women with Robert Barnwell, doing all the servic possible in the circumstances.

---

3. **cars:** railroad cars.
4. **Robert Barnwell:** nephew of the Confederate senator with the same name; a professor and chaplain at South Carolina College.

July 14, 1861. *Mr. C remained closeted with them—the president and General Lee, etc., all the afternoon. The news does not seem pleasant. At least, he is not inclined to tell me any of it. Satisfied himself with telling me how sensible and soldierly this handsome General Lee is. . . .*

I did not care a fig for a description of the war council. I wanted to know what is in the wind now. . . .

July 24, 1861. *They brought me a Yankee soldier's portfolio⁵ from the battlefield. One might shed a few tears over some of his letters. Women—wives and mothers—are the same everywhere . . .*

August 4, 1861. *Hope it is so with us. Who knows what is going on at the executive office?*

Every day regiments march by. The town is crowded with soldiers.

August 5, 1861. *They require 600,000 to invade us. Truly we are a formidable power!*

August 18, 1861. *Went to the hospital with a carriageload of peaches and grapes. Made glad the hearts of some men thereby. When my supply gave out, those who had none looked so wistfully as I passed out that I made a second raid on the market. Those eyes sunk in cavernous depths haunted me as they followed me from bed to bed.*

Camden, South Carolina

September 9, 1861. *Home again. Left Richmond September 2nd, 1861.*

---

5. **portfolio:** portable case for holding papers.

Columbia, South Carolina

March 10, 1862. Congaree House.[6] *Second year. Confederate independence. I write daily for my own distractions. These memoirs may some future day afford dates, facts, and prove useful to more important people than I am. I do not wish to do any harm or hurt to anyone. If any scandalous stories creep in, they are easily burned. It is hard, in such a hurry as things are in, to separate wheat from chaff. . . . Read* Uncle Tom's Cabin *again.*

June 3, 1862. Now, for the first time in my life, no book can interest me. But life is so real, so utterly earnest—fiction is so flat, comparatively. Nothing but what is going on in this distracted world of ours can arrest my attention for ten minutes at a time.

June 4, 1862. Battles near Richmond.

Bombardment of Charleston. Beauregard said to be fighting his way out—or in.

June 11, 1862. General Scott on Southern soldiers. He says we have élan, courage, woodcraft, consummate horsemanship, endurance of pain equal to the Indians, but that we will not submit to discipline. We will not take care of things or husband our resources. Where we are, there is waste and destruction. If it could all be done by one wild desperate dash, we would do it. But he does not think we can stand the long blank months between the acts—waiting! We can bear pain without a murmur, but we will not submit to be bored, etc.

Now for the other side. They can wait. They can bear discipline. They can endure forever—losses in battle nothing to them, resources in men and materials of war inexhaustible. And if they see fit *they will fight to the bitter end.*

---

6. **Congaree House:** a Columbia hotel.

January 1st, 1864. God help my country.

Table talk.

"After the battles around Richmond, hope was strong in me. All that has insensibly drifted away."

Camden, South Carolina

May 27, 1864. It is impossible to sleep here because it is so solemn and still. The moonlight shines in my window, sad and white.

And the wind, the soft south wind, literally comes over a bank of violets, lilacs, roses, orange blossoms, and magnolia flowers thrown in.

July 26, 1864. When I remember all the true-hearted, the lighthearted, the gallant boys who have come laughing, singing, dancing in my way in the three years past, I have looked into their brave young eyes and helped them as I could every way and then seen them no more forever. They lie stark and cold, dead upon the battlefield or moldering away in hospitals or prisons—which is worse. I think, if I consider the long array of those bright youths and loyal men who have gone to their deaths almost before my very eyes, my heart might break, too.

Is anything worth it? This fearful sacrifice—this awful penalty we pay for war?

Chester, South Carolina

April 7, 1865. Richmond has fallen—and I have no heart to write about it. Grant broke through our lines. Sherman cut through them. Stoneman is this side of Danville.

They are too many for us.

Everything lost in Richmond, even our archives.

Blue-black is our horizon . . .

Questions

1. Why did Mary Chesnut decide to keep a journal?
2. Why did Mary Chesnut decide to return to the market on August 18, 1861?
3. What events are described by Mary Chesnut on April 7, April 12, and April 15 of 1861?
4. Do you think people in the twenty-first century will read Mary Chesnut's journal? Why or why not?

Applying Reading Skills

Reread the excerpts from Mary Chesnut's journal listed below. Then follow the directions.

1. February 18, 1861
   Which of Mary Chesnut's remarks are examples of the bandwagon technique?

2. June 11, 1862
   Which of General Scott's remarks are examples of name-calling? Which are examples of glittering generalities?

3. July 14, 1861
   How did Mr. Chesnut try to persuade his wife that events were not as bad as they seemed?

4. April 17, 1865
   Richmond was the capital of the Confederate states. It was a symbol of the Confederacy. The city became a specific target for attack by Union forces. Union leaders believed that the fall of Richmond would break the spirit of the Confederates and persuade them that they could never win. Was their strategy successful? Did the fall of Richmond affect the Confederates as the Union leaders hoped it would?

WRITING ACTIVITY

WRITE A PERSUASIVE PARAGRAPH

Prewrite

History is a record of events and of the people who participated in them. History can seem very real when you read personal documents such as the journal Mary Chesnut wrote. Journals, letters, and diaries are examples of original sources of historical information. These original sources are a valuable part of the historical record.

Many times when new buildings are built, a metal box called a time capsule is put into the cornerstone or foundation of the building. This box contains items that will help people hundreds of years from now, when the box is opened, better understand what life was like when the capsule was buried. The contents of the time capsule are original sources.

Suppose that a time capsule for the cornerstone of a new school is being planned. The time capsule will be a box 8 inches wide, 12 inches long, and 8 inches deep. All area students are being asked to participate in a contest to determine which items will be placed in the capsule. Participants will choose ten items and write a persuasive paragraph explaining why items they choose should be placed in the capsule.

In your opinion, what items will help students in the next century understand what school life is like today? You may want to discuss some opinions and supporting reasons with other students. Then prepare your entry for the contest.

Remember, you are trying to persuade the judges of the contest that your choice of items will be the most representative of school life and the most helpful to future students. Completing a chart may help you organize your thinking. Read the example.

Item	Reason
1. A history textbook	1. A source of information used by most students in an average school

Write

1. Reread your list and supporting reasons.
2. Begin your paragraph with a sentence that introduces the topic, preparing a time capsule for students of the future.
3. The supporting-detail sentences in the paragraph should describe your items and give reasons.
4. Use clue words and phrases such as *because*, *so*, *therefore*, and *for this reason* to help readers identify your reasons.
5. Use your Glossary or dictionary for spelling help.

Revise

Read your persuasive paragraph. Do your reasons for each item sound convincing? Since the box for the time capsule is small, be sure to consider whether all ten items will fit.

1. Your contest entry is judged on original ideas, grammar, spelling, punctuation, and neatness. Check each sentence.
2. Check the subject-verb agreement in each sentence.
3. Can you combine some short choppy sentences using the clue words?
4. Rewrite your contest entry in your best handwriting to share.

PREPARING FOR READING

Learning Vocabulary

1. Mathew Brady felt he should photograph the Civil War to <u>preserve</u> moments of experience for the future.
2. The equipment provided for each photographic team was <u>extensive</u>—it included glass plates, dishes, cups, funnels, chemicals, and bottles.
3. The Library of Congress has <u>acquired</u> most of Brady's photographic plates.
4. Brady's photographs captured the <u>desolation</u> and cruelty of war.
5. They show <u>grotesquely</u> positioned bodies, ruined buildings, and abandoned weapons.

preserve   extensive   acquired
desolation   grotesquely

Developing Background and Skills
Make Generalizations

You know that a **generalization** is a general statement based on many facts or particular examples. Read the paragraph below. Think of a generalization you might make, based on the information.

The Civil War ended in 1865, and the United States was whole again. But it was a very different place from what it had been in 1861. Thousands of soldiers—both Northerners and Southerners—had died or been severely wounded. Many civilians, too, had perished in the war. The South was a ruined land. Many of its great cities had been reduced to rubble. The plantation system had collapsed. Although the slaves had been freed, they had no jobs, no homes, and no money. Families had been divided as they chose to support different sides. There was much bitterness between the winners and the defeated.

To make a generalization you must think about the facts in the paragraph. Your generalization must be supported by the facts. What facts are included in the paragraph?

1. The Civil War ended in 1865.
2. The United States was whole again.
3. Many people from the North and South had died.
4. The South was a ruined land.
5. Many Southern cities were reduced to rubble.
6. The plantation system had collapsed.
7. The slaves were free, but they had no jobs, homes, or money.
8. Families were divided.
9. There was bitterness between the North and the South.

The first two facts describe the outcome of the war. The next seven facts describe the unfortunate results of the war.

A generalization about all the facts should include both the outcome and the results. Which generalization below would you choose?

a. The Civil War did not lead to a victory for the South.
b. The nation suffered greatly because of the Civil War.
c. At the end of the Civil War, the nation was at peace, but there were still many problems to be solved.

Would you agree that **c** describes both the outcome and the results of the Civil War?

In the next selection you will learn about a man who went to the Civil War—not as a soldier, but as a recorder of the events of the war. As you read, think about what generalizations you can make based on the information.

BRADY OF BROADWAY

FIRST PRESS PHOTOGRAPHER

JEAN-RAE TURNER

Brady captured a quiet moment in 1864 for these officers of the 1st Connecticut Artillery.

Mathew B. Brady, a native of Warren County, New Jersey, was born in 1823. When he was only 16, he moved to New York City with a friend, William Page, who was an artist. Brady worked as a jeweler's helper during the day and studied the new art of daguerreotype photography* at night with another artist, Samuel F. B. Morse (who would later become famous as the inventor of the telegraph). In 1844, Brady believed he knew enough to establish his own studio, and he soon became known as "Brady of Broadway." Many rich and famous people—John Quincy Adams, Edgar Allan Poe, singer Jenny Lind—came to his studio to have their portraits made. They had to sit very still for long periods of time, because the cameras Brady used needed a long exposure time.

Just before the start of the Civil War, Brady opened a second studio in Washington, D.C. Even though he was busy photographing princes, presidents, and poets, he wanted to go to war when the Civil War started.

"I felt I had to go," he told a friend later, "to preserve the moment of experience for the future." Brady began to dog the steps of General Winfield Scott, head of the Army of the Potomac, to get permission to accompany him to face the Confederate Army. When Brady learned that Scott was going to be replaced, he went to President Abraham Lincoln and Allen Pinkerton, the famous detective, for the desired permission. President Lincoln scrawled "Pass Brady" on a piece of paper for him, but told Brady he must stay out of the way of the troops and pay for his own equipment.

---

*daguerreotype (də gär′ ə tīp′) photography: an early photographic process in which light-sensitized, silvered copper plates were exposed and then developed with mercury vapor.

The "What-is-it?" wagon got its name because most people had never seen anything like it before. Their question when they did see it was, "What is it?" (top) President Abraham Lincoln posed for Brady when he visited Union officers at an unidentified site in 1862. (bottom)

Brady did. Before the war's end, Brady had 22 of his odd-looking, hearse-like "What-is-it?" wagons assigned to many of the battlefields, including Bull Run, Antietam, Fredericksburg, Gettysburg, and Second Manassas. One of his photographers, J. F. Coonley, even photographed the last days of the Confederacy from a train that was specially equipped. He accompanied General William T. Sherman.

Each of Brady's photographic teams included a driver, the "What-is-it?" wagon pulled by two horses, the photographer, the photographer's assistant, and the printer to make the photographs from the glass plates.

The cameras by today's standards were huge and heavy. Instead of film, glass plates were used. Since no enlarging to speak of was done at that time, the cameras' plates were the same size as the photographs. Most of these plates were 8 by 10 inches in size, but some were bigger.

Because exposures took about 30 seconds each, there were no action photographs, and the photographers had to use heavy tripods to hold their cameras still during the exposure time.

Each team's equipment was extensive. There were glass plates, bottles containing the various chemical solutions, dishes in which to mix the solutions and develop the plates and photographs, measuring cups for the solutions, funnels, and a pail for rinse water. Some of the teams even carried barrels with their own water supply.

Brady and his men faced danger daily in their marches and more than once a "What-is-it?" wagon team found itself caught between the two armies. Brady told his photo teams, "The camera is the eye of history . . . you must never make bad pictures."

Brady wore a white linen duster (like those early automobile drivers were to favor some 40 years later), an artist's straw hat, and sturdy military boots, called

The Civil War, fought mostly on Southern soil, left many places in ruins.
The photograph shows what was left of a railroad station in Charleston,
South Carolina. (top)
Women and children helped with cooking and laundry for the 31st Pennsylvania
Regiment at Fort Slocum near Washington, D.C. (bottom left)
Brady photographed General Robert E. Lee after his surrender to General Ulysses S.
Grant in 1869. (bottom right)

jackboots, that reached above his knees. Because the name "Brady" was stamped on most of the photographs, it is difficult to determine which ones he took and which ones E. L. Handy, his nephew-in-law, and other assistants took.

Brady's health and eyesight, which had always been poor, became worse after the Civil War. In addition, he was faced with many debts from outfitting the photography wagons. Although he had published two earlier photo books, he was unable to find a backer to publish his Civil War photographs during his lifetime. In 1871, he went bankrupt. He died in 1896 and was buried in Arlington National Cemetery.

After his death, many of Brady's famous "wet plates" were seized by people in lieu of debts. Some of them were broken and chipped when improperly stored in various government warehouses. Some of them were found in a barn in upstate New York. Others were lost forever.

A large collection was sold for $5,000 to the Library of Congress in 1954 by Brady's heirs. The library also has acquired all the other known plates. They have been catalogued, and in 1964 they were finally available for use by the public as Brady had wished.

While Mathew Brady was not the first war photographer, he was the first to put teams of photographers into the field to photograph all aspects of the battle. His teams are the forerunners of today's press photographers. Brady's photographs showed the grim visage of war. They captured the utter desolation and cruelty of the war for the first time. They showed the grotesquely sprawled bodies of men, horses, and dogs in death; roofless crumbled houses, barns, and fences; the wounded; the wrecked wagons; and unmanned cannon. They preserved the facts of war for future historians and carved a permanent niche in American history for Brady.

Questions

1. Who was Mathew Brady and what part did he play in the Civil War?

2. Why did Brady go to President Lincoln when he learned General Scott was to be replaced?

3. Do you think Lincoln gave too much or too little assistance to Brady?

4. Think how you might catalogue the Brady collection so that a particular plate might easily be found. Describe the kind of arrangement you would use.

Applying Reading Skills

Choose the generalization that is supported by the information given in the passages listed below. Write the answer on your paper. Then list two facts that support each generalization.

1. The first two paragraphs on page 207
   a. Samuel Morse was a famous inventor.
   b. Brady was a successful photographer.
   c. The Civil War disrupted civilian activities.

2. The second, third, fourth, and fifth paragraphs on page 209
   a. Modern photography has come a long way.
   b. Early photography involved unwieldy equipment and lengthy processes.
   c. The most important member of Brady's team was the photographer himself.

3. The first complete paragraph on page 211
   a. Brady's Civil War venture proved to be very costly.
   b. After the war, Brady suffered misfortunes.
   c. By the end of the war, the novelty of photography had worn off.

THE GETTYSBURG ADDRESS

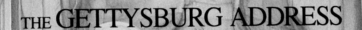

Four score and seven years ago our fathers brought forth on this continent a new nation, conceived in liberty, and dedicated to the proposition that all men are created equal.

Now we are engaged in a great civil war, testing whether that nation, or any nation so conceived and so dedicated, can long endure. We are met on a great battlefield of war. We have come to dedicate a portion of that field as a final resting place for those who here gave their lives that that nation might live. It is altogether fitting and proper that we should do this.

But, in a larger sense, we cannot dedicate—we cannot consecrate—we cannot hallow—this ground. The brave men, living and dead, who struggled here, have consecrated it far above our poor power to add or detract. The world will little note nor long remember what we say here, but it can never forget what they did here. It is for us the living, rather, to be dedicated here to the unfinished work which they who fought here have thus far so nobly advanced. It is rather for us to be here dedicated to the great task remaining before us—that from these honored dead we take increased devotion to that cause for which they gave the last full measure of devotion—that we here highly resolve that these dead shall not have died in vain—that this nation, under God, shall have a new birth of freedom—and that government of the people, by the people, for the people, shall not perish from the earth.

Abraham Lincoln

Jethro Creighton watched as his relatives and friends went off to fight in the Civil War. His brothers John and Tom, his cousin Eb, who had grown up with him, and his schoolteacher, Shad Yale, joined the Union Army. His favorite brother, Bill, joined the Confederates. Jethro was too young to enlist, and he was needed at home.

In this excerpt from the book **Across Five Aprils,** *Jethro is tested on a battlefield of his own.*

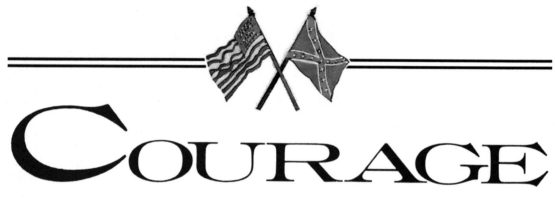

COURAGE

IRENE HUNT

There was an early spring that year. By the first of March the weather was warm, and the higher fields were dry enough for plowing. Jethro carried a rifle with him when he went down to John's place to work; his mother fretted a great deal about it, but his father insisted. Jethro had learned how to handle a gun properly, and it was always possible that he might bring down some kind of wild game for the table, or that he would have need to defend himself against a desperate man.

The field he plowed that day in early March was bordered on the east by dense woods, and Jethro became conscious that every time he approached the woods side of the field, the sharp, harsh call of a wild turkey would sound out with a strange kind of insistence—almost as if some bird demanded that he stop and listen. Once when he halted his team and walked a little distance toward the woods, the calls came furiously, one after the other; then when he returned to his team and moved toward

the west, they stopped until he had made the round of the field.

After several repetitions of this pattern, Jethro tethered his team and, taking up his rifle, walked into the woods. His heart beat fast as he walked, and his slim hand clutching the rifle was wet with sweat.

He walked slowly and carefully, pausing now and then to listen. The calls stopped for a while, and he was half convinced that they had actually come from a wild bird; he made no move for a few minutes, and they began again, softer now and more certainly coming from the throat of a man.

Jethro stood quite still. "Hello," he called finally. "What is it you want of me?"

There was no answer. Then the call came again, softly, insistently, from a clump of trees, one of which was a tremendous old oak.

Jethro walked closer, his gun raised, and after a minute, the human voice which he had been half expecting to hear called out to him.

"Put yore gun down, Jeth; I ain't aimin' to hurt ye. I didn't dast take the chancet of anyone hearin' me call to ye."

"Who is it?" he asked again. "Come out and let me see your face."

Then a skeleton came out from among the trees. It was the skeleton of a Union soldier, though the uniform it wore was so ragged and filthy it was difficult to identify. The sunken cheeks were covered with a thick scattering of fuzz; the hair was lank and matted. It fell over the skeleton's forehead and down into its eyes. The boy stared at it without speaking.

"Jeth, you've growed past all believin'. I've bin watchin' you from fur off, and I couldn't git over it—how you've growed."

Then Jethro realized who it was. "Eb," he exclaimed in a voice hardly above a whisper. "It's Eb, ain't it?"

There was utter despair in the soldier's voice.

"Yes," he said. "I reckon it's Eb—what there's left of him."

For a few seconds Jethro forgot the Federal Registrars[1] and the fact that not only the word which preceded Eb, but his method of announcing himself gave credence to

---

1. **Federal Registrars:** representatives of the Union army who were assigned to hunt down deserters. They had visited the Creighton home searching for Eb.

the suspicion that he was a deserter. But for those first few seconds Jethro could only remember that this was Eb, a part of the family, the boy who had been close to Tom, the soldier who would have more vivid stories to tell of the war than ever a newspaper would be able to publish. He held out his hand.

"Eb, it's good—it's so good to see you. Pa and Ma will be—" he stopped suddenly.

"Yore pa and ma will be scairt—that's what you mean, ain't it? Scairt fer themselves and ashamed of me." He paused for a second and then added defiantly, "I deserted, you know; I up and left Ol' Abe's Army of the United States."

Jethro could only stare at his cousin; he could find no words.

"Desertin' ain't a purty word to you, is it? Well, I done it—I don't jest know why. We'd had another skirmish and there was dead boys that we had to bury the next day—and we'd bin licked agin. All at oncet I knowed I couldn't stand it no longer, and I jest up and left. Oncet a man has left, he's done fer. I've bin a long time gittin' home, and now that I'm here, it ain't no comfort."

"Eb, couldn't you just come up to the house and see them for a few hours or so? Couldn't you have a good meal and get cleaned up and tell the folks all you know about Tom?"

"I caint. I could git 'em into awful trouble. Besides, they would prob'ly jest as soon not set eyes on the likes of me agin."

"But, Eb, if you can't come up to the house, what *did* you come for?"

Eb's face showed quick anger. "I come because I couldn't help myself, that's why. *You* don't know what it's like. There be things that air too terr'ble to talk about—and you want to see the fields where you used to be happy, you want to smell the good air of old Illinois so much that you fergit—you go crazy fer an hour or so—and then you don't dare go back."

He shivered and leaned back against a tree trunk as if just talking had taken more strength than he had to spend.

"Have you been down to the Point Prospect camp?"[2] Jethro asked after a while.

"A couple days. It's worse than the war down there with fellers gittin'

meaner as they git more afraid. I didn't come back to be with soldiers anyway. I'm sick of soldiers, livin' and dead; I'm sick of all of 'em." He threw himself down on a thick padding of dead leaves and motioned Jethro to do the same.

"I want ye to tell me about 'em, Jeth—Uncle Matt and Aunt Ellen, Jenny . . . "

"You knew Pa had a heart attack; he's not been himself since. Ma's tolerable, and Jenny's fine. We do the work of the farm together, Jenny and me."

"And John, Shad—where air they? They joined up, didn't they?"

"Yes, John's in Tennessee. And Shad's in the East with the Army of the Potomac. He was at Antietam Creek and Fredericksburg; you heard of them two battles, didn't you?"

"We hear precious little except what's happenin' in the part of the country we're in." Eb seemed absorbed in his angry thoughts for a while; then he looked up at Jethro again.

---

2. **Point Prospect:** a campground of men who had deserted from the Union army.

"And Bill, did you hear from him?"

"Not a word," Jethro replied in a voice that was hardly audible.

"I guess you took that hard. You was allus a pet of Bill's."

"All of us took it hard."

"Yore paw wrote Tom and me about it. Tom tried to pertend he didn't keer, but I know he did. He cried oncet—I wouldn't tell that 'cept now it's no matter."

"No," Jethro agreed dully, "now it's no matter."

Eb took a dry twig and broke it up into a dozen pieces, aimlessly.

"How did you git the word that Tom was killed?" he asked finally.

"Dan Lawrence was home on sick leave. His pa brought him over; he told us all about it."

"I was at Pittsburg Landing too, but I didn't know about Tom—not fer two or three days. I wanted to write, but somehow I couldn't do it. Tom and me had bin in swimmin' the day before the Rebs su'prised us; we was both of us in good spirits then, laughin' and carryin' on like we done in the old days back home. Somehow all the spirit in me has bin gone ever since. I could stand things as long as I had Tom along with me."

219

He ran his hand across his eyes as if to shut out a picture or a memory. "Tell me about little Jenny; is she still in love with Shad Yale?"

"More than ever, I guess."

Jethro studied Eb's sunken cheeks and dull eyes.

"How do you manage to eat, Eb?"

"I don't do it reg'lar, that's shore. I live off the land, shoot me a rabbit or squirrel and cook 'em over a low fire late at night. It ain't good eatin', but nothin's good these days like it used to be."

Jethro's insides twisted in sympathy. "Are you hungry now, Eb?"

"I'm allus hungry. Ye git used to it after a while."

"John's wife, Nancy, fixed me some grub to bring to the field with me; I'll go get it for you."

He ran to the fencerow where he had left two pieces of bread and the cuts from a particularly tender haunch of beef that Nancy had wrapped in a white cloth for him. He returned to Eb minutes later with the food and a jug of water.

They sat together in the shadows, while Eb ate with an appetite that was like a hungry animal's.

"Eb, I've got to tell you," Jethro said quietly after a while. "The Federal Registrars was at the house lookin' for you last month."

Eb seemed to shrink within himself. He looked at his hands carefully, as if he really cared about inspecting them, and his mouth worked in a strange, convulsive grimace. He wouldn't look at Jethro when he finally spoke.

"I was an awful fool—at least you got a chancet in battle—maybe it's one in a hundred, but it's a chancet. This way, I got none. There's no place on this earth fer me to go. Even the camps of deserters don't want fellers as weak and sick as I am; they let me know that quick at Point Prospect. I'll either freeze or starve—or be ketched. I'd give jest about anythin' if I could walk back to my old outfit and pitch into the fightin' agin. A soldier don't have to feel ashamed."

Jethro sat for a while trying to think of some way out of the situation; it appeared more hopeless the more he thought. He was frightened—for the despairing man in front of him, for himself, and his family. When he finally spoke, he tried hard to sound reassuring, but

the pounding of his heart made his voice shake.

"Well, you stay here till we can think of somethin', Eb. I'm goin' to get you some quilts and things from Nancy's place; I'll bring you what grub I can lay hands on—I can always get eggs and a chicken for you. I think you'd best eat all you can and rest for a spell; we'll think of what's to be done once you get stronger."

Eb looked up then. "You all but fool me into believin' that somethin' *kin* be done, Jeth, but I know better. You ner no one else kin help me now—not even Ol' Abe hisself."

Ol' Abe. Mr. Lincoln. Mr. President.

"I ought to go back to work now, Eb."

"I guess so." Eb looked at him with a suggestion of a smile. "I cain't git used to it—you bein' big enough to handle a team alone. You seem almost a man these days, Jeth."

Jethro walked back to his waiting team; there was still time to plow a dozen furrows before sunset—and to think.

He had faced sorrow and fear; he had felt a terrible emptiness the day Shad and John went away. But he had never been faced with the responsibility of making a fearful decision like the one confronting him.

The authority of the law loomed big in his mind; he remembered, "You and your family will be in serious trouble." Loyalty to his brother Tom and the many thousands who had fought to the last ditch at Pittsburg Landing and all the other places that were adding length to the long list—how could loyalty to these men be true if one were going to harbor and give comfort to a man who simply said, "I quit."

But, on the other hand, how did one feel at night if he awoke and remembered, "I'm the one that sent my cousin to his death." Eb was not a hero, certainly—not now, anyway. People scorned the likes of Eb; sure, so did Jethro, and yet—

"How do I know what *I'd* be like if I was sick and scared and hopeless? We got to remember that Eb has been in battles for two years; maybe he's been a hero in them battles, and maybe to go on bein' a hero in a war that has no end in sight is too much to ask. . . . Sure, deep down in me, I want Eb to get out, to leave me free

of feelin' that I'm doin' wrong to give him grub, or takin' the risk of keepin' it a secret that he's here. Yes, it would leave me free if he'd just move on— but no, it wouldn't—I ain't goin' to be free when he moves on; I can't set down to a table and forget that someone sick as Eb looks to be is livin' off the land, that he's livin' scared like a wild animal that's bein' hunted.

"But what's it goin' to be like if more and more soldiers quit and go into the woods and leave the fightin' to them that won't quit? What do you say to yourself when you remember that you fed and helped someone like Eb and maybe you get a letter from the East that Shad is killed and you see Jenny grievin', or that John is killed and Nancy and her little boys is left alone—how do you feel when things like that come up?

"Of course, right now I could say to Pa, 'I leave it up to you'—and then what could he do? Why, he'd be caught in the same trap I'm in now; I'd wriggle out of it and leave the decidin' to a sick old man; I'd put him in the spot where any way he decided would be bad—hurtful to a man's conscience. No, there ain't an

223

answer that's any plainer to an old man than it is to me."

Jethro lay awake in his room that night and wrestled with his problem. He wondered if, after all, it wouldn't be better to ask his father's advice, but he decided against that as firmly as he had rejected the idea that afternoon. What about Ed Turner, staunch, level-headed neighbor? No, Ed had two sons in the army; it wouldn't do to lay this responsibility upon Ed's shoulders. He thought of Eb's words, "You ner no one else kin help me now—not even Ol' Abe hisself."

Ol' Abe. Mr. Lincoln. Mr. President. Not even Mr. Lincoln himself!

Jethro turned restlessly in his bed. What if one said, "I will abide by the word of him who is highest in this land"? But wasn't that word already known? Wasn't the word from the highest in the land just this: turn in deserters or there will be terrible trouble for you and your family?

But Mr. Lincoln was a man who looked at problems from all sides. Mr. Lincoln had plowed fields in Illinois; he had thought of the problems men came up against; he was not ready to say, "Everything on this side of the line is right, and everything on the other side is wrong."

But would one dare? A nobody, a boy on a southern Illinois farm— would he dare? Mr. Lincoln held the highest office in the land; what would he think? Would it vex him that a boy from southern Illinois could be so bold?

Jeth realized he was not going to be able to go to sleep. There was a candle in his room; there was some ink and an old pen. Jethro began to write on a piece of rough lined paper.

The next morning he hid Jenny's sandwiches inside his coat, and at the barn he picked up a few eggs.

Eb was feeling a little better that morning. The quilts Jethro had taken from Nancy's house had made the long night more comfortable; he had washed himself in the creek and looked refreshed.

"You've brung me a feast, Jeth," he said gratefully.

They sat together for a while and talked.

"I'll be gittin' out in a day or so, Jeth. I caint hev you takin' all this risk for me."

"If you could go back to the army, you would, wouldn't you, Eb?"

"You're askin' a man if he had a chancet to live, would he take it. But I've told you, Jeth—a deserter caint go back. I'll be hunted the rest of my days—but the rest of my days ain't goin' to be too many."

Jethro said nothing, but as he plowed that morning he made up his mind to send the letter. It was a frightening thing to do, but if one did nothing—well, that was frightening too. He knew Eb was not really planning to leave—Eb was a lost and frightened boy, and there was nowhere else to go. For Jethro there was nothing to do but send the letter.

The plowshares needed sharpening, Jethro told his father that noon. Hadn't he better drive over to Hidalgo and get that work done?

Matt assented to the trip readily, and Jethro, with the letter in his pocket, drove off down the road, his heart pounding with excitement.

In Hidalgo the old man who took care of the mail glanced sharply at Jethro when he noticed the inscription on the envelope. But he was a silent man with problems of his own; as long as a letter was properly stamped and addressed it was no affair of his.

The long wait for an answer was interminable. Jethro tossed at night and wondered: had he done an impudent thing, had he laid himself open to trouble, had he been a fool to think that a boy of his age might act without the advice of his elders? Sometimes he got up and walked about his narrow room.

The tensions within him mounted, and the necessity of providing for Eb's needs in strictest secrecy became a task that seemed to grow in magnitude as the days went by.

The letter came one noon when they were all seated at dinner. As so often happened, it was Ed Turner who brought the mail out from town. Jenny ran to the door, eager for a letter from Shadrach; Nancy's eyes pleaded for word from John.

But Ed held only one envelope, and that was addressed to Jethro in a small, cramped handwriting done in very black ink. It was postmarked Washington, D.C.

"Looks like purty important mail you're gittin', Jethro," Ed said quietly. His eyes were full of puzzled concern.

Jethro's head swam. This was the showdown; now, all the family, Ed Turner, and soon the neighborhood would know everything. In the few seconds that passed before he opened the envelope, he wished with all his heart that he had not meddled in the affairs of a country at war, that he had let Eb work out his own problems, that he, Jethro, was still a sheltered young boy who did the tasks his father set for him and shunned the idea that he dare think for himself.

He read the letter through, word for word, and while he read, there wasn't a sound in the cabin beyond the slight rustle of the page in the shaking hand that held it. When he was through, he held the letter out to Jenny.

"You can read it out loud, Jenny."

Jenny stared at him as if he were a stranger; then she shook her head.

"It's your letter, Jeth; you'd best do the readin'."

He didn't know whether he could or not—there was a great pounding in his ears and his breath was short—but he ran his hands across his eyes and swallowed hard. After the first few words, his voice grew steady, and he read the letter through without faltering.

Dear Jethro:

Mr. Hay has called my attention to your letter, knowing as he does the place in my affection for boys of your age and the interest I have in letters coming from my home state of Illinois.

The problem which you describe is one, among so many others, that has troubled both my waking thoughts and those that intrude upon my sleep. The gravity of that problem has become of far-reaching significance and is one in which the authority of military regulations, the decline of moral responsibility, and the question of ordinary human compassion are so involved as to present a situation in which a solution becomes agonizingly difficult.

I had, however, made a decision relative to this problem only a few days before receiving your letter. There will be much criticism of that decision, but you will understand when I say that if it be a wrong one, I have then erred on the side of mercy.

The conditions of that decision are as follows: all soldiers improperly absent from their posts, who will report at certain points designated by local recruit offices by April 1, will be restored to their respective regiments without punishment except for forfeiture of pay and allowances for the period of their absence.

This information you may relay to the young man in question, and I pray that the remorse and despair which he has known since the time of his desertion will bring his better self to the cause for which so many of his young compatriots have laid down their lives.

May God bless you for the earnestness with which you have tried to seek out what is right; may He guide both of us in that search during the days ahead of us.

Yours, very sincerely
and respectfully,
Abraham Lincoln

UNIT THREE
LEVEL 14

MYSTERIES
AND
MARVELS

PREPARING FOR READING

Learning Vocabulary

1. Travelers who had heard about the family's <u>hospitality</u> would stop at their house for the night.
2. One day the wind blew fiercely and did not <u>abate</u> at nightfall.
3. At the height of the storm, an <u>agitated</u> stranger appeared at the door.
4. The stranger went to a chair and sat down wearily in a <u>disconsolate</u> manner.
5. Without any notice, the stranger rose to leave, and no one could <u>intercept</u> him on his way out.
6. The oldest son was concerned about his mother's fears and wanted to <u>assuage</u> them, but he could not succeed in his attempt at <u>reassurance</u>.

| hospitality | abate | agitated | disconsolate |
| intercept | assuage | reassurance | |

Developing Background and Skills
Draw Conclusions

Have you ever thought about the part *you* play in the stories you read? Authors seldom tell you everything. They may leave many of your questions unanswered. But by using the information given and by drawing on your own experience, you can reach certain conclusions. A **conclusion** is a decision based on information and experience. Your conclusions are *your* part of the story.

Read the passage below. What conclusion can you draw?

Friends stopped often at the Otero (ō tãr′ ō) house. Even strangers on a journey used to stop and spend the night there.

The author tells you that both friends and strangers stopped at the Oteros. From your own experience you know that people are not likely to stop where they are not welcome. You can therefore conclude that the Oteros were hospitable, or made people welcome.

Drawing conclusions is an important reading skill. As you read, think about the information presented and about your own experiences. Reason carefully to avoid the following kinds of errors:

- **Jumping to Conclusions**
  Information: The Oteros invited the stranger to spend the night and treated him well.
  Incorrect Conclusion: The Oteros were kind to all strangers.

A single example is not enough to reach the conclusion stated.

- **Choosing the Wrong Reason**
  Information: The Oteros were rich and had a large house. Friends and strangers were always welcome there.
  Incorrect Conclusion: The Oteros were hospitable because they had a large house and were rich.

While it may be true that the Oteros were rich, had a large house, and were hospitable, their wealth and large house were not the reasons for their hospitality.

As you read the next selection, think about what conclusions you can draw. Ask yourself how the author makes the story more interesting by leaving certain things unstated. See how your conclusions change as the story unfolds. What questions still remain unanswered at the end of the story?

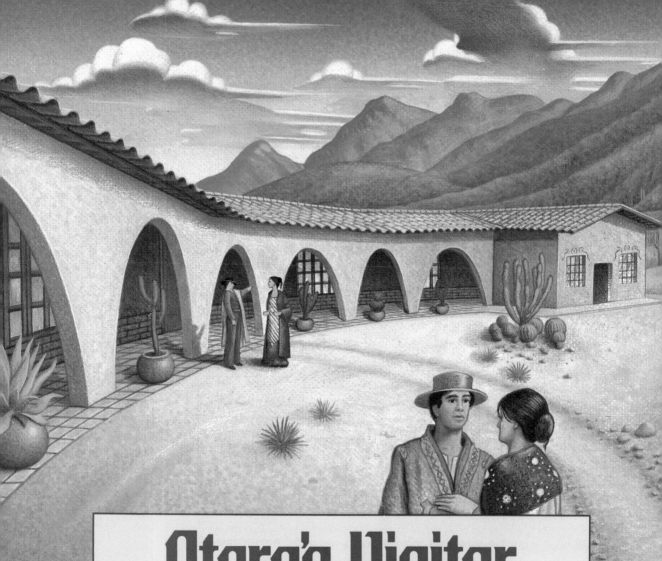

Otero's Visitor

MANUELA WILLIAMS CROSNO

Many years ago there came to this country from Spain a noble family named Otero (ō tãr′ ō). They came with much gold claimed from conquest, so that the family was able to establish itself well in the new world. One of the sons, Adolfo, built for himself a beautiful hacienda[1] and furnished it with possessions the family had brought with them from Spain.

1. **hacienda** (hä′ sē en′ də): landed estate or ranch.

The walls of the long, low building were made of adobe. The rooms were built about a patio, and many of the doors opened out to it. These doors were of heavy, hand-hewn wood. There were lace curtains at the windows, and the greatest of luxuries, an organ, stood in one corner of the long living room near the fireplace. It was beautifully made of carved wood and was supported with heavy carved legs. The organ had been brought from Spain by way of Mexico City.

There were many sons and daughters born in the hacienda of Adolfo Otero, and it became a place of laughter and song and music. Young people and old for miles about found it a place in which to make merry, and always there was about it the feeling of warm hospitality.

As Don[2] Adolfo grew older and could no longer count the white hairs among the black, but could more easily count the black ones among the white, he thought that life had given him all that he could desire. One by one the sons and daughters had married and established haciendas for themselves, and now Don Adolfo lived alone except for his wife and two servants. But still there came to the house many who were friends and some who were strangers, for the weary traveler who had heard about the open hospitality was accustomed to stop here on his journeys and spend the night.

Now this is a country of many winds. Sometimes the soft winds blow from the southwest and travel close to the ground. They are the winds that sing songs in the yucca[3] and grasses that grow on the mesa. But sometimes the hard winds blow from the east and bring snow, if it is winter, or sand, if it is summer. The sand blows hard into the face of the traveler and beats against his horse so that he is driven to seek shelter.

---

2. **Don**: Spanish form of respectful address for a man.
3. **yucca** (yuk′ ə): a group of desert plants that grow in the southwestern United States.

One day, there came such a wind. All day it beat about the hacienda of Don Otero and blew the sand against the doors and windows. No one ventured out on this day, and even when the sun vanished behind the mountains, leaving a trail of smoldering fire, the wind did not abate. In the darkness of night, it seemed even worse than it had been in the daytime.

The two servants and Doña[4] Otero retired early, but Don Adolfo remained in the living room. Two or three times he paced back and forth with an assured step, as if to tell the elements he was calm and at peace. Then he seated himself before the fireplace, where he sat looking into the embers, dreaming who-knows-what dreams. A handsome figure he made sitting there, smoking his pipe, his hair falling down to his shoulders in soft whiteness like snowbanks in the early morning. His eyes were black and still sparkled with the vitality of living. Like coals they glowed as the light before him flickered and threw shadows upon the wall. Suddenly his reverie was interrupted by a hasty pounding on the door. Don Adolfo pulled back the heavy bars that formed the lock, and the great carved door swung open to admit a stranger. He seemed greatly agitated and would not remove his hat; nor would he partake of the warmth before the fire. He was a young man, well formed. His black beard stood out in sharp contrast to the white face beneath it.

"They are coming," he said, seeming to assume that Don Adolfo knew who "they" might be. "This they must not find!" And he drew from his coat a small box of carved wood and thrust it into the hands of Don Adolfo.

"You shall hide it for me, and when I come again you shall give it to me! Guard it with your life! Hide it carefully and tell no one!" With these words, the man turned, opened the door, and it closed quickly behind him. In a moment Don

---

4. **Doña** (dōn′ yə): Spanish form of respectful address for a married woman.

Adolfo heard the sound of horse hooves as the stranger rode quickly away.

Amazed, Otero stood closer to the firelight and examined the little carved box. It was curiously carved, but whether or not it was locked, Otero never knew, for he was a Spanish gentleman—a caballero (kab′ əl yär′ ō)! Then, recalling the command of his visitor, he walked over to the old organ, opened a secret panel in one of the wooden legs, carefully inserted the box, and closed the panel. Don Adolfo smiled to himself with satisfaction because he had been able to hide the box so well. Even his wife did not know of this place.

He went back and sat down before the fire. Soon there was a clatter of hooves, and three armed men stood in his doorway.

"Has someone stopped here?" they asked, glancing around the room. "Have you heard anyone pass?"

Otero held his head to one side as if thinking. "A few minutes ago I heard horse hooves flying down the road in a great hurry!" he said.

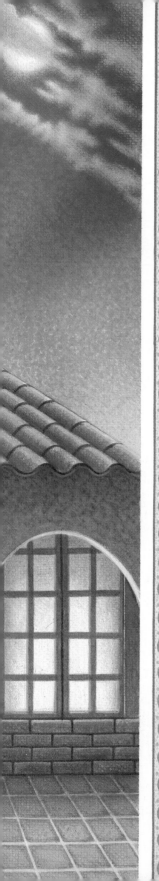

The years continued to throw their days across the path of Don Adolfo, but he did not forget the stranger who had placed a box in his keeping, nor did he forget to guard the trust that had been given him. He waited for the return of the man, and, indeed, he never thought to open the secret panel, until the stranger should return to claim his property. And one day Don Adolfo died, taking with him the secret of the little carved box and its hiding place. His estate was settled by his sons, and all of his obligations known to them were dutifully discharged.

The eldest son, Reyes (rā′ ēs), moved into the hacienda with his wife in order to be with his mother, who had also grown quite old. Reyes was much like his father, an honorable man, but times were different. With the oncoming of American civilization, ranchos sprang up along the old road, which was now repaired often. Here and there little villages grew, so that it was no longer necessary for strangers to seek hospitality in the open countryside. For days at a time, however, the hacienda would ring with the laughter of young people and of old, when Reyes would call them there for a fiesta to honor the old days. And the good people would sit about with lighted faces, speaking of Don Adolfo and of the many fine times they had enjoyed under that very roof.

One moonlit night when the wind was blowing, Carla, the wife of Reyes, was awakened by a sound in the house. She arose quickly and walked to the living room door. Just outside the room she listened. Yes, she was sure of it! There were footsteps walking up and down the room, back and forth! Quiet, assured footsteps! They sounded as if they knew where they were going! She opened the door, but could see no one in the moonlit room. She walked across to the organ and back, but no one was there.

The next morning she told her husband, and that night he, too, listened, but they heard nothing. Smiling at her, he told her he thought she had been mistaken, but she implored him to listen with her again. On this night, too, they heard nothing. For six nights they listened, and on the seventh night, when the wind was blowing, they heard the footsteps walking back and forth the full length of the living room and then pausing before the organ. But when they entered the room, no one was there. Soon they learned to expect the footsteps just before ten o'clock each night that the wind blew, and promptly at ten-thirty they would cease and not be heard again. Reyes and Carla might have been frightened, but there was a reassurance in the walk that quieted their fears.

They said nothing to the old Doña, thinking that it would alarm her. Great was the surprise of Don Reyes, therefore, on a certain morning, to come upon his mother, walking back and forth in the living room. For a moment he thought it might have been she whom he and his wife had heard, but his mother's footsteps were much lighter, and besides, she could not have disappeared so quickly. He and his wife had never been able to intercept their visitor.

So he asked, "Mamacita,[5] what do you do here?"

She looked at him a moment, quietly. "Don Adolfo, your father, walks this room many nights," she said. "I am trying to find what is disturbing his spirit!"

There was conviction upon her face, and Don Reyes knew then that the footsteps he had heard were the footsteps of his father. Many times he had heard him walk in just this fashion; that, he thought, was why the footsteps did not frighten or alarm him. They were familiar ones! He needed time to think about this! So he said to his mother, "Do not be perturbed, Mamacita! My father was a good man. We will find out what is disturbing him."

So Don Reyes remained alone in the living room each evening when the wind brought sand, and he sat quietly before the fireplace, looking almost like his father. But nothing happened, although Don Reyes sat there for many evenings, hearing the footsteps.

One Friday there came a sandstorm. All day the wind beat sand and whirled it in heaps about the hacienda; there

---

5. **Mamacita** (mä′ mə cē′ tə): Spanish word for *mother*.

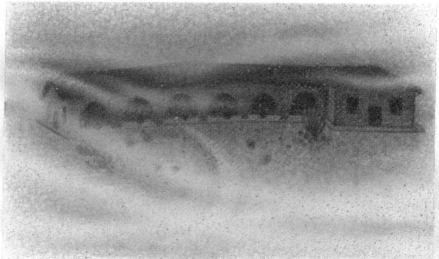

was a constant pelting of sand against the windows. No one ventured to leave the house. After the sun had set, the wind seemed to increase in its fury. But before the fireplace sat Don Reyes, waiting for he knew not what—hoping only to assuage the concern of his mother for his father.

Suddenly there came a quick knock at the door, and he opened it to admit a stranger. The man looked at him uncertainly in the dim light. Reyes closed the door and pushed the heavy bars against it to keep out the wind and sand. The stranger seemed greatly upset. He was a middle-aged man, well formed. A black beard stood in sharp contrast to his white face.

Without sitting down, he began, "But I thought you were Otero—Señor Adolfo Otero! As I came past the window and saw you sitting there, I thought—"

And Reyes added, "He was my father."

The man hesitated as if weighing in his mind whether to inform Reyes of the purpose of his visit. Then he spoke, "A son of Adolfo Otero could not be other than trustworthy. I come for a box left in the keeping of your father."

"Come," said Reyes, "sit here."

And he pointed the stranger to a chair before the fireplace. The man sat down without removing his coat, as one in a daze, and said something under his breath in a queer mumble that Reyes did not understand.

"Come," Reyes said again, "make yourself comfortable. You are but chilled from the wind! I do not know where my father left your box, but I will try to think where it might be. Let me bring some wine for you."

The stranger did not answer. He sat stooped over in his chair toward the fire in a disconsolate manner.

As Reyes reached the door leading out of the room, he heard footseps. That the man by the fireplace heard them also, he knew by the startled look in his eyes as he rose quickly to his feet and stared at Reyes.

Reyes smiled. "Do not be alarmed," he said reassuringly.

The footsteps had walked over to the organ and stopped. Reyes closed the door behind him and went to bring the wine. In a short time, he returned.

The outside door stood open. The stranger had disappeared. As Reyes stood in the room and looked about him, he saw a small panel in the leg of the organ slide softly shut. Then he heard the footsteps for the last time. The wind from the entrance blew the door open leading to the patio, and the curtains parted as if someone walked through them and closed them gently.

Reyes Otero closed the outer door against the fury of the wind and hastened to the organ, where he stooped to examine the place in which he had seen the opening close. When his fingers found the secret panel and slid it open, he knew that his father's last trust had been honorably discharged. The little enclosure was empty!

Questions

1. What did the stranger leave with Don Adolfo? What "rules" did he ask Don Adolfo to follow?
2. Why did Don Adolfo tell the armed men only that he had heard horse hooves flying down the road?
3. Do you think Don Adolfo should have told someone about the box he had hidden? Why or why not?
4. Has anyone ever asked you to keep a secret? What were the circumstances? Were you tempted to tell the secret to someone else? Explain what you did.

Applying Reading Skills

A. The conclusions below are based on "Otero's Visitor." Read each conclusion. Then list two facts from the story that support each conclusion.

1. Don Adolfo was convinced that the stranger was an honest man who was being pursued unjustly.
2. Don Reyes was a man much like his father.
3. Don Reyes thought that the mysterious footsteps were those of his father's ghost.
4. The stranger trusted both Don Adolfo and Don Reyes.
5. While Don Reyes was out of the room, his father's ghost led the stranger to the hidden box.

B. The conclusions below are based on "Otero's Visitor." Read each conclusion. Then explain why the conclusions are not supported by the information in the story.

1. The stranger was a criminal who was escaping from officers of the law.
2. At first, Don Reyes was sure that his wife was only imagining the footsteps she said she heard.
3. The family will probably continue to hear footsteps in the night.

PREPARING FOR READING

Learning Vocabulary

1. The ghost was a watery creature who <u>saturated</u> everything she touched.
2. She appeared on Christmas Eve when the lakes and ponds began to <u>congeal</u>, and <u>extinguished</u> the cozily burning fires.
3. The ghost admitted that she had never <u>aspired</u> to being a ghost, let alone a shower bath.
4. These were the <u>consequences</u>, however, of having jumped from a cliff as a young girl.
5. The master of Harrowby Hall could not <u>tolerate</u> the ghost and thought up an <u>ingenious</u> plan to get rid of her.

saturated	congeal	extinguished	aspired
consequences	tolerate	ingenious	

Developing Background and Skills
Context Clues

What do you do when you come across an unfamiliar word? You may be able to figure out its meaning by using **context clues**. Semantic context clues are found in nearby words, phrases, and sentences.

Read the sentences below and pay special attention to the underlined word.

Oglethorpe knew the house was haunted, and he was not surprised when the pale <u>apparition</u> appeared by his bed.

What familiar words and phrases helped you decide that an apparition is a ghost or phantom?

Syntactic context clues are clues found in word order and sentence structure. The position of a word in a sentence can help you figure out what part of speech it is. Let's review the main parts of speech.

NOUN—word that names a person, place, thing, or idea
often comes after *the*, *a*, *an*, or an adjective
VERB—word that tells what a noun does, feels, or is
often follows a noun
ADJECTIVE—word that describes a noun
often comes before a noun or follows a verb such as *is* or *was*
ADVERB—word that describes an adjective or verb
often tells how or how much and comes before an adjective
and before or after a verb

The sentence below includes each of these parts of speech.

The ghost thoroughly saturated the ancient wool rug.

     NOUN   VERB   NOUN

ADJECTIVE   ADVERB   ADJECTIVES

Knowing what part of speech a word is can help you to
figure out its meaning. Read the following example.

> The ghost darted wildly about the room, knocking things
> to the floor, disarranging papers, and causing general
> <u>havoc</u>.
>
> a. disturb: to destroy   b. amusing: entertaining
> c. clamor: a noisy outcry   d. destruction: ruin

The position of the word *havoc*, following an adjective,
indicates that it is a noun. You can eliminate **a** and **b** as
answer choices because **a** is a verb and **b** is an adjective.
Both **c** and **d** are nouns. Which one best fits the meaning of
the sentence? The semantic clues *darted wildly about*,
knocking things to the floor, and disarranging papers should
help you decide that *destruction* is the correct answer.

As you read the next selection, you will probably come
across several unfamiliar words. See how many meanings
you can figure out by using both semantic and syntactic
context clues.

The Water Ghost of Harrowby Hall

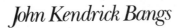

John Kendrick Bangs

The trouble with Harrowby Hall was that it was haunted. What was worse, the ghost appeared at the bedside of the person who saw it and remained there for one hour before it would disappear.

It appeared in the best spare bedroom on Christmas Eve, as the clock was striking twelve. The owners of Harrowby Hall had done their utmost to rid themselves of the damp and dewy lady. They had tried to stop the clock, so that the ghost would not know when it was midnight. But she made her appearance just the same. There she would stand until everything about her was thoroughly saturated.

Then the owners of Harrowby Hall caulked up every crack in the floor. The walls were made waterproof, and the doors and windows likewise. But even this did not suffice. The following Christmas Eve, she frightened the occupant of the room quite out of his senses by sitting down alongside of him. He noticed, too, that in her long, bony fingers bits of dripping seaweed were entwined, the ends hanging down. These ends she drew across his forehead until he swooned away. The next morning he was found by his host unconscious in his bed.

The next year the master of Harrowby Hall decided not to have the best spare bedroom opened at all. However, the ghost appeared as usual in the room. That is, it was supposed she did, for the hangings were dripping wet the next morning. Finding no one there, she immediately set out to haunt the owner of Harrowby himself. She found him in his own cozy room.

Now it so happened that the master of Harrowby was a brave man. He intended to find out a few things he felt he had a right to know. He would have liked to put on a dry suit of clothes first, but the apparition declined to leave him for an instant. Every time he would move she would follow him, with the result that everything she came in contact with got a ducking. In an effort to warm himself up, he approached the fire. This brought the ghost directly over the fire, which immediately was extinguished.

"Far be it from me to be impolite, madam, but it would please me if you'd stop these infernal visits of yours to this house. Go sit out on the lake if you like that sort of thing. Do not, I implore you, come into a gentleman's house and saturate him and his possessions in this way. It is disagreeable."

"Henry Hartwick Oglethorpe," said the ghost in a gurgling voice, "you do not know what you are talking about. You do not know that I am compelled to haunt this place year after year. It is no pleasure to me to enter this house, and ruin and mildew everything I touch. I never aspired to be a shower bath, but it is my doom. Do you know who I am?"

"No, I don't," returned the master of Harrowby.

"I am the Water Ghost of Harrowby Hall. I am the ghost of that fair maiden whose picture hangs over the mantelpiece in the drawing room. It was my father who built Harrowby Hall. The haunted chamber was to have been mine. My father had it furnished in pink and yellow, knowing well that blue and gray were the only colors I could tolerate. He did it merely to spite me. I refused to live in the room. Whereupon my father said I could live there or on the lawn, he didn't care which. That night I ran from the house and jumped over the cliff into the sea."

"That was rash," said the master of Harrowby.

"So I've heard," returned the ghost. "If I had known what the consequences were to be I should not have jumped. But I really never realized what I was doing until after I was drowned. I had been drowned a week when a sea nymph came to me. She informed me that it should be my doom to haunt Harrowby Hall for one hour every Christmas Eve throughout the rest of eternity. I was to haunt that room on such Christmas Eves as I found it inhabited. If it should turn out not to be inhabited, I was and am to spend the allotted hour with the head of the house."

"Do you mean to tell me that on every Christmas Eve that I don't happen to have somebody in that guest chamber, you are going to haunt me wherever I may be, and soak me through to the skin?" demanded the master.

"You have stated the case exactly, Oglethorpe," said the water ghost.

Here the clock struck one, and immediately the apparition faded away.

When Christmas Eve came again, the master of Harrowby was in his grave. He never recovered from the cold contracted that awful night. Harrowby Hall was closed, and the heir to the estate was in London. To him in his chambers came the same experience that his father had gone through. Everything in his room was ruined. What was worse, the apartments below his were drenched with the water soaking through the floors. This resulted in his being requested by his landlady to vacate the premises.

So the heir of Harrowby Hall resolved, as his ancestors before him had resolved, that something must be done.

The thought came to the heir to have the fireplace in the room enlarged, so that he might evaporate the ghost at its first appearance. But he remembered what his father had told him—that no fire could withstand the lady's extreme dampness. And then he thought of steampipes. These could lie hundreds of feet deep in water and still retain sufficient heat to drive the water away in vapor. As a result of this thought, the haunted room was heated by steam to a withering degree.

The scheme was only partially successful. The water ghost appeared at the specified time and found the heir of Harrowby prepared. But hot as the room was, it shortened her visit by no more than five minutes in the hour. It was then that the natural action of the mind, in going from one extreme to the other, suggested to the ingenious heir of Harrowby the means by which the water ghost was ultimately conquered.

The heir provided himself with a warm suit of fur underclothing. He placed over it a rubber garment, tight-fitting. On top of this he placed a suit made of wool, and over this a second rubber garment. Upon his head he placed a light and comfortable diving helmet. On the following Christmas Eve, he awaited the coming of his tormentor.

It was a bitterly cold night. The air outside was still, but the temperature was below zero. The master was

lying on the bed in the haunted room, dressed as has already been indicated, and then—

The clock clanged out the hour of twelve.

There was a sudden banging of doors, a blast of cold air swept through the halls, and the door leading into the haunted chamber flew open. A splash was heard, and the water ghost was seen standing at the side of the heir of Harrowby. From her outer dress there streamed rivulets of water. But the master, deep down under the various garments he wore, was as dry and as warm as he could have wished.

"Ha!" said the young master of Harrowby. "I'm glad to see you. We will go out on the lake."

"But, my dear sir," returned the ghost, "it is fearfully cold out there. You will be frozen hard before you've been out ten minutes."

"Oh, no, I'll not," replied the master. "I am very warmly dressed. Come!"

And they started.

They had not gone far before the water ghost showed signs of distress.

"You walk too slowly," she said. "I am nearly frozen. My knees are so stiff now I can hardly move."

"My clothes are rather heavy," returned the master, "and a hundred yards an hour is about my speed. Indeed, I think we had better sit down here on this snowdrift."

"Do not! Do not do so, I beg!" cried the ghost. "Let me move on. I feel myself growing rigid as it is. If we stop here, I shall be frozen stiff."

"That, madam," said the master slowly, and seating himself on an ice cake—"that is why I have brought you here. We have been on this spot just ten minutes; we have fifty more. Take your time about it, madam, but freeze, that is all I ask of you."

"I cannot move my right leg now," cried the ghost, in despair. "My overskirt is a solid sheet of ice. Oh, kind Mr. Oglethorpe, light a fire, and let me go free."

"Never, madam. It cannot be. I have you at last."

"Alas!" cried the ghost, a tear trickling down her frozen cheek. "Help me, I beg. I congeal."

"Congeal, madam, congeal!" returned Oglethorpe coldly. "You have drenched me and mine for two hundred and three years, madam. Tonight you have had your last drench."

"Ah, but I shall thaw out again, and then you'll see," cried the lady threateningly.

"No, you won't either," returned Oglethorpe. "When you are frozen quite stiff, I shall send you to a cold-storage warehouse, and there shall you remain an icy work of art forever more."

"But warehouses burn."

"So they do, but this warehouse cannot burn. It has fireproof walls. Within those walls the temperature is now and shall forever be 416 degrees below the zero point. Low enough to make an icicle of any flame in this world—or the next," the master added, with an ill-suppressed chuckle.

"For the last time let me beseech you. I would go on my knees to you, Oglethorpe, were they not already frozen. I beg of you do not doo-"

Here even the words froze on the water ghost's lips and the clock struck one. The moon, coming out from behind a cloud, shone down on the rigid figure of a beautiful woman sculptured in clear, transparent ice. There stood the ghost of Harrowby Hall, conquered by the cold, a prisoner for all time.

Questions

1. Who was the water ghost and why did she haunt Harrowby Hall?
2. Why did the young master of Harrowby Hall want to get rid of the ghost?
3. What plan would you have tried to get rid of the ghost?
4. Do you enjoy reading ghost stories? Tell why or why not.

Applying Reading Skills

A. Write the underlined word in each sentence below and give its meaning.

1. At first nothing seemed amiss in the room. Then Henry noticed that a shade left drawn was now partly raised.
   a. missing   b. wrong   c. right   d. incredible
2. A ghostly presence pervaded the room. Every sight, smell, and sound indicated that an unnatural being was there.
   a. was spread throughout   b. came into
   c. illuminated   d. shared

B. Write the word that completes each sentence below.

1. The ghost replied ____ to each question by asking another question.
   a. ardently: enthusiastically
   b. perversely: in a stubborn manner
   c. negotiate: to conduct or carry out
   d. effect: an impression
2. ____ would be an important part of Oglethorpe's plan. A word to the wrong person might result in failure.
   a. Prudently: carefully
   b. Mislead: to guide in the wrong direction
   c. Caution: carefulness
   d. Frivolity: unconcern

THE LISTENERS

"Is there anybody there?" said the Traveller,
  Knocking on the moonlit door;
And his horse in the silence champed the grasses
  Of the forest's ferny floor:
And a bird flew up out of the turret,
  Above the Traveller's head:
And he smote upon the door again a second time;
  "Is there anybody there?" he said.
But no one descended to the Traveller;
  No head from the leaf-fringed sill
Leaned over and looked into his grey eyes,
  Where he stood perplexed and still.
But only a host of phantom listeners
  That dwelt in the lone house then
Stood listening in the quiet of the moonlight
  To that voice from the world of men:
Stood thronging the faint moonbeams on the dark stair,
  That goes down to the empty hall,
Hearkening in an air stirred and shaken
  By the lonely Traveller's call.
And he felt in his heart their strangeness,
  Their stillness answering his cry,
While his horse moved, cropping the dark turf,
  'Neath the starred and leafy sky;
For he suddenly smote on the door, even
  Louder, and lifted his head:—

"Tell them I came and no one answered,
   That I kept my word," he said.
Never the least stir made the listeners,
   Though every word he spake
Fell echoing through the shadowiness of the still house
   From the one man left awake:
Ay, they heard his foot upon the stirrup,
   And the sound of iron on stone,
And how the silence surged softly backward,
   When the plunging hoofs were gone.

—*Walter de la Mare*

PREPARING FOR READING

Learning Vocabulary

1. Opie was <u>sorely</u> disappointed that Professor Pepper didn't reward him with money.
2. Instead, Pepper gave him a ticket that would <u>admit</u> two people to his show.
3. Advertisements said Pepper would raise the ghost of the thief and <u>scoundrel</u> Crookneck John.
4. Pepper asked for <u>absolute</u> silence as he began the show.
5. Even though the professor gave Opie only one cent for his help, Obie said he was much <u>obliged</u> for it.

sorely   admit   scoundrel
absolute   obliged

Developing Background and Skills
Figurative Language

Have you ever thought about the different meanings we give to the words and phrases we use? Read the sentences below, paying special attention to the underlined words.

LITERAL: Aunt Etta was <u>very clever</u>.

FIGURATIVE: Aunt Etta was <u>as clever as forty crickets</u>.

The first sentence is an example of literal language. It means exactly what it says. The second sentence is an example of figurative langauge. The phrase *as clever as forty crickets* has a special meaning. You should be able to figure out that it means "very clever." The meaning of both sentences above, although expressed differently, is exactly the same.

Figurative language adds interest and variety to writing. Writers use figurative language to express their ideas more vividly and clearly.

Several common kinds of figurative language, called figures of speech, are explained below.

SIMILE: a comparison of two things unlike in nature, using the word *like* or *as*. Example: Opie groaned like a banshee. ("Opie groaned loudly and wildly.")

METAPHOR: a comparison between two things unlike in nature, without the use of *like* or *as*. Example: The fog was a blanket over the earth. ("Fog covered the earth.")

IDIOM: a common expression whose meaning, learned through use, cannot be understood by the individual words that make it up. Example: The dog got the lion's share of the chicken. ("The dog got the largest or best part of the chicken.")

PERSONIFICATION: giving human feelings, motives, or actions to non-human things. Example: The sun allowed itself to be seen for a moment. ("The sun could be seen for only a moment.")

HYPERBOLE: intentional exaggeration. Example: The audience stopped breathing when the ghost appeared. ("The audience was frightened by the ghost's appearance.")

What figure of speech describes the phrase *as clever as forty crickets*? Can you think of a metaphor to describe an untalkative person? What do the idioms "down in the dumps" and "escaped by a hair" mean? Which of the following sentences uses hyperbole and which uses personification? *A lifetime passed while Opie waited. Laughter is a merry companion.*

The author of the following selection includes many examples of figurative language. Notice them as you read. Think about how the use of figurative language gives the story a special flavor.

THE GHOST ON SATURDAY NIGHT

SID FLEISCHMAN

There's nothing bashful about a tule fog. It'll creep inside your clothes and get right into bed with you.

When I got home from the schoolhouse on Tuesday, there wasn't a wisp of fog. I lived with my Great-Aunt Etta, and she was waiting for me.

"Opie," she said. "How would you like chicken for supper?"

"Yes, *Ma'am!*" I said.

"Splendid. I've got the chicken. You go out back and pluck it."

I gave a groan. She gave me the chicken. She had a way of foxing me into doing pesky chores.

I sat myself on the chopping stump and began to pull feathers. I passed the time thinking up names for my horse. I already had a list a mile-and-a-half long.

I didn't own a horse—yet.

But I had one promised. Aunt Etta had struck a bargain with me. When I earned enough money to buy a good saddle, she'd buy a good horse to fit under it.

The trouble was I was only ten and kind of runty in size. The older, bigger boys seemed to get all the after-school jobs.

"Wild Charlie," I said aloud. I liked the sound of that. I could see myself galloping across the meadow on Wild Charlie. But when I looked up, I couldn't see the meadow. Or the trees. Or the barn. And before long I couldn't even see the chicken in my hands.

A tule fog had sprung up.

My heart gave a mighty leap. There was saddle money to be made in a good thick fog! I had already saved $2.11. But I needed heaps of money—$17.59 exactly.

I guess there's nothing thicker and wetter than a ground-hugging California tule fog. Aunt Etta was always saying not to stand in one too long. You'd grow webbed feet.

I felt my way back to the house and handed the bird to Aunt Etta.

"I'll be back for supper," I said.

I lifted my feet for town. I guess I was the only boy in Golden Hill who'd gone into the fog business.

I'd gotten the idea from Aunt Etta.

Even in the thickest tule she was sure-footed as a mountain goat. She knew every brick, every post, and every building by heart. So did I. I could streak through town with my eyes shut.

I passed one end of the Horseshoe Mine tunnel. I couldn't see it, but I knew it was there because of the dip in the road. Before long I reached the hotel hitching rack. I crossed the dirt street and counted forty-seven strides. That brought me to Muldoon's General Store.

"Any special errands you want run, Mr. Muldoon?" I asked. He was one of my best tule customers.

"Opie," he said, "if that fog gets any thicker, you'd be able to drive a nail into it and hang your coat. Think you can find the barbershop in it?"

"Yes, sir."

He filled a can with lamp oil, and I set out to deliver it. I turned the corner and kept going until I reached the livery stable. I knew it by the smell. Then I crossed the street. When I sniffed hair tonic, I knew I was at Russell's barbershop.

It turned out there was a stranger in town. Mr. Russell had just finished cutting his hair.

"Opie," he said, "you could do this gentleman a service if you scouted him back to the hotel."

"Be pleased to," I said.

That stranger was a big man and uglier than homemade soap. He clasped my shoulder with one hand as I led him out along the wooden sidewalk.

He followed along behind me without saying a word.

I didn't say much either. He was kind of scary. But when we passed the bank, I said, "You ever hear of anyone buying a horse with a penny?"

He didn't answer.

"Well, sir, that's what my Great-Aunt Etta is going to do," I added.

He wasn't interested—that was clear. So I didn't tell him it was an 1877 Indian-head penny. Rare as a hen's tooth, that date. And mighty valuable. She had Mr. Whitman, the banker, keep it in his safe.

"Here we are, sir," I said. We reached the hotel porch. I hoped I would be a nickel closer to getting my saddle.

He dug in his vest pocket. He handed me a card. And he disappeared through the door.

I was sorely disappointed. He was not only big and ugly; he was stingy too. What did I want his card for?

It was kind of hard to read in the fog. The sun was giving off about as much light as an orange cat. But as I held it closer I saw that it wasn't a calling card. It was a ticket of some sort.

Compliments of
Professor Pepper
ADMIT 2

Admit two to what? Not a word about that. I might have thrown it away if I hadn't been so puzzled. I jammed it into my pocket and went about my fog business.

By the time I reached home, I had the jingle of thirty-five cents in my pocket. I hoped the tule fog would hang on for weeks.

But it lifted around noon the next day. And all over town signs had been tacked up.

THE GHOST IS COMING!

See the ghost of
CROOKNECK JOHN!
Famous Outlaw • Bank Robber
Thief & Scoundrel

HUNG THREE TIMES BEFORE HE CROAKED!

THE GENUINE GHOST
BROUGHT BACK BY PROFESSOR PEPPER, THE FAMOUS GHOST-RAISER. DON'T MISS THIS EVENT. STARTLING! EDUCATIONAL! NO CHILDREN UNDER TWELVE ALLOWED!

SATURDAY NIGHT   8 P.M. SHARP
MINERS' UNION HALL 50 CENTS ADMISSION

Professor Pepper!

I ran home and showed my ticket to Aunt Etta.

"He gave it to me himself!" I said.

"Who did?"

"Professor Pepper, the famous ghost-raiser!"

She looked at me over the tops of her glasses. "What on earth is a ghost-raiser?"

"Haven't you seen the signs? He's going to raise the ghost of Crookneck John on Saturday night. Right here in the Miners' Union Hall."

"Poppycock," Aunt Etta said.

"The signs say so."

"I'll believe that when I see it," she snorted.

"But they won't let *me* in."

"Why not?"

"I'm not old enough."

Aunt Etta stared at me. I didn't have to tell her how much I wanted to have a peek at the ghost of Crookneck John. She could see that for herself.

"Well, I'm old enough for both of us," she said. "We'll go. You don't think I'd visit a spook show *alone*, Opie. We'll see it together. That's that. Leave it to me."

Saturday night arrived at last.

Aunt Etta put on her best hat, and we set out for the Miners' Union Hall.

261

We climbed the wooden stairs to the hall. A toad-faced man stood at the door. He was taking folks' money and tossing it into a box.

When he saw me, he shook his head. "That boy isn't old enough to be twelve," he said.

"Correct," Aunt Etta said.

"Then he can't go in."

"Nonsense," she said.

"Ma'am, that ghost will scare him skinny."

"He's already skinny."

"Then his hair will turn white," the man said.

"Horsefeathers, sir." She handed him my ticket from Professor Pepper himself. "Will you kindly read that."

"It says admit two."

Aunt Etta straightened to her full height. "Exactly. I'm *one* and he's *two*. And the ticket orders you to *admit* us. Step aside, sir, before I call the sheriff."

The man turned white at the mention of the sheriff.

"Come along, Opie," Aunt Etta said.

We breezed right through the door. Oh, she was clever as forty crickets, my Great-Aunt Etta.

The hall was long and shadowy. Two oil lamps burned and smoked in front of the curtain. That's all the light there was.

We took chairs near the front and waited. Before long all the chairs were taken. And folks were standing along the walls.

We could hear noises behind the curtain. There were creaking sounds. And sawing sounds. And hammering sounds.

"Maybe it's the ghost," I said.

Aunt Etta shook her head. "Crookneck John was an outlaw— not a carpenter."

We waited.

At ten minutes to nine, Professor Pepper stepped through the curtains.

"I will ask you not to scream out," he announced in a deep voice.

Professor Pepper took a grip on the lapel of his fancy coat. "What you will see tonight is stranger than strange. Odder than odd. Aye, a man deader than dead will walk among you. A cutthroat, he was. Bank robber. The most feared outlaw of the century!"

I scrunched down in my chair.

"Hung once, he was," Professor Pepper went on. "Hung twice, he was. Hung three times! Aye, that's how he came to be known as Crookneck John."

Professor Pepper lowered his heavy brows. "I would advise the faint-hearted to leave before the ghost-raising begins."

He paused. Everyone seemed to look at everyone else.

"Now, then, I must have absolute silence!" Professor Pepper said. He clapped his hands sharply.

The curtains parted.

A pine coffin was stretched across two sawhorses. It looked old and rotted, as if it had been dug out of the ground.

"Aye, the very box holding the bones of Crookneck John," the professor declared. "The coffin is six feet long. Crookneck John was almost seven feet. Buried with his knees bent up, he was."

Then Professor Pepper clapped his hand again. His assistant, the toad-faced man, appeared and blew out the two oil lamps.

Darkness closed in on the hall.

Professor Pepper's voice came rolling out through the blackness.

"Crookneck John," he called. "I have your bones. Is the spirit willing to come forth, eh? Give us a sign."

Silence. All I could hear was my own heart beating. Then there came a hollow rap-rap-rapping from the pine box.

"Aye, I hear the knock of your big knuckles, Mr. Crookneck John. Now rise up. Rise up your bones and stretch your legs, sir."

My eyes strained to see through the darkness.

A minute went by. Maybe two or three. When Professor Pepper spoke again, he was getting impatient.

"Rise up, you scoundrel! Ashamed to show your crooked neck to these honest folks, eh?

263

This is Professor Pepper himself speaking. Aye, and I won't be made a fool of, sir!"

Seconds ticked away. Then a minute or two. Professor Pepper became as short-tempered as a teased snake.

"Rise up, I say!" he commanded. "I've a hanging rope in my hand and I'll string you up a *fourth* time!"

And then there came a creaking of wood. And a groaning of nails. My neck went cold and prickly. *The lid of that pine coffin was lifting!*

"I can't make out a thing," Aunt Etta said.

Suddenly the snarl went out of Professor Pepper's voice. "No! No!" he gasped. "Down! Back, sir! Not the rope!" Gurgling sounds escaped from his throat. "Help! Help! The lamps! Light the la—!"

I was sitting so straight by then I must have shot up six inches taller. The toad-faced man struck a match to the nearest lamp.

The air lit up. And there, against the curtain, staggered Professor Pepper. A noose was pulled tightly around his neck.

The lid of the coffin stood open. Professor Pepper clawed at the rope around his throat and caught a breath. "Save yourselves," he croaked. "Run for your lives! Lock your doors! Shut your windows! Stay off the streets! The Crookneck Ghost is loose!"

"Come on, Aunt Etta!" I said.

She was calm as an owl at midnight. "Sit where you are."

The hall emptied in a whirlwind hurry. Even the toad-faced man was gone.

There was no one left but Professor Pepper and us.

"Madam," he said. He'd freed himself of the rope and was hammering the lid back on the coffin. "Your lives are in terrible danger!"

"Pish-posh," she answered. "I'll expect you to refund everyone's money, sir."

At that, he banged his thumb with the hammer. "What!"

"Other folks paid at the door to *see* a ghost. They have been flimflammed."

"Really, Madam!"

"*I* didn't see a ghost. *Opie* didn't see a ghost. No one *saw* that ghost of yours."

"Unfortunately, Madam, my assistant appears to have flown for his life. And with the box full of money."

"Pay up, sir," was all Aunt Etta would say. "Come along, Opie."

"Hold on," Professor Pepper said with sudden politeness. "I've been nearly strangled. Aye, short of breath I am. Perhaps that lad will help me carry the coffin downstairs."

"What on earth for?" Aunt Etta said.

"Why, Crookneck John must return to his dry bones before the crow of dawn, Madam. That's the way of ghosts, you know. I'll have the burying box moved to the jailhouse. He'll wake up behind bars, the scoundrel!"

Then he turned an eye on me. "I'll reward you for your trouble, lad. Cash money."

"Yes, sir," I answered.

Aunt Etta could read my thoughts. "I've seen enough play-acting for one night," she said. "It's past my bedtime. I'm going home, Opie."

That pine box was heavy. I didn't think dry old bones could weigh so much.

The moon was rising and full.

When we struggled down to the foot of the stairs, Professor Pepper's breath gave out.

"This'll do, lad," he said. "Oh, I should have known better than to raise the Crookneck Ghost on a full moon night. Turns him wild."

Then he dug in his coat pocket and handed me a coin. A mighty small one.

"Run home fast as you can, hear? Make sure that fine lady of yours is safe. I'll manage for myself."

"Much obliged for the cash money," I said politely. But I could tell from the feel it was only a cent piece.

I didn't run home. I wasn't worried about Aunt Etta. She'd said it was all play-acting. Professor Pepper *himself* could have done the rap-rap-rapping on the coffin. And he could have tied the noose around his *own* neck.

I wasn't even past the hotel when the moon faded out of the sky. The tule fog was creeping back.

I gave the cent piece a flip in the air and caught it. I put it in my pocket and then took it out again. Awfully clean and shiny, I thought, as if it had never been in use. Like Aunt Etta's rare Indian-head penny in a bank safe.

There was just enough moonlight left to make out the date.

My breath caught. It was an 1877 Indian-head cent. It appeared to be Aunt Etta's very own penny.

But how had it come to be in Professor Pepper's coat pocket?

Just then I heard the snort of a horse and the creaking of wagon wheels.

"Bah! This fog's so thick I couldn't find my nose with both hands and a lantern."

I knew that voice. It belonged to the toad-faced man.

"I'm not interested in your nose, idiot!" It was the snarl of Professor Pepper himself. "Find the road. And quick before this town has the law on us."

The law? Suddenly I knew the only way Aunt Etta's rare cent could have gotten into the professor's pocket.

He'd robbed the bank!

I had to do something. I felt my way along the hotel hitching post until I could make out the faint glow of their wagon lamp.

"Stop, sir!" I called out. "You're heading straight into a tree. Need help?"

"Help indeed!" said Professor Pepper. "Where's the road out of town, eh?"

Then he paused.

"Don't I know that voice?"

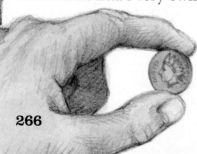

I was having a time to keep my teeth from clacking now. "Yes, sir," I said. "I'm Opie. I scouted you from the barbershop to the hotel."

"Well, take that nag by the nose and lead us out of here. When Crookneck John wakes up in the jailhouse, he'll be after me."

More play-acting, I thought. Oh, he was full of tricks. He'd scared folks into staying off the streets while he got away. But he hadn't counted on the tule fog.

Or me. An idea had already sprung into my head.

I led the horse and wagon step by step along the road toward home. When I came to the dip, I stopped. We were at one end of the old Horseshoe Mine.

"There's a big tunnel on the left, sir. About two miles long. It's kind of a shortcut through the fog."

"Aye, a shortcut would please me!" The professor laughed.

A moment later I left them and they went clattering into the mine.

I was in such a hurry to reach Mr. Whitman's house that I must have barked my shins six times and run into something at least once.

Mr. Whitman owned the bank. I showed him Aunt Etta's 1877 one-cent piece. I told him I thought Professor Pepper had robbed the safe. And we went for the sheriff.

Sure enough, the bank safe was empty.

Mr. Whitman said, "But how did he get in?"

I had already noticed bits of sawdust. I looked up. The sheriff looked up.

"Yup," he said. "Professor Pepper cut through the floor of the Miners' Union Hall upstairs. Probably let himself down with the rope and up again. Then hammered the wood back into place."

I remembered hearing hammer sounds behind the curtain during the long wait for the show to start.

"And he must have hoped we'd believe it was the Crookneck Ghost who'd robbed the bank," the sheriff said. "Well, Pepper can't have got far in this fog."

"Not far at all," I said. "He's in the Horseshoe Mine."

"The Horseshoe Mine! Doesn't he know it makes a perfect horseshoe and comes out about forty feet from the jailhouse?"

"No, sir," I said. "I didn't tell him that."

The end of the tunnel was dark as a sack of black cats. The sheriff waited. His three deputies waited. And I waited too.

Before long we could hear the echo of horse's hooves. My heart began to beat a little faster. The glow of a lantern appeared like a firefly deep in the tunnel.

The sheriff lifted his shotgun and nodded to his deputies. "Get ready, boys."

The wagon lantern grew larger and brighter. Then I could see Professor Pepper himself— chuckling and singing.

But when he saw the law waiting for him, he gave a gasp and a groan.

"Great jumping hop-toads!" he cried out. He grabbed the reins and tried to turn the wagon around. But the mine shaft wasn't wide enough.

The sheriff charged forward and caught the horse by the halter.

"That will do, gents," he said. "Welcome back to Golden Hill."

"Thunder and lightning," the professor snarled. "We've been outfoxed!"

His helper was still clutching the box full of flimflam money. The deputies led him away, together with Professor Pepper.

The sheriff climbed onto the wagon and called to me.

"Opie. Did you say this coffin was uncommon heavy?"

"Yes, sir."

"Hold the lantern."

As I held the lantern, he pried off the lid. There were no bones in that pine box at all.

It was full of money. The stolen bank money.

The sheriff looked through his reward posters.

"Sorry, Opie," he said finally. "There's no reward offered for Professor Pepper. You do deserve one though."

"That's all right," I said. "I got Aunt Etta's penny back for her. Rare as a hen's tooth, that penny. She's going to buy me a horse with it someday."

Mr. Whitman was sitting nearby counting the stolen money. He looked up. "A horse," he said. "Well, a horse has got to have something on it."

When I got home from school on Monday, a saddle was waiting for me in the parlor. The whole room smelled of fresh leather.

"Aunt Etta," I said, "That's the finest looking saddle I *ever* saw!"

"Not much use without a horse under it," she said. "I've already plucked a chicken for supper. If you've got nothing better to do we could go looking for your horse."

"Yes, Ma'am!"

Questions

1. How was Opie able to earn money on foggy days?
2. How did Professor Pepper plan to flimflam the audience at the ghost-raising? How was his plan spoiled?
3. How might the story have turned out if Opie hadn't looked carefully at the penny the professor gave him?
4. If you were making a movie of "The Ghost on Saturday Night," whom would you choose to play the parts of Opie, Aunt Etta, and Professor Pepper? Why?

Applying Reading Skills

A. Read each sentence below based on "The Ghost on Saturday Night" and decide if it is an example of figurative language. If so, write the figure of speech used from the list on page 257. If not, write *literal*.

1. Opie's list of names for his horse was a mile-and-a-half long.
2. Aunt Etta was as sure-footed as a mountain goat.
3. The coffin looked as if it had been dug up.
4. The professor's voice was a drumroll.
5. Aunt Etta was as calm as an owl at midnight.

B. Write the lettered sentence that means the same as each numbered sentence below.

1. Opie could streak through the town with his eyes shut.
   a. Opie couldn't see as he streaked through town.
   b. Opie shut his eyes as he streaked through town.
   c. Opie knew the layout of the town very well.
2. Indian-head pennies are as rare as hens' teeth.
   a. Indian-head pennies are very rare.
   b. Hens' teeth are rare.
   c. Indian-head pennies are sharp.

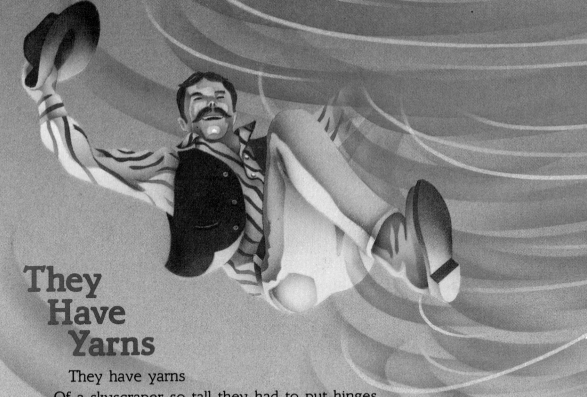

They
Have
Yarns

They have yarns
Of a skyscraper so tall they had to put hinges
On the two top stories so to let the moon go by,
Of one corn crop in Missouri when the roots
Went so deep and drew off so much water
The Mississippi riverbed that year was dry,
Of pancakes so thin they had only one side,
Of "a fog so thick we shingled the barn and six feet out on
    the fog,"
Of Pecos Pete straddling a cyclone in Texas and riding it to
    the west coast where "it rained out under him,"
Of the old man's whiskers: "When the wind was with him his
    whiskers arrived a day before he did."
        "Do tell!"
        "I want to know!"
        "You don't say so!"
        "For the land's sake!"
        "Gosh all fish-hooks!"
        "Tell me some more!"

—*Carl Sandburg*

WRITING ACTIVITY

WRITE A DESCRIPTIVE PARAGRAPH

Prewrite

The writer of "The Ghost on Saturday Night" created a vivid picture of a tule fog by the figurative language used by the characters in the story. Mr. Muldoon describes the fog as getting thick enough "to drive a nail into it and hang your coat." Aunt Etta says the tule is "so thick you'll need a compass to cross the road."

A writer must work at creating vivid descriptions. A well-written description is one that makes readers see, feel, and even smell exactly what the author had in mind. Skim pages 256 and 257 to review the different kinds of figurative language authors use in writing descriptions.

You are going to write a description of an object or an event. Choose a topic from one of the following, or think of your own topic.

1. Lost in a tule fog
2. My messy bedroom
3. The first winter snow
4. My pet ____

Your five senses will help you to create your description. First, close your eyes and try to see exactly what you will describe. Try to recall sights, sounds, colors, and even your feelings about the topic. Completing a sensory map may help you organize your information. Some possible phrases and sentences are shown to help you put your imagination to work.

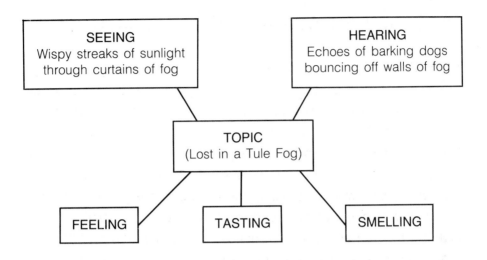

Write

1. Begin your paragraph with a sentence that introduces the topic. Try to use an example of figurative language. For example, *Wispy streaks of sunlight colored the tule fog a dirty mustard yellow, but it still seemed I could see no further than the end of my nose.*
2. Write sentences using examples from your sensory map.
3. Use a thesaurus to find synonyms for "overworked" words.
4. Use your Glossary or dictionary for spelling help.

Revise

Read your description. Is it so clear that your reader could draw a picture of the event or object you describe? Can you combine or move any sentences to help your readers draw clearer pictures?

1. Proofread for end punctuation and capitalization in each sentence.
2. Check the subject-verb agreement in each sentence.
3. Rewrite your paragraph to share.

PREPARING FOR READING

Learning Vocabulary

1. Sherlock Holmes and Dr. Watson listened to Mr. Wilson's <u>narrative</u> of his unusual experience.
2. Mr. Hopkins was a <u>benefactor</u> of the Red-Headed League, who contributed money to the organization.
3. Ross explained that Wilson would have to <u>forfeit</u> his job if he failed to abide by the league's terms.
4. Wilson wondered if copying encyclopedia articles was a real job or just a <u>hoax</u>.
5. Holmes believed that the more <u>bizarre</u> a thing appears to be, the less mysterious it proves to be.
6. Spaulding was Ross's <u>accomplice</u> in a clever scheme.
7. Watson thought Holmes's solution was remarkable; Holmes felt it was <u>elementary</u>.

narrative	benefactor	forfeit	hoax
bizarre	accomplice	elementary	

Developing Background and Skills
Draw Conclusions

Read the passage below.

Dr. Watson took the key to 221b Baker Street from his pocket, inserted it into the lock, and let himself into the house. Upon entering the hallway, he took off his coat and hung it on the rack. A glance into the living room showed him his friend Sherlock Holmes seated in front of the fire, wearing a lounging robe and slippers. Holmes appeared to be in conversation with someone. Watson shifted his position slightly and saw that an agitated stranger was seated opposite Holmes. The stranger was talking rapidly and throwing nervous glances at the window. "It appears," thought Watson, "that Holmes has a new case."

Watson's thought, *Holmes has a new case*, is a conclusion. A **conclusion**, as you know, is a decision based on facts and experience. Watson based his conclusion on the fact that Holmes was talking with an agitated and nervous stranger *and* on his experience of Holmes.

You can use the information in the paragraph to reach two conclusions of your own.

1. Watson and Holmes shared the house at 221b Baker Street.
2. Sherlock Holmes was a detective.

The facts that help you reach conclusion 1 are: *Watson had a key to the residence, let himself in, and hung up his coat. Holmes was dressed in a robe and slippers, sitting by the fire.* Conclusion 2 is based on the information *Watson thought Holmes had a new case.* You must combine this fact with your own knowledge that a mystery or crime is often called a *case*, and is sometimes referred to a detective.

Detective stories present many opportunities for drawing conclusions. In most detective stories, the reader is presented with the same information the detective has. The reader, too, must draw conclusions. In a way, the reader matches wits with the detective to solve the mystery or figure out who the criminal is.

The following selection is a detective story written as a play. In it you will meet the famous detective Sherlock Holmes, the creation of Arthur Conan Doyle. As you read, see what conclusions you can draw from the facts presented. Look for the conclusions Holmes draws and compare them with your own. Notice how Holmes reasons from conclusion to conclusion to solve the mystery.

SHERLOCK HOLMES
AND THE
RED-HEADED LEAGUE

by Arthur Conan Doyle   adapted by Lewy Olfson

Characters

NARRATOR

SHERLOCK HOLMES

DR. WATSON

JABEZ WILSON

VINCENT SPAULDING

DUNCAN ROSS

LANDLORD

NARRATOR: Dr. Watson, opening the door of Sherlock Holmes's Baker Street rooms, finds Holmes seated beside a man with the reddest hair he has ever seen. . . .

HOLMES: Ah, Watson, you could not have come at a better time. Here is a gentleman I should like you to meet. Mr. Wilson, this is Dr. Watson, my partner and helper in many of my most successful cases. Watson, this is Mr. Jabez Wilson.

WATSON: How do you do, Mr. Wilson?

WILSON: I'm so glad to meet you, Dr. Watson.

HOLMES: I'm sure you will particularly enjoy the details of this case, Watson.

WATSON: What is this case about, gentlemen?

HOLMES: Mr. Wilson here has begun a narrative which promises to be one of the most singular which I have listened to for some time. Perhaps, Mr. Wilson, you would be kind enough to begin your tale again.

WILSON: I shall be happy to do so, Mr. Holmes.

HOLMES: Can you find the advertisement you spoke of in that newspaper again?

WILSON: Yes, here it is. This is what began it all, Dr. Watson. Just read it for yourself.

WATSON (Reading aloud): "To the Red-Headed League. On account of the bequest of the late Ezekiah Hopkins, of Lebanon, Pennsylvania, U.S.A., there is now another vacancy open which entitles a member of the League to a salary of four pounds a week for purely nominal services. All red-headed men who are sound in body and mind, and above the age of twenty-one, are eligible. Apply in person on Monday, at eleven o'clock, to Duncan Ross, at the offices of the League, Seven Pope's Court, Fleet Street."

HOLMES: Very good. Now, Mr. Wilson?

WILSON: I have a small pawn-broker's business at Colburg Square. Of late years it has not done more than give me a bare living.

HOLMES: Do you work it alone?

WILSON: No, I have an assistant—though, to tell the truth, I should not be able to employ him if he did not agree to work for such low pay.

HOLMES: What is his name?

WILSON: His name is Vincent Spaulding, and I should not wish a smarter assistant. He has his faults, too. Never was such a fellow for photography. Snapping away with his camera, and then diving down into the cellar to develop his pictures. That is his main fault, but on the whole he's a good worker.

WATSON: He is still with you, I presume, sir?

WILSON: Yes, he is. We live very quietly, the two of us—for I'm widowed, with no family. The first thing that interrupted our dull and quiet lives was this advertisement. As a matter of fact, it was my assistant who called it to my attention.

HOLMES: How was that?

WILSON: Spaulding came into the office just this day eight weeks ago with this very paper in his hand, and he said. . . .

SPAULDING (*A young, vigorous voice*): Mr. Wilson, I wish that I were a red-headed man.

WILSON: Why, Vincent?

SPAULDING: Why, here's another vacancy in the Red-Headed League. It's worth quite a little fortune to any man who qualifies.

WILSON: I've never heard of it. What is it then?

SPAULDING: I wonder that *you* do not know of it, for you are eligible yourself for one of the vacancies, what with your flaming red hair.

WILSON: What are the vacancies worth?

SPAULDING: Merely a couple of hundred pounds a year—but the work is slight, and wouldn't interfere with other occupations.

WILSON: Tell me about it. A couple of hundred a year would certainly come in handy.

SPAULDING: As far as I can make out, the League was founded by an American millionaire who was very peculiar in his ways. He himself had red hair, and he wanted to make life easier for those who were like him.

WILSON: There would be millions of red-haired men that would apply.

SPAULDING: Not so many as you might think. It is confined to grown men, from London, which was the American's native city. And as for color, why the man's hair must be bright, blazing, fiery red like yours. . . .

WILSON: "Bright, blazing, fiery red like yours." Yes, you can readily see for yourselves that my hair is of a full, rich color, so I decided, upon Spaulding's urging, that I would have a try at it.

HOLMES: What happened then?

WILSON: I went to the specified address at the appointed time, accompanied by my assistant. From all corners of London had come every man who had a shade of red in his hair. Every shade of color, they were—orange, brick, Irish-setter, clay—but, as Spaulding pointed out, none was as bright as my own. Well, sir, we pushed and pulled and jammed our way forward, and finally found ourselves next in line at the office door.

HOLMES: Your experience has been a most entertaining one, Wilson.

WATSON: Indeed! Pray continue!

WILSON: The office itself was a small one—nothing particular about it. Behind the desk sat a man whose hair was redder than mine—a Mr. Duncan Ross, he told me later. As we entered the office, he shut the door, and said. . . .

ROSS: Your name, sir?

WILSON: Mr. Jabez Wilson, and willing to fill a vacancy in the League.

ROSS: You are admirably suited for it, Mr. Wilson. I cannot recall when I have seen a red head so fine. May I take hold of your hair?

WILSON: Certainly, if you like.

ROSS (*As if pulling*): Ugh! Mph! No, it's yours all right. I am sorry to have had to take this precaution, but we have twice been deceived by wigs.

279

WILSON: My hair is my own, sir.

ROSS: Well, then, Mr. Wilson. My name is Duncan Ross, and I am myself one of the pensioners upon the fund left by our noble benefactor. I am pleased to tell you that the position is yours. When shall you be able to enter upon your new duties?

WILSON: It is a little awkward, for I have a business already.

SPAULDING: Never mind that, Mr. Wilson. I shall look after it.

WILSON: What would the hours be, Mr. Ross?

ROSS: From ten to two.

WILSON: A pawnbroker's business—for that is my trade—is done mostly at night. So I suppose I can trust my shop to my assistant here. And the pay?

ROSS: Four pounds a week.

WILSON: And the work?

ROSS: The work is to copy out the *Encyclopedia Britannica*.

Don't ask me why: it is the terms of the will. You must provide your own pens, paper, and ink, but we provide the table and chair. Also, you forfeit the position if you once leave the building during the hours of ten to two. Will you be ready tomorrow?

WILSON: Certainly.

ROSS: Then goodbye, Mr. Jabez Wilson, and let me congratulate you once more on the important position which you have been fortunate enough to obtain.

WILSON: With those words, gentlemen, he bowed me and my assistant out of the room. I was, at the same time, both pleased and puzzled.

WATSON: Pleased and puzzled?

WILSON: Well, you see, Mr. Watson, I was pleased with my new source of income, but puzzled over why anyone should want me to copy out the encyclopedia. In fact, by nightfall I had almost convinced myself that it was all

a hoax. The next day, when I reported for work, there was the encyclopedia laid open upon the table, the page at letter "A." Mr. Duncan Ross was there, and he started me off, then left. At two o'clock he returned, complimented me upon the amount that I had written, and bade me good day.

HOLMES: How long did this procedure continue?

WILSON: This went on day after day, Mr. Holmes, and on Saturday, the manager came in and plunked down four golden sovereigns for my week's work. It was the same the next week, and the same the week after. Every morning I was there at ten, and every afternoon I left at two. Eight weeks passed away like this, and I had written about Abbots and Archery and Armour and Architecture and Attica. Then suddenly—

WATSON: Yes?

WILSON: The whole business came to an end.

HOLMES: To an end!

WILSON *(A bit puzzled)*: Yes, sir. This very morning. I went to my work as usual at ten o'clock, but the door was shut and locked, with a little square of cardboard hammered onto it. Here it is, and you can read it for yourself.

WATSON: What does it say, Holmes?

HOLMES: "The Red-Headed League is dissolved. June 22, 1890." (WATSON *laughs*, and HOLMES *joins in*.)

WILSON *(Indignantly)*: I cannot see that there is anything funny. If you can do nothing other than laugh at me, I can go elsewhere.

HOLMES: Oh, no, no, I shouldn't miss your case for the world. But you must admit that it has a slightly comical side to it. Pray, what steps did you take when you found this card?

WILSON: I was staggered, sir. I did not know what to do. Then I called at the landlord's, and asked if he could tell me what had become of the Red-Headed League. He looked at me, astonished, and said. . . .

LANDLORD *(Puzzled)*: Red-Headed League, you say? I never heard of such a body.

WILSON: Well, then, can you tell me what happened to Mr. Ross?

LANDLORD: Ross? I know of no one of that name.

WILSON: Well, then, what happened to the gentleman who rented number four?

LANDLORD: Oh, you mean the red-headed man. His name was William Morris. He was a solicitor and was using my room as a temporary convenience until his new premises were ready. He moved out yesterday.

WILSON: Where could I find him, sir?

LANDLORD: He's at his new offices. He did tell me the address. What was it now? Ah, yes. Seventeen King Edward Street.

HOLMES *(Muttering)*: I'll make a note of that, Mr. Wilson.

WILSON: Well, I already checked there, but there was no one there of either the name of William Morris *or* Duncan Ross. It was a manufacturer of artificial kneecaps. Well, at that, I knew not what to do, so decided to take the advice of my assistant, Spaulding, who said simply to wait. But I got impatient, sir, and hearing that Sherlock Holmes was very clever at such things, I decided to come here for aid.

HOLMES: And you did wisely, Mr. Wilson. From what you have said, I think it is possible that a far more serious issue may be at stake than might at first appear.

WILSON: The issue is quite serious enough as it is. I have lost four pounds a week!

HOLMES: Watson and I will do our best to help you, Mr. Wilson. But first, a few questions. This assistant of yours—how long has he been with you?

WILSON: He'd been with me about a month at that time. He answered an advertisement that I placed in the paper.

HOLMES: And was he the only applicant?

WILSON: No, I had a dozen.

HOLMES: Why did you pick him?

WILSON: Because he was intelligent and handy, and would come at half wages, in fact.

WATSON: What is he like?

WILSON: Small, stout-built, very quick in his ways, no hair on his face—though he's not short of thirty. He has a white splash of acid upon his forehead.

HOLMES (*Excitedly*): Acid, you say? Yes, I thought as much. Hm-m. He is still with you?

WILSON: Oh yes, sir; I have only just left him. But I must be on my way. Will there be anything else you require to ask of me?

HOLMES: Yes, I have one more question. All the mornings that you were out—did your assistant attend to your business?

WILSON: Yes, sir, and he's honest and careful enough. Nothing to complain of, sir. There's never very much to do of a morning.

HOLMES: I believe you have given us all the information we shall need. I shall be happy to give you an opinion on the subject in a day or two. Good day, Mr. Wilson.

WILSON: Good day, sirs.

HOLMES (*After a pause*): Watson, what do you make of it all?

WATSON: It is a most mysterious business.

HOLMES: As a rule, the more bizarre a thing is, the less mysterious it proves to be.

WATSON: What are you going to do, then?

HOLMES: We are going to the pawnbroker's shop of Mr. Wilson.

WATSON: Whatever for?

HOLMES: To investigate, my dear Watson. To investigate!

NARRATOR: Holmes and Watson set out at once for Wilson's shop.

HOLMES: There, Watson. That is the place.

WATSON: Yes, Wilson's name is painted over the door. But now what are you going to do?

HOLMES: First, an experiment.

NARRATOR: Holmes pounds his walking stick on the pavement.

WATSON (*Taken aback*): Pounding your stick on the pavement?

HOLMES: And now, to knock on the door. I hope that Spaulding fellow answers.

SPAULDING: Won't you step in, gentlemen?

HOLMES: Thank you, but I only wished to ask you how one would go from here to the Strand.

SPAULDING: Oh. Third right, fourth left, sir. Good day.

HOLMES: Smart fellow, that. He is, in my judgment, the fourth smartest man in London, and for daring I am not sure that he has not a claim to be third. I have known something of him before.

WATSON: Evidently Mr. Wilson's assistant counts for a good deal in this mystery. I am sure that you inquired your way merely that you might see him.

HOLMES: Not him. The knee of his trousers.

WATSON: And what did you see?

HOLMES: What I expected to see.

WATSON: Why did you beat the pavement before knocking?

HOLMES: Watson, this is a time for observation, not for talk. Let us now explore the area.

NARRATOR: Holmes and Watson continue on down the street and around the corner. Holmes observes each building they pass.

HOLMES: Let me see. I should just like to remember the order of the houses here. There is the tobacconist's, the little newspaper shop, the Coburg branch of the City and Suburban Bank, the restaurant, and the carriage-builder's. That carries us right onto the other block, on which stands the pawnbroker's establishment of Jabez Wilson. This business is serious. A considerable crime is in contemplation. I have every reason to believe that we shall be in time to stop it. But today being Saturday rather complicates matters. I shall want your help tonight, Watson. Will you come to Baker Street at ten? Goodbye for now, Watson.

NARRATOR: Promptly at ten, Watson arrives at Baker Street, and he and Holmes set off into the night.

WATSON: Will you not tell me, Holmes, where we are going, or whom we seek?

HOLMES: I shall gladly do both. We are now going to the Coburg branch of the City and Suburban Bank. The man we seek is none other than John Clay.

WATSON: John Clay! You mean the thief and forger who has escaped the police so many times?

HOLMES: The same. His brain is as cunning as his fingers.

WATSON: Why, all of London has been on his trail for years!

HOLMES: I hope that I may have the pleasure of introducing you to him tonight!

NARRATOR: Leaving the carriage some distance away, Holmes and Watson cautiously enter the bank with a key that Holmes produces without an explanation. They descend to the cellar. . . .

HOLMES (*Softly*): Here, Watson.

WATSON (*Quietly*): Is this the cellar of the bank, then?

HOLMES: It is. We must act quickly, for time is of the essence. I perceive that the ceiling is thick enough. We are not vulnerable from above.

WATSON: Nor from below. The floor seems . . . why, dear me! A hollow sound!

HOLMES: I must really ask you to be a little more quiet. Sit down on one of those boxes while I shade the light.

WATSON: What is in these great packing-cases, Holmes?

HOLMES: French gold from the Bank of France.

WATSON: What!

HOLMES: It has become known that this gold was being stored in the cellar where we now find ourselves. The directors of the bank began to have misgivings about leaving so large a quantity of gold about, and now it appears that their fears were justified. The bank is to be robbed tonight, if I am not mistaken.

WATSON: How so? And only the two of us to stop the thieves?

HOLMES: I have ordered an inspector and two officers to be at the one possible retreat—the front door.

WATSON: How, then, will the thieves enter?

HOLMES: Through a hole in the floor.

WATSON: What!

HOLMES (*Whispering*): Huddle in the shadows! They are coming!

NARRATOR: Vincent Spaulding's voice is heard faintly, talking to another. . . .

SPAULDING: It's all clear. Have you the chisel and the bags?

HOLMES (*Suddenly*): I have you, John Clay!

SPAULDING (*Calling out*): Run, Archie! I'm caught!

HOLMES: It's no use, John Clay. You have no chance at all. You did not reckon with Sherlock Holmes. It is no use!

SPAULDING: So I see. I fancy my friend has escaped though. At least my struggle with you gave him that chance.

WATSON: The door was guarded. There are three men waiting.

SPAULDING: Oh, you seem to have done the thing completely. I must compliment you.

HOLMES: And I you. Your red-headed idea was very clever.

WATSON: Ah, Clay, you'll be seeing your friend soon—in court, you scoundrel!

SPAULDING (*With dignity*): I beg your pardon. You may not be aware that John Clay has royal blood in his veins. Have the goodness when you address me always to say "sir" and "please."

HOLMES (*Laughing*): As you wish, John Clay. Well, would you please, sir, march upstairs, sir, where we can please to get a cab, sir, to carry Your Highness to the police station—sir?

NARRATOR: A short time later, back at Baker Street, Holmes explains to Watson. . . .

HOLMES: It was obvious from the start that the purpose of the Red-Headed League was to get our friend, Jabez Wilson, out of the way for a few hours every day. The plot was suggested, I'm sure, by Wilson's own hair. The four pounds a week was a lure. They put in the advertisement. One accomplice posed as Duncan Ross, the other insured that Wilson would apply. From the time I heard that the assistant had come for half wages, I knew he had some strange motive for securing the station.

WATSON: How could you guess what the motive was?

HOLMES: Wilson's business is very small. It must be, then, the house itself that was of value.

When I thought of the assistant's fondness for photography and his vanishing constantly into the cellar, I realized at once that that was it.

WATSON: Yes, I remember now. Wilson mentioned that.

HOLMES: The description of the assistant convinced me that it was the notorious Clay himself. But what could he be doing in the cellar of a pawnbroker? Why, digging a tunnel, of course, each day for months. Then I wondered, what building could he be tunneling into? Our visit to the actual scene itself showed me that. Remember I observed that the bank was right around the corner from Wilson's?

WATSON: I do indeed.

HOLMES: I surprised you by tapping my stick on the pavement. That was to determine whether the cellar extended to the front of the buildings. Then I paid a call on John Clay himself—at that time known to us as Spaulding.

WATSON: Yes. You said you wanted to observe his knees. What did you see?

HOLMES: You yourself must have noticed how worn, wrinkled and stained they were—which was a natural consequence of his burrowing. All my conclusions assembled, I called Scotland Yard and the bank, and secured permission and a key for our admittance.

WATSON: How could you tell that they would make their attempt tonight?

HOLMES: When they closed their League offices, that was a sign that they cared no longer about Wilson's presence—in other words, that they had completed their tunnel. But it was essential that they should use it soon, as it might be discovered. Saturday would suit them best, as it would give them two days for their escape. For these reasons I expected them to come tonight.

WATSON: Ah, you reasoned it out beautifully. It is so long a chain, and yet every link rings true. It was indeed remarkable, Sherlock Holmes. Remarkable.

HOLMES: On the contrary, it was elementary, my dear Watson. Elementary!

Questions

1. What was the Red-Headed League?
2. Why did Wilson take a job with the league? Why did he later come to consult with Sherlock Holmes?
3. Do you think the explanation of the mystery supports Holmes's generalization that the more bizarre a thing appears, the less mysterious it proves to be? Explain your answer.
4. Think of a problem or mystery that you would want Sherlock Holmes to solve. Describe the problem or mystery as you would present it to Holmes.

Applying Reading Skills

Sherlock Holmes, like many detectives, might have kept a case-book of his conclusions. Copy and complete the "case-book" below by giving one or more reasons for each of Holmes's conclusions.

CASE: The Red-Headed League Mystery

CONCLUSION	REASONS
1. The purpose of the Red-Headed League was to get Wilson out of the way.	
2. Spaulding had some strange motive for becoming Wilson's assistant.	_____
3. Spaulding was really John Clay.	_____
4. Spaulding was digging a tunnel.	_____
5. The tunnel led to the bank.	_____
6. Spaulding and Ross would attempt to rob the bank on Saturday.	_____

PREPARING FOR READING

Learning Vocabulary

1. Agatha Christie's stories are noted for their clever and complicated, or intricate, plots.
2. She decided to incorporate people she met or observed into her stories.
3. Christie admired Sherlock Holmes, but she felt she could not emulate him in the detective she would create.
4. She decided on a Belgian detective—a former inspector who would be both brainy and very tidy, or meticulous.
5. Once the characters were chosen, Christie had to decide on the ramifications, such as false clues and motives.
6. The detective would have to be involved in the plot in a natural and plausible way.

intricate	incorporate	emulate
meticulous	ramifications	plausible

Developing Background and Skills
Context Clues

You know that you can often figure out the meanings of unfamiliar words by using **context clues**. *Context* refers to the setting in which a word appears.

Writers provide context clues by using direct definitions, synonyms, and antonyms. Read the examples below.

DIRECT DEFINITION — Christie worked in the dispensary, a room where medicine and medical supplies were given out, so she thought of murder by poison.

SYNONYMS — The murder would take place among intimates. The victim, the murderer, and the suspects would be close friends or associates.

ANTONYMS — She considered an exotic setting but decided instead on one that was ordinary.

Using the context clues, how would you define *dispensary*? What are two synonyms for *intimates*? How would you define *exotic*?

Direct definitions, synonyms, and antonyms are examples of semantic context clues. Syntactic context clues are another kind of context clue. Syntactic context clues can be found in word order and sentence structure. Read the sentences below. Notice the labels for the parts of speech.

Agatha Christie became a famous novelist and playwright.

NOUNS   VERB   NOUNS

ADJECTIVES

Knowing what part of speech a word is can help you figure out its meaning. For example, it is helpful to know that an unknown word is an adjective, or describing word, instead of a verb, or action word.

In most cases, you will use both semantic and syntactic context clues to define an unknown word. Try it on the example below.

It was uncertain when or how the murder would take place. The police prepared for every contingency.
- a. occur: to happen
- b. possible: capable of happening
- c. appearance: coming into view
- d. possibility: that which can happen

Because of its position in the sentence (after a preposition—*for*—and an adjective—*every*), you know that *contingency* is a noun. Choices **c** and **d** are both nouns. Which word fits best into the context?

As you read the following selection, try to figure out the meanings of unfamiliar words by using both semantic and syntactic context clues. Use the strategies you have learned.

AGATHA CHRISTIE

Writing a deTective StOry

Agatha Christie was a well-known English writer of mystery and detective fiction. Her stories are noted for their intricate plots. Her most famous detectives are Jane Marple and Hercule Poirot (pwä rō'). In this excerpt from her autobiography, Christie tells how she came to invent Hercule Poirot as she wrote her first mystery novel during World War I.

It was while I was working in the dispensary[1] that I first conceived the idea of writing a detective story. . . . My present work seemed to offer a favorable opportunity. Unlike nursing, where there always was something to do, dispensing consisted of slack or busy periods. Sometimes I would be on duty alone in the afternoon with hardly anything to do but sit about. Having seen that the stock bottles were full and attended to, one was at liberty to do anything one pleased except leave the dispensary. I began considering what kind of a detective story I could write. Since I was surrounded by poisons, perhaps it was natural that death by poisoning should be the method I selected. I settled on one fact which seemed to me to have possibilities. I toyed with the idea, liked it, and finally accepted it. Then I went on to the *dramatis personae.*[2] Who should be poisoned? Who would poison him or her? When?

---

1. **dispensary**: room where medicine and medical supplies are given out.
2. *dramatis personae* (dram' ə tis pər sō' nē): list of characters.

Where? How? Why? And all the rest of it. It would have to be very much of an *intime*[3] murder, owing to the particular way it was done; it would have to be all in the family, so to speak. There would naturally have to be a detective. At that date I was well steeped in the Sherlock Holmes tradition. So I considered detectives. Not like Sherlock Holmes, of course: I must invent one of my own, and he would also have a friend as a kind of butt or stooge—that would not be too difficult. I returned to thoughts of my other characters. Who was to be murdered? A husband could murder his wife—that seemed to be the most usual kind of murder. I could, of course, have a very *unusual* kind of murder for a very *unusual* motive, but that did not appeal to me artistically. The whole point of a *good* detective story was that it must be somebody obvious but at the same time, for some reason, you would then find that it was *not* obvious, that he could not possibly have done it. Though really, of course, he *had* done it. At that point I got confused, and went away and made up a couple of bottles of extra hypochlorous lotion[4] so that I should be fairly free of work the next day.

I went on playing with my idea for some time. Bits of it began to grow. I saw the murderer now. He would have to be rather sinister-looking. He would have a black beard—that appeared to me at that time very sinister. There were some acquaintances who had recently come to live near us—the husband had a black beard, and he had a wife who was older than himself and who was very rich. Yes, I thought, that might do as a basis. I considered it at some length. It might do, but it was not entirely satisfactory. The man in question would, I was sure, never murder anybody. I took my mind away from them and decided once and for all that it is no good thinking about real people—you must create your characters for yourself. Someone you see in a tram or a train

---

3. *intime* (aN tēm′): French for *intimate*.
4. **hypochlorous** (hī′ pə klôr′ əs) **lotion**: a disinfectant.

or a restaurant is a possible starting point, because you can make up something for yourself about them.

Sure enough, next day, when I was sitting in a tram, I saw just what I wanted: *a man with a black beard, sitting next to an elderly lady who was chatting like a magpie.* I didn't think I'd have *her*, but I thought *he* would do admirably. Sitting a little way beyond them was a large, hearty woman, talking loudly about spring bulbs. I liked the look of her, too. Perhaps I could incorporate her? I took them all three off the tram with me to work upon—and walked up Barton Road muttering to myself.

Very soon I had a sketchy picture of some of my people. There was the hearty woman—I even knew her name: Evelyn. She could be a poor relation or a lady gardener or a companion—perhaps a lady housekeeper? Anyway, I was going to have her. Then there was the man with the black beard whom I still felt I didn't know much about, except for his beard, which wasn't really enough—or *was* it enough? Yes, perhaps it was; because you would be seeing this man from the *outside* —so you could only see what he liked to show—not as he really was: that ought to be a clue in itself. The elderly wife would be murdered more for her money than her character, so she didn't matter much. I now began adding more characters rapidly. A son? A daughter? Possibly a nephew? You had to have many suspects. The family was coming along nicely.

I left it to develop, and turned my attention to the detective. Who could I have as a detective? I reviewed such detectives as I had met and admired in books. There was Sherlock Holmes, the one and only—I should never be able to emulate *him*. Whom could I have? A schoolboy? Rather difficult. A scientist? What did I know of scientists? Then I remembered our Belgian refugees. We had quite a colony of Belgian refugees living in the parish[5] of Tor. Everyone had

---

5. **parish**: in Great Britain, a district that is a subdivision of a county.

been bursting with loving kindness and sympathy when they arrived. People had stocked houses with furniture for them to live in, had done everything they could to make them comfortable. Why not make my detective a Belgian? I thought. There were all types of refugees. How about a refugee police officer? A retired police officer. Not too young a one. What a mistake I made there. The result is that my fictional detective must really be well over a hundred by now.

Anyway, I settled on a Belgian detective. I allowed him slowly to grow into his part. He should have been an inspector, so that he would have a certain knowledge of crime. He would be meticulous, very tidy, I thought to myself, as I cleared away a good many untidy odds and ends in my own bedroom. A tidy little man. I could see him as a tidy little man, always arranging things, liking things in pairs, liking things square instead of round. And he should be very brainy—he should have little gray cells of the mind—that was a good phrase: I must remember that—yes, he would have little gray cells. He would have rather a grand name— one of those names that Sherlock Holmes and his family had. Who was it his brother had been? Mycroft Holmes.

How about calling my little man Hercules? He would be a small man—Hercules: a good name. His last name was more difficult. I don't know why I settled on the name Poirot; whether it just came into my head or whether I saw it in some newspaper or written on something—anyway it came. It went well not with Hercules but Hercule—Hercule Poirot. That was all right—settled, thank goodness.

Now I must get names for the others—but that was less important. Alfred Inglethorpe—that might do; it would go well with the black beard. I added some more characters. A husband and wife—attractive—estranged from each other. Now for all the ramifications—the false clues. Like all young writers, I was trying to put far too much plot in one book. I had too many false clues—so many things to unravel that it might make the whole thing not only more difficult to solve, but more difficult to read.

In leisure moments, bits of my detective story rattled about in my head. I had the beginnings all settled, and the end arranged, but there were difficult gaps in between. I had Hercule Poirot involved in a natural and plausible way. But there had to be more reasons to explain why other people were involved. It was still all in a tangle.

It made me absent-minded at home. My mother was continually asking why I didn't answer questions or didn't answer them properly. I knitted Grannie's pattern wrong more than once; I forgot to do a lot of things that I was supposed to do; and I sent several letters to the wrong addresses. However, the time came when I felt I could at last begin to write. I

Margaret Rutherford as Miss Jane Marple in *Murder Ahoy.*

Albert Finney (center) as Hercule Poirot investigating in *Murder on the Orient Express.*

Hercule Poirot as portrayed by Peter Ustinov in the movie *Death on the Nile.*

told Mother what I was going to do. Mother had the usual complete faith that her daughters could do anything.

"Oh?" she said. "A detective story? That will be a nice change for you, won't it? You'd better start."

It wasn't easy to snatch much time, but I managed. I had the old typewriter still and I battered away on that, after I had written a first draft in longhand. I typed out each chapter as I finished it. My handwriting was better in those days and my longhand was readable. I was excited by my new effort. Up to a point I enjoyed it. But I got very tired, and I also got cross. Writing has that effect, I find. Also, as I began to be enmeshed in the middle part of the book, the complications got the better of me instead of my being the master of them. It was then that my mother made a good suggestion.

"How far have you got?" she asked.

"Oh, I think about halfway through."

"Well, I think if you really want to finish it, you'll have to do so when you take your holidays."

"Well, I did mean to go on with it then."

"Yes, but I think you should go away from home for your holiday, and write with nothing to disturb you."

I thought about it. A fortnight[6] quite undisturbed. It *would* be rather wonderful.

"Where would you like to go?" asked my mother. "Dartmoor?"

"Yes," I said, entranced. "Dartmoor—that is exactly it."

So to Dartmoor I went. I booked myself a room in the Moorland Hotel at Hay Tor. It was a large, dreary hotel with plenty of rooms. There were few people staying there. I don't think I spoke to any of them—it would have taken my mind away from what I was doing. I used to write laboriously all morning till my hand ached. Then I would have lunch, reading a book. Afterwards I would go out for a good walk on the moor, perhaps for a couple of hours. I think I learned

6. **fortnight**: two weeks.

to love the moor in those days. I loved the tors[7] and the heather and all the wild part of it away from the roads. Everybody who went there—and of course there were not many in wartime—would be clustering round Hay Tor itself, but I left Hay Tor severely alone and struck out on my own across country. As I walked I muttered to myself, enacting the chapter that I was next going to write; speaking as John to Mary, and as Mary to John, as Evelyn to her employer, and so on. I became quite excited by this. I would come home, have dinner, fall into bed and sleep for about twelve hours. Then I would get up and write passionately again all morning.

I finished the last half of the book, or as near as not, during my fortnight's holiday. Of course that was not the end. I then had to rewrite a great part of it—mostly the overcomplicated middle. But in the end it was finished and I was reasonably satisfied with it. That is to say it was roughly as I had intended it to be. It could be much better, I saw that, but I didn't see just how *I* could make it better, so I had to leave it as it was. I rewrote some very stilted chapters between Mary and her husband John who were estranged from some foolish reason, but whom I was determined to force together again at the end so as to make a kind of love interest. I myself always found the love interest a terrible bore in detective stories. Love, I felt, belonged to romantic stories. To force a love motif into what should be a scientific process went much against the grain. However, at that period detective stories always had to have a love interest—so there it was. I did my best with John and Mary, but they were poor creatures. Then I got it properly typed by somebody, and having finally decided I could do no more to it, I sent it off to a publisher, who returned it. It was a plain refusal, with no frills on it. I was not surprised—I hadn't expected success— but I bundled it off to another publisher.

---

7. **tors**: high, rocky hills.

Questions

1. What kinds of books did Agatha Christie become famous for?
2. Why did Christie decide to write a book? How did she happen to decide on a detective story?
3. Did Christie seem to have more difficulty with characters or plot? Explain your answer.
4. If you were going to write a mystery story, what kind would you write? Explain the characters, plot, and setting you would choose to write about.

Applying Reading Skills

Read each incomplete sentence below. Use semantic and snytactic context clues to choose the word that best completes each sentence.

1. Some fictional detectives are razor-sharp and utterly _____. Others are equally brilliant, but all out for themselves.
   a. masterminds: people displaying great intelligence
   b. disguised: changed in appearance or dressed to make recognition difficult
   c. altruistic: unselfishly devoted to the welfare of others
   d. impeach: to question or cast doubt on
2. Many early mystery writers have fallen into _____. For example, few readers today have heard of Arthur Morrison or Guy Boothby.
   a. oblivion: state of being forgotten
   b. unpopular: not favorably viewed
   c. revival: an increased interest (in something)
   d. undeservedly: not according to merit; not rightfully
3. Ashden wrote early mysteries under the name Freed. Later, when he became famous, he _____ denied being the author of books of which he was ashamed.
   a. successfully: fortunately
   b. ingenious: done or executed with cleverness
   c. pretended: claimed or attempted
   d. vehemently: in a manner showing strong feeling

PREPARING FOR READING

Learning Vocabulary

1. <u>Colossal</u> drawings cover an area of more than 4,500 square miles (11,655 sq. km) in the Peruvian desert.
2. Scientists agree that these drawings must have been important, but they do not agree on their <u>significance</u>.
3. Mysterious round stones—almost perfect <u>spheres</u>—have been found in the forests of Central America.
4. The spheres vary from a few inches to eight feet in <u>diameter</u>.
5. How could ancient mapmakers know the <u>circumference</u> of the earth before any sailor had ever sailed around the world?

colossal   significance   spheres
diameter   circumference

Developing Background and Skills
Main Idea

In a well-written paragraph the sentences are all related to one another. They tell about the same subject or topic. The most important information in the paragraph is called the **main idea**. Sometimes a writer states the main idea in a sentence that may come at the beginning, in the middle, or at the end of a paragraph. Read the paragraph below.

Easter Island has long been famous for the gigantic stone heads found there. The statues are carved from a local rock called tufa. They range in height from ten to forty feet. Some weigh more than fifty tons. The statues originally stood on stone platforms.

Which sentence states the main idea?
   a. Easter Island has long been famous for the gigantic stone heads found there.
   b. The statues are carved from a local rock called tufa.

c. They range in height from ten to forty feet.
d. Some weigh more than fifty tons.
e. The statues originally stood on stone platforms.

If you chose **a**, the first sentence of the paragraph, you were right. The other sentences provide the details that support, or tell more about, the main idea. In a well-written paragraph, the main idea is always supported by details.

Sometimes the main idea is stated in two or more sentences, as in the paragraph below.

The statues, though remarkable, are not the only remains found on Easter Island. There are also tombs, towers, cave pictures, and wooden tablets. The towers may have marked land boundaries. The writing on the tablets is unlike any writing known today.

To state the main idea, you must combine the information in the first two sentences: *In addition to the remarkable statues, several other kinds of remains are found on Easter Island.*

Many times the writer does not state the main idea at all. You must summarize the information given and state the main idea in your own words. Read the paragraph below.

No one knows who built the large stone circles or when they were built. Scientists do not agree on how the stones were transported to the site. The purpose of the circles also remains unknown, although several theories have been proposed.

If you consider the information carefully, you might state the main idea in this way: *Several mysteries surround the stone circles.* This statement sums up the information in all the sentences.

As you read the following selection, look for the main ideas. Find the details that support each main idea.

MYSTERIES FROM THE PAST

Who traced the mysterious lines in the desert at Nazca, in Peru, and why? What is the secret of the stone spheres found in a tropical forest in Central America? How could a map showing part of the outline of Antarctica have been drawn hundreds of years before the continent was supposedly discovered?

Questions like these have haunted archaeologists for centuries. Research provides some of the answers, but questions still remain about these mysteries from the past.

No one knows who first discovered the huge drawings in South America's coastal desert. Travelers walking through the region would have noticed strange lines in the sand. But they could make nothing of these lines.

When airplanes began to fly regularly over the desert, the pilots noticed that the desert floor seemed to be covered with huge drawings. Some were geometric figures like rectangles and

squares. More fantastic were the figures of birds, spiders, monkeys, whales, and a host of strange-looking creatures that it has been impossible to identify. There were also straight lines that ran for hundreds of yards, but seemed to begin and end nowhere.

The lines that had been seen by people on the ground were a part of these drawings. The drawings themselves were so huge that their true shape could not be

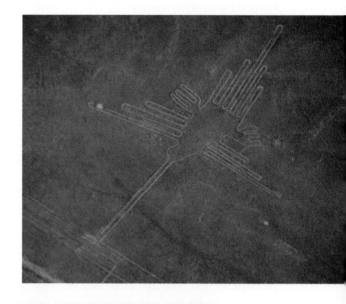

Aerial view of a hummingbird etched on the desert floor. (top) Ground view of a monkey's paw. (opposite left) "Owl man" figure etched on a sand dune. (left)

303

made out from the surface. Thus the drawings had gone unnoticed for centuries.

These colossal drawings are located in the desert some 250 miles (400 km) south of Lima, the capital of Peru. They are scattered over an area about sixty miles (100 km) long and between five and ten miles (8 and 16 km) wide. Most of the drawings are found on plateaus between two valleys, the Içá (ē sä') and the Nazca. Practically every flat spot in this region contains some sort of drawing.

The floor of the desert is covered by a layer of dark rock and pebbles. To make the lines, the surface pebbles were removed to expose the lighter rocks and soil beneath them. The surface material was then piled in a uniform way on both sides of the line. Because it almost never rains in the desert, the lines and drawings have survived. The lines and figures were fairly easy to etch into the surface of the desert. But first the figures would have to have been drawn as scale models, then traced in final form on the desert floor. So the moving and piling of all those rocks and

stones must have involved thousands of hours of work in the broiling sun.

These figures must have been important to those who made them. They were important enough for the Içá-Nazca people to take a large number of laborers away from the hard job of growing food. What could their significance have been? Some scientists say that the lines and figures were part of a system for studying the stars. Others say it was a vast desert calendar to help tell the seasons for planting. Or some of these lines may really have been the outlines of roads, ceremonial avenues along which religious processions passed.

Most puzzling of all are the drawings of spiders, whales, birds, monkeys, and other figures. What could their purpose have been? Even from a high platform only a part of the figures can be seen. Only with the invention of the airplane have people been able to see the huge figures in their entirety. Perhaps the figures were not meant to be seen by humans. Perhaps they were meant to be seen only by the Içá-Nazca's gods who lived in the sky.

THE SECRET OF THE STONE SPHERES

James O. Harrison

In a hot, tropical forest in Central America, some workers for a banana company were cutting their way through a thick tangle of vines about thirty-five years ago. They were searching in Costa Rica for new land where they could plant bananas. Coming to a small clearing, they found a big round stone about six feet (2 m) in diameter. It was almost perfectly round, and it was resting on a small platform paved with river stones.

Fascinated, the workers looked around in the underbrush and found many more stones—some of them large, some of them small. But all of them were amazingly round and smooth. The workers wondered who had made these stone spheres and where they were made. They had found no places nearby where bedrock was exposed. When they described to others what they had found, they learned that few

Stone sphere that is 3.5 feet (1 m) in diameter found in a tropical forest in Costa Rica. (top)
Stone sphere on display at the National Museum of Costa Rica at San Jose. (bottom)

people had ever seen these strange spheres, and no one knew where they came from.

As trees and underbrush were cleared away, more of the stone spheres were found, as well as other small areas paved with river stones. But the spheres have remained a mystery. When scientists in other parts of the world learned about the stone balls, they came to see them and tried to find out more about them. They found that most of the stone balls were made of granite, but a few were made of limestone. Some of the balls were only a few inches in diameter and weighed only a few pounds. Others were as large as eight feet (2 1/2 m) in diameter and weighed more than sixteen tons (14,500 kg). Some of them were so remarkably round that it took very careful measurements to show that they were not quite true spheres.

The spheres were mostly in groups of at least three and sometimes as many as forty-five. Some were arranged in long straight rows, others in circles, and others in triangles. Some of the straight lines point north and south. Could it be that by looking along some of the lines formed by the stones, people were able to keep track of the positions of the sun and other stars? Such information could help them predict when the seasons would change, and therefore when they should plant crops. Maybe the stones were made for religious uses. Some of the stones were found inside graves, together with pottery and gold jewelry. Scientists think this may mean that the stones belonged to persons buried in the graves.

One thing the scientists agree on is that the spheres must have been very important to the people that made them. Using the tools they had, it must have taken many years to make just one ball, even with many people working on it. Scientists think that groups of workers may have been sent away from their villages to stay for years at a time in stony areas where they could work on the spheres.

Who made these round stones, how were they made and moved to the places they were found, and what did they mean to the ancient people who made them? The answers to these questions are yet to be found.

THE PIRI RE'IS MAP

Diane Sherman

Captain Arlington Mallery, a retired sea captain, was examining an old Turkish map in 1956 when he made a startling discovery. Part of the map's outline seemed to show islands and bays along the coast of Antarctica.

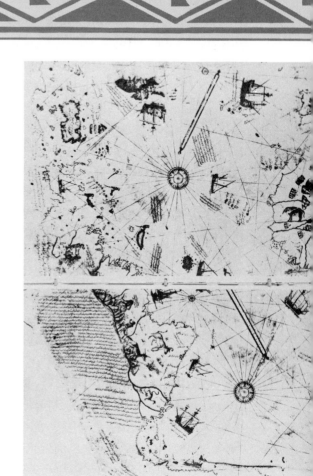

The original Piri Re'is map. (top) Map showing the names of the areas on the Piri Re'is map. (left)

What made this so extraordinary is that the Antarctic coast is under a thick covering of ice. Since 1954, scientists have been mapping the shape of Antarctic bays and islands by bouncing echoes off the ground below the ice. But the Turkish map was dated 1513. It seemed that someone before that time had either mapped the coast through hundreds of feet of ice, or else had drawn the map *before* there was any ice.

How could this be? Most scientists think that ice has covered Antarctica for thousands of years. Yet the map, called the Piri Re'is (pē' rē rī' is) map for the name of the Turkish admiral who drew it, appears to be genuine. It was found in Istanbul, Turkey, in 1929, and has been seen by many scientists. One scientist has pointed out that the map could not have been forged, because even in 1929 no one knew the shape of the land covered by Antarctic ice.

In 1956, Charles Hapgood, a New Hampshire history professor, heard about the map. He decided to study it as a project in his classes. For almost ten years he and his students worked on the problem.

They studied the map and looked over other old maps as well.

It began to look as though the Piri Re'is map might go back to the time of the ancient Greeks. The mathematics used in the map making told Professor Hapgood and his students something else. To draw the map accurately, the mapmakers had to know the distance around the earth, or its circumference. When the ancient Greeks figured this out, they made an error which shows up in all their calculations. Yet the Piri Re'is map was drawn without the mistake. So it would seem that the Greeks could not have drawn the original map. Could the map have been drawn *before* the Greeks lived?

Perhaps there was some ancient people of whom we have no record. If so, they must have been highly advanced. Their ships must have sailed oceans and charted shores not visited by European explorers until the 1500s and later. Some day, perhaps, we will know whether there was a great prehistoric civilization whose sailors roamed the world. In the meantime, the hunt for clues will go on.

Questions

1. What do the Nazca drawings, the stone spheres of Central America, and the Piri Re'is map have in common?
2. What did the invention of the airplane have to do with the discovery of the Nazca drawings?
3. Why do you think the Nazca drawings, the stone spheres, and the Piri Re'is map came to light only relatively recently?
4. If you could help investigate one of the "mysteries from the past" described, which would you choose and why?

Applying Reading Skills

A. Find the paragraph in which each sentence below appears in "Mysteries From the Past." Tell whether it is a main idea or a supporting detail.

1. When airplanes began to fly regularly over the desert, the pilots noticed that the desert floor seemed to be covered with huge drawings.
2. These colossal drawings are located in the desert some 250 miles (400 km) south of Lima, the capital of Peru.
3. They found that most of the stone balls were made of granite, but a few were made of limestone.
4. One thing the scientists agree on is that the spheres must have been very important to the people that made them.
5. It was found in Istanbul, Turkey, in 1929, and has been seen by many scientists.
6. To draw the map accurately, the map makers had to know the distance around the earth, or its circumference.

B. Write the main idea of each paragraph listed below.

1. Second complete paragraph on page 304
2. First paragraph on page 308

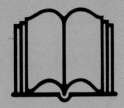

PREPARING FOR READING

Learning Vocabulary

1. Some people believe that the story of Atlantis is <u>authentic</u> history; others believe it is only a legend.
2. According to one account, the island of Atlantis was first ruled by a god who married a <u>mortal</u> woman and founded the royal family.
3. The center of the island was completely surrounded by five <u>concentric</u> rings of land and water.
4. The temples and buildings of Atlantis were <u>symmetrical</u>, or balanced; each section was in harmony with the other sections.
5. The <u>prosperous</u> inhabitants of Atlantis grew wealthy from the gold, copper, and other minerals found on the island.

authentic   mortal   concentric

symmetrical   prosperous

Developing Background and Skills
Main Idea

You know that the **main idea** of a paragraph is the most important information in the paragraph. In a well-written paragraph, the main idea is supported by details that give more information about the topic or help explain it.

Sometimes the main idea is directly stated in a single sentence. Sometimes you have to combine the ideas found in two or more sentences to state the main idea.

To find the main idea, think carefully about the facts presented. Ask yourself, *What is the most important information given?* The answer will help you state the main idea. Ask yourself, *What information tells more about the main idea?* The answer will help you identify the supporting details.

Read the paragraph, question, and answer choices below.

   Did Atlantis really exist? Many writers in the past have tried to prove that it did. Even today the legend of the large island that was destroyed by an earthquake persists. Writers, scientists, and organizations continue the search for Atlantis. Some believe that the Greek island of Santorini is the lost Atlantis. Plato's description of an Atlantean town built of red, white, and black stones fits a Bronze Age town unearthed in Santorini in 1967. The strange coloring of the island's cliffs, too, corresponds to Plato's account. Perhaps the most compelling evidence is the volcanic explosion of 1450 B.C. At that time, the center of Santorini sank, the surrounding rim split, and sea water poured over the island.

Which sentence best states the main idea of the paragraph?
a. People who have searched for Atlantis believe that it is the Greek island of Santorini.
b. Atlantis was destroyed by an earthquake, as was Santorini.
c. Although it is not known whether Atlantis really existed, many people believe Santorini is Atlantis.

Do you agree that **c** is the best choice? What details support it?

As you read the next selection, try to remember the main ideas presented by the author. What information supports or explains these ideas?

ATLANTIS
THE LOST CONTINENT
DAVID MCMULLEN

Was there ever such a place as Atlantis? Or, like the dragons that breathe fire and the unicorn, is Atlantis just a legend? Can we find proof that Atlantis ever existed? If so, where was it and what was it like?

Our very first clue to the Atlantis mystery is more than 2,000 years old. In those days, history was told in stories passed from parent to child. If you wanted to know what happened in earlier times, you went to wise old storytellers. You listened to their tales. The Greek philosopher Plato wrote the story of Atlantis as it was told to a Greek named Solon. Solon was known as the wisest of Greek statesmen and believed the story of Atlantis was authentic.

Solon traveled across Africa from Greece to talk to the wise men of Egypt. They told Solon that the Greeks came from what was left of a much older nation. They said that the people of Egypt had records that were more than 8,000 years old. These Egyptian records told the story of Atlantis—a lost continent.

Before the flood, the records showed there had been a great island off the coast of Africa in what is now the Atlantic Ocean. It was just beyond the Strait of Gibraltar,

Atlantic Ocean

NORTH
AMERICA

ATLANTIS

Bermuda Island   Azores

Strait of Gibraltar

EUR

Bahama   Madeira Islands
Islands

CUBA   Canary Islands

AFRICA

West Indies

SOUTH AMERICA

guarded by the great Rock of Gibraltar. The island had been called Atlantis.

Atlantis was ruled by a series of great and wise kings. Whenever its neighbors were attacked, the armies of Atlantis came to their aid. Everything went well, Solon was told, until Atlantis was struck by earthquakes and floods. Volcanoes erupted and rocked the island.

Then, in one violent day and night of destruction, most of the people were swept into huge cracks in the earth. When the quakes and tidal waves passed, the whole island of Atlantis had vanished beneath the sea. The sea beyond the Strait of Gibraltar was still blocked, which made it difficult for ships to pass. The shallow waters were caused by the island as it settled down into the ocean.

Those Atlanteans who survived the flood went to North Africa and Greece. It may even be that the great pyramids and the Sphinx of Egypt were designed by these survivors. The Atlanteans are thought to have used the sun as the source of all energy. Early Egyptians worshiped the sun and called it the god Ra (rä). Did the Egyptians learn of the sun's greatness from the Atlanteans?

The early Greeks built beautiful buildings at a time when the people of France, Germany, and Britain were still wearing animal skins and living in caves and huts.

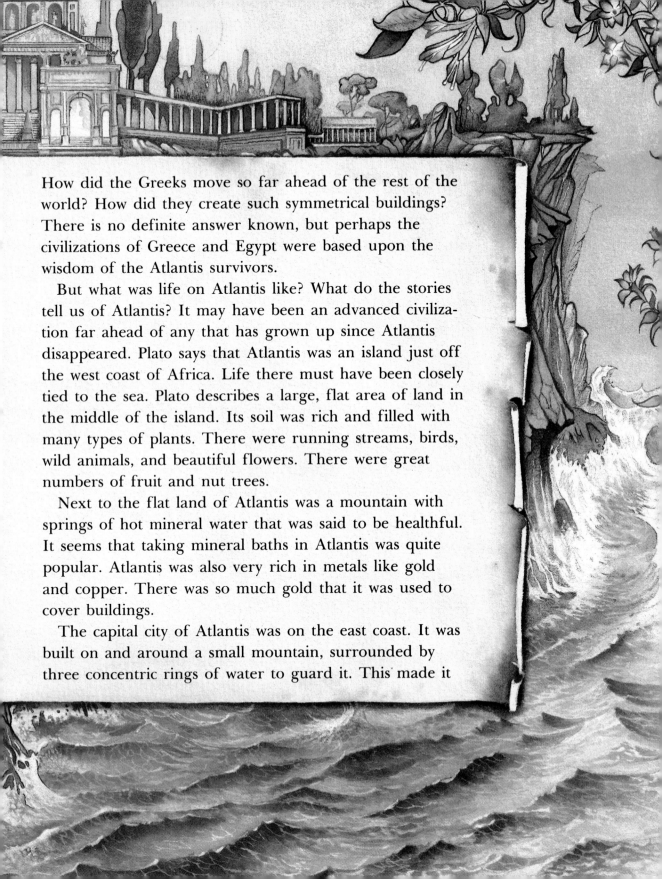

How did the Greeks move so far ahead of the rest of the world? How did they create such symmetrical buildings? There is no definite answer known, but perhaps the civilizations of Greece and Egypt were based upon the wisdom of the Atlantis survivors.

But what was life on Atlantis like? What do the stories tell us of Atlantis? It may have been an advanced civilization far ahead of any that has grown up since Atlantis disappeared. Plato says that Atlantis was an island just off the west coast of Africa. Life there must have been closely tied to the sea. Plato describes a large, flat area of land in the middle of the island. Its soil was rich and filled with many types of plants. There were running streams, birds, wild animals, and beautiful flowers. There were great numbers of fruit and nut trees.

Next to the flat land of Atlantis was a mountain with springs of hot mineral water that was said to be healthful. It seems that taking mineral baths in Atlantis was quite popular. Atlantis was also very rich in metals like gold and copper. There was so much gold that it was used to cover buildings.

The capital city of Atlantis was on the east coast. It was built on and around a small mountain, surrounded by three concentric rings of water to guard it. This made it

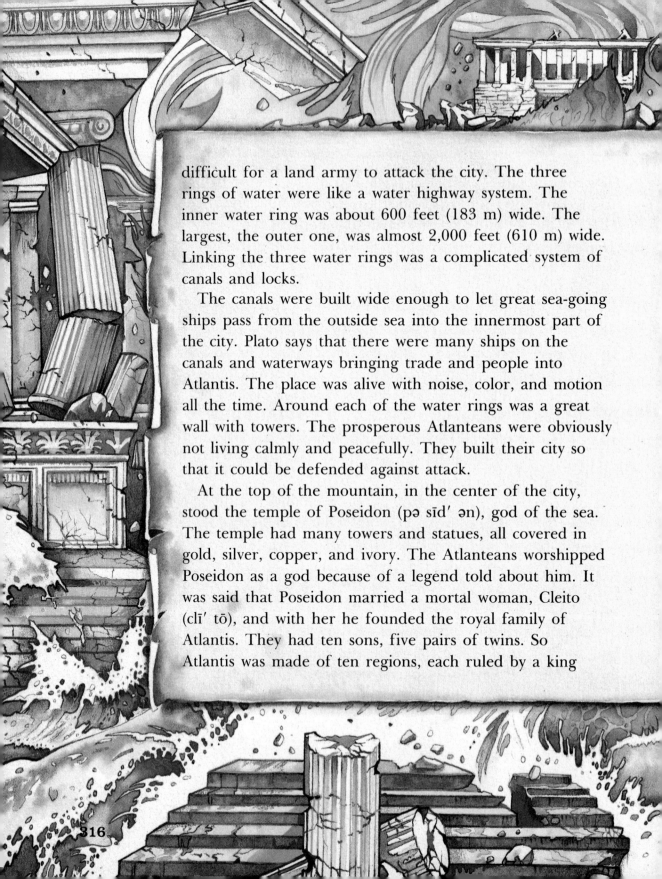

difficult for a land army to attack the city. The three rings of water were like a water highway system. The inner water ring was about 600 feet (183 m) wide. The largest, the outer one, was almost 2,000 feet (610 m) wide. Linking the three water rings was a complicated system of canals and locks.

The canals were built wide enough to let great sea-going ships pass from the outside sea into the innermost part of the city. Plato says that there were many ships on the canals and waterways bringing trade and people into Atlantis. The place was alive with noise, color, and motion all the time. Around each of the water rings was a great wall with towers. The prosperous Atlanteans were obviously not living calmly and peacefully. They built their city so that it could be defended against attack.

At the top of the mountain, in the center of the city, stood the temple of Poseidon (pə sīd′ ən), god of the sea. The temple had many towers and statues, all covered in gold, silver, copper, and ivory. The Atlanteans worshipped Poseidon as a god because of a legend told about him. It was said that Poseidon married a mortal woman, Cleito (clī′ tō), and with her he founded the royal family of Atlantis. They had ten sons, five pairs of twins. So Atlantis was made of ten regions, each ruled by a king

descended from the first ten twins. The most famous king was Atlas. It was from Atlas that Atlantis got its name. And from Atlantis comes the name of the Atlantic Ocean. Atlas and his descendants ruled Atlantis from a palace built around the temple of gold and silver.

Plato also tells us about the life of the people in Atlantis. The rich had a life filled with fine clothes, good food, and beautiful jewelry. They spent their time at the mineral baths and at leisure. The rulers of Atlantis came from the ranks of the rich. The not-so-rich were less lucky. They found themselves in the army or navy, protecting the nation's wealth.

From Plato, we know that the end of Atlantis came about 11,500 years ago. In the beginning it had been a place of peace, a place of beauty where people respected the truth and each other. But as time went by, the Atlanteans became greedy, violent people. They put pleasure before everything else. Legend says that Poseidon, unhappy about such a change, took Atlantis into the sea. But that's only legend.

Is all Atlantis a legend? Did Atlantis exist? If we are to believe the ancient Greek stories of Atlantis, why can they not tell us what happened to that mysterious land? If Atlantis did exist, *where is it now?*

Questions

1. Explain how the story of Atlantis has come down to us.
2. What information supports the idea that Atlanteans settled in Egypt after Atlantis was destroyed?
3. What moral, or lesson, can be learned from the destruction of Atlantis?
4. How might the Atlanteans have protected their city from natural disasters such as floods or earthquakes? Describe a plan they could have developed to protect the island.

Applying Reading Skills

Reread the paragraphs listed below. Then follow the directions.

1. Third paragraph on page 312
   Write the sentence that best states the main idea.
   a. Solon was an ancient traveler who visited Egypt.
   b. The Egyptians told Solon the story of the lost continent of Atlantis.
   c. Ancient Egyptian records described Atlantis.
2. Second paragraph on page 315
   Write three details that support the main idea statement below.
   Atlantis was rich in natural resources.
3. Second paragraph on page 316
   Write the sentence that best states the main idea.
   a. The Atlanteans were concerned about the defense of their island home.
   b. The canals and waterways of Atlantis were important for trade and for defense.
   c. The canals between water rings were wide enough to allow large ships to sail into the innermost part of the city.
4. Third paragraph on page 316
   Write a sentence that states the main idea.

Atlantis

There was an island in the sea
That out of immortal chaos reared
Towers of topaz, trees of pearl,
For maidens adored and warriors feared.

Long ago it sunk in the sea;
And now, a thousand fathoms deep,
Sea-worms above it whirl their lamps,
Crabs on the pale mosaic creep.

—Conrad Aiken

WRITING ACTIVITY

WRITE A FRIENDLY LETTER

Prewrite

Atlantis—was it a marvel of the ancient world or a myth from the mind of Plato? Perhaps no one will ever know for sure what the end of this mystery story is, unless *you* write it.

What do you think happened to ancient Atlantis? What event caused it to disappear? Was it a flood, an unusual tidal wave, a volcanic eruption? Use your imagination and come up with an explanation for the destruction and disappearance of this island continent.

You are going to write a letter to a friend presenting a first-person account of the end of Atlantis. To prepare for writing, reread the article and poem about Atlantis. You will have to plan the body of your letter as if it were the plot of a story. Think about events and their sequence for your "plot."

A diagram of your trip to Atlantis might look like this.

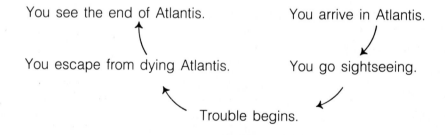

You see the end of Atlantis.　　　　　You arrive in Atlantis.

You escape from dying Atlantis.　　　You go sightseeing.

Trouble begins.

Now, using these events, try a different sequence involving a flashback.

PLOT SEQUENCE

1. Begin your letter with a paragraph relating your escape from the destruction of Atlantis. Describe what happened, how you escaped, and how you felt.
2. Then, in a flashback in time, explain how your visit began and the many beautiful sights you saw.
3. Next, describe one or two events that led to the destruction of Atlantis. Make sure that these events lead sensibly to the events described in the first part of your letter.

Write

1. Create a heading and a greeting for your letter.
2. Write the body of your letter using your plot sequence.
3. Create a closing for the letter and add your signature.
4. You are writing in first person, so use pronouns such as *I*, *me*, *mine*, and *my*.
5. Use your Glossary or dictionary for spelling help.

Revise

Read your letter. Can you change any words or move sentences around to make your story easier for your readers to understand? Try using signal words such as *before*, *then*, *meanwhile*, *following*, *later*, or *immediately* to make sure your reader is clearly informed about when you are switching back in time. Try to use a sentence such as: *I will never forget the day I arrived.* . . . Or *Two weeks before I had come to Atlantis* . . . .

1. Proofread each part of your letter for the use of correct punctuation.
2. Make sure you did not use run-on sentences or incomplete sentences.
3. Check the capitalization and spelling of all words.
4. Rewrite your letter to share.

PREPARING FOR READING

Learning Vocabulary

1. When Bob's fist went through the creature, the creature said apologetically, "Force is useless."
2. Janice did not believe in ghosts or spirits: she was a realist.
3. At first the creature answered all the questions cheerfully, but he soon became tired and started to respond sullenly.
4. All of Janice's doubtfulness, or skepticism, came back, and she replied, "I don't believe a word of it!"
5. Janice was very angry and did not want to answer, but she found herself nodding "yes" involuntarily.
6. "I think I've done rather well," said the creature, as he ran his hand complacently over his crewcut.

apologetically   realist   sullenly
skepticism   involuntarily   complacently

Developing Background and Skills
Synonyms and Antonyms

How many times have you found yourself using the word *great*?

"It was a great game!"
"Great dinner, Mom."
"That's a great idea!"

Have you ever thought about what other words you might substitute for *great* in such cases? If you did, you were thinking about synonyms. A **synonym** is a word that has the same or nearly the same meaning as another word. *Great*, in the sense it is used in the sentence above, has many synonyms. Read the sentences below.

"It was a <u>fabulous</u> game!"

"<u>Outstanding</u> dinner, Mom."

"That's a <u>terrific</u> idea!"

Fabulous, outstanding, and *terrific* are all synonyms of *great.* What other synonyms for *great* can you think of?

Substituting synonyms for words you commonly use can add variety and interest to what you say and write. Synonyms can also be important context clues as you read. Reread the fourth sentence under Learning Vocabulary. What synonym for *skepticism* is given?

Antonyms, or words with opposite meanings, can also be useful context clues. Reread the third sentence under Learning Vocabulary. What word is an antonym for *cheerfully*?

An antonym adds the meanings "not" to a word. Prefixes such as *in-, im-, mis-,* or *un-* when added to a base word can change the word to its antonym. For example, *voluntarily* means "willingly." *Involuntarily* means "not willingly."

Both synonyms and antonyms have shades of meaning. One word may be closer to the meaning you want to convey than another. For example, if something is confusing you, would you describe the situation as a puzzle, a mystery, a problem, or a dilemma? *Puzzle, mystery, problem,* and *dilemma* are synonyms. Which word would you choose to describe the most confusing situation? Which would you choose to describe the least confusing? *Explanation, solution,* and *answer* are antonyms for *mystery.* Which word would you choose as an antonym for *problem*?

As you read the next selection, keep in mind the author's use of synonyms and antonyms. Notice how the author's choice of words influences the way you "see" what he describes.

THE KING'S WISHES

ROBERT SHECKLEY

After squatting behind a glassware display for almost two hours, Bob Granger felt his legs begin to cramp. He moved to ease them, and his number-ten iron[1] slipped off his lap, clattering on the floor.

"Shh," Janice whispered, her mashie[2] gripped tightly.

"I don't think he's going to come," Bob said.

"Quiet, honey," Janice whispered, peering into the darkness of their store.

There was no sign of the burglar yet. He had come every night in the past week, mysteriously removing generators, refrigerators, and air conditioners. Mysteriously—for he tampered with no locks, jimmied no windows, left no footprints. Yet somehow he was able to sneak in and slink out with a good part of their stock. "I don't think this was such a good idea," Bob whispered. "A man capable of carrying several hundred pounds on his back—"

"We'll handle him," Janice said, with the certainty that had made her a master sergeant in the WAC Motor Corps.[3] "Besides, we have to stop him—he's postponing our wedding day."

Bob nodded. He and Janice had built and stocked the Country Department Store with their army savings. They were planning on getting married, as soon as the profits enabled them to. But when someone stole refrigerators—

"I think I hear something," Janice said.

There was a faint noise somewhere in the store. They waited. Then they heard the sound of feet, padding over the linoleum.

"When he gets to the middle of the floor," Janice whispered, "switch on the lights."

Bob switched on the lights, shouting, "Hold it there!"

"Oh, no!" Janice gasped, almost dropping her mashie. Bob turned and gulped.

---

1. **number-ten iron**: irons are a series of golf clubs.
2. **mashie**: a golf club; specifically, a number-five iron.
3. **WAC Motor Corps**: the section of the Women's Army Corps responsible for repairing vehicles.

Standing in front of them was a being at least ten feet tall. He had budding horns on his forehead and tiny wings on his back. He was dressed in a pair of dungarees and a white sweatshirt with EBLIS TECH written across it. Scuffed white buckskins were on his tremendous feet, and he had a blond crewcut.

"Rats," he said. "Knew I should have taken invisibility in college."

"What do you want?" Janice asked, drawing herself to her full five foot three.

"Want? Let me see. Oh, yes. The fan." He walked across the room and picked up a large floor fan.

"Just a minute," Bob shouted. He walked right up to the giant, his golf club poised. Janice followed close behind him. "Where do you think you're going?"

"To King Alerian," the giant said. "He wished for it."

"Oh, he did, did he?" Janice said. "Better put it down." She poised the mashie over her shoulder.

"But I *can't*," the young giant said, his tiny wings twitching nervously.

"You asked for it," Janice said, swinging the club. "Ouch!" she said. The mashie bounced off the being's head, almost knocking Janice over with the recoil. At the same time, Bob swung his club at the giant's ribs.

It passed *through* the giant, ricocheting against the floor.

"Force is useless against a ferra," the young giant said apologetically.

"A what?" Bob asked.

"A ferra. We're first cousins of the jinn."[4] He started to walk back to the center of the room, the fan gripped in one broad hand. "Now if you'll excuse me—"

"A spirit?" Janice stood open-mouthed. Her parents had allowed no talk of ghosts or spirits in the house, and Janice had grown up a hard-headed realist. She was skilled in repairing anything mechanical; that was her part of the partnership. But anything more fanciful she left to Bob.

"You mean you're out of the *Arabian Nights*?"[5] Bob asked.

"Oh, no," the ferra said. "The jinn of Arabia are my cousins. All spirits are related, but I am a ferra."

"Would you mind telling me," Bob asked, "what you are doing with my generator, my air conditioner, and my refrigerator?"

"I'd be glad to," the ferra said. He felt around the air, found what he wanted, and sat down on nothingness.

"I graduated from Eblis Tech just about three weeks ago," he began. "And of course, I applied for civil service. I come from a long line of government men. Well, the lists were crowded, so I—"

"Civil service?" Bob asked.

"Oh, yes. They're all civil service jobs. You have to pass the tests, you know."

"Go on," Bob said.

"Well—promise this won't go any farther—I got my job through pull." He blushed orange. "My father is a ferra in the Underworld Council, so he used his influence. I was appointed over four thousand higher-ranking ferras to the position of ferra of the King's Cup. That's quite an honor, you know.

"I wasn't ready," he said sadly. "The ferra of the cup has to be skilled in all branches of magic. I had just graduated from college —with only passing grades. I thought I could handle anything, but . . . "

"Just a minute," Janice said. "Has this king commanded you to get our fan?"

---

4. **jinn**: spirits (either good or evil) that appear in human or animal form.
5. ***Arabian Nights***: The *Arabian Nights' Entertainments* (also known as *The Thousand and One Nights*), a collection of Eastern folk tales from the tenth century.

"In a way," the ferra said, turning orange again.

"Is this king rich?" Janice asked.

"He's very wealthy."

"Then why can't he buy this stuff?" Janice wanted to know. "Why does he have to steal it?"

"Well," the ferra mumbled, "there's no place where he can buy it."

"Why can't he import the goods?"

"This is all so embarrassing," the ferra said.

"Out with it," Bob said.

"If you must know," the ferra said sullenly, "King Alerian lives in what you would call two thousand B.C."

"Then how—"

"Oh, just a minute," the young ferra said crossly. "I'll explain everything. As I told you, I got the job of ferra of the King's Cup. Naturally I expected the king would ask for jewels, or beautiful women, either of which I could have supplied easily. But the king had all the jewels he wanted, and more wives than he knew what to do with. So what does he do but say, 'Ferra, my palace is hot in the summer. Do that which will make my palace cool.'

"I knew right then I was in over my head. It takes an advanced ferra to handle climate. I guess I spent too much time on the track team. I was stuck.

"I hurried to the master encyclopedia and looked up 'Climate.' The spells were just too much for me. But I read that there was artificial climate control in the twentieth century. So I walked here, along the narrow trail to the future, and took one of your air conditioners. When the king wanted me to stop his food from spoiling, I came back for a refrigerator. Then it was—"

"You hooked them all to the generator?" Janice asked.

"Yes. I may not be much with spells, but I'm pretty handy mechanically."

It made sense, Bob thought. After all, who could keep a palace cool in two thousand B.C.? But what still bothered Bob was, what kind of spirit was he?

"No, I don't get it," Janice said. "In the *past?* You mean time travel?"

"Sure. I majored in time travel," the ferra said with a proud, boyish grin.

"Well," Janice said, "why don't you go somewhere else?"

"This is the only place the trail to the future leads," the ferra said.

He picked up the fan. "I'm sorry to be doing this, but if I don't make good here, I'll never get another appointment."

He disappeared.

Half an hour later, Bob and Janice were in a corner booth of an all-night diner, talking in low tones.

"I don't believe a word of it," Janice was saying, all her skepticism back in force. "Spirits! Ferras!"

"You have to believe it," Bob said wearily. "You saw it."

"I don't have to believe everything I see," Janice said staunchly. Then she thought of the missing articles, the vanishing profits, and the increasingly distant marriage. "All right," she said. "What'll we do?"

"You have to fight magic with magic," Bob said confidently. "He'll be back tomorrow night. We'll be ready for him. Good, strong magic, that's what we need. A dose of his own medicine."

"What kind of magic?" Janice asked.

"To play safe," Bob said, "we'd better use all kinds. I wish I knew where he's from. To be really effective, magic—"

"Let's go," Janice said to Bob. "If anyone hears us, we'll be laughed out of town."

They met at the store that evening. Bob had spent the day at the library, gathering his materials. They consisted of twenty-five sheets covered on both sides with Bob's scrawling script.

At eleven forty-five, the ferra appeared.

"Hi," he said. "Where do you

keep your electric heaters? The king wants something for winter."

"Begone," Bob said, "in the name of Idpa!"

"Oh, here they are," the ferra said. "This is the electric model, isn't it? Looks a little shoddy."

"I invoke Rata."

"Shoddy nothing," Janice said, her business instincts getting the better of her. "That stove is guaranteed."

"I call on the Heavenly Wolf," Bob went on.

"Let's see, I have a broiler," the ferra said. "And I need a bathtub."

"I call Forcas, Marchocias, Astaroth—"

"These are bathtubs, aren't they?" the ferra asked Janice, who nodded involuntarily. "I think I'll take the largest. The king is a good-sized man."

"—and Thetus," Bob finished. The ferra looked at him with respect.

Angrily Bob invoked Ormazd, Persian king of light.

"That's all I can carry, I suppose," the ferra said.

Bob called upon the gods of Arabia. He tried Africa, Madagascar, India, Ireland, Malaya, Scandinavia, and Japan.

"That's impressive," the ferra said, "but it'll do you no good." He lifted the bathtub, broiler, and heater.

"Why not?"

Bob gasped, out of breath.

"You see, ferras are affected only by their own spells. Just as jinn are responsible only to magic laws of Arabia. Also, you don't know my true name, and you can't do much of a job exorcizing anything if you don't know its true name."

"What country are you from?" Bob asked.

"Sorry," the ferra said. "But if you knew that, you might find the right spell to use against me. And I'm in enough trouble now."

"If the king is so rich, why can't he pay?" Janice asked.

"The king never pays for anything he can get free," the ferra said. "That's why he's so rich."

Bob and Janice glared at him, their marriage fading off into the future.

"See you tomorrow night," the ferra said. He waved and vanished.

"Well, now," Janice said, after the ferra had left. "What now? Any more bright ideas?"

"All out of them," Bob said, sitting down heavily on a sofa.

"Any more magic?"

"That won't work," Bob said. "I couldn't find *ferra* or *King Alerian* listed in any encyclopedia. He's probably from some place we've never heard of."

"Just our luck," Janice said. "What are we going to do? I suppose he'll want a vacuum cleaner next." She closed her eyes and concentrated.

"I think I have an idea," Janice said, opening her eyes.

"What's that?"

"First of all, its *our* business that's important, and *our* marriage. Right?"

"Right," Bob said.

"All right. I don't know much about spells," she said, rolling up her sleeves, "but I do know machines. Let's get to work."

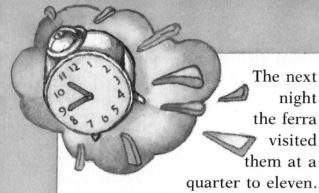

The next night the ferra visited them at a quarter to eleven.

"The king is in a rush for this," he said. "His newest wife has been pestering him. It seems that her clothes last for only one washing. Her servants beat them with rocks."

"Sure," Bob said.

"Help yourself," Janice said.

"That's awfully decent of you," the ferra said gratefully. "I appreciate it." He picked up a washing machine and vanished.

Bob and Janice sat down and waited. In half an hour the ferra appeared again.

"What did you do?" he asked.

"Why, what's the matter?" Janice asked sweetly.

"The washer! When the queen started it, it threw out a great cloud of evil-smelling smoke. Then it made some strange noises and stopped."

"In our language," Janice said, "we would say it was gimmicked."

"Gimmicked?"

"Rigged. Fixed. Strung. And so's everything else in this place."

"But you can't do that!" the ferra said.

"You're so smart," Janice said venomously. "Go ahead and fix it."

"I was boasting," the ferra said in a small voice. "I was much better at sports."

Janice smiled and yawned.

"Well, gee," the ferra said, his little wings twitching nervously. "This puts me in an awful spot. I'll be demoted. I'll be thrown out of civil service."

"We can't let ourselves go bankrupt, can we?" Janice asked.

Bob thought for a moment. "Look," he said. "Why *don't* you tell the king you've met a strong countermagic? Tell him he has to pay a tariff if he wants his stuff."

"He won't like it," the ferra said doubtfully.

"Try it anyhow," Bob suggested.

"I'll try," the ferra said, and vanished.

"How much do you think we can charge?" Janice asked.

"Oh, give him standard rates. After all, we've built this store on fair practices."

"He's so rich," Janice said dreamily. "It seems a shame not to—"

"Wait a minute!" Bob shouted. "We can't do it! How can there be refrigerators in two thousand B.C.? It would change the whole course of history! Some smart guy is going to look at those things and figure out how they work. Then the whole course of history will be changed!"

"So what?" Janice asked practically.

"So what? So research will be carried out along different lines. The present will be changed."

"You mean it's impossible?"

"Yes!"

"That's just what I've been saying all along," Janice said triumphantly.

"Oh, stop that," Bob said. "I wish I could figure this out. No matter what country the ferra is from, it's bound to have an effect on the future."

At that moment the ferra appeared.

"The king has agreed," the ferra said. "Will this pay for what I've taken?" He held out a small sack.

Spilling out the sack, Bob found that it contained about two dozen large rubies, emeralds, and diamonds.

"We can't take it," Bob said. "We can't do business with you."

"Don't be superstitious!" Janice shouted, seeing their marriage begin to evaporate again.

"Why not?" the ferra asked.

"We can't introduce modern things into the past," Bob said. "It'll change the present. This world may vanish or something."

"Oh, don't worry about that," the ferra said. "Nothing will happen."

"But why? If you introduced a washer in ancient Rome—"

"Unfortunately," the ferra said, "King Alerian's kingdom has no future."

"Would you explain that?"

"Sure." The ferra sat down on the air. "In three years King Alerian and his country will be completely destroyed by forces of nature. Not a person will be saved. Not even a piece of pottery."

"We'd better unload while he's still in business," Janice said, holding a ruby to the light.

"I guess that takes care of that," Bob said. Their business was saved, and their marriage was in the immediate future. "How about you?" he asked the ferra.

"Well, I've done rather well on this job," the ferra said. "I think I'll apply for a foreign transfer."

He ran a hand complacently over his blond crewcut. "I'll be seeing you," he said, and started to disappear.

"Just a minute," Bob said. "Would you mind telling me what country you're from? And what country King Alerian is from?"

"Oh sure," the ferra said, only his head still visible, "I thought you knew. Ferras are the spirits of Atlantis."

And he disappeared.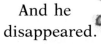

Questions

1. Explain the problem that Bob and Janice had.
2. Why did the spells Bob tried on the ferra have no effect?
3. Who—Bob and Janice or the ferra and King Alerian—was more satisfied with the bargain that was struck at the end? Give your reasons.
4. If you had lived in 2000 B.C. and knew about the inventions of the 20th century A.D., what things would you most want and why?

Applying Reading Skills

Read the sentences below from "The King's Wishes." Write each underlined word. Then write a synonym for each word in Part A, and an antonym for each word in Part B.

A. 1. "We'll handle him," Janice said, with the certainty that had made her a master sergeant in the WAC Motor Corps.
   2. Scuffed white buckskins were on his tremendous feet, and he had a blond crewcut.
   3. She was skilled in repairing anything mechanical; that was her part of the partnership. But anything more fanciful she left to Bob.
   4. "Just a minute," Janice said. "Has this king commanded you to get our fan?"

B. 1. "I was appointed over four thousand higher-ranking ferras to the position of ferra of the King's Cup. That's quite an honor, you know."
   2. "You have to fight magic with magic," Bob said confidently.
   3. "That's impressive," the ferra said, "but it'll do you no good."
   4. "This puts me in an awful spot," the ferra said. "I'll be demoted. I'll be thrown out of civil service."

FIRE AND ICE

PREPARING FOR READING

Learning Vocabulary

1. Everything reflected in the magical mirror was so distorted that no one could recognize even the most familiar things.
2. Gerda hoped to revive Kai from his enchanted state and break the spell of the Snow Queen.
3. In the eerie light of the northern sky, the gigantic, icy castle appeared unreal.
4. The Snow Queen's home was a bleak place with thousands of immense, cold, empty rooms and corridors.
5. Kai sat alone in the icy void at the center of the frozen maze of empty rooms and halls.

distorted   revive   eerie
bleak   void

Developing Background and Skills
Author's Purpose and Point of View

Have you ever thought about the many reasons you have for reading? Have you ever read a comic book for amusement? An encyclopedia article to get facts for a report? Directions to understand how to do something?

Just as you have different purposes for reading, authors have different purposes, or reasons, for writing. Authors of comic books write to entertain. Authors of encyclopedia articles write to give factual information. Authors of directions write to explain. Sometimes authors write to describe something. They may also write to persuade, or convince, people to do something or to think in a certain way.

Read each of the numbered passages below. Decide which **author's purpose** best describes each.

a. to entertain   b. to persuade   c. to explain

d. to give factual information   e. to describe

1. Hans Christian Andersen was born in Odense, Denmark, in 1805. He was the son of a poor shoemaker who died when Hans was 11. At 14, Andersen moved to Copenhagen, where he continued his education. He published his first fairy tale in 1835 and continued writing until his death in 1875. Andersen's stories made him one of Denmark's most famous authors.

2. The Snow Queen's castle was a gigantic, brooding place. It was as big as a mountain with walls of ageless ice and drifted snow.

3. There is just one word for the new Super Press edition of Andersen's fairy tales—SUPERB! This single volume including *all* the stories is a must for every home library. Be sure to order your copy of what is certain to become a collector's item. Do it today—while the supply still lasts.

Did you choose these answers: 1.d, 2.e, 3.b? If you did, you were right.

In addition to a purpose, authors usually have a point of view. The **author's point of view** refers to the author's way of viewing things or his or her attitude toward something. The words an author chooses to describe something often offer clues about how the author feels about it. For example, in 3 above, the author uses the words *superb, a must, collector's item.* All of the words create a positive impression.

As you read the following story, try to determine what purpose the author had in writing it. See if you can figure out the author's point of view or his opinions.

"My own dear Northern Lights. See how they flash and shine. They are the lights the Snow Queen burns at the top of the world to brighten the winter night."

340

The
Snow Queen

Hans Christian Andersen
Retold and illustrated by Richard Hess

Long, long ago, there lived a wicked demon who created a looking glass. It showed everything to be the opposite of what it truly was. All that was good appeared evil; all that was evil appeared good. The demon smashed his mirror, and the winds carried the tiny pieces far and wide. One piece lodged in the eye of a boy named Kai. From that day on, Kai was no longer his true self. His friend Gerda could not believe how he had changed.

One winter's night, Kai unknowingly followed the evil Snow Queen. Many thought he was dead when he couldn't be found, but Gerda believed he was alive. She set out to find him, bringing a rosebud from the garden where they had spent so many happy hours. Along the way, she was captured by robbers. Although the robbers meant to keep her, a girl in the group helped Gerda to escape on a reindeer.

The reindeer leapt off, through the great forest, over rivers and valleys, as fast as he could go. Around them, the wolves howled and the ravens screamed as they sped on through a sky full of strange fire. "My Northern Lights," said the reindeer peering back over his shoulder at Gerda. "My own dear Northern Lights. See how they flash and shine. They are the lights the Snow Queen burns at the top of the world to brighten the winter night."

Day and night, he rushed on and on. By the time they arrived in Lapland, they were tired and hungry.

Just beyond the border they stopped at a poor and simple hut to rest and ask directions. They were greeted by an old Lapp Woman who was drying strips of codfish over a whale-oil lamp. Gerda was so overcome by cold and exhaustion that she could hardly speak. The reindeer told her story for her.

"You poor creatures," said the kindly Lapp Woman, when he had finished. "You've got a long way yet to go. You must now travel hundreds of miles to the top of the world to the Snow Queen's northern palace. For that is where she is now, burning her Bengal lights for us to see to the south."

When they had eaten and warmed themselves by her fire, the old Lapp Woman took up one of the codfish she had been drying. She wrote some strange markings upon it. Then she gave it to Gerda, saying, "Take this, child, and if you find her, give it to my sister, the Finn Woman. She will help you to reach the Snow Queen's castle."

Next morning they thanked the old woman, and she wished them a fond good-by. Then the gallant reindeer sprang away again toward the tracery of beautiful lights flickering in the northern sky.

Over lakes and valleys they sped once more. Then the reindeer stopped and pointed with his right antler to a curious spot in a deep valley below. All they could see was a thin thread of smoke curling out of the deep mantle of snow. When they came nearer, they saw a chimney poking up from a large snowdrift. Gerda knocked on the chimney. Right up through the smoke appeared a large, round face smiling gaily in welcome. Gerda knew immediately that they had come to the right place. The face was smudged with soot and surrounded by matted hair, but it looked uncannily like that of the old Lapp Woman. "Excuse me," Gerda said, "but are you the Finn Woman?"

"Oh, yes," said the woman, pulling herself up to the lip of the chimney.

Gerda gravely handed her the message from her sister, written on the strip of dried codfish. The woman read it quickly, then said, "Come in," before disappearing back through the smoke. Again it struck Gerda that she was the same woman with whom they had spent the night in Lapland.

Gerda and the reindeer made their way down the chimney as best they could and found themselves in a large and cozy room with a very high ceiling. The room was very warm. Indeed, it was so hot below the ice and snow that the Finn Woman wore hardly any clothes at all. Gerda at once took off her coat and mittens to cool down. Since the reindeer had no clothes to shed, the Finn Woman gave him a piece of ice to put on his head. Then three times she reread the message that was written on the codfish, until she knew it by heart. When she was done, she popped the fish into the supper pot that was steaming on the stove, since she made it a habit never to waste anything.

Gerda sat wearily by the warm fire and soon fell asleep. So once more the reindeer told their stories. The Finn Woman winked, but she said nothing.

Finally the reindeer said into the silence, "You are so wise and clever. I have heard it told that you can bind the four winds of the world with a single strand of your sewing thread. Won't you give the little girl a potion so that she will be able to overcome the wiles of the Snow Queen and rescue Kai?"

"The strength of a hundred men would not help her," said the Finn Woman slowly, putting another piece of ice on the reindeer's head. Then she stood up and leaned over the stove. She lifted the lid on her cook pot, and the dried codfish swimming within it seemed to whisper in her ear. "Little Kai," she said, turning, "is with the Snow Queen, and he is delighted with everything that he finds there. He thinks that he is in the best place in the world for he has a splinter of demon glass in his eye and his heart has turned as cold as ice. If the sliver be not taken from his eye, he will never become truly human again, and the Snow

Gerda was all
alone. There
she stood,
without shoes
or gloves in the
middle of the
freezing cold
at the top of
the world.

Queen will keep her power over him."

"But can't you help little Gerda with something that will give her the power to bring the Snow Queen to defeat?"

"I can give her no greater power than she already has," the Finn Woman said. "She is powerful already because her heart is pure, because she is an innocent child. She alone can conquer the Snow Queen and remove the splinter from little Kai's eye."

With this, she gently awakened Gerda and fed her some of the special codfish from the pot. Then she led Gerda and the reindeer back up the chimney to the deep snow outside.

"The Snow Queen's gardens," she said, "begin just two leagues to the north. There," she said, turning to the reindeer, "you will find a large bush with red berries growing upon it. You must leave Gerda there and return here as fast as you can. Go quickly now, for the Queen is presently away. Gerda must find Kai and revive him before she returns."

The Finn Woman turned back toward Gerda and smiled. Without saying another word, she kissed the girl's cheek and lifted her up onto the reindeer's back. As they sped furiously northward, Gerda could see her standing by the smoking chimney waving to them.

Gerda clung to the reindeer's back. "But wait," she cried. "I've forgotten my boots." And, "Oh," she said, "I haven't got my mittens. We must go back."

But the reindeer dared not stop after the Finn Woman's urgent words. He ran until he came to the bush with red berries. There he gently set Gerda down. Great tears trickled down his cheeks and froze on his whiskers. Then he turned and sped back the way they had come.

Gerda was all alone. There she stood, without shoes or gloves, in the middle of the freezing cold at the top of the world.

Slowly she began to run. She ran toward the lights in the northern sky. She ran through what the Finn Woman had called the Snow Queen's gardens, which were great spreading trees with snow-laden branches bent and frozen into fantastic shapes and forms. She ran over one hill and then another. Then, from the top of the last hill, she saw in the eerie light a gigantic, brooding, icy castle. It was as big as a mountain and topped with craggy turrets and towers with walls of ageless ice and drifted snow. The windows and doors were piercing winds.

Gerda's heart nearly stopped at the sight of the Snow Queen's stronghold. But she knew that somewhere within was her beloved Kai. She summoned her remaining strength and courage and plunged on.

Meanwhile, inside the endless halls of the Snow Queen's bleak palace, a small figure sat alone. It was Kai. The palace had more than a thousand rooms and an equal number of corridors, the longest stretching several miles. Each room, each corridor, was lit by the Northern Lights, and each was immense and cold and glitteringly empty. In the middle of this icy maze of rooms and corridors, there was a great frozen lake that had cracked and buckled into a thousand thousand pieces of ice—each exactly like all the others. And here it was, at the cold heart of the never-ending empty halls, that the Snow Queen sat when she was at home.

Here, now, sat Kai. He was blue with cold, but he did not know it, for the Snow Queen had kissed away his feelings and his heart was little better than a block of ice.

As Gerda struggled toward him, he was sluggishly moving about, dragging together into a clump the sharp, flat pieces of ice, trying to fit them together into a pattern.

Laboriously he moved the pieces into new arrangements, first one and then another, for the Snow Queen had told him that if he could discover the pattern that spelled *eternity*, he would become

Gerda flung her arms about him, crying, "Kai, oh, Kai, oh dearest Kai, I have found you at last!" But Kai responded not at all.

347

his own master and have all the world for his own. Try how he might, he could not discover it. No pattern he found satisfied him.

He was alone, alone in a world of ice. The Snow Queen had flown off to sprinkle the snow on volcanoes far to the south. And she had left him in the dreary isolation of her magic castle, to work his puzzle by the vast, frozen lake. He sat and pondered, moved an endless succession of pieces, and then sat and stared again. You might have thought him frozen solid there, alone in the icy void.

That was how Gerda found him as she stepped out of the maze into the great frozen hall at last. She looked across the icy waste, and for all his distance, for all his eerie stillness and the blueness of his skin, she knew him at once. She ran across the field of ice toward him and flung her arms about him, crying, "Kai, oh, Kai, oh, dearest Kai, I have found you at last!"

But Kai responded not at all. He sat there, still, rigid, cold, and unspeaking.

Great tears spilled from Gerda's eyes, down her cheeks, and onto Kai's neck and breast as she held him, sobbing. And little by little the warmth of her tears falling on his chest reached Kai's heart, thawing and melting the coldness within him. He shifted and stirred. From where she had hidden it, Gerda took out the rosebud she had brought with her from the garden. She held it steadily before his eyes. "Kai," she said, "do you remember? Oh please remember." And she sang the little verse that had meant so much to them:

> *Rose, Rose, Rose, Rose*
> *Will I ever see thee red?*
> *Aye, merrily, I will,*
> *If spring but stay.*

The sound of her sweet voice and the words she sang touched Kai's newly warmed heart. His eyes slowly came alive as he remembered. And he, too, burst into tears. So thick and fast did the tears come, coursing down his cheeks, that in their passage they dislodged and swept away the little piece of demon glass that had so long distorted his vision. For the first time now, he saw Gerda clearly and knew her. He shouted for joy. "Gerda, Gerda, my beloved Gerda! Where have you been so long? And where have I been? What's happened to us?"

Slowly he looked around. "How cold it is here!" he said. "How empty and horrid!" But then he hugged Gerda and they laughed and wept and danced for joy. They whirled about over the pieces of ice that littered the lake. They kicked the pieces and spun them and bounced about on them. And soon the pieces of ice were moving with them, leaping with a rhythm of their own, flying through the air, shaking and trembling with the children's joy.

When Gerda and Kai were finally exhausted, they flopped down, laughing, upon the ground beside the lake. And when they did so, the pieces of ice settled down upon the surface of the lake, forming the perfect shape that Kai, by himself, had never been able to find, the pattern that spelled *eternity*. The pieces of ice had come to rest in the shape of an enormous heart. For only true love is eternal. And only the truly human heart can know true love.

Outside, the winds were still and a bright sun appeared on the horizon. As they walked toward the sunrise, the castle behind them seemed to shudder and groan and heave. They turned to look, and there in the doorway they saw the frightful specter of the Snow Queen. Angry mists swirled about her. At her back was a gigantic, shapeless mass whose piggish red eyes flashed and glowed with rage and frustration. It was the demon king.

Fear-stricken, the children turned to run. But the two furies seemed rooted to the spot, unable to pursue them. Then Gerda and Kai realized that the demon king and the Snow Queen could do them no further harm. The sign of Kai's release, the symbol of love, stood out on the frozen lake. Thus it would stand forever while the sliver of glass from the evil mirror would remain frozen in the eternal ice at the top of the world.

Questions

1. What effect did the piece of demon glass have on Kai?
2. Why did Kai change back to his old self?
3. Do you think Gerda could have reached the kingdom of the Snow Queen and found Kai without the help of the reindeer, the Lapp woman, and the Finn woman? Explain.
4. Fairy tales often teach a lesson, reveal some truth, or convey a message. What do you think the lesson, truth, or message of "The Snow Queen" is?

Applying Reading Skills

Choose the word or phrase that best completes each sentence below. Write the word, phrase, or phrases on your paper. The sentences are based on "The Snow Queen."

1. The author's purpose in writing the story was to _____.
   a. explain   b. entertain   c. persuade
   d. describe   e. give factual information
2. From the author's point of view, _____.
   a. love is a stronger emotion than hate
   b. hate is a stronger emotion than love
   c. true love and a pure heart give us great power
   d. what is good always appears evil, and what is evil appears good
3. The author would probably agree that _____.
   a. nothing succeeds without love
   b. real love is eternal
   c. good always overcomes evil
   d. bad things always happen to good people
   e. changes are permanent
   f. evil may befall us by chance

BEYOND WINTER

Over the winter glaciers
I see the summer glow,
And through the wild-piled snowdrift
The warm rosebuds below.

Ralph Waldo Emerson

PREPARING FOR READING

Learning Vocabulary

1. The polar bear appeared yellow against the stark, white snow.
2. It stalked past the frightened boys lying flattened against the ice.
3. The bear stood poised at the edge of the ice, waiting for a seal to appear.
4. It swiftly struck a killing blow, hauled the seal out of the water, and began to devour it hungrily.
5. The boys built a crude shelter using blocks of ice.
6. By putting seal fat and a homemade wick into the cavity of the frozen seal heart, they fashioned a lamp stove.
7. The rescue helicopter appeared through the fog and hovered above the icy landscape.

stark	stalked	poised	devour
crude	cavity	hovered	

Developing Background and Skills
Author's Purpose and Point of View

An **author's purpose** is his or her reason for writing. You know that authors may write for many different reasons. The author's purposes you have learned about are listed below.

AUTHOR'S PURPOSE

1. to entertain or amuse
2. to explain
3. to describe
4. to give factual information
5. to persuade

What is the purpose of the author of a textbook? A mystery story? A political advertisement? The directions included in a model kit?

Sometimes an author may combine two or more purposes in writing. For example, the writer of a travel book may describe a particular place in an entertaining way, give factual information about it, explain how to get there, and persuade you to visit the place. Usually, however, an author has a single overriding purpose. Read the example below.

Matthew tilted his head back and watched the helicopter until it became only a tiny red speck in the snowy sky—a spark in the midst of the bleak coldness. Matthew's thoughts were with his father as he trudged across the stark plain. There was beauty in this frozen land, he thought, but there was also danger. The helicopter would have to fight its way through, and that would not be easy.

One of the author's purposes for writing the passage was to describe. What other purposes could the author have had?

The **author's point of view** is the way the author feels about his or her subject. Point of view has to do with the author's way of viewing things and his or her attitude about things. Read the sentences below.

The idea of the two teen-age boys setting out on a search in the raging storm seemed foolish to Mrs. Ross. The boys, however, felt that their experience and knowledge made them the logical choice for the mission.

Mrs. Ross and the boys felt differently about the rescue mission because they were looking at it from different standpoints. Their points of view were not the same.

As you read the next selection, think about the author's main purpose in writing it. Look for clues that will help you determine his point of view about what he narrates.

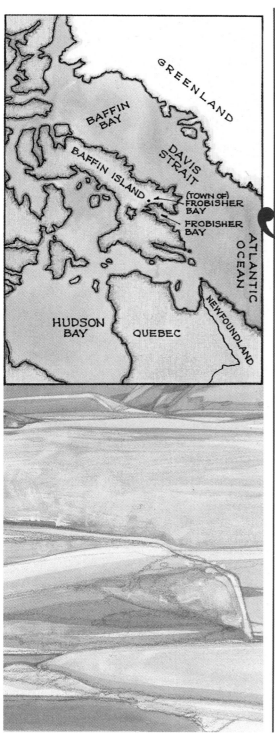

FROZEN *fire*

JAMES HOUSTON

The land around Frobisher Bay in the Canadian Arctic is a forbidding frozen landscape for much of the year. But to Ross Morgan, it is a geologist's dream. Even a bitter Arctic storm does not prevent him and Charlie, his helicopter pilot, from attempting a prospecting expedition. When the men do not return and weather conditions prevent an air search, Morgan's son, Matthew, decides to take action. With his Eskimo friend, Kayak, Matthew sets out in a snowmobile to find his father. When the gas supply is exhausted, the boys have to abandon their search and return to Frobisher Bay on foot.

Matthew dreaded the look of the black water that stood gaping before them, sometimes eight feet, sometimes twelve feet wide. The crack stretched like a long ragged tear in a piece of white paper for as far as Matthew could see.

"There's a seal," whispered Kayak.

Matthew saw a head as round and black as a bowling ball floating in the icy water not thirty paces from them.

"Oh I wish I had my father's rifle," whispered Kayak. "Here we are, helpless, starving, and all that meat and fat staring at us. Even if I had a harpoon."

As though the seal had heard the dreaded word "harpoon," its head ducked beneath the ice and did not reappear.

Matthew saw his friend run forward and kick hard at a four-foot chunk of ice that had cracked away from the main ice and then frozen fast again. Carefully, Kayak knelt and cleared the snow away. Then seeing the weak fault where the ice pan had refrozen, he started chipping with the snow knife at the crack.

"Help me," he called to Matthew, who opened the largest blade of his Swiss Army knife.

Kneeling, they worked desperately. Small chips of ice flew up their sleeves, melted and ran along their arms in icy rivulets. Suddenly with a soft swoosh the small pan of ice let go and drifted. Kayak caught it with his knife and slowly drew it to him.

"I'll go first," he said, cautiously putting one foot on the ice pan.

Matthew saw it shudder and sink a little.

"It should hold me," Kayak said.

As though he trod on eggs, he carefully eased one knee and then the other onto the trembling pan of ice.

"Now push the ice," he said to Matthew. "Not so hard you'll tip

me in, but hard enough to float me over to the other side."

Matthew lay on his stomach and with both hands he gave the ice a steady push. Kayak was on his hands and knees. A light breeze whipped across the ice and caught him like a sail, so the ice pan turned half around. Matthew closed his eyes and prayed.

"*Nakomik*, thanks a lot," he heard Kayak shout, and when Matthew opened his eyes, he saw Kayak scrambling onto the strong ice on the other side of the widening crack.

Kayak then began to chip two holes in the ice pan about four inches apart. He worked downwards in a V shape until the two holes touched. Then he forced the piece of tent line through the ice and tied it tight.

"Get ready," he called to Matthew and, pushing the ice with his foot, sent it drifting back across the crack.

"You're heavier than I am and that ice is very tippy even though it's thick," shouted Kayak. "You be mighty careful how you climb onto it."

With the deadly cold black water all around him, Matthew felt like an elephant balancing on a cold round ball. Slowly, cautiously, Kayak drew Matthew toward him across the widening gap between the heavy shore ice of the bay and the great central body of ice, until Matthew, too, could crawl onto the strong ice.

"I think we're going to be all right now," Kayak called to Matthew. "The wind should make it easier to get onto the shore ice across the bay near Frobisher."

He was wrong. Dead wrong. For the next six hours they hurried across the vast broken ice fields, driving the knife in before taking every step, testing. In the late afternoon, they watched with terror as the huge tide flooded the ice creating deadly lakes just south of them. With each step Matthew imagined he could feel the broken ice beneath them moving south toward the Hudson Straits where they would be swept to certain death in the North Atlantic Ocean.

"It's no use going any farther," said Kayak. "I can feel it, we are being swept away. The tide is carrying us too far south. We will never reach the other side."

"What do you mean?" said Matthew, horrified.

"See that hill," said Kayak. "It was far to the south of us this morning, when we crossed the tide crack. Now it is so far to the north I can scarcely see it. We have moved fifteen miles south already. By morning we will have drifted thirty, almost forty miles away. We are lost, I tell you. Lost forever. Look. Look how the ice has split." Kayak showed him. "We were once on pans a mile square in size. Look how all of them have broken. You could not walk fifteen paces now without falling into water. I am sorry, Mattoosie, we are truly finished."

A cruel blast of wind swept out of the north, driving chilling swirls of ice fog around them.

"We must build an igloo," said Matthew, taking out Kayak's snow knife.

"It is too difficult out here," Kayak mumbled. "The snow is wet with salt water."

"Still we must try our best," said Matthew, and he paced out the small circle as he had seen Kayak do and began to cut the thin damp blocks. Big wet flakes of snow came driving on the wind.

"Come and help me," Matthew called to Kayak.

"Don't move," answered Kayak in a whisper. There was terror in his voice.

Cautiously, Matthew turned and saw the white head and black beady eyes as it moved snakelike through the icy water. When it reached the small ice pan on which they stood, the huge polar bear heaved its bulk out of the water and shook itself like an immense dog. It looked yellow against the stark white snow.

Matthew and Kayak lay like dead men on the ice, both their heads turned so that they could watch the bear. Matthew clutched the snow knife like a dagger and trembled inside, as he felt the wet salt water seep up from the snow and soak his clothing.

The bear did not even pause to look at them as it stalked past. They saw it crouch down flat against the snow.

Cautiously, Matthew looked ahead and saw a seal's dark head poised alert and motionless in the water. Seeing nothing but a yellowish heap of snow, the seal swam cautiously along the edge of the ice.

Matthew watched it sniff the dead seal all over, then roll it on its back and, holding it steady, tear its throat open with its powerful jaws. It started to devour its prey.

At last Matthew saw that the big bear was finished eating. He and Kayak watched it as it licked its lips and, like a huge cat, carefully wiped the seal fat from his mouth. It turned and shambled toward them, paused and

Suddenly, with lightning swiftness, the bear's right paw shot out and struck the seal's head a killing blow. The left paw lunged forward and hooked the seal inward with its great curved claws. Using its teeth, the bear easily hauled the hundred-pound seal up onto the ice pan.

sniffed the air. With its belly rumbling, it padded once more to the edge of the ice and slipped silently into the freezing water.

Kayak rolled stiffly onto his hands and knees, then crouched like an animal, still watching the place where they had last seen the bear.

In the half darkness, Matthew saw him cut the dead seal's big artery, pull its heart out, and set it on the ice.

"Quick, we've got to build a shelter. Work hard and it will warm you up a little. Move your arms and legs," Kayak said, "so your clothing won't freeze stiff."

On one end of their pan, sheets of ice the size of tabletops lay scattered like playing cards forced there by the pressures of the rising tides. Kayak stood three sheets upright, leaning them against each other. Then together they hauled two more into place to form a rough circle.

"Now gather snow," said Kayak, kicking it into wet piles with his soaking boots. "We'll chink up the holes and cracks between the ice to make it strong."

When their crude shelter was finished, it looked like nothing but another miserable pile of ice.

Kayak hurried away and returned with the frozen heart and the torn remains of the seal. He dragged them inside.

Matthew saw Kayak take the snow knife, hack white chunks of seal fat from the inside of the carcass, and set the frozen heart up in the snow like a small melon with its top cut open.

"Give me your little knife," Kayak said and with it he trimmed a narrow piece off the back tail of his shirt in a place where it was still dry.

"I hope I didn't lose it," Kayak said, searching his pockets with his freezing hands. "I've found it. My little piece of flintstone." He handed it to Matthew. "Hold it carefully. Don't drop it. It's worth more to us than gold."

Matthew had to help Kayak cut open the freezing front of his parka, so that he could reach into his inside breast pocket to get the little carving file and the wad of fine steel wool, the ones Matthew had seen him using in school.

"They're soaking wet," said Kayak. "Feel in your hip pockets. They're still dry. Can you find any pieces of lint or string?"

"Only just this bit of string," said Matthew. "Nearly nothing."

"It may be enough. Roll it into a loose ball," Kayak said. "Now Mattoosie, you do everything

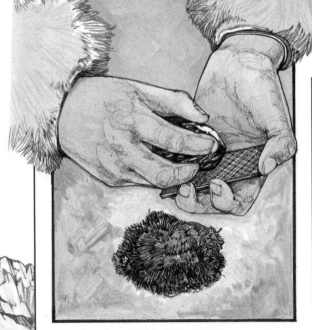

exactly how I tell you. If you get your hands a little bit burned, don't mind it, understand me?"

Matthew wanted to laugh at him or cry. "How are you going to burn my hands? They're almost frozen."

He watched as Kayak struck the flint along the steel teeth of the little file. On the third try sparks flew into the wet steel wool and Matthew gasped in surprise as he saw the fine steel wire spark and begin to flare red and burn. The fire fizzled out.

"Now," said Kayak. "If I can light it again, you put the dry string in the spark with your finger. Do it right! My hands are freezing."

He struck the file again a dozen times before the steel wool sputtered into running sparks. Matthew held the wad of string against the tiny flame.

"Hold it there. Don't let it go out."

Kayak took the shirttail wick that he had made, rubbed it with seal fat, and held it in the tiny glow.

"Don't breathe on it just yet," he said, and waited.

Matthew felt a blister beginning to rise on his finger, but he didn't cry out.

"Don't move it," Kayak ordered.

Slowly the seal fat sizzled, then a real flame burst into life. Kayak blew gently on it, then carefully stuffed one end of the wick into the well of glistening seal fat that he had stuffed into the open cavity of the frozen seal's heart. The flame expanded, as the seal fat softened and soaked upward into the homemade wick.

"I would never have believed that," Matthew said quietly. "That you could make a lamp stove out of a frozen seal's heart and make wet steel wool burn. It smells good," he said. "Like my mother's burning toast!"

"It's something," said Kayak, "I didn't learn in school."

With Matthew's knife he cut strips of rich red seal meat from the carcass where the bear had scarcely touched it. Together they warmed the strips over the little lamp and ate them. Matthew thought that he had never tasted anything so good.

"Tonight we sleep resting on our knees and elbows," Kayak said. "The snow's too wet to lie down."

Kayak pulled off his parka and beat it with a piece of jagged ice until the sheath of ice fell away, then he put his parka on backwards.

"Why are you doing that?" asked Matthew.

"Because I'm going to pull up my hood and breathe into it. That way I catch all my body heat. You do the same. It's a trick I heard about from my mother's relatives. It might help to save our lives."

In the first light of morning, Matthew heard the ice grinding and had the uneasy sense that their whole house was slowly turning. Kayak pushed out the piece of ice that he had used to block the entrance.

Matthew, still crouching stiffly, looked up and in the sky saw a long thin white contrail.

"It's the big plane," said Kayak, "going into Frobisher Bay or maybe over to Greenland."

Matthew whirled around, dived back through the entrance, reached into his pack and leaped outside holding the snowmobile's mirror.

"Give me the knife, the knife!" he shouted.

With its point he scratched a small cross in the mercury behind the glass. Then, standing in the rays of the morning sun, he placed it against his eye and sighted it on the plane. Through the tiny opening, he could see it moving through the cold blue sky like a slow silver bullet. He tipped the glass back and forth, back and forth, back and forth. He continued to watch the airplane through the hole until it was out of sight.

"What's that? Some kind of magic you are doing?" Kayak asked him.

"No," answered Matthew. "It was nothing, I guess. My dad told me that sometimes a pilot can see a mirror flashing from a very long way off. You know, it's that old Indian trick."

"Well, it didn't make them turn around," said Kayak.

"I guess you're right," said Matthew, and he dropped the mirror in the snow.

A steady wind blew out of the north and the cold spring sun glared off the snow-covered ice. They pumped their feet and swung their arms about their bodies to keep their blood circulating. Matthew watched the tide go slack, then turn, and all too soon they felt the pull of the outgoing tide carrying them toward destruction in the open sea.

The cold that comes with night swept in, and with it ghostly vapors appeared like steam between the cracks of broken ice. The full moon rose, staring at them like a dead man's face, and once more they heard the dreadful grinding as the tide drove them south with awesome force.

Kayak started to pull the last remains of the seal into their little house and then suddenly changed his mind and began to circle around the house, pressing down hard, leaving a dark red trail of seal blood in the snow.

"What good will that do?" Matthew cried.

Kayak didn't answer him. The only sound was the moaning of the ice in the gathering gloom. Together they crawled inside the hut, huddled side by side, and ate some seal meat.

"Aren't you going to light the lamp?" said Matthew.

"Maybe later. What's the use? . . . Oh, I'll try to light it if you want me to."

They slept, crouching like animals in the lamp's faint glow, until the first light of morning filtered faintly through their icy shelter.

"What's that?" gasped Kayak. He cocked his head and listened.

"I don't hear anything," said Matthew. "Wait! Wait! Yes, I do. I do!"

They kicked away the thin ice door and scrambled out the narrow entrance.

"Thug-thug-thug-thug-thug!" They heard a helicopter's engine driving the whirling blades through the glittering ice fog overhead.

"It's going! It's going. It can't see us in the fog," said Kayak.

"And we were in the house."

"Thug-thug-thug-thug-thug!"

"It's turning! It's coming back!" Matthew shouted and danced upon their pan of ice that was now shaped like a broken marble tombstone.

Suddenly, the red helicopter loomed through the fog, hovered like a giant bird, then swept toward them. Like a pair of partly frozen scarecrows they danced a jig together.

"It's Matilda!" Kayak yelled. "It's the *Waltzing Matilda*. She's all patched up on one side."

They could see Charlie in the gleaming blister,* waving at them wildly. One door of the helicopter slid open and Charlie flipped out a short rope ladder with metal rungs. Kayak staggered across the ice pan and grabbed it.

---

* **blister:** a transparent dome or bulge on an aircraft.

"Get in!" Charlie shouted over the roar of the engine.

Kayak grabbed Matthew by the hood of his parka and helped pull him up the ladder. Matthew slumped down behind them. There was very little room inside.

Charlie pointed down and said, "Whoever made that red circle around that ice shack of yours certainly saved your lives. I would have never found you without that bull's eye. Where did you get the paint?"

"It's not paint," said Matthew. "He thought of the idea." Matthew nodded toward Kayak. "He saved us."

"It worked like magic," Charlie shouted. "And where did you get the mirror? The one you flashed at the Nordair flight that was coming into Frobisher. If they hadn't seen that mirror shining, we'd never have found you. The aircraft and the rescue teams were looking for you inland. That mirror saved your lives!"

"He thought of that," said Kayak. "Mattoosie saved us with his Aree-zoona Indian trick."

"There's lots of people who are going to be mighty glad to see you two."

Questions

1. What two things did the boys do to help the rescue teams find them?
2. How long a period does the story cover?
3. Which boy—Kayak or Matthew—do you think was better prepared to survive by himself? Explain.
4. What would you have done to survive and to attract the rescue teams if you had been in Kayak and Matthew's situation? Assume that you had only the things that they had.

Applying Reading Skills

A. Use complete sentences to answer the question (1) and follow the directions (2).

1. For which reason listed on page 352 do you think the author wrote "Frozen Fire"? Support your answer.
2. From information presented in the story, describe in your own words how to make a frozen-seal-heart lamp stove or how to give mirror-flash signals.

B. Write the statements below you think the author of "Frozen Fire" would agree with.

1. Luck plays the most important role in getting out of difficult situations.
2. The area around Frobisher Bay is one of the most dangerous places in the world.
3. Courage is important in seeing people through times of danger.
4. We learn many things that we never need to use.
5. You never know when or where your knowledge and experience will come in handy.
6. It is better not to be alone in a dangerous or possibly dangerous situation.
7. Even when things seem to be at their worst, something good always turns up.

THERE IS JOY

There is joy in
Feeling the warmth
Come to the great world
And seeing the sun
Follow its old footprints
In the summer night.

There is fear in
Feeling the cold
Come to the great world
And seeing the moon
—Now new moon, now full moon—
Follow its old footprints
In the winter night.

Eskimo Chant translated by
Knud Rasmussen

PREPARING FOR READING

Learning Vocabulary

1. One of the <u>theories</u> about Antarctica held by the ancient Greeks was that it was a warm land covered with thick and <u>lush</u> vegetation.
2. The land of Antarctica is eternally frozen and lies <u>perpetually</u> under a layer of ice.
3. Ice, unlike water, cannot absorb and then <u>retain</u> heat.
4. No grass or trees grow there, and strong winds whip across its <u>barren</u> surface.
5. The Arctic tern is an astonishing bird that <u>migrates</u> annually between the Arctic and the Antarctic.

theories	lush	perpetually
retain	barren	migrates

Developing Background and Skills
Cause and Effect

As you read, you often learn how things are related to one another. One way in which things are related is called cause and effect. In a **cause-and-effect relationship**, one event, action, or situation—the cause—results in another event, action, or situation—the effect. The sentence below states a cause-and-effect relationship.

The mountains can be located only by scientific instruments because they are buried beneath the icecap.

In this sentence, *they are buried beneath the icecap* states the cause. *The mountains can be located only by scientific instruments* states the effect. The signal word *because* helps you recognize the cause-and-effect relationship. Other commonly used signal words include *so*, *so that*, *as a result*, *in order to*, *in order that*, and *since*.

When writers do not use signal words to indicate a cause-and-effect relationship, you must figure out how events or actions are connected. Read the sentences below.

The waters of the oceans around Antarctica are colder, less salty, and heavier than those of the oceans to the north. At the boundary where they meet, the cold Antarctic waters sink below the warmer waters of the northern seas.

You probably realize that a cause-and-effect relationship exists between the two sentences. How do you know which is the cause and which is the effect?

You should ask yourself "What happens?" The answer tells you the effect. (The Antarctic waters sink below the warmer waters of the northern seas.)

The answer to the question "Why does this happen?" will tell you the cause. (Waters around Antarctica are colder, less salty, and heavier than the waters to the north.)

An event, action, or situation can be both a cause and an effect. Read the example below.

Cook's ship, *Resolution*, was fragile. It was unable to smash its way through the pack ice. Cook never sighted the continent of Antarctica.

CAUSE: Cook's ship, *Resolution*, was fragile.
EFFECT: It was unable to smash its way through the pack ice.

CAUSE: It was unable to smash its way through the pack ice.
EFFECT: Cook never sighted the continent of Antarctica.

As you read the following selection think about how the events, actions, and situations are connected. See if you can figure out the cause-and-effect relationships.

POLES APART

Ellesmere Island in Canada (shown above) lies within the Arctic Circle approximately 450 miles (724 km) from the North Pole.

An iceberg drifts by the coast of Antartica.

EDWARD F. DOLAN, JR.

"Poles apart" is an old saying that means two things are vastly different from each other. The saying springs from the fact that the North and South Poles are separated by the entire earth. But the saying can be applied also to the differences between these areas.

The North Pole is located in the midst of the Arctic Ocean, circled by the lands of three continents:

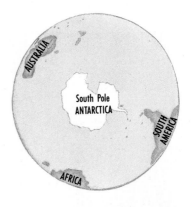

North America, Europe, and Asia. The South Pole, on the other hand, is located in the midst of a huge continent, surrounded by three oceans: the Indian, Pacific, and Atlantic.

Other differences also exist between the two regions. One of these is the weather. Both regions are unbelievably cold, but Antarctica is the colder. Antarctica is a giant land mass covered over with a sheet of ice. This ice is unable to do what any ocean can do: absorb whatever heat there is, retain it, and then re-radiate it. Furthermore, no warm ocean currents enter the waters around Antarctica. Without the protection of any large surrounding islands, it lies exposed to the world's fiercest winds. Its temperatures often plunge to 85 degrees below zero and averages 40 degrees below zero. That is 10 degrees lower than those of the Arctic. Winds of up to 200 miles an hour (320 km) frequently scream across its barren face.

In the Arctic, the ice melts in the summer. The temperatures there move up close to the freezing point and, in places, above it. But Antarctic temperatures always remain well below the freezing

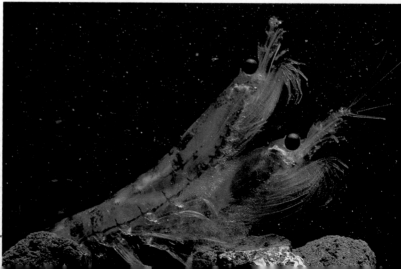

Creatures who live in the polar regions include the black-browed albatross and walrus (top left to right). Krill (bottom center) are small, shrimplike animals that live in oceans. In the Antarctic region, krill are food for seals, penguins, and whales.

point. All but a few hundred miles of the continent are perpetually under a layer of ice. Because the land is eternally frozen, there is no rain and only light snowfall.

Both the Arctic and Antarctic are regions of endless light and then of endless darkness. However, their seasons are reversed. Winter darkness comes to the Arctic in October. But in the Antarctic, it begins in the final week of March and lasts until the closing week in September. The rest of the time, the sun never sets.

Climate accounts for still another striking difference between the Arctic and the Antarctic. There is enough warmth in the Arctic to support a population of humans and land animals. Antarctica, though, has no permanent human inhabitants. The Arctic has such land animals as reindeer, caribou, fox, and polar bears. The Antarctic's chief resident is the waddling penguin. He is found in several species, weighs as much as 80 pounds (36 kg), and stands 4 feet (1.2 m) tall. He resembles a tiny man in a black suit and yellowish shirt bowing to his friends and giving out a trumpetlike call.

Scientists believe the penguin

is the sole survivor of a host of animals that once lived on Antarctica. In the eighteenth and nineteenth centuries, deposits of coal and the fossil imprints of plant leaves were first found. These discoveries have led scientists to believe that Antarctica was a warm place of forests and swamps inhabited by dinosaurs and pre-historic mammals. Then came the Ice Age, killing many of the animals or driving them away to other places. Unable to fly or to swim great distances, the penguin was forced to remain behind.

Other land animals found in Antarctica are a small wingless fly and a tiny spider. Both come alive only in the summer months. The rest of the time they remain frozen in the ice. Even germ life cannot survive the cold and great quan-tities of ultraviolet light. Con-sequently, many scientists have said that Antarctica would be one of the most healthful lands in which people could live. They would not suffer the common cold or any of the diseases caused by microbes. They would be just fine—if only they could keep from freezing to death.

The intense cold freezes every-

thing swiftly and preserves it. In 1947, Navy explorers located a camp left behind by explorer Robert Falcon Scott thirty-five years earlier. A hut was found that looked as if it had been built the day before. The timbers showed no sign of rot, and there was not a trace of rust on the nails. Inside were biscuits and canned beef, still perfectly edible.

The Arctic and Antarctic support much sea and winged life. Both have their share of fish, seal, and whale. Antarctic waters also have such residents as shrimp, squid, jellyfish, octopi, five kinds of seals,

the giant blue whale, and the vicious grampus whale, which also inhabits the Arctic seas. Both have a wide variety of birds, including the stormy petrel, the albatross, and the Arctic tern. Of all of them, the Arctic tern is the most astonishing. It migrates from Pole to Pole annually, traveling 22,000 miles (35,200 km) to escape the winter of one and enjoy the short summer of the other.

As for the continent itself, Antarctica covers 5 million square miles (13 million sq. km). It consists of mountains and plateaus. Some of its peaks rise to 12,000

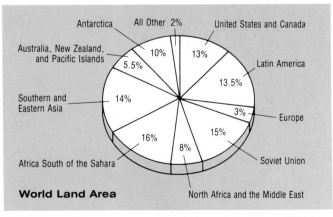

World Land Area

Antarctica 10%   All Other 2%   United States and Canada 13%

Australia, New Zealand, and Pacific Islands 5.5%

Latin America 13.5%

Southern and Eastern Asia 14%

Europe 3%

Soviet Union 15%

Africa South of the Sahara 16%

North Africa and the Middle East 8%

feet (3,657 m) and 15,000 feet (4,572 m). In all this vast continent, not a tree grows. Plant life is limited to a few mosses and lichens on which the spiders and wingless flies feed. The layer of ice spread over the continent is 2 miles (3.2 km) thick in some places.

Though there are striking differences between the roof and the basement of the world, there is one thing they have in common. Both have fascinated people for centuries. The ancient Greeks had their ideas about what the Arctic must be like, and they had a few theories about Antarctica. Correctly, they imagined it to be a continent. They felt it was needed to keep the world in balance because of all the heavy lands in the Northern Hemisphere. Incorrectly, however, they thought of it as a warm land—just as they first envisioned the Arctic. They guessed that it was covered with thick, lush vegetation. Both of their ideas became suspect when people finally figured out that the world was round and began to sail from the Atlantic to the Pacific by going south of South America.

Top left to right: Lichens are flowerless plants made up of two parts: algae and fungus; most polar bears live on the sea ice surrounding the North Pole which breaks apart during the summer; (right) seals have thick layers of fatty blubber which allows them to keep warm even while resting on ice and snow.

Questions

1. On what continent is the South Pole located? What three continents surround the North Pole?
2. When does summer begin in the Arctic? Fall? Winter? Spring? When do these seasons begin in the Antarctic?
3. Would travel and exploration be easier in the Arctic or in the Antarctic? Give the reasons for your answer.
4. If you had a chance to visit either the Arctic or the Antarctic, which would you choose? Explain why.

Applying Reading Skills

A. Copy the sentences below. Draw one line under the cause. Draw two lines under the effect.

1. Because the North and South poles are located at opposite extremes of the earth, the expression "poles apart" refers to two things that are vastly different from one another.
2. In the Arctic, the ice melts in the summer. The temperatures there move up close to the freezing point and above it.
3. Antarctica would be a healthful place for people to live. They would not suffer colds or diseases caused by microbes.
4. The penguin was forced to remain behind. Penguins cannot fly or swim great distances.
5. The Greek theories about Antarctica became suspect when people began to sail into and explore the region south of South America.

B. Follow the directions given. Use the information given in "Poles Apart."

1. Give three causes of this effect: *Antarctica is colder than the Arctic.*
2. Give two effects of this cause: *The land of Antarctica is eternally frozen.*

WRITING ACTIVITY

WRITE AN ARTICLE OF CONTRAST

Prewrite

"Poles Apart" is an article that contrasts the North and South poles. You are going to write an article contrasting two states: Alaska and Florida. You can use the chart below to organize your information. You may want to add other categories or kinds of information in each category. Before you write, make your own chart with notes in each category.

	ALASKA	FLORIDA
LOCATION (including bordering states or countries, and water boundaries)		
SIZE (area in square miles, rank among states)		
CLIMATE (average temperature, yearly rainfall or snowfall, seasons)		
PHYSICAL FEATURES (mountains, lakes, rivers)		
PLANT AND ANIMAL LIFE		

Where can you look for information for your article?
1. An atlas will give you information on maps of the states.
2. An almanac can give you facts on climate, seasons, and size.

3. An encyclopedia can give you information on all categories.
4. Library books can be found about each state.

Write

1. You may follow this plan for paragraph organization. For your first paragraph, write a main idea sentence introducing your topic: contrasting Alaska and Florida. Continue giving contrasting facts about the location and size of the two states.
2. Write a paragraph contrasting climate, one on physical features, one on plant and animal life, and one on any other categories you may have added.
3. Help your reader identify contrasting information easily by using clue words and phrases such as *but, rather, opposite, however, contrasted with,* and *while.*
4. Use your Glossary or dictionary for spelling help.

Revise

Read your article. Did you begin each paragraph with a main idea sentence that states the categories you are contrasting? Can you combine sentences to help your readers understand the comparison more clearly? For example, instead of this:

Florida ranks ____ in size among the states. Alaska ranks ____ in size among the states.

Try this: Florida ranks ____ in size among the states, while Alaska ranks ____.

1. Proofread for the correct use of numbers and spelling.
2. Check the capitalization and end punctuation in each sentence.
3. Rewrite your article. You may want to look for photographs or magazine pictures as well as a map to make your article even more interesting.

PREPARING FOR READING

Learning Vocabulary

1. Karen was selected as an <u>alternate</u> to take part in the Antarctic program, in case Robin, the first choice, was unable to do so.
2. Both girls attended a three-day <u>orientation</u> program to prepare them for the trip.
3. Robin's first impression of Antarctica was a place where cold and light <u>permeated</u> everything.
4. Twelve nations maintain <u>facilities</u> in Antarctica where scientists <u>committed</u> to their work carry out research.
5. The penguins were so <u>inquisitive</u> that they followed Robin and Karen everywhere.

alternate	orientation	permeated
facilities	committed	inquisitive

Developing Background and Skills
Main Idea

You know that the most important information in a paragraph is called the **main idea**. The main idea may be developed through details or examples. The details support the main idea. Sometimes a single sentence in the paragraph states the main idea. Find the sentence that states the main idea of the paragraph below.

The International Geophysical (jē' ō fiz' i kəl) year, or IGY, was a special period of time for scientists to study the earth and sky. *Geophysical* means "related to the study of the earth and the forces that affect or change it." Ten thousand scientists from about seventy nations took part.

If you chose the first sentence, you were right.

Sometimes the main idea of a paragraph is found in two or more sentences. Read the paragraph below.

During the IGY, several nations set up bases in Antarctica for collecting scientific data. After the IGY ended, most of these nations continued their research there. The question then arose as to who should control the continent. In 1959, the 12 nations that had worked there during the IGY signed a treaty. They agreed that Antarctica should remain free for scientific observation and be used only for peaceful purposes.

By combining information from the last two sentences, you can state the main idea: *The twelve nations that had worked in Antarctica during the IGY signed a treaty stating that the continent should remain free and be used only for scientific purposes.* What details in the paragraph explain why the treaty came to be written?

Sometimes the main idea is not stated at all. All the information in the paragraph may consist of details or examples. Read the paragraph below.

During the IGY, scientists set out to measure tides, map the heavens, and probe beneath the earth's crust. They explored the Arctic and the Antarctic. They collected facts about earthquakes, hurricanes, droughts, and currents. They used satellites to take measurements of oceans and continents. Engineers observed the sun and tested its rays, hoping to learn how the rays might be used to furnish power.

All of the sentences in the paragraph tell about the projects carried out during the IGY. How could you sum up the details in a main idea statement?

As you read the following selection, look for the main ideas the author presents. Which does the author state directly? Which must you infer, or figure out for yourself?

SCOUTING THE BOTTOM OF THE WORLD

Marilyn Z. Wilkes

Suppose you were offered a chance to go to a place that only 25,000 Americans have visited. Robin Moyle of Scarsdale, New York, and Karen Prentice of Portland, Oregon, were offered just such an opportunity as part of the Girl Scouts' program of Wider Opportunities. And they took it!

The Antarctic Research Project, or ARP, is a program co-sponsored by the National Science Foundation and the Girl Scouts. It offers one girl between the ages of seventeen and nineteen the chance to spend two months as part of the American scientific team in Antarctica. This girl has to be an outstanding student with an interest in science. She has to be a citizen of the United States and a Girl Scout. And she has to be in excellent health and physical condition.

"The application was harder than my college applications," remembers Robin. Nevertheless, she and Karen were among sixty-six girls to apply. They had to write pages of information about themselves, including several essays. They also underwent thorough medical and dental examinations to prove their fitness.

In April, 1985, a certified letter notified Robin that she had been chosen. Karen had been selected first alternate. She would go if something prevented Robin from doing so.

In September, both girls went to Arlington, Virginia, for an intensive three-day group orientation given by the Navy and the National Science Foundation. "We lived and breathed Antarctica," says Robin. "They told us everything from how to get mail to the types of clothes we'd be wearing." They also told Karen that the Project would like to send her as well as Robin.

"I hadn't had the mind set that I was going," says Karen. "Then all of a sudden, I had three weeks to contemplate going to Antarctica! It took some getting used to."

On October 14, the girls met at the American naval base in Christchurch, New Zealand, where their flight to Antarctica would originate. They met a lot of people and were issued their polar clothing, forty pounds of it! There were thick, solid rubber "Bunnyboots," a type of hat that can be pulled over the face called a balaklava (bal′ ə kläv′ ə), long underwear, wool shirts, canvas wind pants, huge "bear paw" mittens, and a massive hooded parka. "It took twenty minutes to get it all on," says Robin. "We looked like a herd of elephants. Movement was rather difficult."

It took three tries to get to Antarctica from New Zealand because the weather, even in summer, is so bad. "The half hour before landing was one of breathless anticipation and excitement!" Robin wrote in her journal. "We coasted and stopped. This was it! They opened the door, and cold and light permeated everything. The temperature was -23 degrees Centigrade. I stepped out of the plane and into another world. I was completely awestruck. Nothing I had ever felt in my life could compare with that first impression. I was on another planet!"

The landscape was a brilliant white as far as the eye could see. Mountains loomed faintly in the distance. Snow and ice were everywhere. "I started taking pictures like crazy," remembers Robin, "and within about ten minutes, my camera froze!"

Karen Prentice works in a laboratory analyzing water samples from Lake Hoare.

The new arrivals were whisked away in orange vans down a flag-lined "road" to McMurdo Naval Air Station. McMurdo is located at the base of Mt. Erebus (ãr′ ə bəs), a huge volcano that still spurts steam. It is the largest Antarctic station and one of four operated by the United States year-round. Other research facilities are maintained by each of the twelve nations that participate in the Antarctic Treaty. This treaty, which was signed in 1957, reserves the region for peaceful purposes and encourages international cooperation in scientific research. It comes up for renewal in 1990.

McMurdo's eighty-five buildings house up to a thousand people each summer. Its winter population is about ninety. It boasts an excellent library, gym, radio station, hospital, a satellite tracking station, laboratories, and an aquarium. It looks like a small industrial city. Helicopters come and go daily, weather permitting. Everything, from food and medical supplies to fuel and building materials, must be brought in by cargo plane or icebreaker ships. Helicopters also fly people to other research locations.

Antarctic summer lasts from late October until the end of December. During that time, the sun never sets. This allows scientific teams to work in shifts around the clock. The girls were allowed to choose work projects that reflected their own interests. But before they could be "turned loose" in the frigid, hostile Antarctic environment, they had to undergo three days of survival training. They learned how to climb glaciers, deal with frostbite and hypothermia (a severe drop in body temperature), and avoid crevasses (kri vas′ əz)—deep cracks in the ice that are often hidden by loose snow.

Life soon took on a rhythm for Robin and Karen. Each followed her own schedule, often not seeing the other for weeks at a time. Each explored the huge ice caves formed by cracks in glaciers that get covered over. "There are no words that describe the aqua blue of the ice caves," Karen wrote of her visit. "With the tinkle of ice crystals clattering on the floor (and) the icy smoothness of huge, ice walls, it was the Snow Queen's Castle brought to life."

Robin's first work assignment was to join the seal census team near Mt. Erebus, weighing and tagging Weddell seals. She was transported in a track vehicle similar to a tank. She stayed at the site for two weeks, living with the team in their tiny hut and using another as a lab. There were no showers, and all the food was dried, canned, or frozen. Despite the hard living conditions, Robin loved the work. "The seals were adorable. Big, fat, and very charming. They just rolled over and looked at you very funny." It was pupping season, so there were mothers and babies everywhere. Adult seals "have a series of different noises—chirps, belches, barks, groans— all very different." Adults weigh about 1,000 pounds (454 kg). When they are born, pups weigh from thirty to sixty pounds (14 to 27 kg). They gain five pounds (2 kg) a day on their mothers' rich milk.

Wildlife is protected in the Antarctic. Scientists are not allowed to interfere in any way, even to help an animal in distress. However, studies are constantly conducted to increase our knowledge of the unique animal and marine life found there. For example, another of the experiments Robin worked on involved large fish called Mawsoni. These fish live in sub-freezing waters, yet they don't freeze. Scientists have found that a "natural antifreeze" is produced in the fish's bodies, enabling them to live in conditions that would otherwise be impossible. They hope the substance can be useful to human medicine, perhaps in preserving blood in bloodbanks for longer periods of time.

Karen also worked with the Weddell seals, but her favorite project was at frozen Lake Hoare. She helped take water samples and analyze them in a laboratory. For some reason, the water at Lake Hoare is supersaturated with oxygen. Sci-

entists melt holes in the ice with a burner and take samples in an effort to discover why.

An important assignment for both girls took them by helicopter to New Harbor. There they acted as aides or "tenders" for divers who descend into the subfreezing water to study the marine life. Holes are blasted in the ice with dynamite and reopened each day with saws and axes. The tender's job is to help the diver, checking equipment, making sure air lines are clear and functioning, and staying alert to danger. If divers don't resurface within thirty minutes, a pulse of light is sent down. If that gets no response, the tender calls for help. Since divers go down without a tether, there is always the danger that they won't be able to find the hole, or that their equipment will freeze up. One young woman diver Robin was tending suffered frozen air lines sixty feet (18 m) underwater. Her safety equipment also failed, and she was barely able to surface in time.

A high point for both Robin and Karen was their visit to Amundsen-Scott Station[1] at the South Pole. It was an 800 mile (1,287 km) flight from McMurdo. When they landed,

---

1. **Amundsen-Scott Station:** named after explorers Roald Amundsen of Norway, first explorer to reach the South Pole in December 1911, and Robert Scott of England, who reached the South Pole one month after Amundsen.

the temperature was −46°C (−51°F) with winds of 20 miles (32 km) per hour. They walked quickly to the ceremonial South Pole for pictures. The ceremonial pole is a red and white striped barber pole with a silver ball on top! Next to it stands a painted wooden likeness of Opus, the penguin in the comic strip "Bloom County." In the five minutes they had been there, Robin's nose and cheeks had turned yellow-white and numb!—frostbite! She pulled up her balaklava, and they continued with the pictures as fast as possible. Then they drove to the geographic pole[2] a short distance away and, literally, ran around the world.

Once indoors at Amundsen-Scott Station, Robin's frozen skin "turned red and really hurt a lot. Later it peeled off like a bad sunburn." If she had been exposed longer, the consequences would have been more severe—blistering, possible infection, and even gangrene.

Robin and Karen had many unforgettable experiences during their eight weeks in Antarctica. They skied down glaciers and witnessed a solar eclipse. They attended a Thanksgiving Day "Penguin Bowl" football game, complete with parade, in the middle of a storm. They saw two of the continent's eight species of penguins, the little Adelies and the Emperors. The penguins were so inquisitive that they followed their visitors everywhere. As a departing helicopter rose in the sky, the penguins watched until they fell over backwards. Robin also worked with the lively dog sled teams, now rarely used in this age of snowmobiles and other vehicles.

Most important to both girls, however, were the people they met. Those who go to the Antarctic are a rare breed—vital, interesting, and committed to their work. Both Robin and Karen hope to go back again. They also hope that other Scouts will follow them in this Wider Opportunity.

---

2. **geographic pole:** the point at which all the earth's lines of longitude meet.

Questions

1. What did Robin Moyle and Karen Prentice have to do in order to go to Antarctica?
2. Why did the girls go to Antarctica in October?
3. In what ways do you think Robin and Karen's experiences will help them in their future careers?
4. Which of the projects Robin and Karen worked on would you like to work on if you were to take part in the ARP? Explain your answer.

Applying Reading Skills

A. Read the paragraphs in "Scouting the Bottom of the World" listed below. Write the sentence that best states the main idea of the paragraph.

1. The second paragraph on page 382
   a. The ARP is a program co-sponsored by the National Science Foundation and the Girl Scouts.
   b. The ARP offers a Scout between ages 17 and 19 the chance to spend two months in the Antarctic as part of the American scientific team.
   c. The girl chosen to participate in the ARP must be a citizen of the U.S., a Girl Scout, and a person in good health and physical condition.
2. The second paragraph on page 385
   a. The population of McMurdo varies greatly from summer to winter.
   b. McMurdo is completely dependent on the outside world for all of its necessities.
   c. McMurdo Station is like a small city.

B. Read the paragraphs in "Scouting the Bottom of the World" listed below. Write the main idea of each.

1. The first complete paragraph on page 386
2. The complete paragraph on page 387

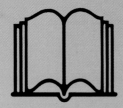

PREPARING FOR READING

Learning Vocabulary

1. The balloons needed to lift the escape platform would be filled with hydrogen kept <u>compressed</u> in steel <u>cylinders</u>.
2. Levers would control the <u>valves</u>, opening them to allow the gas to enter the balloons, and closing them to prevent the gas from escaping.
3. The flying platform was rocked back and forth at high angles by the <u>concussions</u> of the explosions.
4. For the entire <u>duration</u> of the journey, the escape platform traveled at a fabulous speed.

compressed   cylinders   valves
concussions   duration

Developing Background and Skills
Diagrams

Stories and articles you read sometimes include diagrams. A **diagram** is a special kind of drawing that helps you to visualize something by showing its essential parts or by showing how it works. The drawing on the next page is a diagram. Refer to this diagram as you read the passage below.

A hot-air balloon is a bag filled with heated air. The balloon rises and floats in the air because the hot air inside is lighter than the surrounding air. After the bag is inflated, the pilot fires the burner to ascend. To stay aloft, the burner is fired at frequent intervals. To rise even higher, the burner is fired more frequently for longer periods. To descend to lower altitudes, the burner is fired less frequently, or the cooling vent is opened. Upon landing, the pilot opens the rip panel to let all the air out of the bag.

A Hot-Air Balloon

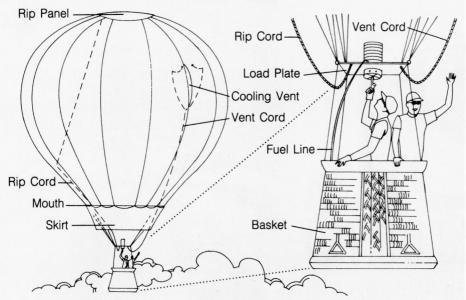

The diagram shows you what a hot-air balloon looks like. The important parts of the balloon are labeled, and you can see where each is in relation to the others. The diagram actually provides you with information additional to that given in the passage. What parts of the balloon labeled in the diagram are *not* mentioned in the passage?

The diagram on the left shows the entire balloon. That on the right shows a part of the balloon in greater detail. Use the diagrams to answer these questions.

- How does the pilot open the cooling vent?
- Where is the burner located?
- Where is the fuel stored?
- Where does the pilot ride?

The story that follows is a fantasy written primarily to amuse and entertain. However, a good part of the story involves the description and explanation of a fabulous invention. Two diagrams accompany the story. As you read, refer to the diagrams and see if they help you better understand what the author tells you about the invention and how it works.

THE 21 BALLOONS

WILLIAM PÈNE DU BOIS

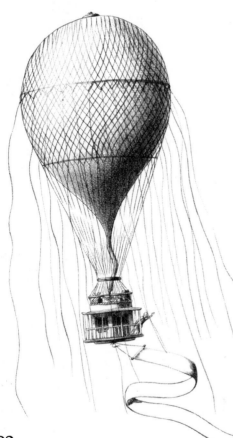

After teaching school in San Francisco for 40 years, Professor William Waterman Sherman constructs a giant hot-air balloon, the Globe, and decides to spend a year floating around the world. His plans change, however, when a sea gull punctures the balloon, and he plummets to a small

volcanic island called Krakatoa. There he meets a group of twenty families with names from **A** to **T** (Mr. A. and Mrs. A. and their son, A-1, and daughter, A-2; Mr. B. and Mrs. B.; and so on). He learns about the fabulous diamond mines on the island and the dormant volcano that erupted there once not so very long ago.

As the excerpt begins, Professor Sherman is on the beach talking things over with Mr. F. The Professor wonders why the citizens of Krakatoa are willing to risk their lives by staying on an island that may become an exploding volcano at any moment.

"How can you live happily here under the constant threat of being blown sky high? Now that I think of it, this whole Island is like a turkey stuffed with nitroglycerin."

"It troubles me just to hear you mention it.

However, if we have a warning, which we all somehow expect to have, there is a quick escape from Krakatoa. Given as little time as ten minutes to get off the Island, we'll all be safe and on our way to some other country."

"What is this escape?" I asked.

"It's the invention I promised to show you yesterday," said Mr. F. "This is an invention we all worked carefully on for many months, starting right after the big explosion in 1877. It's a flying platform, a huge platform big enough to take us all swiftly into the air within ten minutes of a warning from the mountain."

"A platform capable of lifting twenty families of four?" I asked. How do you hope to get it off the ground?"

"With balloons," answered Mr. F.

This idea appealed to me immensely. I walked over to where Mr. F. was lying, sat down beside him, and watched him as he sketched the platform in the sand. He made a bird's-eye view of it and drew the twenty balloons around its outside edge. It was rectangular in shape. He started writing numbers in the sand. "I don't know how much the actual platform weighs by itself," he said, "it is made of the lightest pine wood in the world, imported by us especially for this purpose from South America. It is made of light beams, and the floor boards are laid with spaces between them for greater lightness. The balustrade around the platform is of hollowed wood— the woodwork couldn't possibly have been made lighter.

"The balloon platform is lifted by ten large balloons of 32,400 cubic feet each; and ten balloons,

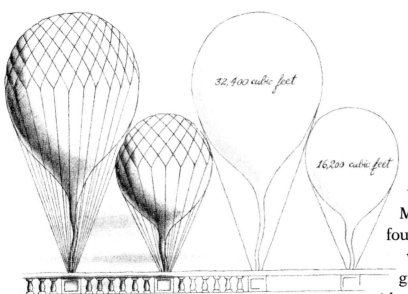

32,400 cubic feet

16,200 cubic feet

The huge platform was situated here. Mr. F. showed me four great wooden vats, one on the ground near each side of the balloon platform. There were hoses leading from the vats to the balloons in what Mr. F. described as "pitchfork connections." The hoses were large and single as they left the vats, then branched off into smaller hoses, each one attached to a balloon.

"This is how we believe we have solved the problem of a quick takeoff," he said, "compressed hydrogen. Each of these vats contains three hundred thousand cubic feet of hydrogen compressed at sixteen hundred pounds to the square inch. The hydrogen is kept in steel cylinders which are submerged in water in the vats to keep leakage down to a minimum and keep the hot rays of the sun from direct contact with the cylinders. In the event of

half as big as the larger ones, of 16,200 cubic feet each. The larger balloons will fly higher than the smaller ones which will be situated in the spaces between the larger ones, thus alternating around the platform, one large, one high, and one small, one low, etc."

"I see," I said. "How do you get the balloons filled with hydrogen and the platform off the ground in ten minutes?"

"That was our most difficult problem. Come with me. I'll show you the platform and how we think we have solved the question of a fast getaway."

After a good long walk, we came to a clearing which was as far away from the mountain as it was possible to get on the Island.

an emergency, we will all rush to the platform, jump on, and each family will stand by a balloon. The big valves in the four vats will be turned on full force. Each family will have to see that its balloon is carefully handled so that the tremendous rush of hydrogen into it won't cause any tears, rips, or snarls. The smaller balloons will fill first. There is a lever near each balloon which controls the valve allowing gas to enter it. When the small ones are three quarters full, their valves will be shut off. Shutting off the smaller balloons' valves will speed the filling of the big ones since they will be receiving all of the pressure."

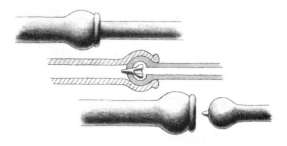

Mr. F. then picked up one of the hoses and showed it to me. There was a sort of ball-and-socket connection in each hose, and it took a hundred-and-fifty-pound pull to separate the hose at this connection.

"Each hose has a connection such as this," he explained. "Twenty hoses makes a total pull of three thousand pounds. The balloon platform isn't tied down with ropes before the takeoff. It is held down only by these hoses. Gas rushes into the balloons until the platform rises and there is a three-thousand-pound pull on the twenty hoses. The platform then tears itself away from the hose connections and leaps into the air. There is a valve in the ball end of each ball-and-socket connection. It allows gas to be forced into the balloon but prevents gas from escaping when the connection with the vats is broken. When the balloon platform is in the air, the hoses will be pulled in and attached to hoses from this smaller compressed hydrogen tank on the platform itself. It is with the hydrogen on the platform that flight will be controlled."

"How can you control the flight of the platform?"

"By adding hydrogen to the balloons we can go higher to a certain extent. By detaching the hoses from the tank on the platform and releasing hydrogen from the balloons, we can make the platform descend. Where we go is, as usual, left entirely to the winds. However, since we carry our own hydrogen supply, there is no reason why, with any sort of a wind and a minimum of luck, we can't travel a tremendous distance."

I walked around on the platform. The floor boards were springy underfoot, and you could see grass underneath through the spaces between them. I tried to imagine this huge floor in flight, looking through the boards at a city underneath. How frightening and incredible it would be, to be moving through space on such a huge piece of construction. The balloons were carefully folded under tarpaulins. I took a look at several of them. They were magnificent, made of beautiful rubberized silk, and each balloon was painted many different iridescent colors.

Mr. F. then asked, "Have you a parachute?"

"Of course not," I answered. "I threw everything overboard on the *Globe*. I didn't carry one anyway; I didn't feel I needed one."

"Each family here has a family parachute, another invention of ours. A family parachute is built so as to keep a family of four together during a descent," explained Mr. F.

"Isn't it possible to land the balloon platform?"

"Hardly so," said Mr. F. "In the first place, it would be hard to find enough level space in which to land such a huge aircraft; and in the second place, it wouldn't be possible to deflate the balloons fast enough to prevent the wind from blowing it and dragging it across the countryside. We wouldn't dare risk a landing in this; we plan to jump off, picking our countries and spots with care—if we ever have to take a trip on it. Professor Sherman, I would advise you to get a parachute as soon as you possibly can."

"How can I get one in Krakatoa?" I asked.

See Mrs. M. She and her husband designed and made the family parachutes. I am sure she has enough silk left over to make you an ordinary one."

We went together to the M.'s Moroccan house, and I told Mrs. M. my problem.

"Why, certainly," she said, "I can make you a parachute. But it will take me about two weeks. But then I doubt if you'll be needing it before then. I hope not anyway," she said, laughing.

"Of course not," I said. "Take your time—there's no rush at all."

I spent the morning of August 26, 1883, as I had spent the morning before, swimming and sun bathing with Mr. F. on that delightful little fine coral beach.

"Up to now," said Mr. F., as the movement of the earth's surface rolled him over near me, "you have asked me many questions which I have done my best to answer. I think you now know just about all there is to know about life on the Island. Now I have a wonderful idea. Everybody here is from San Francisco, and I am sure they would get a thrill hearing of their old friends and of their friends' children. Would you possibly consider giving us all a talk in the dining room after lunch?"

"I would be only too delighted," I said.

"Wonderful," said Mr. F. "You can't imagine how much they'll like this. Our conversation here always seems eventually to get around to San Francisco, and we haven't had any real news of our old friends in years."

We took a swim and returned to Mr. F.'s house. While I was dressing, Mr. F. ran around to all the houses preparing everybody for the talk I was going to give. I was very pleased that in this simple way I was perhaps going to be able to repay them somewhat for their fabulous hospitality.

We had a delicious lunch which consisted simply of huge portions of Javanese rice cooked and curried as the Dutch do it in the Dutch

East Indies. Krakatoa is actually part of the Dutch East Indies, though no Dutchman has ever cared to set foot on the Island.

Mr. F. waited until all of the tables had been cleared by the D. family, then placed a chair on one of the tables. He silenced the crowd, introduced me as the speaker in a most informal and nice way, looked at me, and pointed to the chair. I climbed up on the table, sat down, and after the twenty families were all comfortably settled, began my talk. The response to it was amazing and most gratifying. While I was talking, all eyes were attentively fixed on me, and I was looking around the room catching the reactions to each new name I mentioned and thinking up incidents to talk about next. Looking out of the window, I noticed that the ground seemed a little more active than usual. Being a new citizen of the Island, I didn't know whether there was anything unusual about this at first. I went on with my talk.

Suddenly—and this was a sight which is as vivid to me now as it was when I first saw it—the wall opposite me slowly and almost noiselessly opened up in a crack large enough to allow the sun to shine through. It was the most terrifying and sinister sight I have ever seen. A considerable amount of powdered plaster dropped on the heads of the families in the room and the windows near the cracked wall broke open.

Mr. M. rushed to the table where I was sitting, leaped onto it, and immediately started shouting instructions. "I want all of the women and little children to run to the platform at once and start taking the covers off the balloons! I want all of the men to run quickly to their houses and grab their family parachutes (hearing the word 'parachute' at that moment came to me like a blow on the head) and dash to the balloon platform! I want the six boys who are fifteen years old to take whatever food Mrs. D. has prepared for tonight and rush it to the platform!" He clapped his hands loudly, and the room was emptied at once. He turned to me and said, "We've rehearsed this a thousand times; don't be alarmed. Everything will turn out all right. We'll be off in less than fifteen minutes. Now," he said, "you're the only man with no particular job at this time. We all have pretty large amounts of diamonds sewn into a pouch attached to our family parachutes. Why don't you take a bucket and see if you can get to the mines and grab some diamonds? A few big ones will take care of you quite nicely. *But don't go near the mines if it's too dangerous, please, Sherman, don't go near the mines if. . . ."*

He was shouting after me, for I was off for the mines like a madman as soon as I got the gist of his suggestion. Unfortunately for me this was a waste of time. It was impossible to approach the mountain. I knew I had just a little over ten minutes time, the time needed to fill the balloons. I tried running—the action of the earth's surface threw me to the ground. I tried walking—I doddered, staggered, floundered, and tumbled. I tried crawling, but the earth's rumblings and heavings kept rolling me over on my side. I looked up at the mountain ahead and saw that it would be impossible to reach in the time allotted me. I threw away my bucket, turned, and ran through the village for the platform, reeling, buckling, and falling every few feet of the way. I was the last to see the Village of Krakatoa from the ground.

When I arrived at the balloon platform, it was straining at the hoses ready to leap. There were many hands extended my way. I reached up, and my arms were grabbed just as the balloon platform tore itself away. I was lifted onto the platform. I remember twenty pops like champagne corks in rapid succession as the rubber ball-and-socket connections were broken, and the eighty-one Krakatoans swiftly bounded off into the air.

We flew directly over the crater. Here, we were greeted by a roaring swift upward blast of hot air which catapulted us far up into the sky. When we were about a half mile up, we were comparatively still. There might have been a little wind, but it wasn't strong enough to blow us off this hot sulphurous airshaft.

We spent seventeen hours over the volcano, from five o'clock in the afternoon of the 26th until ten o'clock the following morning. At that time the shaft of hot air seemed to have lost its strength. We were lowered to an altitude of about one hundred feet above the mountain, or roughly fifteen hundred feet above sea level; and there a wind cleared us of that dreadful crater.

We flew until we were a mile over Java when, with stunning

suddenness, the Island of Krakatoa in seven rapid ear-splitting explosions blew straight into the air for as far as we could see. Our flying platform was rocked back and forth at thirty-degree angles by the concussions. Those of us who were near the balustrade hung on for life. A few of those who were in the middle of the platform were tossed about like flapjacks in a skillet. We were twenty-seven miles away from the Island when it happened, which was just about far enough for safety. Any closer and we would have been dumped right off the platform into the Sunda Strait. We couldn't see what was left of Krakatoa because it was wrapped in a thick, huge, tremendously tall black cloud of pumice, ashes, smoke, lava, dirt, with, I suppose, a few billion dollars worth of diamonds thrown in.

We were afraid that ashes, rocks, or even diamonds might fall on us and pierce our balloons, but all that actually happened of that nature was that we were soon enveloped by the thick, black dust cloud which was so dense that it was almost impos-

sible to see through, making it extremely difficult to keep the platform level. We traveled with this cloud for hours, not being able to see whether ground or sea was beneath us and fearing the horrible fate of crashing into a mountaintop in Java. We tied handkerchiefs around our faces so that we wouldn't breathe too much of the thick concentration of powdered ashes and pumice we were traveling with, and it seemed for a while that as long as the wind was with us, the powdered remains of Krakatoa would follow along and that we would be forever enveloped in this ghost of a dead island. The wind generated by the explosion was tremendous, and for the entire duration of this extraordinary journey, we were hurtling through space at a fabulous speed.

You can find out what happened to Professor Sherman and his friends if you read the final chapters in The Twenty-One Balloons.

Questions

1. How did Professor Sherman get to Krakatoa?
2. Why do you think the design of the balloon platform called for alternating large and small balloons?
3. Why did Mr. M. suggest to Professor Sherman that he go to the mines for more diamonds even though the volcano was beginning to explode?
4. Imagine that you had been put in charge of the emergency escape from Krakatoa. Think how you would organize the escape and what jobs you would assign to each person. Write up your plan as a set of "Emergency Evacuation Instructions" to be posted in different parts of the island.

Applying Reading Skills

Use complete sentences to write the answers to the questions below.

1. What does the diagram at the top of page 395 show?
2. If the balloon platform has 10 large balloons and 10 small balloons, how much hydrogen will be needed to fill all the balloons?
3. In the diagram of the hoses on page 396, which ends (right or left) are connected to the balloon? To the compressed hydrogen cylinders?
4. Use the diagram on page 391 to explain how heated air enters the balloon.
5. Refer again to the diagram on page 391. Would you expect the cooling vent to be bigger than the rip panel? Why or why not?

Fifteen Reflections on
VOLCANOES

I

Out of all the quiet mountains,
All the silent giants,
Only one speaks

II

A thousand gallant steeds,
Over a wooden bridge

III

An orchestra of slide whistles,
Tuning for an unknown symphony.

IV

A million black genies
Billowing in the wind

V

Oil and tomato soup
Bubbling in a black bowl.

VI

The blood of the earth, pours forth
From an open wound

VII

A lush tropical island . . .
Suddenly a hot black desert.

VIII

Coloring the sunset,
Like a child let loose with a paint box.

IX

A hundred mighty rivers,
Transformed into steam,
Are soon gone

X

And tell me, what is it
That you object so violently to?

XI

Ageless mountains
Sinking slowly into the sea,
Cry out, at the young upstart.

XII

The baby was throwing little stones,
And boulders

XIII

Tired of its old surroundings,
The fickle child, changes them every day.

XIV

When Mt. Vesuvius let down her hair
She smothered her loved ones,
In her fiery tresses.

XV

Oh mighty men . . . RUN!!!

Pamela Burnley, 9th grade

WRITING ACTIVITY

WRITE A REPORT

Prewrite

In "The Twenty-One Balloons" Professor Sherman is amazed at the flying platform, a most unusual invention for transportation. Suppose you could invent your own original form of transportation. What would you design? To be original it must not be a copy of any known form of transportation, although like the flying platform, it might use other forms of transportation such as balloons, bicycles, or automobiles in unique ways.

You are going to write a report on your form of transportation and include a diagram with labels. To prepare for writing, reread the lesson on diagrams on pages 390 and 391. Read the story again to find what kinds of facts Mr. F. told Professor Sherman about the flying platform.

Your report should present the important facts about your invention and explain why it would be a useful form of transportation. The sample outline below can serve as a guide as you plan your own outline. Add headings and subheadings as you choose. Then complete each subheading of the outline with the appropriate facts about your invention.

My Invention: The ___

I. General Information
   A. Shape (What will it look like?)
   B. Size (What are the exact measurements? How many people can ride on or in it?)
   C. Building materials (What is it made of?)

II. Power
    A. Form of Power (How does it move?)
    B. Speed (How fast can it travel?)
III. Uses
    A. Transportation (Why is it better than other forms?)
    B. Other Uses (What other ways can it be used?)

Write

1. Think about the paragraphs in your report. Each paragraph should have a main idea sentence at the beginning or end of the paragraph. The facts from the subheadings of your outline should be used as detail sentences.
2. You may want to write a paragraph for each heading in the outline, or combine Parts I and II for one paragraph and use Part III for a second paragraph.
3. Prepare your diagram and write the labels.
4. Use your Glossary or dictionary for spelling help.

Revise

Read your report and look at your diagram. Make sure the information in your report matches the information in the diagram. Does each paragraph have a main idea sentence? Did you write run-on sentences? Stringing too many facts together with *and* can make your information confusing and difficult to read.

1. Proofread for spelling and capitalization.
2. Check the end punctuation in your sentences.
3. Rewrite your report and prepare your diagram to share.

PREPARING FOR READING

Learning Vocabulary

1. A <u>dispatch</u> from Batavia, Java, to London in 1883 described the <u>havoc</u> in that part of the world caused by the eruption of Krakatoa.
2. Clouds of smoke from the volcano <u>obscured</u> the sun for hours.
3. An eyewitness reported that the eruption began on a Sunday and that a shower of ashes <u>commenced</u> to fall before daybreak on Monday.
4. He ran to escape the great tidal wave that <u>engulfed</u> everything along the shore.
5. Even so, a <u>torrent</u> of water overtook him and washed him inland.

dispatch	havoc	obscured
commenced	engulfed	torrent

Developing Background and Skills
Main Idea

You know that the **main idea** is the most important information in a paragraph. A well-written paragraph is made up of a main idea and details that support it. You also know that the main idea

(1) may be stated in a single sentence
(2) may be found in two or more sentences
(3) may not be stated directly at all

In case (2), you must combine information to state the main idea. In case (3), you must think about all the information given in the paragraph and state the main idea in your own words.

At times you may be asked to find the main idea and supporting details in a group of several paragraphs. You can go about finding the main idea and supporting details by using the same strategy you used for a single paragraph. Ask yourself what the most important information is, and then ask yourself what details support this idea.

In reading newspaper stories, you may have noticed that the headlines often state the main idea of a story. Read the two paragraphs below and think about how the main idea could be expressed in a headline.

KANTAN ISLAND, September 14.—The region around Laketa lay in ruins in the aftermath of yesterday's tidal wave. Scenes of destruction were everywhere. A foot of mud covered the entire area. Nothing is left of Laketa and the surrounding villages. The sea carried away everything.

At least 36 Europeans were among the victims, but the total number of human casualties is still not known. In addition, hundreds of farm animals—cattle, horses, pigs, and chickens—were destroyed.

Which of the following headlines expresses the main idea of the story?
a. DEATH TOLL STILL NOT KNOWN
b. DISASTER STRIKES ISLAND
c. TIDAL WAVE DESTROYS LIFE AND PROPERTY IN LAKETA

You would probably agree that **c** expresses the main idea of the two-paragraph story. What details support or explain this idea?

The following selection is a collection of accounts of a disaster that took place in Indonesia more than one hundred years ago. Some of the accounts are newspaper stories. Others are personal eyewitness reports. As you read the selection, look for the main ideas presented in each account. Find the details that support the main ideas.

KRAKATOA-
THE REAL STORY

"The Twenty-One Balloons" is a fictional account of the volcanic eruption of Krakatoa in 1883. To discover the real story of this dramatic event, read the newspaper and eyewitness accounts that follow.

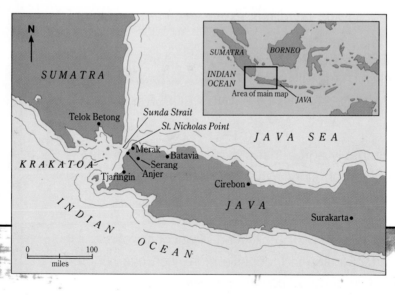

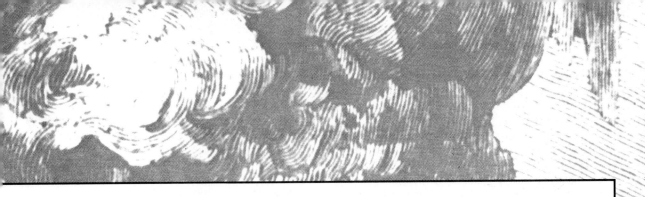

The New York Times

BATAVIA, Java, Aug. 27—Terrific detonations were heard yesterday evening from the volcanic island of Krakatoa. They were audible at Soerakrata, on the Island of Java. The ashes from the volcano fell as far as Cheribon and the flashes proceeding from it were visible in Batavia. Stones fell in a shower on Serang, which was in total darkness throughout the night. Batavia was nearly so, all the gaslights having been extinguished during the night. Communication with Anjer is stopped, and it is feared that there has been a calamity there. Several bridges between Anjer and Serang have been destroyed and a village has been washed away, the rivers having overflowed their banks.

BATAVIA, Java, August 28—The eruption of the volcano on the island of Krakatoa continues. North Bantam, in Java, is covered with ashes, mud, and stones. The crops are ruined and roads and bridges are damaged. The European quarter of Anjer and the Chinese camp at Merak have been swept away by the overflow of the rivers. The tidal-wave also swamped the lower quarters of Batavia.

The map (left) shows the area around Krakatoa. The modern spellings of cities and other places are used. In the newspaper and eyewitness accounts, the spellings are those used in the 1800s. For example, today the city in central Java is known as Surakarta. In 1883, this city was known as Soerakrata.

The New York Times

NEW YORK, THURSDAY, AUGUST 30, 1883

EVENTS BEYOND THE SEA.
TOWNS IN JAVA DESTROYED BY TIDAL WAVES.
GREAT DESTRUCTION OF LIFE AND PROPERTY IN THE STRAITS OF SUNDA—DISAPPEARANCE OF A MOUNTAIN.

LONDON, Aug. 29.—A dispatch from Batavia, Java, to Lloyds* says that the towns of Anjer, Tjiringine, and Telokbelong have been destroyed by tidal waves caused by the volcanic eruptions. It also says that all the light-houses in the Sunda Straits have disappeared, and that where the mountain of Kramatan formerly stood the sea now flows. The aspect of the Sunda Straits is much changed and navigation is dangerous.

---

*Lloyds: a London-based group that specializes in providing shipping news and many kinds of insurance.

NEW YORK, TUESDAY, OCTOBER 2, 1883

A VOLCANO'S FIRST EFFORT.
A VESSEL'S RECENT EXPERIENCE IN THE STRAITS OF SUNDA.

Capt. Weupper, of the German ship Herschel, which arrived from Manila yesterday, reports that on May 20, when in the Straits of Sunda, he witnessed one of the first of the great volcanic disturbances which are reported as having caused so great havoc in that portion of the world. At 11 o'clock on the morning of May 20 the Herschel was becalmed in the Straits of Sunda. About six miles distant from her was the island of Krakatoa, which is about two miles wide, and is a short distance from Java. Two peaks rise side by side on

Krakatoa. From the smaller of these was pouring a dense column of snow-white smoke which rolled upward in huge clouds. The vessel lay with her sails flapping idly while the sailors watched the unusual sight.

The outpouring smoke about 2 o'clock in the afternoon suddenly became black, and the sky darkened. A sulphurous smell began to steal over the atmosphere. Volumes of dark smoke spread over the sky until it wore the appearance of night, but still no breath of air touched the sails of the becalmed ship. Ashes dropped from the clouds and the decks were soon covered with this volcanic snow. The fall of ashes soon became as dense as a snow-storm. Some of the sailors were greatly alarmed, although they were assured that there was no danger. At 6 o'clock, while the black volcanic clouds still obscured the sun, a light breeze sprang up and the ship got under steerage way. She headed toward the Cape of Good Hope, and the dark outlines of the volcanic peaks on Krakatoa grew gradually fainter until they were lost in the still deeper blackness of the night. Ashes to the depth of three inches lay on the decks of the Herschel, and the water appeared to be covered with the same substance. Ashes fell steadily for over 48 hours after Krakatoa was last seen.

THIS EYEWITNESS REPORT IS TAKEN FROM THE LOGBOOK OF THE FIRST OFFICER ON THE AMERICAN SHIP *W. H. BESSE.*

Sunday, August 26, 1883.—The day commenced with strong breezes and thick cloudy weather; atmosphere very close and smoky. At 5 P.M. heard a quick succession of heavy reports sounding like the broadside of a man-of-war* only far louder and heavier; heard these reports at intervals throughout the night. The sky was intensely dark, the wind having a dull moaning; through the rigging also noticed a light fall of ashes. The sun when it rose next morning (*Monday, August 27*) had the appearance of a ball of fire, the air so smoky, could see but a short distance. Was in hopes to get out clear of the straits before night. At 10 A.M. were within 6 miles of St. Nicholas Point, when we heard some terrific reports; also observed a heavy black bank rising up from the direction of Krakatoa Island. By the time the squall struck us, it was darker than any night I ever saw; this was midnight at noon. A heavy shower of ashes came with the squall, the air being so thick it was difficult to breathe. The terrible noises from the volcano, the sky filled with forked lightning, the howling of the wind through the rigging formed one of the wildest and most awful scenes imaginable. At 4 P.M. wind moderating, the explosions had nearly ceased, the shower of ashes was not so heavy. The ship was covered with tons of fine ashes resembling pumice stone. It stuck to the sails, rigging and masts. . . . It was weeks before it was all removed, some of it still remaining on the wire backstays.

All day—*Tuesday, August 28*—crew were employed in shovelling the ashes off the decks and clearing the cables and heaving up one anchor.

———
*Reports sounding like the broadside of a man-of-war:** shots from all the guns on the side of a war ship

AN ELDERLY DUTCH PILOT, EMPLOYED IN GUIDING SHIPS THROUGH THE STRAITS, GAVE THIS ACCOUNT OF HIS EXPERIENCE.

I have lived in Anjer all my life, and little thought the old town would have been destroyed in the way it has. I am getting on in years, and quite expected to have laid my bones in the little cemetery near the shore. But not even that has escaped, and some of the bodies have actually been washed out of the graves and carried out to sea. The whole town has been swept away, and I have lost everything except my life. The wonder is that I escaped at all. I can never be too thankful for such a miraculous escape as I had.

The eruption began on the Sunday afternoon. We did not take much notice at first, until the reports grew very loud. Then we noticed that Krakatoa was completely enveloped in smoke. Afterwards came on the thick darkness, so black and intense that I could not see my hand before my eyes. Towards night everything became worse. The reports became deafening, and a red fiery glare was visible in the sky above the burning mountain. Although Krakatoa was twenty-five miles away, the concussion and vibration from the constantly re-

A painting of the W.H. Besse.

peated shocks was most terrifying. Many of the houses shook so much that we feared every minute would bring them down. There was little sleep for any of us that dreadful night. Before daybreak on Monday, on going out of doors, I found the shower of ashes had commenced. This gradually increased in force until at length large pieces of pumice-stone kept falling around. About 6 A.M. I was walking along the beach. There was no sign of the sun, as usual, and the sky had a dull, depressing look. Some of the darkness of the previous day had cleared off, but it was not very light even then. Looking out to the sea I noticed a dark, black object through the gloom.

At first sight it seemed like a low range of hills rising out of the water, but I knew there was nothing of the kind in that part of the Sunda Strait. A second glance—and a very hurried one it was—convinced me that it was a lofty ridge of water many feet high, and worse still, that it would soon break upon the coast near the town. I turned and ran for my life. My run-

ning days have long gone by, but you may be sure that I did my best. In a few minutes I heard the water with a loud roar break upon the shore. Everything was engulfed. Another glance showed the houses being swept away and the trees thrown down on every side. Breathless and exhausted, I still pressed on. As I heard the rushing waters behind me, I knew that it was a race for life. Struggling on, a few yards more brought me to some rising ground, and here the torrent of water overtook me. I gave up all for lost, as I saw with dismay how high the wave still was. I was soon taken off my feet and borne inland by the force of the resistless mass. I remember nothing more until a violent blow aroused me. Some hard firm substance seemed within my reach, and clutching it I found I had gained a place of safety. The waters swept past, and I found myself clinging to a coconut palm tree. Most of the trees near the town were uprooted and thrown down for miles, but this one fortunately had escaped and myself with it.

Questions

1. What disaster do the accounts in the selection "Krakatoa—The Real Story" describe?
2. If the Krakatoa disaster had occurred in 1983 rather than in 1883, do you think it would have resulted in the same great loss of life? Explain your answer.
3. By reading the accounts, what conclusions can you come to about how the tidal waves were related to the volcanic eruptions?
4. Make your own "Krakatoa Chronology." List all the dates mentioned in the selection in chronological order and write a phrase about the events that took place.

Applying Reading Skills

Follow the directions given below.

1. Write a headline that expresses the main idea of the *New York Times* story for August 28, 1883.
2. In your own words, state the main idea of the *New York Times* story for October 2, 1883.
3. State the main idea of the second paragraph beginning on page 415 and continuing on page 416. List three details that support the main idea.
4. Write a sentence stating the main idea of the entire selection "Krakatoa—The Real Story." Try to have your main idea sentence answer the questions *what*, *when*, *why*, and *where*.

PREPARING FOR READING

Learning Vocabulary

1. Just as Jupiter <u>revolves</u> around the sun, the moons Callisto (kə lis′ tō), Ganymede (gan′ ə mēd′), Europa (ū rō′ pə), and Io (ī′ ō) revolve around the planet Jupiter.
2. Scientists have learned a great deal about Jupiter from the spacecraft that <u>probed</u> the planet and sent back photographs.
3. Beneath its ocean of liquid hydrogen, Jupiter may have a solid <u>core</u> of rock and iron.
4. The dark patches on Callisto's surface may be dirt left behind as ice turned to <u>vapor</u> and drifted away.
5. Europa may be heated by <u>friction</u> as its surface heaves up and down.
6. <u>Molten</u> sulfur erupts from the volcanoes of Io into space, where it cools into particles that fall like snow.
7. Grooves and ridges of Ganymede may mark deep <u>fractures</u> along which plates of ice moved.

revolves	probed	core	vapor
friction	molten	fractures	

Developing Background and Skills
Cause and Effect

To understand what you read, you need to think about how things are connected. You know that one way in which events, actions, and situations are connected is a cause-and-effect relationship. A **cause** is the reason something happens. An **effect** is the result, or the thing that happens.

Writers sometimes use words such as *because, so that, in order to,* and *as a result* to signal a cause-and-effect relationship.

Read the sentence below. The part of the sentence that states the cause is underlined once. The part that states the effect is underlined twice.

Jupiter's surface cannot be seen from the earth because layers of dense clouds surround the planet.

Writers, as you know, do not always use signal words. Sometimes they do not even write about a related cause and effect in one sentence. You can still figure out the connection. If you ask, "What happened?" the answer will tell you the effect. The answer to the question "Why did it happen?" tells you the cause. Read the sentences below. The cause is underlined once. The effect is underlined twice.

Layers of dense clouds surround Jupiter. The surface of this planet cannot be seen from the earth.

Sometimes the cause may be separated from the effect by one or more sentences. Read the example below. Again, the cause is underlined once, and the effect is underlined twice.

Layers of dense clouds surround the planet Jupiter. The clouds appear like a churning sea of pink, tan, yellow, blue-green, and gray. Many of them stretch around the planet in bands. Jupiter's surface cannot be seen from the earth.

The following selection is a science article about the planet Jupiter. As you read, think about how the events, actions, and situations are connected. See if you can figure out the cause-and-effect relationships that exist.

*A composite photograph showing **Jupiter** (top), **Io** (far left), **Europa** (closest to Jupiter), **Ganymede**, and **Calisto** (foreground).*

JUPITER
FIRE AND ICE IN SPACE

PATRICIA LAUBER

Agiant among giants, Jupiter is truly enormous. Eleven Earths could be lined up along its diameter. More than a thousand Earths would fit inside it. Jupiter contains twice as much material as all the other planets together. It is so big and bright in our sky that it can easily be seen without a telescope. Through even a small telescope, it appears as big as the moon does to the unaided eye.

We see only the top of Jupiter's atmosphere. It is a churning sea of colored clouds—pink, tan, yellow, blue-green, gray. Many stretch around the planet in bands. The top of the atmosphere is also marked by plumes, streaks, spots, and patches that range in color from white to red to reddish brown.

Beneath its cloud deck, Jupiter is a hot planet. Scientists think the heat is left over from the time when Jupiter formed. The heat warms gases, which rise in the atmosphere. Winds, caused by the planet's rapid spin, stretch the rising gases into long bands of high pressure. But the top of the atmosphere is a chilly 200 degrees Fahrenheit below zero. The warm gases cool and flow into the low-pressure bands. They descend through the atmosphere, are heated, and rise again.

A PLANET OF MYSTERY

The colors remain mysterious. No one yet knows what they are, where they come from, or why they don't mix together. Jupiter is made mostly of hydrogen and helium, which are colorless gases, with traces of other gases that are also colorless. Some scientists think the colors must come from chemicals of some kind. Perhaps the chemicals change color when they are acted on by lightning in Jupiter's atmosphere. Perhaps they change when acted on by sunlight, somewhat in the way a person's skin tans when acted on by sunlight.

Another mystery of Jupiter's atmosphere is the Great Red Spot. It was first seen in 1655, but no one knows when it first appeared. It is a big, reddish, football-shaped, swirling mass of gas that has changed color and size as astronomers have watched it over the years. The spot varies from brick red to grayish red. Sometimes it is so big you could line up three Earths across it. At other times it shrinks by a third. The Great Red Spot revolves around Jupiter along with other cloud features, but it travels more slowly. It may be some sort of storm.

Astronomers have long known that Jupiter has a magnetic field because the planet gives off continuous radio static. There are also great bursts of radio noise caused by lightning. Jupiter's magnetic field traps vast numbers of charged particles from the sun, creating a sea of deadly radiation.

Scientists feel sure that Jupiter has no solid surface beneath its clouds. It has an atmosphere that is mostly hydrogen gas. Deeper down, where the pressure of the atmosphere is very great, the molecules of gas are pushed together, or compressed. They are so compressed that they form a liquid. This layer of liquid hydrogen is 43,000 miles (68,800 km) deep.

The photograph of Jupiter's red spot was taken by Voyager 2 on July 3, 1979. The spacecraft was 3.72 million miles (6 million km) above Jupiter's surface.

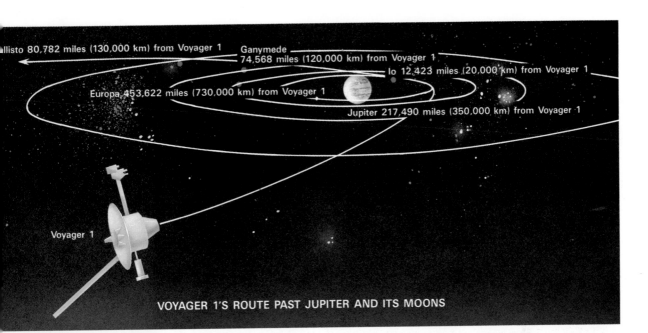

llisto 80,782 miles (130,000 km) from Voyager 1

Ganymede
74,568 miles (120,000 km) from Voyager 1

Io 12,423 miles (20,000 km) from Voyager 1

Europa 453,622 miles (730,000 km) from Voyager 1

Jupiter 217,490 miles (350,000 km) from Voyager 1

Voyager 1

VOYAGER 1'S ROUTE PAST JUPITER AND ITS MOONS

Beneath that layer, pressures are believed to be 3 million times the air pressure on Earth. Here the hydrogen may be so compressed that it acts like a liquid metal. There is a great, dark ocean of it, 29,000 miles (46,400 km) deep. Here Jupiter's magnetic field is probably produced by electric currents.

Beneath the ocean of metallic hydrogen, there may be a solid core of rock and iron. If so, it is trapped in pressures we could not even imagine at temperatures higher than those on the sun's surface.

Jupiter has at least 15 moons. The eight small outer moons are probably asteroids that mighty Jupiter captured. Among the inner moons are four big ones: Callisto (kə lis′ tō), Ganymede, (gan′ ə mēd′), Europa (ū rō′ pə), and Io (ī′ ō). Together they are called the Galilean moons, in honor of the great Italian astronomer, Galileo, who discovered them in 1610. *Voyagers 1* and *2*[2] gave us our first good look at these moons.

---

1. **Voyagers 1 and 2**: two unmanned spacecraft that probed and sent back photographs of Jupiter and its moons in 1979.

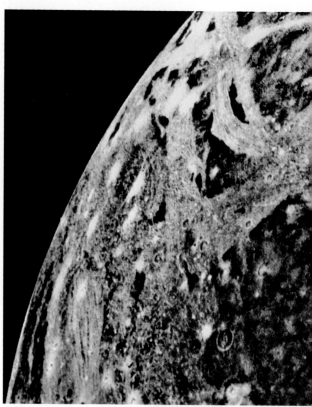

CALLISTO

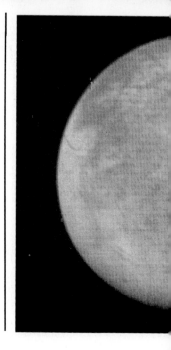

allisto is the outermost of the Galilean moons. It is nearly twice the size of Earth's moon. Its dark surface is ice perhaps mixed with dust. Under its deep frozen ocean is a rocky core. Callisto's battered face shows that the surface is very old. The big moon probably formed when the planets did and was bombarded by rocks and other leftover matter.

There are signs of large meteorites that slammed into Callisto and briefly melted the icy crust. The dark surface suggests that dirt has been left behind as ice turned to vapor and drifted away. Recent craters are marked by bright rays, but Callisto looks much as it did 4 billion years ago.

Calisto (far left), Ganymede (left), Europa (below).

GANYMEDE

The next moon is Ganymede, Jupiter's biggest moon. At first glance, Ganymede looks very much like our moon. It is peppered with craters and has large, dark patches. But the dark areas are not plains, as they are on our moon. They are cratered crust, broken by bands of strange grooves and ridges that look as if they had been made by a giant rake. The grooves are hundreds of miles long, a few miles wide, and about a hundred yards deep. The ridges are about 3,000 feet (914 m) high. Nothing like the grooves and ridges has been seen anywhere else in the solar system.

Some bands of grooves run across big craters. Some big craters lie on top of grooves. So scientists think the grooves and craters were formed in the same period of Ganymede's history. The craters must be very old because few young craters are that big. Therefore, the grooves must be very old.

What are the grooves? No one knows. Ganymede has an icy crust that may float on a layer of slush. At its center is a solid core of rock. Perhaps young Ganymede heated up inside, expanded, and tore its crust apart. Perhaps the grooves and ridges mark fractures where plates of ice moved and jostled one another. Perhaps they are signs of mountain building. For now, they remain a mystery.

EUROPA

Europa looks like a billard ball with cracks. Its smooth surface is ice, perhaps 60 miles (96 km) thick. There are no mountains, no ancient, giant craters. There are only the cracks or streaks, a dark network of lines that run on for hundreds of miles.

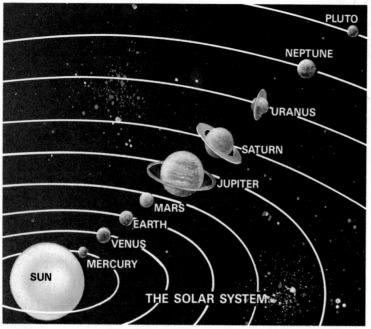

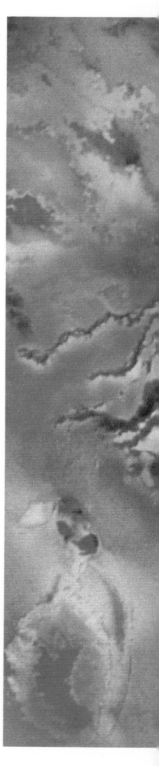

The surface of *Io* from a distance of 77,100 miles (124,053 km).

PLUTO

NEPTUNE

URANUS

SATURN

JUPITER

MARS

EARTH

VENUS

MERCURY

SUN

THE SOLAR SYSTEM

The smoothness suggests that the surface is young. Like its neighbors, Europa must have been bombarded by huge chunks of rock long ago. But the scars do not show. Somehow the surface has been renewed. How this happened is not understood, but one idea is that Europa was heated inside. It expanded and cracked its crust of ice. Hot springs of water erupted onto the surface and froze. Over millions or billions of years, a thick surface of ice built up, and the craters disappeared under it. If this idea is right, Europa may still be heated inside. Perhaps it has geysers that we have not seen.

Europa might be heated by radioactivity in its rocky core. Or it might be heated by friction. Scientists think that Jupiter's strong gravity raises land tides in Europa, just as our moon raises tides in our oceans. Europa's surface heaves up and down. The pumping action stretches and compresses the inside of the moon and heats up the inner materials. That, scientists are sure, is what happens on Europa's neighbor Io, the innermost of the big moons.

Io

When the first pictures of Io were received, watching scientists were astounded. "It looks like a pizza!" one of them said. Io was mostly orange-red with large white patches and small dark spots.

Before the arrival of *Voyager 1*, scientists had known that Io was red, redder even than Mars. They did not expect it to be red, orange, yellow, white, and black. They were also surprised not to see any craters. What could be erasing them? It couldn't be the atmosphere because Io's atmosphere escaped into space long ago. It couldn't be running water because Io's surface temperature is too cold. The answer turned out to be the biggest surprise of all: volcanoes. In the whole solar system, no other moon is known to have active volcanoes.

There are at least nine active volcanoes on Io—and hundreds of extinct ones. Their outpourings are more than enough to have buried Io's craters. Io is a moon on which the landscape is always being renewed.

The colors of Io show that sulfur is erupting out of the volcanoes. Once molten, sulfur changes its color at different temperatures. At low temperatures it is yellowish-white. As temperatures rise, it changes from white to yellow to orange to red to black. If molten sulfur is cooled quickly, it keeps its color. On Io, plumes of molten sulfur erupt 60 or 70 miles (104 km) into space where they cool. The particles of cool sulfur fall like snow onto Io's surface.

When the volcanoes erupt, most of the material colors Io and lays down a new surface. Some of it does other things. For example, Jupiter has a tiny inner moon named Amalthea (am əl thē′ ə). Amalthea is potato-shaped and deep red. The color probably comes from sulfur that erupted out of Io's volcanoes, cooled, and snowed onto Amalthea.

Jupiter's ring illuminated by sunlight coming from behind.

THE RING

Another big surprise from *Voyager 1* was the discovery that Jupiter has a ring. Earth-based astronomers have never seen it. It did not appear in the photographs from the *Pioneer*[2] flybys. But both *Voyager 1* and *Voyager 2* photographed it.

The ring is faint. The outer edge is some 34,000 miles (54,400 km) out from the cloud tops of Jupiter. The inner edge seems to reach all the way down to the clouds. About 18 miles (28.8 km) thick, the ring is made of fine particles that glimmer like dust specks in a beam of light. You could say that the particles are millions of tiny moons that orbit Jupiter.

The ring was not only a surprise but also a mystery that raised many questions. Where do the particles come from? Why don't they fall into Jupiter? Or, if they do fall into Jupiter, what is the source of new particles that replace old ones? The best guess is that the particles come from material thrown out by Io's volcanoes.

---

2. **Pioneer**: an unmanned spacecraft that flew by and probed Jupiter in 1973.

Questions

1. Write five facts about Jupiter.
2. Why are Callisto, Ganymede, Europa, and Io called the Galilean moons?
3. What modern inventions have helped us learn more about Jupiter? Explain your answers.
4. On the basis of the information in "Jupiter—Fire and Ice in Space," draw and label a diagram of the planet, its moons, and its other features.

Applying Reading Skills

Copy and complete the chart below. Use the information in "Jupiter—Fire and Ice in Space."

CAUSE	EFFECT
	Jupiter can easily be seen without a telescope.
The top of Jupiter's atmosphere is −200° F.	
	Astronomers know that Jupiter has a magnetic field.
Scientists did not expect Io to be red, orange, yellow, white, and black.	
	There are no craters visible on Io's surface.

A JOURNEY TO THE CENTER OF THE EARTH

Jules Verne

A Journey to the Center of the Earth *was published in 1864. Jules Verne got the idea for the story when he met a scientist who had spent a week exploring Stromboli, a volcanic island off the coast of Italy. This scientist had descended into the crater of an inactive volcano on the island. In Verne's book, three people descend into a crater in Iceland: Professor Hardwigg; his nephew and story narrator, Harry; and Hans, an Icelandic guide. Their goal is to reach the very center of the earth. After many adventures which take them farther and farther below the earth's surface, they discover an underground sea. After days of sailing across it on a raft, they come to a wall of stone. Convinced that their course lies beyond the rock, Harry sets up a gunpowder charge to blast a passage. When the gunpowder explodes, the raft and its three passengers are carried away on a torrent of water. It doesn't take the travelers long to realize that they are inside a shaft, a shaft much like those that make up the interior of volcanoes.*

"It is just as I thought," said my uncle, after a moment or two. "We are in a narrow well about four fathoms[1] square. The waters of the great inland sea, having reached the bottom of the gulf, are now forcing themselves up the mighty shaft. As a natural consequence, we are being cast up on the summit of the waters."

"That I can see," was my reply. "But where will this shaft end, and to what fall are we likely to be exposed?"

"Of that I am as ignorant as yourself. All I know is that we should be prepared for the worst. We are going up at a fearfully rapid rate. As far as I can judge, we are ascending at the rate of two fathoms a second, or a hundred and twenty fathoms a minute. At this rate, our fate will soon be a matter of certainty."

"No doubt of it," was my reply. "The great concern I have now, however, is to know whether this shaft has any issue.[2] It may end in a granite roof—in which case we shall be suffocated by compressed air, or dashed to atoms against the top. I fancy, already, that the air is beginning to be close and condensed. I have a difficulty in breathing."

After thinking of this and other matters, I once more looked around me. We were still ascending with fearful rapidity. The heat began to increase in a most threatening and exceptional manner. I cannot tell exactly, but I think it must have reached 122 degrees of Fahrenheit.

---

1. **fathom**: unit of measure equal to six feet.
2. **issue**: opening or outlet.

As we progressed, the temperature increased in the most extraordinary degree, and I began to feel as if I were bathed in a hot and burning atmosphere. Never before had I felt anything like it. I could only compare it to the hot vapor from an iron foundry, when the liquid iron runs over. By degrees, and one after the other, Hans, my uncle, and myself had taken off our coats. They were unbearable. Even the slightest garment was not only uncomfortable, but the cause of extreme suffering.

"Are we ascending to a living fire?" I cried; when, to my horror and astonishment, the heat became greater than before.

"No, no," said my uncle, "It is simply impossible, quite impossible."

"And yet," said I, touching the side of the shaft with my naked hand, "this wall is literally burning."

At this moment, feeling as I did that the sides of the extraordinary wall were red hot, I plunged my hands into the water to cool them. I drew them back with a cry of despair.

"The water is boiling!" I cried.

My uncle, the Professor, made no reply other than a gesture of rage and despair.

Something very like the truth had probably struck his imagination.

But I could take no share in either what was going on, or in his speculations. An invincible dread had taken possession of my brain and soul. I could only look forward to an immediate catastrophe, such a catastrophe as not even the most vivid imagination could have thought of. An idea, at first vague and uncertain, was gradually being changed into certainty.

I determined as a last resource to examine the compass. The compass had gone mad! Yes, wholly stark staring mad. The needle jumped from pole to pole with sudden and surprising jerks, ran round, or as it is said, boxed the compass.

"Uncle, uncle!" I cried, "We are wholly, irretrievably lost!"

"What, then, my young friend, is your new cause of terror and alarm?" he said, in his calmest manner. "What fear you now?"

"What do I fear now!" I cried, in fierce and angry tones. "Do you not see that the walls of the shaft are in motion? Do you not see that the solid granite masses are cracking? Do you not feel the terrible, torrid heat? Do you not observe the awful boiling water on which we float? Do you not remark this mad needle? Every sign and portent of an awful earthquake?"

My uncle coolly shook his head.

"An earthquake," he replied, in the most calm and provoking tone.

"Yes."

"My nephew, I tell you that you are utterly mistaken," he continued.

"Do you not, can you not, recognize all the well-known symptoms—"

"Of an earthquake? By no means. I am expecting something far more important."

"My brain is strained beyond endurance—what, what do you mean?" I cried.

"An eruption, Harry."

"An eruption," I gasped. "We are, then, in the volcanic shaft of a crater in full action and vigor."

"I have every reason to think so," said the Professor in a smiling tone, "and I beg to tell you that it is the most fortunate thing that could happen to us."

The most fortunate thing! Had my uncle really and truly gone mad? What did he mean by these awful words? What did he mean by this terrible calm, this solemn smile?

"What!" cried I, in the height of my exasperation. "We are on the way to an eruption, are we? Fatality has cast us into a well of burning and boiling lava, of rocks on fire, of boiling water, in a word, filled with every kind of eruptive matter. We are about to be expelled, thrown up, vomited, spit out of the interior of the earth in a wild whirlwind of flame, and you say—the most fortunate thing which could happen to us."

"Yes," replied the Professor, looking at me calmly from under his spectacles. "It is the only chance which remains to us of ever escaping from the interior of the earth."

It is quite impossible that I can put on paper the thousand strange, wild thoughts which followed this extraordinary announcement.

But my uncle was right, quite right, and never had he appeared to me so audacious and so convinced as when he looked me calmly in the face and spoke of the chances of an eruption—of our being cast upon mother earth once more through the gaping crater of a volcano!

Nevertheless, while we were speaking we were still ascending; we passed the whole night going up. The fearful noise redoubled; I was ready to suffocate. I seriously believed that my last hour was approaching. In such circumstances you do not choose your own thoughts. They overcome you.

It was quite evident that we were being cast upwards by eruptive matter; under the raft there was a mass of boiling water, and under this was a heaving mass of lava.

I often think now of my folly: as if I should ever have expected to escape!

Towards morning, the ascending motion became greater and greater. But though we were approaching the light of day, to what fearful dangers were we about to be exposed?

Instant death appeared the only fate which we could expect or contemplate.

Soon, a dim light penetrated the vertical gallery, which became wider and wider. I could make out to the right and left long dark corridors like immense tunnels from which awful and horrid vapors poured out. Tongues of fire, sparkling and crackling, appeared about to lick us up.

The hour had come!

"Look, uncle, look!" I cried.

"Well, what you see are the great sulphurous flames. Nothing more common in connection with an eruption."

"But if they lap us round!" I angrily replied.

"They will not lap us round," was his quiet and serene answer.

"But it will be all the same in the end if they stifle us," I cried.

"We shall not be stifled. The gallery is rapidly becoming wider and wider, and if it be necessary, we will presently leave the raft and take refuge in some fissure in the rock."

"But the water, the water, which is continually ascending?" I despairingly replied.

"There is no longer any water, Harry," he answered, "but a kind of lava paste, which is heaving us up, in company with itself, to the mouth of the crater."

In truth, the liquid column of water had wholly disappeared to give place to dense masses of boiling eruptive matter. The temperature was becoming utterly insupportable, and a thermometer exposed to this atmosphere would have marked between 189 and 190 degrees Fahrenheit. Perspiration rushed from every pore. But for the extraordinary rapidity of our ascent we should have been stifled.

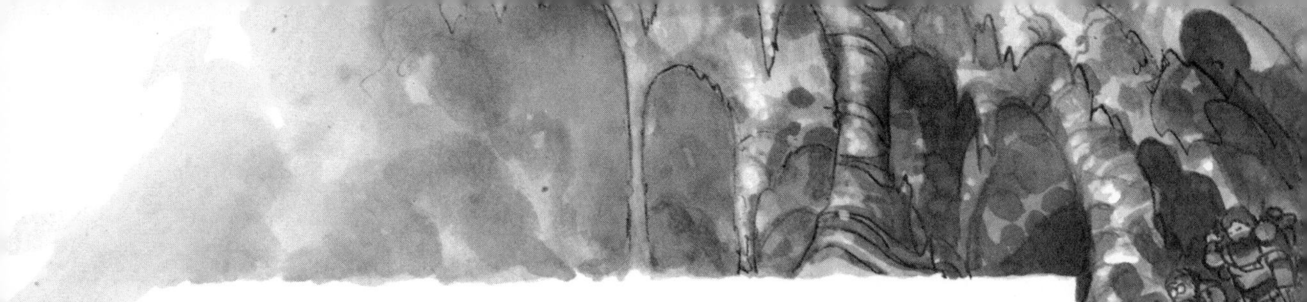

Towards eight o'clock in the morning a new incident startled us. The ascensional movement suddenly ceased. The raft became still and motionless.

"What is the matter now?" I said, very much startled by this change.

"A simple halt," replied my uncle.

"Is the eruption about to fail?" I asked.

"I hope not."

"I tell you, uncle, that the eruption has stopped."

"Ah," said my uncle, "you are wrong. Do not be in the least alarmed; this sudden moment of calm will not last long, be assured. It has already endured five minutes, and before we are many minutes older we shall be continuing our journey to the mouth of the crater."

All the time he was speaking the Professor continued to consult his chronometer.[3] Soon the raft resumed its motion, in a very rapid and disorderly way, which lasted two minutes or thereabout; and then again it stopped as suddenly as before.

"Good," said my uncle, observing the hour. "In ten minutes we shall start again."

"In ten minutes?"

"Yes—precisely. We have to do with a volcano, the eruption of which is intermittent. We are compelled to breathe just as it does."

3. **chronometer** (krə nom′ ə tər): clock or timepiece.

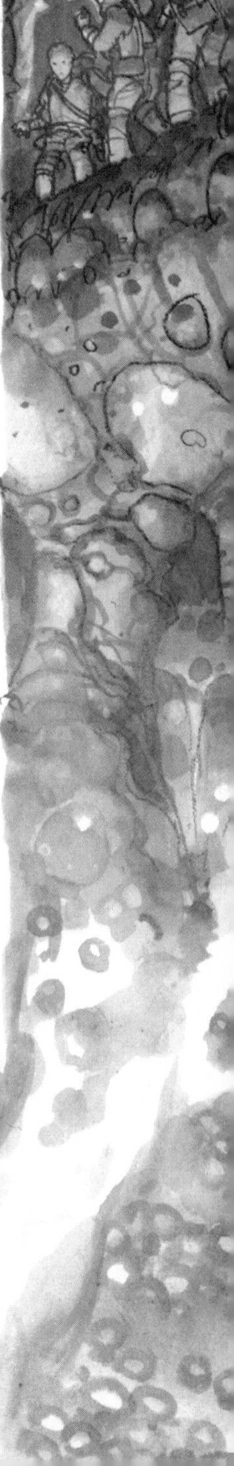

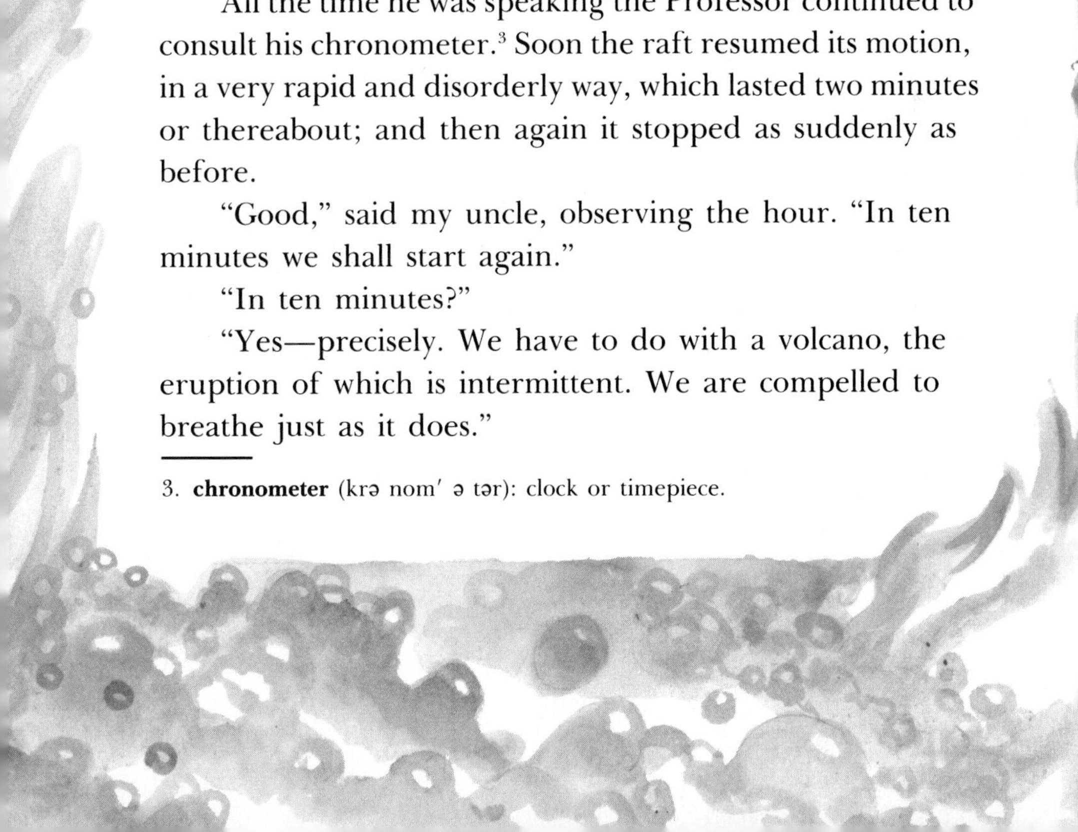

Nothing could be more true. At the exact minute he had indicated, we were again launched on high with extreme rapidity.

It is impossible for me to say how many times this was repeated. All that I can remember is, that on every ascensional motion, we were hoisted up with ever-increasing velocity. During the sudden halts we were nearly stifled; during the moments of projection the hot air took away our breath.

I thought for a moment of the vast snowy plains of the arctic regions, and I was impatient to roll myself on the icy carpet of the north pole.

By degrees, my head, utterly overcome by a series of violent emotions, began to give way to hallucination. I was delirious. Had it not been for the powerful arms of Hans the guide, I should have broken my head against the granite masses of the shaft.

I have, in consequence, kept no account of what followed for many hours. I have a vague and confused remembrance of the shaking of the huge granitic mass and of the raft going round like a spinning-top. It floated on the stream of hot lava, amidst a falling cloud of cinders. The huge flames roaring, wrapped us around.

A storm of wind which appeared to be cast forth from an immense ventilator roused up the interior fires of the earth. It was a hot incandescent[4] blast.

---

4. **incandescent** (in′ kən des′ ənt): glowing with heat.

At last I saw the figure of Hans as if enveloped in the huge halo of burning blaze, and no other sense remained to me but that sinister dread which the condemned victim may be supposed to feel when led to the mouth of a cannon, at the supreme moment when the shot is fired and his limbs are dispersed into empty space.

When I opened my eyes I felt the hand of the guide clutching me firmly by the belt. With his other hand he supported my uncle. I was not grievously wounded, but bruised all over in the most remarkable manner.

After a moment I looked around, and found that I was lying down on the slope of a mountain not two yards from a yawning gulf into which I should have fallen had I made the slightest false step. Hans had saved me from death while I rolled insensible on the flanks of the crater.

"Where are we?" dreamily asked my uncle, who literally appeared to be disgusted at having returned to earth.

"In Iceland?" said I.

"*Nej*," said Hans.

"Hans is wrong," said I, rising.

After all the innumerable surprises of this journey, a yet more singular one was reserved to us. I expected to see a cone covered by snow, by extensive and wide-spread glaciers in the midst of the extreme northern regions. But contrary to all our expectations, I, my uncle, and the Icelander, were cast upon the slope of a mountain calcined[5] by the burning rays of a sun which was literally baking us with its fires.

I could not believe my eyes, but the actual heat which affected my body allowed me no chance of doubting. When our eyes were accustomed to the light we had lost sight of for so long, the Professor spoke.

"Hem!" he said, in a hesitating kind of way. "It really does not look like Iceland. Look, look, my boy!"

Right above our heads, at a great height, opened the crater of a volcano from which escaped, from one quarter of an hour to the other, with a very loud explosion, a lofty jet of flame mingled with stone, cinders, and lava. I could feel the convulsions of nature in the mountain, which breathed like a huge whale, throwing up from time to time fire and air through its enormous vents.

Below, and floating along a slope of considerable angularity, the stream of eruptive matter spread away to a depth which did not give the volcano a height of three hundred fathoms.

Its base disappeared in a perfect forest of green trees, among which I perceived olives, fig-trees, and vines loaded with rich grapes.

Certainly this was not the ordinary aspect of the arctic regions. About that there could not be the slightest doubt.

"Where can we be?" I asked, speaking in a low and solemn voice.

Hans shut his eyes with an air of indifference, and my uncle looked on without clearly understanding.

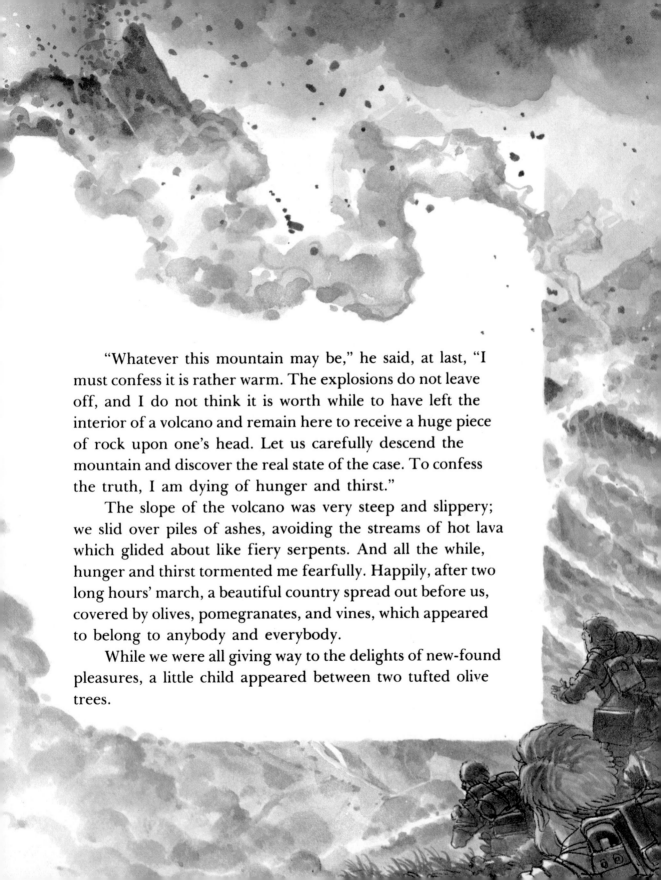

"Whatever this mountain may be," he said, at last, "I must confess it is rather warm. The explosions do not leave off, and I do not think it is worth while to have left the interior of a volcano and remain here to receive a huge piece of rock upon one's head. Let us carefully descend the mountain and discover the real state of the case. To confess the truth, I am dying of hunger and thirst."

The slope of the volcano was very steep and slippery; we slid over piles of ashes, avoiding the streams of hot lava which glided about like fiery serpents. And all the while, hunger and thirst tormented me fearfully. Happily, after two long hours' march, a beautiful country spread out before us, covered by olives, pomegranates, and vines, which appeared to belong to anybody and everybody.

While we were all giving way to the delights of new-found pleasures, a little child appeared between two tufted olive trees.

"Ah," cried I, "an inhabitant of this happy country."

My uncle tried to look as gentle as possible, and then spoke in German.

"What is the name of this mountain, my friend?"

The child made no reply.

"Good," said my uncle, with a very positive air of conviction, "we are not in Germany."

He then made the same demand in English, of which language he was an excellent scholar.

The child shook its head and made no reply. I began to be considerably puzzled.

"I must perforce try him in Italian," said my uncle, with a shrug.

"*Dove noi siamo?*"

"Yes, tell me where we are?" I added, impatiently and eagerly.

Again the boy remained silent.

"My fine fellow, do you or do you not mean to speak?" cried my uncle, who began to get angry. He shook him, and spoke another dialect of the Italian language.

"*Come si noma questa isola?*"—what is the name of this island?

"Stromboli," cried the little shepherd, dashing away from Hans and disappearing in the olive groves.

"Stromboli! Stromboli!" I repeated to myself.

My uncle played a regular accompaniment to my gestures and words. We were singing together like an ancient chorus.

Ah—what a journey—what a marvelous and extraordinary journey! Here we had entered the earth by one volcano, and we had come out by another. And this other was situated more than twelve hundred leagues from that dreary country of Iceland. The wondrous chances of this expedition had transported us to the most harmonious and beautiful of earthly lands. We had abandoned the region of eternal snows for that of infinite verdure,[6] and had left over our heads the gray fog of the icy regions to come back to the azure sky of Sicily!

---

6. **verdure** (vër′ jər): fresh, green color of growing plants.

Glossary

This glossary can help you to pronounce and find out the meanings of words in this book that you may not know.

The words are listed in alphabetical order. Guide words at the top of each page tell you the first and last words on the page.

Each word is divided into syllables. The way to pronounce each word is given next. You can understand the pronunciation respelling by using the key below. A shorter key appears at the bottom of every other page.

When a word has more than one syllable, a dark accent mark (') shows which syllable is stressed. In some words, a light accent mark (') shows which syllable has a less heavy stress.

Information about the history, or etymology, of selected words is presented in brackets following the definition.

The following abbreviations are used in this glossary:

n. noun   *v.* verb   *adj.* adjective   *adv.* adverb   *prep.* preposition   *pl.* plural

Glossary entries were adapted from the *Macmillan School Dictionary* and the *Macmillan Dictionary.*

PRONUNCIATION KEY
Vowel Sounds

/a/	bat	/ō/	rope, soap, so, snow
/ā/	cake, rain, day	/ô/	saw, song, auto
/ä/	father	/oi/	coin, boy
/är/	car	/ôr/	fork, ore, oar
/ār/	dare, hair	/ou/	out, cow
/e/	hen, bread	/u/	sun, son, touch
/ē/	me, meat, baby, believe	/ù/	book, pull, could
/èr/	term, first, worm, turn	/ü/	moon
/i/	bib	/ū/	cute, few, music
/ī/	kite, fly, pie, light	/ə/	about, taken, pencil,
/ir/	clear, cheer, here		apron, helpful
/o/	top, watch	/ər/	letter, dollar, doctor

Consonant Sounds

/b/	bear	/s/	city, seal	/y/	yo-yo
/d/	dog	/t/	tiger	/z/	zoo, eggs
/f/	fish, phone	/v/	van	/ch/	chain, match
/g/	goat	/w/	wagon	/sh/	show
/h/	house, who	/m/	map	/th/	thin
/j/	jar, gem, fudge	/n/	nest	/th/	those
/k/	car, key	/p/	pig	/hw/	where
/l/	lamb	/r/	rug, wrong	/ng/	song

A

a·ban·don (ə ban′ dən) v. to give up something completely.

a·bate (ə bāt′) v. **a·bat·ed, a·bat·ing.** to make or become less in force, intensity, or amount.

ab·o·li·tion·ist (ab′ ə lish′ ə nist) n. one who supported the abolition of slavery in the U. S. in the 1800s.

a·brupt·ly (ə brupt′ lē) adv. suddenly; quickly; unexpectedly.

ab·so·lute (ab′ sə lüt′) adj. complete or perfect.

ab·sorb (ab sôrb′, ab zôrb′) v. to take up and retain; to soak up.

ac·com·plice (ə kom′ plis) n. a person who knowingly helps another in committing a crime or other wrongdoing.

ac·quire (ə kwīr′) v. **ac·quired, ac·quir·ing.** to come into possession of; gain as one's own.

Ad·ams, John Quin·cy (ad′ əmz, jon′ kwin′ sē) 1767–1848, sixth President of the United States, from 1825 to 1829.

ad·journ (ə jėrn′) v. to suspend or temporarily stop work or proceedings.

ad·mit (ad mit′) v. **ad·mit·ted, ad·mit·ting.** to be the means of entrance for; allow in.

ad·vanced (ad vanst′) adj. ahead of others, modern, progressive.

ag·i·tat·ed (aj′ ə tā′ tid) adj. excited; perturbed; disturbed.

ag·ri·cul·tur·al (ag′ rə kul′ chər əl) adj. relating to farms or farming.

aide-de-camp (ād′ də kamp′) n. an officer who serves as an assistant to a superior officer.

al·ba·tross (al′ bə trôs′) n. a type of web-footed sea bird known for its lengthy migratory flights.

al·ter·nate (ôl′ tər nit, al′ tər nit) n. one who takes the place of another; substitute. —v. **al·ter·nat·ed, al·ter·nat·ing.** to do or perform in turns, following one another.

al·ti·tude (al′ tə tüd′, al′ tə tūd′) n. height above a given point, such as ground or sea level.

A·mal·thea (ə mäl′ thē′ ə) a small inner moon of the planet Jupiter. Greek Mythology. goat whose horns became horns of plenty, providing a steady supply of food.

a·mend (ə mend′) v. to change for the better; correct.

an·ar·chy (an′ ər kē) n. the total absence of government and law.

an·ces·tor (an′ ses′ tər) n. one from whom a person is descended; a predecessor.

an·gle (ang′ gəl) n. a figure formed by two lines with one common end point.

angle

Ant·arc·ti·ca (ant ärk′ ti kə, ant är′ ti kə) the ice-covered region surrounding the South Pole, one of the seven continents.

An·tho·ny, Su·san B. (an′ thə nē, sü′ zən) 1820–1906, U. S. reformer, and leader in the women's right-to-vote movement.

an·ti·freeze (an′ ti frēz′, an′ tē frēz′) n. a substance that freezes at a very low temperature, added to other liquids to keep them from freezing.

a·pol·o·get·i·cal·ly (ə pol′ ə jet′ ik lē) adv. in a way that expresses regret or apology.

ap·pa·ri·tion (ap′ ə rish′ ən) *n.* ghost; specter; phantom.

ap·peal (ə pēl′) *v.* to arouse a favorable response; be attractive or interesting.

ap·pli·ca·tion (ap′ lə kā′ shən) *n.* written form used in making a request.

ap·pren·tice (ə pren′ tis) *n.* a person who works for a skilled worker in order to learn a trade or art; any learner or beginner. —*v.* **ap·pren·ticed, ap·pren·tic·ing.** to place as an apprentice.

ap·ti·tude (ap′ tə tüd′, ap′ tə tūd′) *n.* natural ability or talent.

ar·chae·ol·o·gist (är′ kē ol′ ə jist) *n.* one who studies the human past through excavation of former dwelling sites.

ar·chives (är′ kīvz) *n. pl.* public records, papers, or documents, as of a government or institution.

Arc·tic (ärk′ tik, är′ tik) the ice-covered region surrounding the North Pole.

ar·ray (ə rā′) *n.* an orderly grouping or arrangement. —*v.* to set up, marshal, or put in order, as for battle.

ar·ter·y (är′ tər ē) *n., pl.* **ar·ter·ies.** one of the muscular elastic tubes that carry oxygenated blood away from the heart to all parts of the body.

ar·til·ler·y (är til′ ər ē) *n.* a unit of the military that uses large weapons such as cannons and mortars.

as·pire (ə spīr′) *v.* **as·pired, as·pir·ing.** to seek ambitiously to attain something; aim.

as·sent (ə sent′) *v.* to agree to; concur with.

as·suage (ə swāj′) *v.* **as·suaged, as·suag·ing.** to make less severe; ease.

as·sump·tion (ə sump′ shən) *n.* something taken for granted; supposition.

at·mos·phere (at′ məs fir′) *n.* mass of gases that surrounds the earth or any other heavenly body.

au·di·ble (ô′ də bəl) *adj.* loud enough to be heard.

au·then·tic (ô then′ tik) *adj.* being what it appears or claims to be; genuine; real.

a·vert (ə vėrt′) *v.* to prevent; avoid.

awe·struck (ô′ struk′) *adj.* filled with great wonder combined with fear or reverence.

az·ure (azh′ ər) *adj.* clear sky-blue color.

B

back·er (bak′ ər) *n.* one who supports a person or undertaking with money or influence; patron.

bale (bāl) *v.* **baled, bal·ing.** to make into a bundle, and prepare for transportation.

ball-and-sock·et con·nec·tion a joint formed by a ball or knob in a socket, permitting limited circular movement in every direction.

ball-and-socket connection

bal·us·trade (bal′ əs trād′) *n.* a row of posts, or balusters, and the handrail they support, forming a railing on stairs or platforms.

bank·rupt (bangk′ rupt′, bangk′ rəpt) *adj.* one who is without the resources to pay his or her debts.

bar·ren (bār′ ən) *adj.* desolate; bare; empty.

Basque (bäsk) a region in the north of Spain on the Bay of Biscay.

beck·on (bek′ ən) v. to signal, summon, or call by sign or gesture.

bell·weth·er (bel′ we<u>th</u>′ ər) n. a male sheep that leads the flock, usually with a bell around its neck.

ben·e·fac·tor (ben′ ə fak′ tər) n. a person who gives help or financial aid.

ben·e·fit (ben′ ə fit) v. to be useful, profitable, or helpful to.

Ben·gal lights (ben′ gôl līts) **1.** a blue light used formerly for signaling and illumination. **2.** any of various colored lights or flares.

bi·zarre (bi zär′) adj. very odd or strange; fantastic.

bleak (blēk) adj. cold; chilling; cheerless; dreary.

bois·ter·ous (boi′ stər əs) adj. noisy and lively.

bon·dage (bon′ dij) n. involuntary servitude; slavery.

box the com·pass a phrase meaning to make a complete turn of 360 degrees, which is one full circle.

break·through (brāk′ thrü′) n. an important development, achievement, or discovery that helps to further progress in any field of knowledge or activity.

brisk (brisk) adj. sharp in tone or manner.

browse (brouz) v. **browsed, brows·ing.** to feed, as on leaves and twigs.

bud·ding (bud′ ing) adj. at an early or promising stage of development.

Bu·reau of La·bor Sta·tis·tics the U.S. government agency that maintains employment information. Also **(BLS).**

C

cab·al·le·ro (kab′ əl yãr′ ō) n. Spanish. horseman; gentleman. [Spanish caballero, from Late Latin caballārius horseman, from caballus horse.]

ca·det (kə det′) n. a student at a military school.

ca·lam·i·ty (kə lam′ ə tē) n. **1.** great suffering or distress; misery. **2.** accident.

Cal·lis·to (kə lis′ tō) a moon of Jupiter. Greek Mythology. nymph who was turned into a bear and became a constellation (the Big Bear).

ca·nal (kə nal′) n. an inland waterway built for navigation, irrigation, drainage, or power.

Cape of Good Hope (kāp′ uv gùd hōp′) the most southern cape, or tip of land, at the bottom of Africa.

ca·pit·u·late (kə pich′ ə lāt′) v. **ca·pit·u·lat·ed, ca·pit·u·lat·ing.** to surrender or yield; give up.

ca·reer (kə rir′) n. occupation or profession; one's lifework.

car·i·bou (kãr′ ə bü′) n. any of a group of large deer native to the northern regions of the world.

cat·a·logue (kat′ əl ôg′) v. **cat·a·logued, cat·a·logu·ing.** to make an orderly list or record of for identifying items.

cat·a·pult (kat′ ə pult′) v. to hurl or throw.

---

a b**a**t, ā c**a**ke, ä f**a**ther, är c**a**r, âr d**a**re; e h**e**n, ē m**e**, ėr t**e**rm; i b**i**b, ī k**i**te, ir cl**ea**r; o t**o**p, ō r**o**pe, ô s**a**w, oi c**oi**n, ôr f**o**rk, ou **ou**t; u s**u**n, ù b**oo**k, ü m**oo**n, ū c**u**te; ə **a**bout, tak**e**n

cau·tious·ly (kô′ shəs lē) *adv.* in a way that is characterized by care or wariness.

cav·ern·ous (kav′ ər nəs) *adj.* deep-set; hollow. [French *caverne*, from Latin *caverna*, from *cavus* hollow.]

cav·i·ty (kav′ ə tē) *n., pl.* **cav·i·ties.** space within the body or an organ.

cen·sus (sen′ səs) *n.* an official count of the population of a place.

Cen·tral A·mer·i·ca (sen′ trəl ə mär′ i kə) region between the Pacific and the Caribbean, occupying the long isthmus of North America that links that continent with South America.

char·ac·ter (kār′ ik tər) *n.* a pictorial symbol used in writing by Japanese, Chinese, and Koreans; hieroglyphic.

character

chide (chīd) *v.* **chid·ed, chid·ing.** to scold mildly.

cir·cum·fer·ence (sər kum′ fər əns) *n.* the distance around something.

cir·cum·stance (sėr′ kəm stans) *n.* a condition, act, or event accompanying and often affecting another condition, act, or event.

civ·il ser·vice (siv′ əl sėr′ vis) government or public service, other than the military.

civ·i·li·za·tion (siv′ ə lī zā′ shən) *n.* the way of life of a particular people brought about by complex social, economic, cultural, political, and intellectual development.

civ·i·lized (siv′ ə līzd′) *adj.* advanced beyond what is primitive or savage.

Clei·to (klī′ tō) *Greek Mythology.* a mortal woman who married Poseidon.

cli·ent (klī′ ənt) *n.* one who engages the professional advice or services of another.

co-spon·sor (kō′ spon′ sər) *v.* to jointly provide financial support for.

co·los·sal (kə los′ əl) *adj.* extremely large; immense.

com·mence (kə mens′) *v.* **com·menced, com·menc·ing.** to begin; start.

com·merce (kom′ ərs) *n.* business involving the exchanging, buying, or selling of commodities or services; trade.

com·mis·sion (kə mish′ ən) *n.* a group of persons who have been appointed or elected to perform certain duties.

com·mit·ted (kə mit′ id) *adj.* devoted.

com·pla·cent·ly (kəm plā′ sənt lē) *adv.* in a self-satisfied or pleased way.

com·pos·ing room (kəm pōs′ ing rüm′) the room in a printshop where typesetting is done.

com·pressed (kəm prest′) *adj.* pressed or squeezed together; made more compact.

com·pro·mise (kom′ prə mīz) *n.* settlement of a disagreement by having each side agree to give up some part of its demands.

com·rade (kom′ rad) *n.* close friend or companion; co-worker.

con·ceive (kən sēv′) *v.* **con·ceived, con·ceiv·ing.** to form or develop mentally; devise; plan.

con·cen·tric (kən sen′ trik) *adj.* having a common center.

concentric

con·cus·sion (kən kush' ən) *n.* violent shaking or shock.

Con·fed·er·a·cy (kən fed' ər ə sē) the states who seceded from the U. S. in 1860–1861 and formed a political union called the Confederate States of America.

con·form (kən fôrm') *v.* to behave or think in agreement with a rule or standard.

con·geal (kən jēl') *v.* to change from a liquid to a solid by cooling or freezing.

con·science (kon' shəns) *n.* thought or feeling that prompts one to distinguish between right and wrong.

con·se·crate (kon' sə krāt') *v.* **con·se·crat·ed, con·se·crat·ing.** to make or declare holy.

con·se·quence (kon' sə kwens') *n.* result of an earlier action or happening; outcome.

con·serv·a·tive (kən sėr' və tiv) *adj.* moderate; traditional.

con·ster·na·tion (kon' stər nā' shən) *n.* a feeling of alarm or amazement leading to confusion or fear.

con·sti·tu·tion·al (kon' stə tü' shən əl) *adj.* of, or in conformance with, a constitution, especially of a nation or state.

con·sult (kən sult') *v.* to be asked for advice.

con·tem·plate (kon' təm plāt') *v.* **con·tem·plat·ed, con·tem·plat·ing.** to give attention to; consider carefully. [Latin *comtemplātus*, past participle of *contemplārī* to observe, from *con-* with

+ *templum* space marked out in the sky for observation, temple; with reference to the practice of ancient Roman priests of observing a *templum* for omens.]

con·ti·nent (kont' ən ənt) *n.* one of seven great land areas of the earth, traditionally including Asia, Africa, North America, South America, Antarctica, Europe, and Australia.

con·trail (kon' trāl') *n.* a trail of vapor that forms behind an airplane or jet flying at high altitude.

cope (kōp) *v.* **coped, cop·ing.** to struggle; to deal with successfully.

core (kôr) *n.* the innermost or central part of something.

cor·po·rate (kôr' pər it, kôr' prit') *adj.* of or related to a corporation, or legally independent business organization. [Latin *corporātus*, past participle of *corporāre* to make into a body, from *corpus* body.]

Cos·ta Ri·ca (kōs' tə rē' kə) country in Central America, located between Panama and Nicaragua.

Costa Rica

crag·gy (krag' ē) *adj.* steep; rugged.

cri·te·ri·on (crī tir' ē ən) *n., pl.* **cri·te·ri·a** or **cri·te·ri·ons.** a rule or standard by which something or someone can be judged or measured.

cri·tic (krit' ik) *n.* one who judges the work or performance of another.

cru·cial (krü' shəl) *adj.* very important; critical; decisive.

---

a bat, ā cake, ä father, är car, âr dare; e hen, ē me, ėr term; i bib, ī kite, ir clear; o top, ō rope, ô saw, oi coin, ôr fork, ou out; u sun, u̇ book, ü moon, ū cute; ə about, taken

crude (crüd) *adj.* lacking skill or polish; rough.

cu·bic feet (kū′ bik fēt′) a unit of measurement for objects or spaces having length, width, and depth or height. This box can hold 15 cubic feet of sand.

cur·rent (kėr′ ənt) *n.* a portion of a body of water or air flowing continuously in the same direction.

cur·ry (kėr′ ē) *v.* **cur·ried, cur·ry·ing.** to prepare food with various spices.

cyl·in·der (sil′ ən dər) *n.* solid or hollow objects that resemble cans or rollers.

D

da·guerre·o·type pho·tog·ra·phy (də gär′ ə tīp′ fə tog′ rə fē) an early method of photography in which a light-sensitive metal plate was exposed, and served as the finished picture after developing.

dark·room (därk′ rüm′) *n.* room where photographs are developed, arranged so that almost all light is eliminated.

de·bate (di bāt′) *n.* formal discussion of the arguments for and against a question or issue, especially public contests in which two people argue opposite sides of a topic.

de·cent (dē′ sənt) *adj.* kind; considerate.

de·fi·ant·ly (di fī′ ənt lē) *adv.* in a way that is characterized by open resistance; boldly.

del·e·gate (del′ ə gāt′, del′ ə git′) *n.* one given authority to represent or act for another or others.

de·lu·sion (di lü′ zhən) *n.* a false idea or belief.

dense (dens) *adj.* not allowing the passage of light; thick.

des·o·la·tion (des′ ə lā′ shən) *n.* ruined or deserted condition.

de·vote (di vōt′) *v.* **de·vot·ed, de·vot·ing.** to give or apply one's energy or attention to something.

de·vour (di vour′) *v.* to eat up greedily.

di·am·e·ter (dī am′ ə tər) *n.* a straight line that passes through the center of a circle or sphere with both of its ends on the boundary; the width or thickness of something.

diameter

di·e·tet·ics (dī′ ə tet′ iks) *n.* branch of the science of nutrition dealing with meal planning and the preparation of food.

di·e·ti·cian (dī′ ə tish′ ən) *n.* a person trained in dietetics.

din (din) *n.* loud, continuous noise.

dis·a·bil·i·ty (dis′ ə bil′ ə tē) *n., pl.* **dis·a·bil·i·ties.** thing that disables; handicap.

dis·con·so·late (dis kon′ sə lit) *adj.* so sad as to be without cheer, hope, or comfort.

dis·patch (dis pach′) *n., pl.* **dis·patch·es.** written message sent off quickly or promptly; information that is sent somewhere. —*v.* to send off quickly to a specific destination or for a specific purpose.

dis·so·lu·tion (dis′ ə lü′ shən) *n.* separating into parts, disintegration.

dis·suade (di swād′) *v.* **dis·suad·ed, dis·suad·ing.** to keep someone from doing something by persuasion or advice.

dis·tort (dis tôrt′) *v.* to change the natural or usual form of.

dis·trac·tion (dis trak' shən) *n.* that which diverts and relieves the mind; amusement.

dram·a·tis per·so·nae (dram' ə tīs pər sō' nē) list of characters in a play.

drudg·er·y (druj' ər ē) *n.* wearying, boring, or lowly work.

du·ra·tion (dů rā' shən, dū rā' shən) *n.* the period of time during which something exists or persists.

E

e·con·o·my (i kon' ə mē) *n., pl.* **e·con·o·mies.** system by which the production, consumption, and distribution of goods, wealth, and services operates.

ed·i·ble (ed' ə bəl) *adj.* able to be eaten; fit to eat.

ed·i·tor (ed' ə tər) *n.* one who prepares something for publication.

ee·rie (ir' ē) *adj.* strange and frightening.

ef·fi·cient (i fish' ənt) *adj.* producing a desired effect with a minimum of effort.

eggs Ben·e·dict poached eggs on an English muffin covered with broiled ham and a cream sauce.

é·lan (ā län') *n.* enthusiasm; vitality; dash.

e·lec·tor·al vote (i lek' tər əl vōt') a vote in the electoral college, the body that formally elects the President and Vice President of the United States.

el·e·men·ta·ry (el' ə men' tər ē, el' ə men' trē) *adj.* of, or relating to, the simple basic parts or beginnings of something.

em·ploy·er (em ploi' ər) *n.* a person or business that employs, or hires, a person or group of people for pay.

em·u·late (em' yə lāt') *v.* **em·u·lat·ed, em·u·lat·ing.** to try to equal or go beyond.

en·dure (en důr', en dūr') *v.* **en·dured, en·dur·ing.** to undergo without impairment; continue without yielding.

en·gulf (en gulf') *v.* to swallow up; surround.

en·ter·prise (en' tər prīz') *n.* a project or undertaking, especially one that is difficult or important.

en·ti·ty (en' tə tē) *n., pl.* **en·ti·ties.** something with real existence; an actual thing.

e·ques·tri·an sci·ence (i kwes' trē ən sī' əns) the formal study of horseback riding.

e·qui·ta·tion (ek' wə tā' shən) *n.* the art of horseback riding.

es·sen·tial (i sen' shəl) *adj.* necessary for the existence or continuation of something; indispensable.

es·tate (es tāt') *n.* property or possessions, especially those things owned by a person at his or her death. [Old French *estat* possession, state, from Latin *status* position, condition.]

e·ter·ni·ty (i tėr' nə tē) *n., pl.* **e·ter·ni·ties.** a seemingly endless length of time.

Eu·ro·pa (ū rō' pə) a moon of Jupiter.

ewe (ū) *n.* female sheep.

---

a bat, ā cake, ä father, är car, âr dare; e hen, ē me, ėr term; i bib, ī kite, ir clear; o top, ō rope, ô saw, oi coin, ôr fork, ou out; u sun, ů book, ü moon, ū cute; ə about, taken

ex·hil·a·rate (eg zil′ ə rāt′) v.
ex·hil·a·rat·ed, ex·hil·a·rat·ing.
to make cheerful, lively, or excited;
stimulate.

ex·hort (eg zôrt′) v. to try to persuade
by appeal, argument, or warning; urge
strongly.

ex·po·sure (iks pō′ zhər) n. the act of
subjecting a light-sensitive film to light.

ex·ten·sive (eks ten′ siv) adj. large in
amount, degree, or number.

ex·tin·guish (eks ting′ gwish) v. to put
out.

eye·wit·ness ac·count (ī′ wit′ nəs ə
kount′) a description from one who
actually saw something; first-hand
description.

F

fa·cil·i·ty (fə sil′ ə tē) n., pl.
fa·cil·i·ties. thing such as a building
or piece of equipment that serves a
particular purpose.

Fahr·en·heit (fār′ ən hīt′) a temperature
scale on which water freezes at 32
degrees and water boils at 212 degrees. [Named for Gabriel Daniel
Fahrenheit, 1686–1736, German
physicist who devised this scale.]

fa·nat·i·cism (fə nat′ ə siz′ əm) n. excessive or unreasonable enthusiasm
or zeal.

fault (fôlt) n. a break in something, as in
the ice on a lake or the earth's surface.

fer·ra (fār′ ə) n. a spirit.

flank (flank) n. the side of something.
—v. to move around and attack the
side of.

flash·back (flash′ bak′) n. a break in the
normal time sequence of a perfor-

mance, during which events of the
past are inserted.

fore·bod·ing (fôr bō′ ding) n. a feeling
that something bad or evil is going to
happen.

fore·sight (fôr′ sīt′) n. care, provision, or
thought for the future.

for·feit (fôr′ fit) v. to lose as a penalty for
some fault, mistake, or misdeed.

for·ger (fôr′ jər) n. one who copies and
signs another's signature to deceive or
falsify.

fos·sil (fos′ əl) n. a
piece of the
earth's crust that
formed around
an ancient plant
or animal and
preserved its
shape when it
hardened.

fossil

foun·dry (foun′ drē) n., pl. **foun·dries.**
place where metal is melted and cast.

frac·ture (frak′ chər) n. a break; split;
crack.

frag·ile (fraj′ əl, fraj′ īl) adj. easily broken,
damaged, or destroyed; delicate.

fric·tion (frik′ shən) n. rubbing of one
object against another.

Fro·bish·er Bay (frō′ bi shər bā′) **1.** a
bay in the Canadian arctic. **2.** a town
on the bay.

fu·gi·tive (fū′ jə tiv) adj. fleeing or having
fled. —n. a person who is fleeing or
has fled.

fur·row (fèr′ ō) n. a long narrow groove
or channel made by a plow blade by
forcing up the dirt on either side of its
point.

fu·ry (fūr′ ē) n., pl. **fur·ies.** a wild, and
often fierce spirit.

G

Gal·i·le·o (gal′ ə lē′ ō, gal′ ə lā′ ō) 1564–1642, Italian astronomer, physicist, and mathematician; full name, **Galileo Galilei** (gal′ ə lā′).

gan·grene (gang′ grēn′, gang grēn′) *n.* death and decay of body tissue caused by the blood supply being cut off.

Gan·y·mede (gan′ ə mēd′) a moon of Jupiter. *Greek Mythology.* young boy who became cupbearer to the gods on Mt. Olympus.

gen·er·ate (jen′ ə rāt′) *v.* **gen·er·at·ed, gen·er·at·ing.** to produce or cause to be; bring into existence.

ge·o·met·ric (jē′ ə met′ rik) *adj.* consisting of or decorated with straight lines, circles, angles, or other simple forms.

ges·ture (jes′ chər) *v.* **ges·tured, ges·tur·ing.** to express a thought or feeling by moving the head, hands, body, or limbs.

gla·cier (glā′ shər) *n.* large mass of ice moving slowly over land, usually down a valley.

glade (glād) *n.* open space in a forest or woods.

glam·or·ous (glam′ ər əs) *adj.* full of excitement or charm; fascinatingly attractive.

glare (glār) *n.* a strong, usually unpleasant light. —*v.* **glared, glar·ing.** to stare with hostility.

god·fa·ther (god′ fä′ thər) *n.* man who sponsors a child at a baptism.

gram·pus whale (gram′ pəs wāl′) a type of large dolphin, also known as the killer whale. [Middle English *graspeys*, from Old French *graspeis, craspois* whale, seal; literally, fat fish, going back to Latin *crassus piscis* fat fish.]

gran·ite (gran′ it) *n.* a hard, durable igneous rock, often used in buildings, monuments, and other construction.

Grant, Ulysses S. (grant′, ū lis′ ēz) 1822–1885, U. S. general and eighteenth President of the United States from 1869 to 1877.

graph·ic arts all forms of visual artistic representation on a flat surface, as drawing, painting, and photography.

grieve (grēv) *v.* **grieved, griev·ing.** to feel great sadness or sorrow; mourn.

gro·tesque·ly (grō tesk′ lē) *adv.* in a distorted, deformed, or unnatural way. [French *grotesque* strange painting, from Italian *(pittura) grottesca* strange (painting), from *grotta* cave; because of the strange nature of paintings found in certain old grottoes in Italy.]

grov·el (gruv′ əl, grov′ əl) *v.* to crawl or lie face downward, as in fear or humility.

H

ha·ci·en·da (hä′ sē en′ də) *n.* an estate in the Southwestern United States, Mexico, and South America, surrounded and associated with large amounts of cropland or pastures.

hal·low (hal′ ō) *v.* to make holy; sanctify.

hand-hewn (hand′ hūn′) *adj.* carved or cut by hand.

---

a **bat**, ā **cake**, ä **father**, är **car**, âr **dare**; e **hen**, ē **me**, ėr **term**; i **bib**, ī **kite**, ir **clear**; o **top**, ō **rope**, ô **saw**, oi **coin**, ôr **fork**, ou **out**; u **sun**, u̇ **book**, ü **moon**, ū **cute**; ə **about**, **taken**

hand·i·capped (han′ dē kapt) *adj.* hampered or disadvantaged, often referring to a physical disability.

har·poon (här pün′) *n.* a spear with a rope attached and a barbed point, used to spear sea animals.

harpoon

hav·oc (hav′ ək) *n.* general destruction; devastation; ruin.

hearse (hèrs) *n.* a vehicle used to carry dead persons from one place to another, as before or after a funeral.

heart·y (här′ tē) *adj.* of sound health.

heir (ār) *n.* one who inherits or is entitled to inherit property.

he·li·um (hē′ lē əm) *n.* an odorless, colorless, extremely light gas.

Her·cu·les (hèr′ kyə lēz′) *Classical Legend.* a hero celebrated for his exceptional strength. Also, **Heracles, Herakles.**

hes·i·tate (hez′ ə tāt′) *v.* **hes·i·tat·ed, hes·i·tat·ing.** to wait or stop a moment, often because of reluctance or fear.

hoax (hōks) *n., pl.* **hoax·es.** a trick or deception, meant as a joke or to fool others.

hos·pi·tal·i·ty (hos′ pə tal′ ə tē) *n., pl.* **hos·pi·tal·i·ties.** the act, practice, or quality of being friendly and generous to guests or strangers. [Old French *hospitalite,* from Latin *hospitālitās* to receive guests, going back to *hospes* guest, host.]

hos·tile (hos′ təl, hos′ tīl′) *adj.* not hospitable or welcoming; rough.

hov·el (huv′ əl) *n.* small, wretched shelter.

hov·er (huv′ ər) *v.* to remain suspended in the air over or around a particular spot.

Hud·son Straits (hud′ sən strāts) waterway connecting Hudson Bay with the Atlantic Ocean.

hue (hū) *n.* a characteristic of a color based upon its visual relationship to other colors.

hu·mid (hū′ mid) *adj.* containing or characterized by the presence of much water vapor; moist; damp.

hur·tle (hèrt′ əl) *v.* **hur·tled, hur·tling.** to move rapidly, especially with much force.

hy·dro·gen (hī′ drə jən) *n.* a colorless, tasteless, and odorless gas that is the lightest chemical element and also highly flammable. [French *hydrogène,* going back to Greek *hydōr* water + *gennān* to produce, because water is produced when hydrogen is burned.]

I

Ice Age (īs′ āj′) a period of time when glaciers are believed to have covered much of the earth's surface.

id·ly (īd′ lē) *adv.* lazily; without showing much effort.

il·lu·mi·nat·ed (i lü′ mə nā′ tid) *adj.* lit; having light on or in.

im·mi·grant (im′ ə grənt) *n.* one who comes into a place or region from another in order to make a permanent residence there.

im·plore (im plôr′) *v.* **im·plored, im·plor·ing.** to call upon or ask earnestly; beseech; beg for.

im·port (im pôrt′) *v.* to bring in goods from a foreign place for commercial purposes.

im·pres·sion (im presh′ ən) *n.* a feeling or judgment about something or someone.

im·pres·sive (im pres′ iv) *adj.* producing or instilling a strong impression; exciting attention, emotion, or admiration.

im·print (im′ print′) *n.* mark or depression produced by stamping or pressing.

im·pu·dent (im′ pyə dənt) *adj.* offensively forward; saucy; insolent.

in lieu of (in lü′ uv) phrase meaning in place of; instead.

in·au·gu·ral (in ô′ gyər əl, in ô′ gər əl) *adj.* relating to an initiation or formal opening.

in·cor·po·rate (in kôr′ pə rāt′) *v.* **in·cor·po·rat·ed, in·cor·po·rat·ing.** to include (something) as a part.

in·dig·nant (in dig′ nənt) *adj.* filled with controlled anger, usually over injustice.

in·dus·try (in′ dəs trē) *n., pl.* **in·dus·tries.** a particular branch of business, trade, or manufacture.

in·ex·haust·i·ble (in′ ig zôs′ tə bəl) *adj.* that cannot be depleted or used up easily.

in·flu·ence (in flü′ əns) *n.* the effect one has on something or in bringing about a particular outcome or result.

in·gen·ious (in jēn′ yəs) *adj.* having creative ability; imaginative.

in·hab·it (in hab′ it) *v.* to live in or on.

in·no·cent (in′ ə sənt) *adj.* free from evil or wrong; pure; naive.

in·nu·mer·a·ble (i nü′ mər ə bəl) *adj.* too numerous to be counted.

in·quis·i·tive (in kwiz′ ə tiv) *adj.* curious; nosy.

in·scrip·tion (in skrip′ shən) *n.* words or characters written, carved, engraved, or marked on a surface. [Latin *īnscrīptīo, in* in, upon *scrīptiō* to write.]

inscription

in·sen·si·bly (in sen′ sə blē) *adv.* without awareness, reason, or consciousness.

in·sis·tent·ly (in sis′ tənt lē) *adv.* in a manner demanding attention or notice.

in·stinct (in′ stingkt) *n.* unlearned, inborn disposition or tendency.

in·sti·tu·tion (in′ stə tü′ shən, in′ stə tū′ shən) *n.* an organization, society, or establishment devoted to a particular purpose.

in·su·late (in′ sə lāt′) *v.* **in·su·lat·ed, in·su·lat·ing.** to provide for less transfer of heat by surrounding with a nonconducting material. [Late Latin *īnsulātus* made into an island, from Latin *īnsula* island.]

in·te·grate (in′ tə grāt′) *v.* **in·te·grat·ed, in·te·grat·ing.** to bring different parts together into a whole.

in·tense (in tens′) *adj.* very strong.

in·ten·tion (in ten′ shən) *n.* what is intended; plan; purpose.

in·ter·cept (in′ tər sept′) *v.* to stop or seize on the way.

---

a **b**at, ā **c**ake, ä **f**ather, är **c**ar, âr d**are**; e h**en**, ē **m**e, ėr **t**erm; i **b**ib, ī **k**ite, ir **cl**ear; o **t**op, ō **r**ope, ô **s**aw, oi **c**oin, ôr **f**ork, ou **out**; u **s**un, ù **b**ook, ü **m**oon, ū **c**ute; ə **a**bout, tak**e**n

in·te·ri·or de·sign (in tir′ ē ər də zīn′) art or business of designing and furnishing interiors of homes or offices to provide beauty, convenience, and comfort. Also, **interior decorating.**

in·ter·mi·na·ble (in tėr′ mi nə bəl) *adj.* seemingly endless; drawn out.

in·ter·mit·tent (in′ tər mit′ ənt) *adj.* alternately stopping and starting.

in·tern·ship (in′ tėrn ship′) *n.* the position of an intern, or an advanced student or graduate, usually in a professional field, gaining supervised practical experience.

in·ter·val (in′ tər vəl) *n.* intervening time or space; temporary stop in the course of something. [Latin *intervallum* space between ramparts, space between, from *inter* betweèn + *vallum* rampart.]

in·ter·view (in′ tər vū′) *n.* meeting between an employer and applicants for a job to exchange information and permit evaluation.

in·tri·cate (in′ tri kit) *adj.* very involved or complicated.

in·ven·to·ry (in′ vən tôr′ ē) *n., pl.* **in·ven·to·ries.** a list or accounting of something to allow assessment.

in·vin·ci·ble (in vin′ sə bəl) *adj.* not capable of being vanquished or overcome.

in·vol·un·tar·i·ly (in vol′ ən tār′ ə lē) *adv.* not done in a conscious way.

I·o (ī′ ō) a moon of Jupiter.

ir·i·des·cent (ir′ ə des′ ənt) *adj.* displaying shimmering and changing colors.

ir·re·triev·a·bly (ir′ i trē′ və blē) *adv.* in a manner that is not recoverable or retrievable.

i·so·la·tion (ī′ sə lā′ shən) *n.* state of being alone; in solitude.

Is·tan·bul (is′ tan bül′, is täm′ bül) largest city and commercial center of Turkey. Formerly, as Constantinople, capital of the Byzantine Empire, and known in ancient times as Byzantium.

J

Ja·va (jä′ və, jav′ ə) a large island of Indonesia, near Australia.

jinn (jin) *n.* genie; spirit.

joint (joint) *n.* the place or part where two bones meet and bend.

jour·nal (jėrn′ əl) *n.* a record or account; diary. [French *journal* newspaper, diary, from Old French *jornal* daily, from Latin *diurnālis*, going back to *diēs* day.]

Judg·ment Day in some religions, the day of God's final judgment of the earth's people.

jus·ti·fy (jus′ tə fī) *v.* **jus·ti·fied, jus·ti·fy·ing.** to provide adequate grounds for; warrant.

K

keen·ly (kēn′ lē) *adv.* eagerly; intensely.

ki·mo·no (ki mō′ nə, ki mō′ nō) *n.* loose robe or gown tied with a sash, traditionally worn by Japanese men and women.

kin (kin) *n.* one's family; a relative.

kin·dling (kind′ ling) *n.* small pieces of highly flammable wood used to start a fire.

L

la·bo·ri·ous·ly (lə bôr′ ē əs lē) *adv.* with difficulty or much work.

lank (lank) *adj.* straight and flat.

la·pel (lə pel′) *n.* the front part of a coat or jacket, folded back as a continuation of the collar.

Lap·land (lap′ land′) a region in Scandinavia traditionally inhabited by a nomadic people known as Lapps.

la·va (lä′ və, lav′ ə) *n.* **1.** molten material that flows from a volcano, or fissure in the earth's surface. **2.** the rock formed when this material cools.

league (lēg) *n.* **1.** an association of people to foster common interests. **2.** a measure of distance equal to three nautical miles.

leg·end (lej′ ənd) *n.* a story, often about a well-known or heroic person, handed down by tradition and not necessarily factual.

lei·sure·ly (lē′ zhər lē, lezh′ ər lē) *adj.* unhurried; relaxed; slow.

Li·brar·y of Con·gress national library of the United States, in Washington, D. C.

li·chen (lī′ kən) *n.* a group of nonflowering plants, usually growing on tree trunks or rocks.

light (līt) *v.* **light·ed** or **lit, light·ing.** to settle or come to rest.

lime·stone (līm′ stōn′) *n.* a sedimentary rock used extensively in building.

Lind, Jenny (lind′, jin′ ē) 1820–1887, a famous Swedish singer. Also known as the Swedish Nightingale.

li·no·le·um (li nō′ lē əm) *n.* material used as a floor covering, made into sheets or tiles.

lit·er·al·ly (lit′ ər ə lē) *adv.* without exaggeration; actually.

liv·er·y sta·ble (liv′ ər ē, liv′ rē stā′ bəl) place where horses are kept, cared for, and let out for hire.

loam (lōm) *n.* a rich, usually dark soil, containing much organic matter.

lock (lok) *n.* an enclosure in a waterway with gates at each end, in which the water level can be changed to raise or lower vessels.

lock

lodge (loj) *v.* **lodged, lodg·ing.** to settle or embed in something.

lof·ty (lof′ tē) *adj.* extending to a great height; towering.

lon·gi·tude (lon′ jə tūd′, lon′ jə tüd) *n.* distance around the earth's surface, measured in degrees east and west of an imaginary line running through Greenwich, England.

loom (lüm) *v.* to largely, and often suddenly, appear above or in front of.

lug (lug) *v.* **lugged, lug·ging.** to pull or carry with effort.

lunge (lunj) *v.* **lunged, lung·ing.** to move suddenly forward.

lure (lür) *n.* a powerful or irresistible attraction.

lush (lush) *adj.* rich and abundant.

M

mag·net·ic (mag net′ ik) *adj.* having the properties of a magnet.

---

a b**a**t, ā c**a**ke, ä f**a**ther, är c**ar**, âr d**are**; e h**e**n, ē m**e**, ėr t**erm**; i b**i**b, ī k**i**te,
ir cl**ear**; o t**o**p, ō r**o**pe, ô s**aw**, oi c**oi**n, ôr f**or**k, ou **ou**t; u s**u**n, ú b**oo**k, ü m**oo**n, ū c**u**te;
ə **a**bout, tak**e**n

mag·ni·tude (mag′ nə tüd′, mag′ nə tüd′) *n.* size or extent, especially greatness of size or extent.

ma·jor·i·ty (mə jôr′ ə tē, mə jär′ ə tē) *n., pl.* **ma·jor·i·ties.** a number or group larger than another number or group.

make·shift (māk′ shift′) *adj.* used temporarily in place of the proper or usual thing.

man·tel·piece (man′ təl pēs′) *n.* the upper, horizontal portion of a mantel; a shelf over a fireplace.

man·u·al (man′ ū əl) *adj.* relating to, or done by the hands.

mas·sa (mas′ ə) *n. Slang.* formerly a term resulting from a mispronunciation of master and/or mister, common among slaves.

mas·sive (mas′ iv) *adj.* imposing or exceedingly large; great.

me·an·der (mē an′ dər) *v.* to follow a winding course. [Meander, winding river in Turkey.]

mel·an·chol·y (mel′ ən kol′ ē) *n.* sadness; depression.

mem·oir (mem′ wär) *n.* a written account of the incidents and experiences of one's life. Often, **memoirs.**

me·ni·al (mē′ nē əl) *adj.* degrading; lowly.

men·tal·ly re·tard·ed (men′ tə lē rē tärd′ id) *adj.* mentally handicapped by significantly less than average intelligence development.

me·sa (mā′ sə) *n.* a flat-topped hill or mountain with steep sides descending to the plain below; high plateau. [Spanish *mesa*, going back to Latin *mēnsa*, table.]

mesa

me·tic·u·lous (mə tik′ yə ləs) *adj.* characterized by extreme or excessive concern about details.

Mex·i·can War (mek′ si kən wôr′) a war fought between the United States and Mexico from 1846 to 1848. Also, **Mexican-American War.**

mi·crobe (mī′ krōb) *n.* a microscopic living organism; microorganism, especially one that causes disease.

mi·grate (mī′ grāt) *v.* **mi·grat·ed, mi·grat·ing.** to move seasonally from one region or climate to another.

mil·dew (mil′ dü) *n.* any of various fungi that can grow on organic matter and cause a pungent smell. —*v.* to be affected with mildew.

mill (mil) *v.* **milled, mill·ing.** to move in an aimless or confused manner.

min·is·ter (min′ is tər) *n.* a governmental agent, especially one with a diplomatic role.

mi·nor (mīn′ ər) *n.* a field of study in which a student takes many courses, but not enough to qualify it as a major. —*adj.* of small, or comparatively small importance.

mode (mōd) *n.* manner, way, or method of doing something.

mod·er·ate (*n.,* mod′ ər it; *v.,* mod′ ər āt′) *n.* a person who holds views that are not radical or extreme, especially in politics. —*v.* **mod·er·at·ed, mod·er·at·ing.** to lessen or become less excessive, violent, or intense. [Latin *moderātus*, past participle of *moderārī* to regulate, control, from *modus* measure, limit.]

mol·e·cule (mol′ ə kūl′) *n.* the smallest particle of a substance that maintains the properties of the substance, and is made up of two or more atoms.

mol·ten (mōl′ tən) *adj.* melted or liquified by heat.

mo·men·tous (mō men′ təs) *adj.* of great importance.

mon·arch but·ter·fly (mon′ ərk but′ ər flī′) large orange and black butterfly known for its migrations of several thousand miles.

monarch butterfly

moor (mür) *n.* tract of open, rolling, wild land, often wet and covered with heath, and having bogs and marshes.

Morse, Sam·u·el F. B. 1791–1872, U. S. inventor and artist, especially known for the Morse code.

mor·tal (môr′ təl) *adj.* characteristic of human beings; earthly.

mourn (môrn) *v.* to feel sorrow or grief.

mus·ket (mus′ kit) *n.* a type of shoulder gun predating the rifle. [Middle French *mousquet*, from Italian *moschetto* musket, earlier an arrow for a crossbow, from *mosca* fly, from Latin *musca*.]

myr·i·ad (mir′ ē əd) *adj.* an innumerably large number of; countless.

N

nar·ra·tive (nār′ ə tiv) *n.* a story or account, as of an experience.

nar·ra·tor (nār′ āt′ ər) *n.* one who tells or relates something, as a story or sequence of events.

na·tive (nā′ tiv) *adj.* belonging to or originating from.

nav·i·ga·tion (nav′ i gā′ shən) *n.* the practice of directing the course of a water vessel or aircraft.

niche (nich) *n.* a place or position for which one is especially or particularly suited.

ni·tro·glyc·er·in (nī′ trə glis′ ər in) *n.* a colorless liquid organic compound that is very explosive. Weak alcohol solutions of nitroglycerin are used to treat heart disease.

nom·i·nal (nom′ ən əl) *adj.* small; minimal.

non·es·sen·tial (non′ i sen′ shəl) *adj.* not very important or necessary.

North Star (nôrth′ stär′) a bright star in the north sky. It is the last star in the handle of the Little Dipper constellation, and is officially known as Polaris.

North·ern Lights (nôr′ thərn līts) a vivid display of lights and stars in the arctic sky, also known as the aurora borealis.

no·ti·fy (nō′ tə fī′) *v.* **no·ti·fied, no·ti·fy·ing.** to give notice to; inform. [Old French *notifier* to make known, from Latin *nōtificāre*, from *nōtus* known + *facere* to make.]

no·tion (nō′ shən) *n.* idea; theory, belief, or opinion.

no·to·ri·ous (nō tôr′ ē əs) *adj.* well-known for something bad; infamous.

nymph (nimf) *n. Classical Mythology.* any of various female immortals, found primarily in natural settings of sea or forest.

O

ob·lige (ə blīj′) *v.* to make indebted or grateful.

---

a b**a**t, ā c**a**ke, ä f**a**ther, är c**a**r, âr d**a**re; e h**e**n, ē m**e**, ėr t**e**rm; i b**i**b, ī k**i**te, ir cl**e**ar; o t**o**p, ō r**o**pe, ô s**a**w, oi c**oi**n, ôr f**or**k, ou **ou**t; u s**u**n, u̇ b**oo**k, ü m**oo**n, ū c**u**te; ə **a**bout, tak**e**n

ob·scure (əb skūr′) v. **ob·scured, ob·scur·ing.** to hide; conceal.

ob·sti·nate (ob′ stə nit) adj. not yielding to argument, persuasion, or reason; stubborn.

ob·vi·ous·ly (ob′ vē əs lē) adv. seen easily; clearly evident.

oc·cu·pa·tion (ok′ yə pā′ shən) n. the work that a person does to earn a living; profession; trade.

om·i·nous·ly (om′ ə nəs lē) adv. threateningly; forebodingly.

op·pres·sive (ə pres′ iv) adj. overwhelming or depressing to the spirit or senses.

op·tion (op′ shən) n. thing chosen or available for choosing.

or·a·tor (ôr′ ə tər) n. a skilled public speaker.

o·ri·en·ta·tion (ôr′ ē ən tā′ shən) n. introduction or familiarization with new surroundings or circumstances.

o·rig·i·nate (ə rij′ ə nāt′) v. **o·rig·i·nat·ed, o·rig·in·at·ing.** to come into existence; begin.

or·phan (ôr′ fən) n. a child whose natural parents are absent or dead.

Os·we·go (ô swē′ gō) a city in northern New York State, on Lake Ontario.

out·land·ish (out lan′ dish) adj. strange, unfamiliar, or bizarre.

out·set (out′ set′) n. beginning; start.

P

pains·tak·ing (pānz′ tā king) adj. taking pains; showing great care and effort.

pall (pôl) n. that which covers or conceals.

pal·met·to tree (pal met′ ō trē′) a type of palm tree with a soft, pithy trunk found in the South. Also, **cabbage palm.**

par·al·lel (pär′ ə lel′) n. any of the imaginary lines that encircle the earth parallel to the equator, used to measure distance from the equator and define location on the earth's surface.

par·ti·cle (pär′ ti kəl) n. a very small bit or piece of something.

pas·sive (pas′ iv) adj. **1.** submitting without opposition or resistance. **2.** not responsive or reactive.

pat·i·o (pat′ ē ō′) n. **1.** inner court open to the sky, as in a Spanish or Spanish-style house. **2.** any open courtyard. [Spanish patio courtyard, possibly going back to Latin patēre to lie open.]

pa·trol (pə trōl′) v. **pa·trolled, pa·trol·ling.** to go through with the purpose of guarding or inspecting.

pawn·bro·ker (pôn′ brō′ kər) n. one licensed to lend money at interest on articles of personal property left as security.

pe·cul·iar (pi kūl′ yər) adj. strange; odd; unusual.

pelt (pelt) v. to hit or strike repeatedly.

pen·e·trate (pen′ ə trāt′) v. **pen·e·trat·ed, pen·e·trat·ing.** to pass completely into and through.

pen·sion·er (pen′ shə nər) n. one who receives a pension.

per·ceive (pər sēv′) v. **per·ceived, per·ceiv·ing. 1.** to be or become aware of through the senses. **2.** to grasp mentally.

per·man·ent (pėr′ mə nənt) adj. continuing or intended to last forever without change.

per·me·ate (pėr′ mē āt′) v. **per·me·at·ed, per·me·at·ing.** to spread out widely; diffuse.

per·pet·u·al·ly (pər pech′ ū əl ē) *adv.* in a lasting or permanent way.

per·plex (pər pleks′) *v.* to trouble with doubt or uncertainty.

per·se·vere (pėr′ sə vir′) *v.* **per·se·vered, per·se·ver·ing.** to continue in a course of action or pursuit in spite of difficulties or obstacles; persist.

per·spec·tive (pər spek′ tiv) *v.* a point of view.

per·turb (pər tėrb) *v.* to disturb or disquiet greatly.

Pe·ru (pə rü′) country on the western coast of South America.

Peru

pet·rel (pet′ rəl) *n.* any of various hook-billed sea birds with black or brown plumage and white markings. [Possibly diminutive of St. *Peter*, because it seems to walk on water like St. Peter.]

phan·tom (fan′ təm) *adj.* something existing only as an image in the mind or imagination.

phi·los·o·pher (fi los′ ə fər) *n.* one who studies or searches for the fundamental nature, function, and purpose of human beings, existence, and the universe in an orderly fashion.

phys·i·cal ther·a·py (fiz′ i kəl thãr′ ə pē) treatment of an injury or disease through physical methods, as exercise, massage, or exercise.

plain·tive·ly (plān′ tiv lē) *adv.* sorrowfully; mournfully; sadly.

plan·et (plan′ it) *n.* any one of nine massive spherical bodies that revolve around the sun: Mercury, Venus, Earth, Mars, Jupiter, Saturn, Uranus, Neptune, and Pluto.

plan·ta·tion (plan tā′ shən) *n.* large estate or farm where usually a single main crop such as tobacco, cotton, or rice is grown.

pla·teau (pla tō′) *n.* elevated, relatively flat land area.

Pla·to (plā′ tō) c.428–c.347 B.C., Greek philosopher.

plau·si·ble (plô′ zə bəl) *adj.* seeming to be true, honest, or worthy of trust; believable.

plow·share (plou′ shãr′) *n.* leading edge or blade of a plow, which cuts the soil.

plum·met (plum′ it) *v.* to fall or drop straight downward; plunge.

plunge (plunj) *v.* **plunged, plung·ing.** to put, cast, or insert forcefully or suddenly; thrust.

Poe, Ed·gar Al·lan (pō′, ed′ gər al′ ən) 1809–1849, American poet, essayist, critic, and fiction writer.

poise (poiz) *v.* **poised, pois·ing.** to suspend or balance in, or as in, midair.

pome·gran·ate (pom′ gran′ it, pom′ ə gran′ it) *n.* round, reddish fruit containing many small seeds, each of which is enclosed in a red, juicy, edible pulp. [Old French *pome grenate* the fruit, going back to Latin *pōmum* apple, fruit + *grānātum*, neuter of *grānātus* having many grains.]

---

a bat, ā cake, ä father, är car, ãr dare; e hen, ē me, ėr term; i bib, ī kite, ir clear; o top, ō rope, ô saw, oi coin, ôr fork, ou out; u sun, ù book, ü moon, ū cute; ə about, taken

pore (pôr) *n.* very small opening, as in the skin of animals, serving as an outlet for perspiration. —*v.* **pored, por·ing.** to read or study with great attention, care, or absorption.

por·tent (pôr′ tent′) *n.* indication or warning of what is to come; omen.

Po·sei·don (pə sīd′ ən) Greek god of the sea and brother of Zeus and Pluto. Known by the Romans as Neptune.

po·ten·tial (pə ten′ shəl) *adj.* capable of being or becoming; possible but not actual.

Po·to·mac (pə tō′ mək) river in the eastern United States, flowing through West Virginia and separating Virginia and Maryland.

pound (pound) *n.* basic monetary unit of the United Kingdom.

pre·cau·tion (pri kô′ shən) *n.* measure taken beforehand to avoid danger, failure, loss, or harm.

pre·cede (pri sēd′) *v.* **pre·ced·ed, pre·ced·ing.** to go or come before or ahead of.

pref·er·ence (pref′ ər əns, pref′ rəns) *n.* one who or that which is preferred or liked better.

prem·is·es (prem′ is əs) *n. pl.* land and the buildings on it.

pre·serve (pri zėrv′) *v.* **pre· served, pre·serv·ing.** to maintain or keep; make lasting.

pres·sure (presh′ ər) *n.* barometric or atmospheric pressure, the density of the air in one area in relation to the density in another area.

probe (prōb) *v.* **probed, prob·ing.** to investigate, examine, or explore thoroughly.

pro·ces·sing (prô′ ses ing) *v. Photography.* taking exposed film and chemically developing negatives for printing.

pro·fes·sion (prə fesh′ ən) *n.* occupation that requires special education and training; career.

proof sheet (prüf′ shēt′) a sheet of trial photographic prints.

pro·pos·al (prə pō′ zəl) *n.* something put forward for consideration, discussion, or acceptance; suggestion; offer.

prop·o·si·tion (prop′ ə zish′ ən) *n.* a statement in which something is proposed and often affirmed.

pros·pect (pros′ pekt) *n.* chance for future success; opportunity. —*v.* to search or explore.

pros·per·ous (pros′ pər əs) *adj.* having success, wealth, or good fortune.

pro·test (prə test′) *v.* to express strong opposition, disapproval, or dissent.

proviso (prə vī′ zō) *n.* statement making a condition; provision.

pub·lish·er (pub′ li shər) *n.* one who produces and issues printed material for sale to the public.

punc·ture (pungk′ chər) *v.* **punc·tured, punc·tur·ing.** to make a hole in with a sharp or pointed object.

pyr·a·mid (pir′ ə mid′) *n.* massive structure of masonry, usually having a square base and four triangular sides that slope upward to a point at the top.

pyramid

Q

Qua·ker (kwā′ kər) member of the Society of Friends, a Christian denomination founded in the seventeenth century.

qual·i·fy (kwôl′ ə fī′) v. **qual·i·fied, qual·i·fy·ing.** to meet the necessary standards or requirements.

qualm (kwäm) n. sudden feeling of apprehension or doubt; misgiving.

quar·ter (kwôr′ tər) n. particular section or district, as of a city or town.

R

Ra (rä) a hawk-headed sun god of ancient Egypt. Also, **Re.**

ra·di·a·tion (rā′ dē ā′ shən) n. radiant energy emitted in the form of waves or particles. [Latin *radiātus*, past participle of *radiāre* to emit beams, going back to *radius* beam, rod.]

ra·di·o·ac·tiv·i·ty (rā′ dē ō ak tiv′ ə tē) n. the emission of harmful radiation during a process of atom disintegration, in which atoms of one element are transformed into atoms of another element.

ram·i·fi·ca·tion (ram′ ə fi kā′ shən) n. thing or effect that results from a situation or statement.

rash (rash) adj. acting too hastily or with lack of thought.

rat·i·fy (rat′ ə fī′) v. **rat·i·fied, rat·i·fy·ing.** to consent to officially; approve.

ra·ven (rāv′ ən) n. a large black bird with a harsh cry.

re·al·ist (rē′ ə list) n. a person who is concerned with what is actual or practical, instead of what does not or cannot exist.

re·as·sur·ance (rē ə shùr′ əns) n. the act of restoring confidence or courage.

re·bel·lion (ri bel′ yən) n. organized armed resistance against a government; insurrection.

ref·er·ence (ref′ ər əns) n. **1.** that which is referred to as a source of information. **2.** the act of referring, or directing attention to something.

re·flex (rē′ fleks′) n. response that happens without a person's control or effort.

ref·uge (ref′ ūj) n. shelter or protection from danger.

rel·e·vant (rel′ ə vənt) adj. connected or having to do with the matter at hand; appropriate.

re·luc·tant (ri luk′ tənt) adj. unwilling; averse. [Latin *reluctāns*, present participle of *reluctārī* to struggle against, going back to *re-* back + *lucta* wrestling.]

rep·e·ti·tion (rep′ ə tish′ ən) n. that which is repeated.

rep·u·ta·tion (rep′ yə tā′ shən) n. a general or public estimation of someone or something.

re·sent (ri zent′) v. to feel anger or bitterness at or toward.

res·ig·na·tion (rez′ ig nā′ shən) n. formal, usually written, notice that one is resigning, or giving up one's job or position voluntarily.

---

a bat, ā cake, ä father, är car, âr dare; e hen, ē me, ėr term; i bib, ī kite, ir clear; o top, ō rope, ô saw, oi coin, ôr fork, ou out; u sun, ù book, ü moon, ū cute; ə about, taken

re·solve (ri zolv´) v. **re·solved, re·solv·ing.** to decide; determine; settle.

re·source (rē´ sôrs´, ri sôrs´) n. something used for aid, assistance, or support.

re·su·mé (rez´ ü mā´, rez´ ü mā´) n. statement of one's qualifications and work record, used in applying for employment.

re·tain (ri tān´) v. to hold back or contain.

rev·er·ie (rev´ ər ē) n. fanciful musing or daydreaming.

re·vive (ri vīv´) v. **re·vived, re·viv·ing.** to bring back to consciousness; give new strength to.

re·volve (ri volv´) v. **re·volved, re·volv·ing.** to move in a closed curve around a central point or object.

rig (rig) n. equipment or apparatus used for a particular purpose.

rig·ging (rig´ ing) n. all the ropes, chains, and wires of a boat or ship used to support the masts or work the sails.

rigging

riv·u·let (riv´ yə lət) n. a small stream or brook.

S

sat·ur·at·ed (sach´ ə rā´ tid) adj. filled with something to the point where no more can be absorbed.

scoun·drel (skoun´ drəl) n. a dishonest person; villain.

se·ces·sion (si sesh´ ən) n. the act of withdrawing formally from an organization, usually to form another organization.

seg·ment (seg´ mənt) n. one of the parts into which something is, or may be divided; section.

self-es·teem (self´ es tēm´) n. high regard or respect for oneself.

sick·le mow·er (sik´ əl mō´ ər) a piece of equipment pulled behind a tractor and used to cut high grass or other plants.

sig·nif·i·cance (sig nif´ i kens) n. something that is meant; meaning.

skep·ti·cism (skep´ tə siz´ əm) n. a doubting or questioning attitude or state of mind.

so·lic·i·tor (sə lis´ ə tər) n. British lawyer who advises clients and prepares cases for presentation in court, but may only actually plead cases in the lower court, as distinguished from a barrister.

sore·ly (sôr´ lē) adj. very; extremely.

sov·er·eign (sov´ rən, sov´ ər ən) n. a former British coin worth one pound.

sphere (sfir) n. round, three-dimensional figure having all the points of its surface at an equal distance from the center.

stalk (stôk) v. to move or walk in a threatening way.

stark (stärk) adj. barren or desolate.

sul·len·ly (sul´ ən lē) adv. in a withdrawn or gloomy way because of bad humor or anger; sulkily.

su·per·sat·u·rat·ed (sü pər sach´ ə rā´ tid) adj. containing more than a normal amount of something; a degree beyond saturation; more than concentrated.

su·per·vise (sü′ pər vīz′) *v.*
su·per·vised, su·per·vis·ing. to watch over in order to guide, direct, or control; oversee.

sym·met·ri·cal (si met′ ri kəl) *adj.* having beauty, proportion, and harmony of form; balanced.

T

tem·po·rar·i·ly (tem pə rär′ ə lē) *adv.* in a way that is lasting, existing, or used for a limited time only; not permanently.

the·o·ry (thē′ ər ē) *n., pl.* **the·o·ries.** idea that explains a group of facts.

ther·a·peu·tic (thār′ ə pū′ tik) *adj.* of or relating to the treatment or cure of diseases or disorders.

tid·al wave (tīd′ əl wāv′) swift, tall, powerful ocean wave caused by an underwater earthquake.

To·ky·o (tō′ kē ō′) capital and largest city of Japan, on the island of Honshu.

tol·er·ate (tol′ ə rāt′) *v.* **tol·er·at·ed, tol·er·at·ing.** to put up with; bear; endure.

tor·rent (tôr′ ənt, tor′ ənt) *n.* violent, swiftly flowing stream, especially of water.

tri·pod (trī′ pod′) *n.* a three-legged stand for supporting a camera or surveying instrument. [Latin *tripūs* three-legged seat, from Greek *tripous* three-legged table or cauldron, going back to *tri* three + *pod* foot.]

tur·moil (tėr′ moil) *n.* state or condition of confusion, agitation, or commotion.

U

Un·der·ground Rail·way (un′ dər ground′ rāl′ wā′) before the abolition of slavery, a secret system of helping slaves escape to freedom in Canada or the Free States.

u·ni·form (ū′ nə fôrm′) *adj.* unchanging; unvarying.

u·ni·son (ū′ nə sən) *n.* complete or perfect agreement.

V

valve (valv) *n.* device used to control the flow of liquids, gases, or loose materials.

va·por (vā′ pər) *n.* gaseous state of a substance that is a liquid or a solid under normal conditions of temperature or pressure.

vi·o·late (vī′ ə lāt′) *v.* **vi·o·lat·ed, vi·o·lat·ing.** to fail to obey or keep; break.

void (void) *n.* emptiness.

W

wa·ver (wā′ vər) *v.* to hesitate or show doubt; be uncertain.

West Point officially the U. S. Military Academy, a four-year institution providing college-level instruction and officer training for careers in the U. S. Army, located in New York State.

World War II (wėrld′ wôr′ tü′) 1939–1945, war between most of the world's major powers, fought in Europe, Asia, and Africa, and in the Atlantic, Pacific, and Indian oceans.

---

a b**a**t, ā c**a**k**e**, ä f**a**th**e**r, är c**a**r, âr d**a**r**e**; e h**e**n, ē m**e**, ėr t**e**rm; i b**i**b, ī k**i**t**e**, ir cl**e**ar; o t**o**p, ō r**o**p**e**, ô s**a**w, oi c**o**in, ôr f**o**rk, ou **o**ut; u s**u**n, u̇ b**oo**k, ü m**oo**n, ū c**u**t**e**; ə **a**b**o**ut, tak**e**n

This section of *Lofty Achievements* includes a review of letters and the sounds they stand for. Good readers know that letters in a word are clues. Looking carefully at these letters is one way to figure out how to say a word. Some words may look new, but once you say them you may discover that you already know them.

Word Work

Lessons

Beginning Sounds

Letters stand for sounds at the beginning of words.

A. Copy the sentences below. Fill in the missing letters. Choose the letters from those in the box. Be sure the words make sense in the sentence.

| b | d | g | l | m | p | qu | t | v | w | y | z |

"A __ard sale, __et's __ook," Peter said. Molly __asn't fond of them, but she __ielded. She __alked among the __ables, eyeing the __ooks and __ames, __ondering about the jacket with the broken __ipper. She __ought a __aint __urple __ase—just right for __iolets—and a __oo __adge with a __orilla on it. She __ot some old __agazines, a __asket for her __ike, and an old __ainting—a real __asterpiece, she thought.

"So you __on't like __arage sales?" Peter __eased.

"__ell," Molly __aughed. "not __ite as __uch as __ou __o."

Some beginning sounds can be spelled more than one way.

B. Number your paper from 1 to 8. Read each group of words below. Write the two words from each group that begin with the same sound.

1. cancel
   cinder
   kind

2. phase
   fate
   paste

3. rinse
   wreath
   wealth

4. notify
   keyhole
   knight

5. why
   whose
   hermit

6. generate
   galley
   jacket

7. caboose
   salary
   civic

8. savor
   comma
   kettle

Ending Sounds

Letters stand for sounds at the end of words.

A. Copy the sentences below. Fill in the missing letters. Use the letters in the box.

b   d   l   m   p   n   x   dge   g   t

Ann though__ she saw a fo__ ru__ into the he__. She ha__ see__ i__ earlier sitting ato__ a stump in the yar__: a small one. We had had a raccoo__ once in the garde__, but this was something new. I was doubtfu__. Yes, she was sure it was not a do__. I wen__ to look; mew, I hear__. I laughed and reached ou__ one ar__ to gra__ and dra__ out Dick's cat Maggie—pointy ears and a fluffy orange tai__.

Some ending sounds can be spelled more than one way.

B. Copy the sentences below. Fill in the missing letters. Choose the letters from those in the box.

f   ff   ph   k   c   ck   s   ss

1. I woke up this morning with a sti__ ne__ and ba__.
2. For a brie__ moment I began to pani__: Was I getting si__?
3. Then I remembered helping Dad clean the basement yesterday— what a me__ it had been!
4. Ye__, it too__ u__ all day, and there is an enormou__ pile of stu__ for the trash collectors.
5. What a trium__ to have the job done, even i__ I do feel wea__ now.

Short Vowel Sounds

There are five short vowel sounds. Some short vowel sounds can be spelled more than one way.

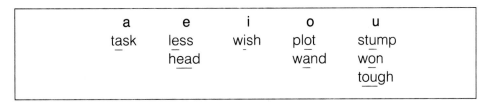

a	e	i	o	u
task	less	wish	plot	stump
	head		wand	won
				tough

Number your paper from 1 to 7. Complete each sentence below with a word that has the same vowel sound as the underlined word. Write the word on your paper. Underline the letter or letters that spell the short vowel sound.

1. The old tree in front of the house was ____ down today.

   taken   chopped   cut

2. It had a disease that would eventually ____ it.

   kill   claim   fight

3. I remembered a lot about that tree as I ____ the workers.

   watched   saw   helped

4. I spent hundreds of ____ hours in that tree.

   happy   pleasant   lonesome

5. In fact, I wore the rough surface of one branch smooth from sitting on it so ____.

   hard   long   much

6. Once I tried to pull the cat up in a ____.

   box   basket   cage

7. ____ the tree fell, I knew I had lost a true friend.

   As   When   Since

Consonant Clusters with *l* and *r*

> Consonant clusters are made up of two or more letters whose sounds blend together.

Read the poem below. Notice the underlined words.

What is the same about
  Slippery and cloak,
  Frightfully and broke,
  Plentiful and clap,
  Gratefully and slap?
Sure you know, don't get flustered,
Each begins with a consonant cluster.

Number your paper from 1 to 13. Read each word clue below. Write your answer, using one of the consonant clusters in the box.

	bl	cl	fl	gl	pl	sl	
br	cr	dr	fr	gr	pr	tr	

1. I am extremely cold. __igid

2. I am a flower. __ossom

3. I am a dried plum. __une

4. I fix the water pipes. __umber

5. I'm a good material for making warm pajamas. __annel

6. I am a formal agreement, a pact. __eaty

7. I'm a black-and-blue sore place. __uise

8. I'm a vacation trip on a ship. __uise

9. I am informal language. __ang

10. I am great honor or high praise. __ory

11. I keep everything down to earth. __avity

12. I'm dull and plain, never fancy. __ab

13. I'm cold and damp. __ammy

Word Work

Consonant Clusters with *s*

> Consonant clusters can be two or three letters whose sounds blend together.

Many consonant clusters begin with *s*. Look for consonant clusters as you read the story below.

Was that someone screaming? . . . No, maybe a screech owl. It wasn't a human sound. . . . It was outside. . . . Oh! What's squeaking? A stranger coming up the stairs? . . . No, outside again . . . Right, that old tree creaking in the wind . . . No, yes, wait. . . . Sleep, I'll just . . . what was that? The tree again, a branch rubbing against the screen . . . Was I . . . No . . . Yes, I mustn't be scared.

Morning came. Sunshine streamed into the room. The sky was light blue. My brother Steve was still sprawled across the mattress, sound asleep. I sniffed; a good smell came from downstairs. I swiftly sneaked out of the room. Dad was cooking eggs in the electric skillet. He looked up.

"How did you spend the first night in the new house?"

"Just fine," I said with a smile.

"Sure," he grinned. And winked.

Number your paper from 1 to 11. Write the consonant clusters below. Next to each, write the word or words from the story that begin with the cluster.

1. sc	2. sn	3. sw	4. squ	5. sk	6. sp
7. scr	8. str	9. sm	10. st	11. spr	

Ending Consonant Clusters

Consonant clusters can come at the beginning or at the
end of words. Some important ending consonant clusters
are listed below.

ld   nd   nk   sk   mp   ft   lt   nt   st

Number your paper from 1 to 9. Write each sentence below. Find
one consonant cluster that will complete all the incomplete words in
the sentence. Use the consonant clusters in the box.

1. The young chi__ hopped from the stu__ to the platform, then
   stared at us as we stared at him.

2. I knew the co__ would bo__ when I first slipped the halter over
   his head.

3. At fir__ we walked three abrea__, but then the path narrowed and
   we walked single file.

4. Quick as a wi__ the rock rolled down the ba__, hit the water with
   a plu__, and sa__.

5. Randy worked from dawn to du__, enjoying the ta__ of cleaning
   out his de__ drawers.

6. I he__ the co__, wet puppy and tried to dry him with a towel.

7. The settlers fou__ the la__ sandy but good grou__ for farming.

8. Tomás bought materials at the cra__ shop to make a gi__ for
   his sister.

9. Mary said the berries were abunda__ but you had to hu__ for the
   best place to pick.

Short Vowel Sounds

Some short vowel sounds can be spelled more than one way.

ô	u̇
st<u>a</u>ll	w<u>oo</u>l
cr<u>aw</u>l	b<u>u</u>sh
c<u>o</u>st	c<u>ou</u>ld
<u>au</u>to	

Number your paper from 1 to 5. Complete each sentence below with a word that has the same vowel sound as the underlined word. Write the word on your paper. Underline the letter or letters that spell the vowel sound.

1. Mr. Wickes, the music teacher, _____ a new <u>song</u> today.

       gave   taught   sang

2. After school I <u>put</u> my _____ in my room and went to find Mom.

       books   stuff   music

3. I knew she <u>would</u> want to hear this _____new song.

       great   good   loud

4. Her <u>jaw</u> dropped open, as it _____ does when she is surprised.

       sometimes   usually   often

5. She laughed and sat down to play the tune <u>all</u> the way

    through _____ the piano. Her grandmother had written it!

       on   with   using

Long Vowel Sounds

> Many words that end in *e* have a long vowel sound.

Read the poem below. Notice the vowel sound in each underlined word.

Spins and spines,
Caps and capes,
Cubs and cubes,
Globs and globes.
How do they differ, can you see?
The difference comes from adding *e*.

The magic *e* changes the short vowel sound to a long vowel sound. The missing word in each sentence below can be discovered by adding the magic *e* to one of the other words in the sentence. Number your paper from 1 to 10. Write the complete sentences.

1. I _____ my foot gets better soon, though I do hop around quite well.
2. Purple hair is another fad that will soon _____.
3. Cleaning the barn was a grim job; years of _____ covered every surface.
4. After I strip the paint, I'll repaint the wagon red with a blue _____.
5. Our travel plan involved going by _____ as far as Dallas.
6. My little sister sure looks _____ with her hair cut short.
7. In the Fish Patrol, Mark's _____ name is Cod; mine is Trout.
8. The hug Fran gave me was so _____, it almost took my breath away.
9. Tim told us it was _____ to start the club meeting.
10. The fir trees just added fuel to the forest _____.

Long *a* Vowel Sound

> The long *a* vowel sound can be spelled more than one way.
>
> st**a**te   s**ai**l   st**ay**   sl**eigh**

Read the poem below.

"I'm late for my date,"
    the rabbit complained,
        as he looked at his watch on a chain.
"I know it's past eight,
    but I can't find my way.
        I've been astray for over a day."

A. Number your paper from 1 to 8. Write the words from the poem that have a long *a* vowel sound. Underline the letter or letters that stand for that sound.

B. Number your paper from 1 to 12. Read each group of words below. Write the two words in each group that have the long *a* vowel sound.

1. awe
   acclaim
   alike
   noonday
	2. craze
	   freighter
	   caught
	   false
		3. scarf
		   decade
		   ailment
		   animal
			4. obtainable
			   drawer
			   happen
			   haystack

5. enrage
   gayly
   measure
   furnace
	6. either
	   hateful
	   neighbor
	   national
		7. peanut
		   stomach
		   statement
		   playroom
			8. brash
			   eighteen
			   rainbow
			   fantasy

9. explain
   although
   station
   answer
	10. announce
	   strait
	   basis
	   recall
		11. ladle
		   plant
		   walnut
		   payment
			12. mayor
			   senator
			   yawn
			   paper

Long e Vowel Sound

> The long *e* vowel sound can be spelled more than one way.
>
> b<u>ee</u>   b<u>ea</u>d   bus<u>y</u>   b<u>e</u>   br<u>ie</u>f

A. Number your paper from 1 to 12. Write each word. Then underline the letter or letters that stand for the long *e* vowel sound.

1. diesel
2. posse
3. meekly
4. fleece
5. thief
6. everyone
7. legally
8. comedy
9. stereo
10. energy
11. meatball
12. degree

B. Number your paper from 1 to 6. Find the word or words with the long *e* vowel sound in each sentence below. Write the long *e* words on your paper. Underline the letter or letters that stand for this sound.

1. My brother's birthday was last week; I gave him an easel.
2. Phil really does paint well; I don't know how he does it.
3. He sketches everything quickly—and easily, it seems.
4. Drawing anything causes me great grief: I simply can't do it.
5. Phil isn't a tease; he's always ready and eager to help.
6. It's an even exchange; he can't keep a musical beat nor sing a note on pitch—I can.

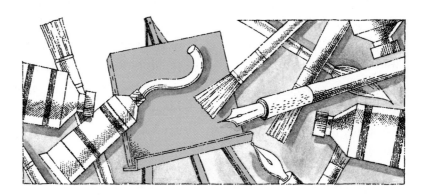

Long *i* Vowel Sound

> The long *i* vowel sound can be spelled more than one way.
>
> b<u>i</u>k<u>e</u>   bl<u>igh</u>t   b<u>y</u>   p<u>ie</u>

"The <u>fine</u> is <u>five</u> <u>dimes</u>," the librarian said,
   for the overdue books,
      I'd lost under <u>my</u> bed.
That's the <u>price</u> I pay since I <u>lie</u> at <u>night</u>
   and read <u>by</u> <u>myself</u>
      <u>while</u> the moon is <u>bright</u>.

The underlined words in the poem show different letters that stand for the long *i* vowel sound: *igh, ie, y,* and *i-e.* Number your paper from 1 to 28. Read the story below. Then write each word that has the long *i* vowel sound. Underline the letter or letters that stand for the long *i* vowel sound.

My sister Meg had to write a paper last night. "Describe a place you know as it might have been long ago," her teacher had said.

Meg looked outside and tried to think. It was hard: our street is lined with high-rise buildings now. Then she thought of Uncle Mike and his old house on Moose Isle.

Our uncle has told us about his life there before the bridge was built. Getting supplies was quite a chore. Cars had to wait until low tide to drive across the wide sand flats to the mainland. People cut ice from the ponds in winter to save for summer. They dried fish in summer to satisfy their need for food in winter. They had to rely on oil lamps for light and wood stoves for heat.

When the snow flies, the power lines are often down for days at a time. Our uncle piles wood into his stoves and turns the old lamps up high and knows exactly what long ago was like.

Long *o* Vowel Sound

> The long *o* vowel sound can be spelled more than one way.
>
> code   loan   hero   slowly

Read the poem below.

"My motto is," spoke the goat, as a joke,
   "Life has no ifs, only butts."
"Not mine," boasted the crow, "I've a practical creed,
   You caw as you go with the flow."

A. Number your paper from 1 to 10. Write the words from the poem that have the long *o* vowel sound. Underline the letter or letters that stand for the long *o* vowel sound.

B. Number your paper from 1 to 12. Look at each group of words. Write the words from each group that have a long *o* vowel sound.

1. wind-blown
   tadpole
   evolve
   horrify

2. oasis
   comical
   logic
   solo

3. mope
   showoff
   nonstop
   profit

4. drowsy
   oatmeal
   owing
   scoff

5. stopwatch
   notebook
   yellow
   allow

6. tolerate
   approach
   hood
   hopeful

7. jumbo
   coastal
   orchestra
   council

8. second
   ostrich
   October
   throat

9. crowd
   overall
   cloak
   strong

10. awoke
    chowder
    oxygen
    mower

11. product
    officer
    radio
    toast

12. problem
    groan
    towel
    whole

The Unusual *u*

There are two short *u* vowel sounds and two long *u* vowel sounds. Each is spelled in more than one way.

Read the words in the box. Look at the underlined letters. Listen for the sounds the underlined letters stand for.

Short Vowels		Long Vowels	
u	u̇	ü	ū
j<u>u</u>st	sh<u>oo</u>k	s<u>oo</u>n	ref<u>u</u>ge
s<u>o</u>n	p<u>u</u>t		d<u>ew</u>
r<u>ou</u>gh	c<u>oul</u>d		b<u>u</u>gle

Number your paper from 1 to 12. Read each key word below. Then find a word in the row that has the same vowel sound. Write the word on your paper.

1. **pew**   sugar   boot   unit
2. **jump**   enough   confuse   value
3. **mood**   balloon   bush   could
4. **took**   cuckoo   pulley   tough
5. **huge**   fuel   fulfill   won
6. **ton**   ruler   usher   museum
7. **zoo**   crooked   butcher   ooze
8. **put**   hundred   would   moonlight
9. **room**   brook   kangaroo   none
10. **few**   humid   hot   lucky
11. **number**   usual   stunt   bulletin
12. **bushel**   armful   tube   uproar

Short and Long Vowel Sounds

A. Read the two underlined words in each sentence below. One is the short vowel sound of a vowel, the other is the long vowel sound of the same vowel. Write the headings *Short Vowel* and *Long Vowel* on your paper. List each underlined word under the correct heading.

1. A parade is a glorious <u>sight</u>, and I had a good place to <u>sit</u>.
2. I could look up the <u>block</u> and see the <u>floats</u> coming.
3. In front of me they turned to <u>head</u> down Water <u>Street</u>.
4. Leading the parade was the mascot of the fire department, a small brown <u>mutt</u>, riding in a cart pulled by a <u>mule</u>.
5. I heard the <u>clank</u> of the <u>chains</u> and bells on the harness before I saw the cart.

B. The underlined word in each sentence below is shown divided into syllables at the end of the sentence. Number your paper from 1 to 6. Write each underlined word, leaving a space between the syllables. Underline each syllable with a short vowel sound once and each syllable with a long vowel sound twice.

1. The <u>pathway</u> went alongside the gardens. (path way)
2. When my cat hears the can opener she makes a <u>beeline</u> for the kitchen. (bee line)
3. It's so hot and <u>humid</u> I can't do anything. (hu mid)
4. Working hard always makes me very <u>hungry</u>. (hun gry)
5. I want to go skating but I <u>cannot</u> go today. (can not)
6. The <u>echo</u> was as clear as our calls had been. (ech o)

Beginning Consonant Digraphs

> Two or three consonants that stand for one sound are called consonant digraphs.

Read the words below. Look at the underlined letters. They are consonant digraphs.

> chimney   shadow   thin   these   wheat

Notice that the letters *th* can stand for two different sounds. Number your paper from 1 to 7. Add a consonant digraph to complete each word below. Write the complete word on your paper. Be sure it makes sense in the sentence.

1. Divers discovered an old __ipwreck just off the __ore of our town last week.
2. __ey __ink it is an old __aling boat.
3. It would be a real __allenge to salvage it, but __e divers __ought it might be worthwhile.
4. They already have brought up a __est of old tools.
5. The boat is stuck in __ick mud but is in good __ape and in fairly __allow water.
6. __en, and if, they can save it, it will be a great addition to the museum being built near the town __arf.
7. The museum director said __ere is a __ance the work could begin in the spring.

Ending Consonant Digraphs

> Consonant digraphs can come at the end of words.

The words below have ending consonant digraphs.

> in<u>ch</u>   di<u>tch</u>   wi<u>ng</u>   pu<u>sh</u>   fif<u>th</u>

Read the story below.

They say you can't teach an old dog new tricks. Well, it's worth trying. My cousin sure taught one oldish dog some fresh tricks.

If you tell Patch, the dog, to be happy, she'll bare her teeth, and you'll hear a low growling sound from her throat. Tell her you wish she'd go away, and you find her sitting at your feet in a flash. Tell her to look alive, and she'll stretch out on the floor with hardly at twitch from any muscle. Want her to catch a ball in her mouth? You'll have to tell her to miss it.

Each command seems the wrong one to me, but to Patch it couldn't be more right. She has simply learned to "sing" a different song.

Write each word below. Next to each word write the words from the story that end with the same sound and are spelled the same way.

1. ri<u>ch</u>   2. pi<u>tch</u>   3. ha<u>ng</u>   5. cra<u>sh</u>   6. bo<u>th</u>

Syllables

Some words can be divided into parts called syllables. You hear a vowel sound in every syllable.

Sometimes two or more vowel letters stand for one vowel sound. For example, in the word *coast* you see two vowels, but you hear only one vowel sound. The word *coast* has one syllable. The word *radio* has three syllables. It has three vowel sounds.

A. Number your paper from 1 to 20. Read each word below. The number of vowel sounds is the same as the number of syllables. How many syllables does each word have? Write your answers.

1. awareness
2. closeness
3. identify
4. individual
5. caboose
6. elastic
7. understandable
8. leapt
9. majority
10. tuna
11. quail
12. vicinity
13. intervene
14. mutiny
15. registration
16. unreal
17. investigation
18. through
19. noonday
20. siege

When you say a word that has more than one syllable, you stress, or emphasize, one syllable more than another. In a dictionary or glossary, the stressed syllable is followed by an accent mark (').

mu' sic   for bid'

B. Number your paper from 1 to 9. Read each word below. Which syllable is stressed: the first, second, third, or fourth? Write your answers.

1. successive
2. scallop
3. speculation
4. zinnia
5. replica
6. protrude
7. penicillin
8. persuade
9. stupidity

Schwa

> The schwa is a special vowel sound. It can be spelled with *a*, *e*, *i*, *o*, or *u*. The schwa vowel sound is often heard in the unstressed syllable of a word.

Read the words below. The underlined letters stand for the schwa vowel sound.

> isl<u>a</u>nd   ag<u>e</u>nt   happ<u>i</u>ly   at<u>o</u>m   circ<u>u</u>s

The schwa vowel sound can also be at the beginning of a word, as in *upon*, or in the middle of a word, as in *definite*.

Number your paper from 1 to 9. Write each underlined word below. Underline the vowel that stands for the schwa vowel sound.

1. I couldn't believe it when I was <u>nominated</u> to run for student <u>council</u> president.
2. I really knew very little <u>about</u> student elections.
3. Keri was my campaign manager and was <u>supremely</u> <u>helpful</u>.
4. She had a <u>method</u> for dealing with any <u>problem</u>.
5. From the beginning I didn't think I had a chance in a <u>thousand</u> of winning.
6. Ben Taylor was on the <u>opposing</u> ticket.
7. This was the <u>second</u> campaign he had run in.
8. An <u>informal</u> poll had him way <u>ahead</u> early in the campaign, but he didn't win by too much—thanks to Keri's help.
9. I'm glad he won; Ben will be a good <u>president</u>.

Vowel Combinations

> Some vowel combinations make the same sound but are spelled with different letters.
>
> boy   down
>
> toil   thousand

A. Write the words *boy* and *down* at the top of your paper. Under each word, write the six words from the list below that have the same vowel sound.

foil	compound	voyager
allowance	enjoyment	coward
flounder	downright	appointment
arouse	coinage	employer

B. *Ou* and *ow* do not always stand for the vowel sound you hear in *count*. Read the words below. Only eight of them have the vowel sound you hear in *count*. Which eight are they? Write them on your paper.

township	courtroom	adventurous
trout	towering	browse
mouthful	bestow	barrow
eyebrow	billow	rainbow
dismount	announcer	perilous

C. Number your paper from 1 to 5. Read the word clues below. Each answer will be a word you wrote in Part B.

1. I am a freshwater fish that is great to eat. _____

2. I'm just above your eye. _____

3. When you bite off more than you can chew, you have me. _____

4. I am very tall. _____

5. You hear me on the radio; you see me on TV. _____

Vowels + *r*

The letter *r* changes the sound of the vowel it follows.

Read the underlined words below. Notice the vowel sounds.

<u>Am</u> and <u>arm</u>
<u>Stand</u> and <u>stare</u>
<u>Chain</u> and <u>chair</u>
<u>Stem</u> and <u>stern</u>
<u>Skit</u> and <u>skirt</u>
<u>Woke</u> and <u>work</u>
<u>Hut</u> and <u>hurt</u>

Look again. Read each pair.
How do their vowel sounds compare?

A. Number your paper from 1 to 5. From each list write the two words that rhyme.

1	2	3	4	5
cut	chart	blunt	faint	worm
curt	chair	blurt	flair	won
flit	smart	shirt	cart	team
flirt	chore	short	care	term

B. Number your paper from 1 to 8. From each row of words, write the words in which *r* changes a vowel sound. HINT: You will not write the same number of words from each row.

1. griddle   brake   starfish   angrily
2. propose   afire   scream   millionaire
3. startle   travel   written   blur
4. track   browse   frozen   tardy
5. already   world   lurch   central
6. wordless   squirt   carve   crayon
7. breach   compare   divert   prank
8. worried   rigid   drizzle   yarn

r-Controlled Vowels

> Some r-controlled vowel sounds can be spelled in different ways.

Read the two groups of words below. Listen for the vowel sounds that are the same in each group.

> 1. inter<u>fere</u>   <u>wea</u>ry   <u>deer</u>
> 2. <u>or</u>chard   s<u>oared</u>   t<u>ore</u>

A. Pick a word from the box above that has the same vowel sound as the underlined word. Write the word that completes each sentence.

1. Aaron's shirt _____ when it got caught on a <u>thorn</u>.
2. We <u>roared</u> with delight when we saw how many apples were on the trees in the _____.
3. Suddenly I could <u>clearly</u> see the _____ through the trees.
4. Larkin bicycled and was _____ when he got <u>here</u>.
5. I tried not to _____ too much and let out a <u>cheer</u> when Peg finally rode her new bike without a wobble.
6. The kite _____ higher as I let out <u>more</u> string.

> The letter r can follow and change the schwa vowel sound.

B. Number your paper from 1 to 6. Write the words that end with the sound you hear at the end of *joker*.

eraser	polar
boxcar	affair
meager	spur
vigor	angular
boar	prior

Short and Long Vowel Sounds

> The letters *a, e, i, o, u,* and sometimes *y* can be used alone or together to spell short or long vowel sounds.

Idioms are groups of words that have meanings that are not the same as the meanings those words usually have. Number your paper from 1 to 8. Copy the sentences below. Choose a word from the box that completes the idiom in each sentence. The word you choose should have the same vowel sound as the underlined word.

lip	clock	hand	green
heavy	shooting	boat	flies

1. It was a very hot day, so we sat under a tree, _____ the breeze and trying to stay <u>cool</u>.
2. I never thought we'd <u>get</u> here; we were stuck in _____ traffic for over an hour.
3. Megan and Nora forgot to keep their eye on the _____, so they <u>got</u> home late.
4. The afternoon passed quickly; <u>time</u> _____ when you're having fun.
5. Losing the tennis match was hard for Ron, but he kept a <u>stiff</u> upper _____ and thought about how he could improve his serve.
6. None of us <u>know</u> the answers to the question, so we are all in the same _____.
7. Mrs. Muller can answer your gardening questions; <u>she's</u> got a _____ thumb.
8. Cora lent me a _____ and helped me <u>stack</u> the pile of wood.

Syllables and Short Vowel Sounds

Learning to divide words into syllables can help you read new words. When you come to a difficult word in your reading, you can work on one small part at a time. Read these one-syllable words.

    jab   jerk   jig   joke   jump

Now read these words.

    center   bitter   commitment

How many vowel sounds are in each word?
How many syllables does each word have?
Below are the same words divided into syllables.

    cen ter   bit ter   com mit ment

Notice that a vowel comes between two consonants in the first syllable of each word. Do you hear a short or a long vowel sound?

> When two consonants stand between two vowels, the word is usually divided between the consonants. The vowel in the first syllable is often short.

Number your paper from 1 to 30. Write each word, leaving a space between the syllables.

1. blanket	2. mammoth	3. fasten
4. captain	5. differ	6. platter
7. fretful	8. hermit	9. slumber
10. poppy	11. magnet	12. summit
13. forgotten	14. cosmos	15. supportive
16. flutter	17. stubborn	18. discontent
19. disrupt	20. occurrence	21. excerpt
22. advantage	23. suspense	24. cascade
25. wander	26. uppermost	27. fitful
28. dictate	29. tactic	30. headquarters

Syllables and Long Vowel Sounds

Read the poem below.

> The otters are playful at the zoo,
>   The penquins are nice and the <u>zebras</u> are too.
> But the <u>polar</u> bears get my attention; I watch them when I can.
>   They're huge and <u>robust</u>, and they swim with such grace!
> In short, I'm a polar bear fan.

Read the underlined words above. How many vowel sounds does each have? How many syllables?

This is how the words are divided into syllables.

> ze bras   po lar   ro bust

Notice that a vowel is at the end of the first syllable of each word. Do you hear a short or a long vowel sound?

> When one consonant stands between two vowels, the consonant usually goes with the second syllable. The vowel in the first syllable is often long.

A. Number your paper from 1 to 16. Write each word, leaving a space between the syllables.

1. easel	2. focus	3. duty	4. vocal
5. motive	6. frequent	7. labor	8. unit
9. prefix	10. crazy	11. future	12. oval
13. private	14. bacon	15. isolate	16. miners

B. Number your paper from 1 to 5. Find five words below that have a long vowel sound in the first syllable. Write them, leaving a space between the syllables.

splendid	turkey	argue	rival	clumsy
vacate	clover	symbol	peanut	humid

Word Work

Syllables, Consonant Digraphs, and Consonant Clusters

Read the list of things Trevor knew lived in the ocean nearby. Look for consonant digraphs and consonant clusters.

Trevor's Ocean Creatures

horseshoe crab	plankton	green fleece
slippery tangle weed	slender sea star	arrow shrimp
smooth cord weed	black scallop	sand dollar
giant squid	cross hatched lucine	dog whelk
sea urchin	disk shell	parchment worm

A. Look at the underlined letters in the list above.

1. Remember that consonant digraphs are two or three letters that stand for one sound. List the consonant digraphs.
2. In a consonant cluster, the separate sounds of the consonants blend together. List the consonant clusters.

Look out for these letter combinations when you are dividing a word into syllables.

> In most cases, do not divide words between the letters in a consonant digraph or in a consonant cluster.

B. Number your paper from 1 to 12. Write the words below on your paper. Underline each consonant digraph or consonant cluster. Then draw a line between the syllables.

1. duchess
2. ketchup
3. fragrant
4. eclipse
5. hydrant
6. mischief
7. fathom
8. folder
9. standstill
10. mongrel
11. celebrate
12. manuscript

Syllables and Prefixes

Read the following sentence.

I <u>disliked</u> what I had written so I <u>rewrote</u> the paragraph.

Look again at the underlined words. Notice that each has a prefix.

How many vowel sounds does each word have?
How many syllables?

This is how those words are divided.

dis liked   re wrote

> In a word with a prefix, the prefix is usually a
> separate syllable.

Number your paper from 1 to 30. Write the words below on your
paper. Underline the prefix in each word. Then draw a line between
the syllables.

1. displease
2. inactive
3. interstate
4. nonmetal
5. misjudge
6. extract
7. multicolor
8. triangle
9. bifocal
10. foreground
11. precede
12. projection
13. reproduce
14. monotone
15. subtitle
16. unimportant
17. uncommon
18. reposition
19. midcycle
20. prescribe
21. intersection
22. refuel
23. nonfiction
24. dislodge
25. postpone
26. pregame
27. relocate
28. misunderstood
29. midday
30. exceed

Syllables and Suffixes

Read the poem below.

> So <u>readily</u> we baked the cake.
>   We even made the stew.
> We so enjoyed the <u>accomplishment</u>
>   of doing something new.
> But oh, were we <u>forgetful</u>
>   of the dishes left to do.

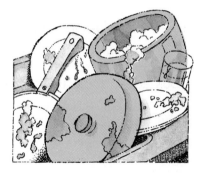

Look again at the underlined words. Notice that each has a suffix.

How many vowel sounds does each word have?
How many syllables?

This is how those words are divided into syllables.

　　　read i ly　　ac com plish ment　　for get ful

> In a word with a suffix, the suffix is usually a
> separate syllable.

Number your paper from 1 to 20. Write the words below on your
paper. Underline the suffix in each word. Draw a line between the
syllables.

1. bitterness
2. stranger
3. consumer
4. mysterious
5. eventful
6. sisterhood
7. ailment
8. happily
9. athletic
10. detective
11. wisdom
12. cartoonist
13. flawless
14. attendance
15. chiefly
16. membership
17. amazement
18. breakable
19. fondness
20. imitation

Stressed Syllables

> When the first vowel in a word is followed by a double consonant, the first syllable is usually accented. In most two-syllable words, the first syllable is accented.
>
> | | | |
> |---|---|---|
> | kit′ ten | din′ ner | griz′ zly |
> | fa′ mous | nick′ el | log′ ic |

Read the story below. Number your paper from 1 to 30. Write the underlined words. Divide each word into syllables. Put an accent mark after the stressed syllable. REMEMBER: In *most,* but not *all,* two syllable words the first syllable is accented.

Traffic was snarled. What is wrong, Barb wondered, as she rode between the two lines of the bicycle lane. She rode slowly, looking at the people in the cars. Some seemed angry at the delay. Some seemed resigned to it and patient. She couldn't figure out why so many people thought honking their car horns would solve the problem. She saw a man lean out his car window and shout to a honker behind him, "Do you think the front cars are being stubborn just to annoy you?"

The cars started moving. Barb realized she might never know what the holdup had been. A police officer stood at the next corner. Barb got off her bike and walked over to him. "What was the matter? I hope nothing serious happened here," she said.

The officer's laughter took Barb by surprise. "No," he said. "It was a mother duck and five ducklings—just like that children's story. I'm going to buy that book for my daughter."

"I remember that story. Maybe I'll buy it too," Barb said. "I bet my little brother would like it."